WHO GOT THE CAMERA?

AMERICAN MUSIC SERIES

Jessica Hopper and Charles Hughes, Editors
Peter Blackstock and David Menconi, Founding Editors

ALSO IN THE SERIES

WHO GOT THE CAMERA?

A HISTORY OF RAP AND REALITY

ERIC HARVEY

UNIVERSITY OF TEXAS PRESS ⧖ AUSTIN

Requests for permission to reproduce material
from this work should be sent to:
Permissions
University of Texas Press
P.O. Box 7819
Austin, TX 78713-7819
utpress.utexas.edu/rp-form

♾ The paper used in this book meets the minimum requirements of
ANSI/NISO Z39.48-1992 (R1997) (Permanence of Paper).

Library of Congress Cataloging-in-Publication Data

Names: Harvey, Eric, author.
Title: Who got the camera? : a history of rap and reality / Eric Harvey.
Other titles: American music series (Austin, Tex.)
Description: First edition. | Austin : University of Texas Press, 2021. |
Series: American music series | Includes bibliographical references and index.
Identifiers:
LCCN 2021005320
ISBN 978-1-4773-2134-8 (cloth)
ISBN 978-1-4773-2394-6 (ebook other)
ISBN 978-1-4773-2395-3 (ebook)
Subjects: LCSH: Gangsta rap (Music)—History and criticism. | Reality television
programs—History and criticism. | True crime television programs—History and
criticism. | Rap musicians. | Crime in music.
Classification: LCC ML3531 .H365 2021 | DDC 782.421649—dc23
LC record available at https://lccn.loc.gov/2021005320

doi:10.7560/321348

CONTENTS

▼

PREFACE

EAVESDROPPING

▼

During a 1993 conversation, bell hooks asked Ice Cube a question that Black artists are commonly forced to confront: "If the major buying audience is white and we want to reach that audience, to what extent do we compromise ourselves in trying to reach that audience?" Cube replied,

> I do records for Black kids, and white kids are basically eavesdropping on my records. But I don't change what I'm sayin'. I won't take out this word or that word because I got white kids buying my records. White kids need to hear what we got to say about them and their forefathers and uncles and everybody that's done us wrong. And the only way they're goin' to hear it uncut and uncensored is rap music, because I refuse to censor anything I have to say about anybody.[1]

I write this book as an eavesdropper. I grew up watching Black entertainment take over popular culture while simultaneously internalizing the local reality of racial difference and separation. The Indianapolis district where I attended middle and high school was desegregated by a federal judge in 1971, after determining it was still practicing de jure segregation in violation of the Supreme Court's 1954 *Brown v. Board of Education* decision. The judge's order wasn't implemented until 1981, when the city started busing Black students nearly an hour each way to attend school amid the vast corn and soybean fields of the city's white, southeastern suburbs. I started high school in 1991, and it did not register until years later that I was participating in a desegregation process that had begun when my parents were children, and that the burden of integration was borne by Black families instead of white ones.

Yet my education in Black popular culture didn't come in the classroom or from my Black peers, many of whom were understandably reticent to engage with their white classmates. My freshman year coincided with hip-hop's simultaneous pop-crossover moment and rebellious punk phase, when stars like Tone Loc, DJ Jazzy Jeff and the Fresh Prince, Vanilla Ice, and MC Hammer were competing with the adult world of rebellious, nationalist hip-hop: Cube's *Death Certificate*, 2Pac's *2Pacalypse Now*, Public Enemy's *Apocalypse 91*, and others. Hip-hop culture was strongly influencing TV—from *A Different World* and *The Fresh Prince of Bel-Air* to *The Arsenio Hall Show*, *In Living Color*, and HBO's *Def Comedy Jam*—as well as Black-directed films like *House Party* and *Boyz n the Hood*. Not only did I listen to a lot of rap and watch a lot of Black TV and movies, but I *interacted* with these cultural artifacts. I borrowed and dubbed rap tapes from my friends, maintained numerous notebooks with my best stabs at lyric transcriptions, and investigated references I didn't understand. I not only learned about South Central and Compton but was introduced to the Black Panthers, Marcus Garvey, Malcolm X, and the Nation of Islam and eavesdropped on realistic portrayals of working-class Black Americans. By scanning the list of samples on rap records, I learned about a world of 1960s and 1970s funk and R&B that would have never entered my life through oldies radio, and I learned that Black stand-up comedy and storytelling had a history that long pre-dated Eddie Murphy and Bill Cosby.

My media habits derived from an urge to more deeply participate in media culture, to bring it closer to me. I didn't just want to consume, I wanted to play along. Reality TV, especially daytime and late-afternoon talk shows, gave me that chance. I watched them all—Oprah, Geraldo, Sally Jessy—but was especially drawn to the beleaguered populism of Phil Donahue, the inventor of the format, forever running around the studio audience with a wireless mic, entertaining topics that the "regular" news wouldn't go near. Through daytime talk, I learned about people who would never appear on the nightly news—transgender people, drag queens, sex workers, and atheists—and developed my argumentation skills at a vicarious remove, particularly on the episodes that dealt with politics and race, for which my hip-hop homework had prepared me well.

During the summer of 1992, I put my autodidactic education to its first test. I was riding in the car with my father, and the story of the controversy surrounding Body Count's "Cop Killer" came on a news break. It had been a bit more than a year since the release of the Rodney King video, and the streets of Los Angeles were still smoldering from the rebellion that greeted the acquittal of King's assailants. Thanks to Vice President Dan Quayle stirring up election-year conservative anger by denouncing it, "Cop Killer," a punk/metal hybrid from Ice-T's mostly overlooked side project, had become a national news story. While the mainstream news media was framing the story through the voices of white officials, I was tracking the "Cop Killer" saga mostly through *Donahue*, *Oprah*, *Rolling Stone* magazine, and MTV News. When the radio story concluded, I took a deep breath and offered my opinion. Ice-T was not literally promoting the killing of police officers, I mumbled in my dad's direction, but expressing his anger at the constant harassment that Black people faced from the cops. My father, a veteran Marion County sheriff's deputy, did not agree.

I idolized my dad growing up and had planned to follow his career path until my early teens. I grew up immersed in cop culture and loved hanging out at the police station, a room full of middle-aged men who drank endless coffee, cracked rude jokes, typed up warrants, and went on calls. The pioneering Fox reality show *Cops* debuted when I was eleven, though my dad wasn't a fan. He joked that the most accurate representation of day-to-day police life was the humdrum office politics of the 1970s sitcom *Barney Miller*, and he watched endless reruns of the kindly southern sheriff Andy Taylor on *The Andy Griffith Show*. I never got to ask my dad what he was thinking at the moment I sided with "Cop Killer." He responded with a deep sigh, and the topic soon changed, or we arrived where we were going—I can't quite remember which. Maybe he was disappointed in me; maybe he resented the fact that an increasing number of people didn't see the cops as *Barney Miller* or *Andy Griffith* characters anymore, and a great many more never had. Regardless, chiming in on "Cop Killer" marked the first time I articulated an informed opinion on a political topic.

Like all fans of popular culture, I had been drawn into a world imagined by others, but what its performers called "reality rap" was far from escapist fantasy. Part of why I developed my "Cop Killer" opinion came from the subversive thrill of freaking out my parents, and part of it grew from my naïve, youthful exoticization of rebellious Black men who didn't give a fuck. But at the same time, eavesdropping through hip-hop had helped me form a cogent opinion on the issue of racist police brutality and an inchoate understanding of the distinction between literal and symbolic expression. I learned these not necessarily from "Cop Killer" itself, which wasn't even rap and which I didn't much like as music, but from the discourse that it generated and the debates that it fostered. And I know I wasn't alone. The last thing anyone needs at this point is to read a white man explaining how hip-hop changed his life, so I'll stop there, with this book's origin myth. I came of age eavesdropping on Black popular culture, watching and listening as the concerns of a generation left behind by a deindustrializing, law-and-order-obsessed society made their way into an ever more fractured national conversation. This profound and thrilling change in popular music and Black representation overlapped with another shift, as the mainstream journalistic establishment gave way to a sensationalistic and often vulgar network of news and information from the outskirts of centrist, corporate news: tabloid culture.

All books have numerous starting points, and I'll briefly note two more. The first came in 2000, when I took my first job out of college with a small documentary production company in Indianapolis. Run by two veterans of Indianapolis's WTHR NBC News affiliate, the company's contract with the Discovery networks allowed me (first as a production assistant, then briefly as chief videographer and editor) to learn the intricacies of nonfiction television, from local news broadcasts to national documentaries. My nearly three years with the company left me with dozens of hours of local and national programming on my résumé and a profound desire to never work in TV production again. The sixty-hour workweeks were bad enough, but I was regularly shocked at the degree of scripting and editing used to elide political controversies and the emphasis placed on expensive technological tricks that signified nothing apart from their own flashy spectacle. At the same time, consumer-level digital cameras were improving and editing software was coming prepackaged with each home computer, and I could see the writing on the wall: my company was failing to meet the changing times, and its days were numbered.

My intellectual curiosity had been piqued, and wanting to learn more about media technologies, storytelling formats, and documentary truth, I decamped for academia: specifically, the graduate programs at Indiana University's (dearly departed) Department of Communication and Culture and the Department of Folklore and Ethnomusicology. This book first came into being in late 2008 as a paper for Portia Maultsby's Theoretical Perspectives on African American Music seminar. In addition to Dr. Maultsby, I want to thank my seminar colleagues, who talked through early versions of this idea with me: June Evans, Mike Lee, Thomas Richardson, and especially Langston Collin Wilkins, whose knowledge of hip-hop is far deeper than mine could ever be.

An equally huge thank you goes out to my Department of Communication and Culture peers and friends, with whom I talked, laughed, debated, and drank during my PhD odyssey: Aleena Chia, E Cram, Seth Friedman, Mack Hagood, Jennifer Jones, Andrea Kelley, Michael Lahey, James Paasche, Landon Palmer, Justin Rawlins, Jason Sperb, and Travis Vogan. I am infinitely grateful for the mentorship of my professors and committee members, Christopher Anderson, Richard Bauman, Ilana Gershon, Jane Goodman, Joan Hawkins, Barbara Klinger, James Naremore, Yeidy Rivero, and Ted Striphas.

Six years after writing that seminar paper, I turned it into a presentation for the annual Experience Music Project (now Museum of Pop Culture) Pop Conference. In the audience was Jessica Hopper, who optioned it for the *Pitchfork Review* (RIP), where it ran in 2015. There are likely dozens of other authors who can say this, but I'll say it anyway: without Jessica, there's no book. Immeasurable thanks go out to Jessica for her encouragement, conversation, and inspiration, both at the *Review* and later in commissioning the book you're reading now for the University of Texas Press. Thanks also to Stuart Berman and the *Pitchfork Review* editorial staff and to Meaghan Garvey for her gorgeous illustrations that accompanied the original piece.

I wrote and delivered that Experience Music Project presentation while employed and funded by the Department of Communication at Weber State University, my first post-PhD appointment. I want to thank my departmental colleagues for their enthusiasm and support, especially Nicola Corbin.

Thank you to Ron Becker and the Miami University Department of Media, Journalism, and Film, which hosted me for a public talk on this material in October 2016.

Thank you to the Vanderbilt Television News Archive and Indiana University's Archives of African American Music and Culture, two incredibly valuable and well-managed archival collections that hosted me for book research. Thanks especially to the head of collections at the Archives of African American Music and Culture, Brenda Nelson-Strauss.

Thank you to my current colleagues in the Grand Valley State University School of Communications, particularly my multimedia journalism partners, who have been incredibly supportive during the process of researching and writing this manuscript. I couldn't ask for a better set of intellectual peers, coworkers, and friends.

Thank you to my remarkably patient and supportive editor, Casey Kittrell, the University of Texas Press staff, and the early reviewers of the manuscript.

Thank you to Kevin Howley, who convinced me to go to grad school in 2003, a few years after he taught me how to take television seriously.

Thank you to all of my students. Over the past two decades, from DePauw University to Indiana, Weber State, and Grand Valley State, I have learned more from you than you'll ever know. Thank you for trusting me with a small part of your education.

Endless thank-yous to my mother and stepfather and to the Auschermans, Harveys, Kingens, Lawtons, and Pontiuses. And to my friends: thanks for listening to music with me, teaching me about music, and tolerating me theorizing about music for the past quarter century. And to Amy, who rode shotgun on this bumpy ride for the past nine years. Without her intellectual example and constant support, this book wouldn't exist.

WHO GOT THE CAMERA?

INTRODUCTION

THE STRENGTH OF STREET KNOWLEDGE

▼

On September 21, 1990, Arsenio Hall welcomed N.W.A to his stage. In their own ways, Hall and N.W.A represented the integration of hip-hop into mainstream pop culture. Hall, the thirty-one-year-old stand-up comedian and actor who had single-handedly modernized the all-white late-night talk show format with his boisterous "dog pound" crowd and rap star guests, had recently been named "TV Person of the Year" by *TV Guide* and had hosted MTV's Video Music Awards telecast a couple weeks earlier. His guests that evening, N.W.A, were, to put it lightly, a different kind of Black cultural icon. "Everything about the four young men I'm about to introduce you to is controversial," Hall said, "from their name to their music, which last year the FBI accused of encouraging violence against the police." As the group and Hall sat on the edge of the stage, their first subject was the song that had spurred a letter from Milt Ahlerich, assistant director of the FBI Office of Public Affairs, a little more than a year earlier. Ahlerich never mentioned "Fuck tha Police" by name in his letter to Priority Records, and naturally Hall could not say it on air, but even its safe-for-broadcast pronunciation, "Eff tha Police," triggered rapturous applause from Hall's audience. The song's author, Ice Cube, had acrimoniously left N.W.A at the end of 1989, so MC Ren explained the song's meaning to Hall's national audience. "Once in everybody's lifetime, they get harassed by the police for no reason, and everybody wants to say it, but they can't say it on the spot, 'cause something will happen to 'em," Ren explained. "In the ghetto, or in the Black community, you get harassed by the police just for what you wear . . . they stereotype you as a gang member . . . that's how it is." The song was not meant as incitement to violence against police officers, he explained, but as a pressure-release valve for residents of overpatrolled Black neighborhoods. Hall, who would later be named a celebrity ambassador for the Drug Abuse Resistance Education (D.A.R.E.) program developed by Los Angeles Police Department chief Daryl Gates, prompted Ren to disavow his claim that *all* cops were bad. "Nah," Ren replied. "Ninety percent of them are."

The interview took an unexpected turn when Hall asked Dr. Dre what the group were planning to perform that night. "We was gonna perform for y'all, right?" Dre said to the crowd. "But [the police] said N.W.A were too radical, so we just get the interview." The audience gasped, but Dre's admission made sense to anyone who'd followed the group's well-documented saga. While touring the country the previous summer, the mere threat that the group would perform "Fuck tha Police" live placed them in the crosshairs of local police departments. Police searched N.W.A fans outside concert venues, and the group was forced to sign a contract at several stops promising not to perform the song, under threat of arrest. When they did briefly break into the song at a Detroit stop, plainclothes police rushed the stage and the plug was pulled. After Dre's announcement, Hall paused for a moment, promised viewers that they would "huddle up" and figure something out, and sent the show to break. A few minutes later, the show returned backstage. As N.W.A enters the studio through a service door, they are aggressively met by police officers who attempt to stop them from performing. They scuffle for a few seconds, the action framed by a shaky handheld camera. The group break free from the police and run up the stairs to the stage door, when the shot cuts to a view from the stage, showing the group running through the audience while Hall's voice booms over the PA system, introducing their performance of "100 Miles and Runnin'," a single that itself dramatized N.W.A's post–"Fuck tha Police" notoriety as a nationwide police chase.

Hall was in on the gag the whole time, of course, but the fact that the brief scuffle between N.W.A and the police was prearranged was less important than how it looked. From the fraught interaction to the jittery handheld camera, it looked like it had been directly modeled on the pioneering reality show *Cops*, which had started its third season on Fox a week earlier. Every bit the upstart cultural sensation as Hall's show, *Cops* paired documentary-style camera crews with local police departments, capturing action-packed, vérité-style footage of everyday police work that was edited into twenty-two-minute episodes. With no actors, script, or narrator, the show's March 1989 debut was billed as an innovative entry into the growing world of "reality" or "reality-based" television programming. While sitcoms and serial dramas about the daily lives of police were nothing new, as the *New York Times* television critic wrote in October 1990, "the difference now is that ... the police officers on the screen really carry guns, really chase drug-dealers through the streets, really save people's lives."[1] Yet, as police and critics alike quickly noted, the reality of *Cops* was just as dramatized and shocking as "Fuck tha Police," but intended to achieve the opposite goal: a wholly positive portrayal of police work. *Cops* did not show officers negotiating mounds of paperwork or sitting around offices and squad cars, activities that comprised dozens of hours of their workweek, nor did it chronicle accusations of racial profiling and brutality that were common to young Black men in cities like Compton and South Central Los Angeles. In the sensationalistic reality of *Cops*, police work was one exciting drug bust, arrest, or chase after another in neighborhoods whose citizens possessed the least economic and political power: usually lower-middle-class, often Black. *Cops* was pro-police propaganda that looked like a wild documentary about the brave men and women of law enforcement who serve as the thin blue line between a safe suburban existence and the ever-present threat of malevolent criminals.

A few months before N.W.A's *Arsenio* appearance, Ice Cube released his first solo album, which he named *AmeriKKKa's Most Wanted* as a play on Fox's other law-and-order-themed reality hit, which had debuted in February 1988. One of Fox's earliest hits, *America's Most Wanted* turned TV viewers into an ad hoc posse led by host John Walsh, who played violent and dramatic reenactments of actual crimes whose perpetrators were still at large and then gave vigilant viewers a 1-800 number to help federal agents track them down. The opportunity to turn Walsh's reality vigilantism on its head was too much for Cube to pass up. On the album's title track, he samples Walsh's voice ("Don't try to apprehend him"), while resignifying the show's original intent into a statement on racist policing ("Every motherfucker with a color is most wanted"). *AmeriKKKa's Most Wanted* made Cube a solo star, and it also put him back in dialogue with the same federal officer whose letter had obliquely threatened his freedom: FBI agent Milt Ahlerich. In addition to being the agency liaison who had convinced his fellow agents to open their cases to Fox's audience, Ahlerich also served as *America's Most Wanted's* public defender during the show's controversial first season. On a 1988 episode of ABC's late-night public affairs show *Nightline*, Ahlerich responded to factual accusations that *Wanted* overrepresented murders, rapes, and assaults to foster the belief that America was far more dangerous than it actually was. To Ahlerich, the slant toward the gruesome was less important than the accuracy of each dramatization. "The fact is that the crimes that were originally committed were very, very violent, and they're portrayed in a very accurate fashion here," he told host Ted Koppel. The implication was tacit but obvious: no one would tune in to a show about fugitives who committed white-collar crimes like wire fraud or corporate embezzlement, even though those transgressions could do as much damage to American families as violent crimes. As with Ice Cube's platinum-selling album, so it went with Fox's reality TV sensation: the more salacious the content, the more profitable the product.

Though Cube initially wanted his former N.W.A bandmate Dr. Dre to produce *AmeriKKKa's Most Wanted*, he was rebuffed by Eazy-E and Ruthless Records, whose iffy accounting methods had caused Cube to leave the group in the first place. Instead, Cube took his lyric notebooks and flew to New York, where he hooked up with his favorite group, the militant Long Island collective Public Enemy, and its production team, the Bomb Squad. Led by the political firebrand Chuck D, PE introduced Black nationalist fervor and political spectacle into hip-hop lyrics, and the Bomb Squad's dense, soul- and funk-infused sample collages established an entirely new bar for production. The influence of PE's second album, *It Takes a Nation of Millions to Hold Us Back*, was audible in Dre's production on *Straight Outta Compton* (released a few months later) and in the political edge of Cube's lyrics. As the most outspoken and political rapper of the moment, at a point when rap was dramatically transforming itself from party and club music to sensationalistic political force in Black popular culture, Chuck tasked himself with defining the music to outsiders. In a 1988 interview with the rock-focused *Spin* magazine, Chuck condensed his thoughts on rap's communicative affordances into an aphorism: "Rap is black America's TV station." Chuck said that rap "gives a whole perspective of what exists and what black life is about. And black life doesn't get the total spectrum of information through anything else. They don't get it through print because kids won't pick up no magazines or no books, really, unless it got pictures of rap stars."[2] Unlike N.W.A's political shock tactics, Chuck saw Public Enemy's music as the key medium of a communications empire with a political benchmark. In another widely circulated quote, Chuck claimed his goal was to create five thousand new Black leaders. What better medium-as-metaphor was there than the one that transmitted a potent mixture of entertainment programming and hard-hitting news to tens of millions of Americans?

Public Enemy's Black TV station was broadcasting a new vision for Black America, one not only in dialogue with the rousing oratory of Malcolm X and the media interventions of the Black Panthers in the 1960s but also squarely at the center of a surging Afrocentrism that was transforming hip-hop lyricism and style while instituting itself at the highest echelons of academia and politics. In early 1990, a lengthy public effort to draw attention to the ravages of South African apartheid led to the momentous release of Nelson Mandela, who had been imprisoned for his political beliefs for three decades. Though the era's hip-hop was suffused with Africanness—from red, black, and green medallions to kente-cloth garments—N.W.A's resident entrepreneur Eazy-E was very much not a participant, dismissing rap's swelling pro-African currents in the April 1990 issue of *Spin*: "Chuck D gets involved in all that Black stuff, we don't. Fuck that Black Power shit: we don't give a fuck. I bet there ain't anybody in South Africa wearing a button saying 'Free Compton.' They don't give a damn about us, so why should we give a damn about them?"[3] When Arsenio Hall brought up Eazy's comments during N.W.A's appearance on his show, Ren handled the response: "All the Black Power stuff, it's like a fad right now...quit fakin'. It's too many problems over here for them to try to be worryin' about over there." The escalating situation in Kuwait and Iraq was on Ren's mind as well: "This crisis in the

Gulf, that's bull to me. It's politics, you know. They makin' money off of all that."

For a minute or so, *The Arsenio Hall Show* had transformed into something closer to *The Phil Donahue Show*, a popular daytime talk show forum for perspectives on current events that often fell outside the range of mainstream news. N.W.A were not nearly as politically informed as Public Enemy, but their notoriety and race permitted them to play the role of Black spokesmen nonetheless. Ren had to speak for Eazy because the group's spirited front man was deep in character that night. During the interview, he sat to the side, wearing a straitjacket and a Jason–style hockey mask while fingering the tip of a switchblade. He was present purely for shock value, a parody of the Black ghetto horror against which Milt Ahlerich, *America's Most Wanted*, and *Cops* were staging their own sensationalistic war.

The term "gangsta rap" first appeared in a *Los Angeles Times* review of a March 1989 N.W.A concert. It was an apt coinage: in "Straight Outta Compton," Ice Cube referred to the group as "the gang called Niggaz with Attitudes," and he penned another single titled "Gangsta Gangsta." A few years after N.W.A's emergence, that same phrase would describe a commercial music juggernaut worth hundreds of millions of dollars, a fashionable lifestyle system that transcended the music, and a societal scourge that triggered multiple congressional hearings about the impact of violent music on children. Yet while it worked well as a consumer genre that drew upon a legacy of "outlaw" mythology in American pop, the rappers themselves disliked the term and preferred a different descriptor. "I still call it reality rap, because...our stuff is much more than just talking about gangsta things," Cube told an interviewer in 1994. "Our stuff is talking about the social climate. To me, it means a network of information." Ice-T agreed: "If anyone asked me at the time, I called it 'reality rap,'" the rapper wrote in his memoir. "To me it was street level journalism, real life observations told in poetry."[4] To Eazy-E, the music was "the real story of what it's like living in places like Compton. We're giving them reality. We're like reporters."[5] Tupac Shakur, the most tragic and transcendent figure of the era, compared his music to the revelatory imagery of frontline war reporters. "Because you had reporters showing us pictures of the war at home, that's what made the war end," he wrote. "So I thought, that's what I'm going to do as an artist, as a rapper. I'm gonna show the most graphic details of what I see in my community and hopefully they'll stop it quick."[6] Even Dr. Dre's protégé Snoop Doggy Dogg—far from a political rapper—defended his controversial debut album with a rationale that stretched the definition of journalism. "The situations I deal with on my albums is reality. The same things the news is bringing you," he told Arsenio in 1994, while awaiting trial for accessory to murder. "But I'm bringing it to you live and direct like the news can't give it to you, 'cause I know it. Know what I'm saying? They just scared of it."

Like reality TV producers and personalities, reality rappers understood their term of art first and foremost as a comparative one. The first listed definition of "reality" in the *Oxford English Dictionary*, after all, is "the world or the state of things as they actually exist, as opposed to an idealistic or notional idea of them." It's the definition that spawns phrases like "the harsh reality of life in the hood," or "stop being polite and start getting real." As a programming format, reality television was pitched as a true-to-life and shocking alternative to the medium's escapist fare, but with an overt entertainment value that distinguished it from the staid evening news. Networks were especially careful to draw a bright line between reality entertainment and news reality: the first wave of reality TV either came from Fox, which had no news division, or was produced by independent companies and licensed by syndicators. When NBC started airing the first network-produced reality show, *Unsolved Mysteries*, in 1987, the network aired a warning before each episode to distinguish the reality from that of its news division: "What you are about to see is not a news broadcast." Rappers' reality emerged from a similar dialogue with their peers, serving as a signal that they were uncovering shocking truths about Black lives that were absent not only from the nightly news but from the safe "urban music" of Black dance-pop and R&B. In much the same way that network news divisions stayed far away from reality TV, Black radio stations kept their distance from vulgar, violent reality rap—becoming, along with the police, a key enemy of Ice-T, Ice Cube, and Public Enemy. In an echo of *Cops'* weekly pre-episode warning that "viewer discretion is advised," Dr. Dre alerts listeners at the start of "Straight Outta Compton" that "you are about to witness the strength of street knowledge." Like their reality entertainment peers, they were warning the squeamish, nodding to the censors, and issuing a tantalizing dare to everyone else.

Nine months before N.W.A's reality-spoofing appearance on *Arsenio*, Public Enemy sounded their own alarm with "Welcome to the Terrordome," a single that reported from the front lines of white-on-Black violence around the country—the murder of Yusuf Hawkins by a white mob in Brooklyn, the police-fueled rioting at a Black fraternity event in Virginia Beach—and provided an update on the group's own notoriety, sparked by its "Minister of Information," Professor Griff, making baldly anti-Semitic remarks to a reporter. Chuck D viewed the dawning decade as a moment of reckoning for Black Americans: "The 1990s are coming [and] if we as a people do the wrong thing the Black situation is out of here at the end of the decade. The terrordome is the 1990s."[7] The explosion of antirap sentiment that year gave credence to Chuck's fear. That year's two most critically acclaimed rap albums, PE's *Fear of a Black Planet* and Cube's *AmeriKKKa's Most Wanted*, were as controversial as they were popular. *Planet* received national news coverage for brushing off Griff's anti-Semitism and embracing the discredited work of a homophobic race scientist, and *AmeriKKKa* earned reproach of its own for Cube's occasional bouts of violent misogyny. Both albums sold platinum.

That summer, an Indiana CD plant refused to duplicate the new album from the Houston trio the Geto Boys because the company found the lyrics on songs such as "Mind of a Lunatic" revolting. Ice-T titled his third album *Freedom of Speech*, and it included an attack on Tipper Gore, whose Parents Music Resource Center, after five years of lobbying, had convinced the record industry to adopt a voluntary "parental advisory" sticker that year. One of the biggest stories of 1990 was the First Amendment case of the Miami sex-rap group 2 Live Crew triggered by Nick Navarro, the flashy Florida sheriff who starred in the pilot episode of *Cops*. Nineteen-ninety was the year that *Newsweek* published its instantly notorious "Rap Attitude" issue, followed by a *Time* cover story devoted to "dirty words," which linked rap to the raunchy stand-up acts of Sam Kinison and Andrew Dice Clay. Inspired by everything from vulgar hip-hop to hypersexualized and ultraviolent Hollywood films and the provocative photography of the gay artist Robert Mapplethorpe,

Newsweek's July 2 cover posed the question that was dividing the nation: "Art or Obscenity?"

On rap albums and on television programs alike, reality entertainment emerged from the red-hot center of the culture wars, which conservatives had raised to a fever pitch in the first full year of the George H. W. Bush administration. Illinois congressman Sidney Yates connected the tumult to the foolhardy crusade to snuff out Hollywood communists in the 1950s. "You've got a fight going on today that is just as emotional as the fight that took place then," Yates said. "Except communism isn't the bogeyman. This time it's pornography and obscenity."[8] America's existential foe since the 1950s had seemingly vanished the previous November, as the world watched the Berlin Wall crumble on live television, a globally televised spectacle representing the end of communism and the global triumph of liberal democracies and free markets. Caught up in the "Fall of the Wall" rapture, foreign policy analyst Francis Fukuyama published an article titled "The End of History?," arguing that the end of the Cold War symbolized not merely the triumph of Western liberalism but "the end-point of mankind's ideological evolution and the universalization of Western liberal democracy as the final form of human government."[9] Though Fukuyama's article was roundly criticized for its multiple blind spots (it was published in a neoconservative journal that promoted American hegemony), it was also true that with the nation's primary foe vanquished, American animosities were quickly turning inward.

A second symbolic moment came on March 3, 1991. On the same day that General Norman Schwarzkopf accepted the Iraqi surrender and ended the Gulf War—the first fully televised war, which Americans watched live on CNN as it happened—a Los Angeles plumber named George Holliday stepped onto his balcony and shot camcorder footage of Los Angeles Police Department officers brutalizing the Black motorist Rodney King. The shaky black-and-white video footage of the Pentagon's "smart bombs" that had proven America's post–Cold War military superiority was swiftly replaced by shaky black-and-white footage of sworn officers declaring war on the flailing body of a Black citizen. Then, in January 1992, the same month that Fukuyama's article was published as a best-selling book, President Bush's attorney general Bill Barr reassigned more than three hundred FBI agents from Cold War–related duties abroad to street gang control in thirty-nine American cities—the largest reallocation of manpower in the bureau's history.[10] The war had come home. Welcome to the Terrordome.

Fukuyama's argument raised an interesting cultural question: What happens to the American imagination, and the national conversation, when the nation-state's existential enemies have been conquered? As the 2000s dawned, a *Vanity Fair* critic ventured a response: The 1990s had been the "tabloid decade," a ten-year period marked by the rise of "advanced technology and increased vulgarity." Fueled by the dramatic expansion of the television universe and the consumer video market (and, later, the rise of the internet), a sensationalist new national mindset had eradicated the boundary between the highbrow world of mainstream journalism and the lowbrow world of supermarket tabloids. Americans spent the decade obsessing over lurid and salacious stories, culminating with the nearly two-year O. J. Simpson saga, "a prolonged Hollywood Babylon spectacle that confirmed the prevailing national interest in sex, death, celebrity, and televised car chases," and the minutely documented affair between President Bill Clinton and his intern Monica Lewinsky.[11]

The tabloid decade's effects were especially visible in the rise of reality TV, alternately called "confrontainment," "tabloid TV," or simply "trash TV." The cultural theorist Kevin Glynn named the brave new world of the late 1980s and early 1990s "tabloid culture" to describe a technologically sophisticated space where "journalism and popular culture intersect."[12] According to Glynn, tabloid culture took shape in three types: Fox's true-crime novelties *Cops* and *America's Most Wanted* (and their dozens of successors); the syndicated sensationalism of daytime talk shows hosted by the erstwhile TV journalists Phil Donahue, Oprah Winfrey, Geraldo Rivera, and others; and the lurid prime-time tabloid news troika of *A Current Affair*, *Hard Copy*, and *Inside Edition*. TV executives gobbled up tabloid programs because of simple economics: the combination of sensationalism and populism drew significant ratings at a bargain. Unlike sitcoms or prime-time dramas, there were no writers or actors to pay, just a few hosts and some skeleton crews. The stars? They were drawn from the growing population of Americans eager to see themselves on television, by any means necessary.

The journalistic establishment were none too pleased about a new crop of pretenders to their throne, where they had reigned since the 1950s as the august arbiters of America's discursive reality. In 1989, pioneering CBS News producer Fred Friendly convened a televised panel titled "Who's a Journalist? Talk Show Sensationalism," during which Phil Donahue, Geraldo Rivera, and the rabble-rousing late-night provocateur Morton Downey Jr. squared off in a roundtable discussion against representatives from the *Los Angeles Times*, the *Chicago Tribune*, and *60 Minutes*. In a representative exchange, the *LA Times'* Jack Nelson opined that he did not consider Downey a journalist, to which Downey replied by calling Nelson a "snob." Tabloid programming had cemented itself in television culture by 1992, when the Pulitzer Prize–winning *Washington Post* reporter Carl Bernstein reprimanded the "idiot culture" of modern news. "For more than fifteen years we have been moving away from real journalism toward the creation of a sleazoid infotainment culture in which the lines between Oprah and Phil and Geraldo and Diane [Sawyer] and even Ted [Koppel] . . . are too often indistinguishable," Bernstein wrote. "In this new culture of journalistic titillation, we teach our readers and our viewers that the trivial is significant, that the lurid and the loopy are more important than real news."[13]

Bernstein was joined in his animus by no less than Chuck D, who condemned the "filth and garbage" news of the "piss press" and regretted that "the commercial success and popularity of tabloid programs . . . have caused the local, national, and world news programs, which used to have more substance in their reporting, to become more tabloidistic in order to keep up their ratings."[14] Chuck was being a bit selective here, given his association with Louis Farrakhan, the headline-hungry leader of the Nation of Islam. The connection does not make Chuck hypocritical as much as it reveals the depth and breadth of tabloid culture's spread: those in the eye of the storm might not recognize its scope. Though TV anchors blanched, there was no stopping tabloid stories from making their way into the eminent realm of the nightly network news. During a 1993 *CBS Evening News* broadcast, Dan Rather found himself having to introduce a report on the Amy Fisher story, a tawdry Long Island love triangle that ended in attempted murder. Signing off the episode, Rather looked squarely at the camera and reminded his viewers, "This is real." He was referring, of course, to the program they were watching.

But the reality revolution was well underway. A year earlier, the media critic Jon Katz spotted the successor to daily newspapers and nightly news not in journalism schools but in TV writers' rooms, Hollywood productions, and hip-hop recording studios. What Katz called "New News" was not actually news at all, but evidence that news-style discourse had spread throughout the entertainment industry. New News was sharply attuned to a younger, more populist perspective on the most important events of the day, not the "official" stories emanating from the corridors of power. The entertainment industry, Katz wrote, had "[seized] the functions of mainstream journalism, sparking conversations and setting the country's social and political agenda." There were more frank discussions of divorce, sex, and AIDS on *Beverly Hills, 90210* and daytime talk shows, Katz observed, than on any mainstream news source, and sitcoms like *Roseanne* and *Murphy Brown* tackled the realities of working-class stress and single motherhood with a must-see mix of social relevance and laugh-track reliability. Katz was particularly enamored of rappers' and Black film directors' ability to force political discourse on race into the heart of national discussions. Public Enemy's 1992 music video for "By the Time I Get to Arizona," he noted, catalyzed the debate over the recognition of Martin Luther King Jr.'s birthday far more effectively than a *Meet the Press* debate; N.W.A had first reported in 1988 what the Rodney King video revealed in 1991; and *Boyz n the Hood* dealt "with race more squarely than *Nightline*" did.[15] The New News had usurped the Old News because a growing percentage of the American population did not feel that TV or print offerings were telling the whole truth—or, at least, *their* truth.

What Katz observed in 1992 had been years in the making. Three years before Chuck D claimed that rap is Black America's TV station, the sociologist Joshua Meyrowitz published an influential study examining how the rise of television occasioned a seismic shift from a print-dominated world of daily newspapers and periodicals to a TV-dominated information landscape constructed by the constant circulation of electronic signals. The impact was felt in far more than an expanded entertainment palette: while the written word created meaning through symbolic abstraction—letters, words, sentences—that required various levels of education to parse, TV told similar stories with the condensed, simplified moving images of other humans doing things. "Television by no means presents 'reality,'" Meyrowitz asserted, "but television looks and sounds much more like reality than sentences and paragraphs do."[16]

Though print reporters broke or covered stories more extensively than television news—civil rights protests, the Watergate scandal, the war in Vietnam—those stories increasingly did not seem "real" until they had been shrunk to bite-size visual narratives and contextualized to living room viewers by trusted TV personalities.

By the late 1970s, the average household had a television set turned on from six to eight hours per day, and television's thorough infiltration of daily life exerted a profound impact on how Americans socialized and experienced cultural difference. "Through television, rich and poor, young and old, scholars and illiterates, males and females, and people of all ages, professions, classes, and religions often share the same or very similar information at the same moment," Meyrowitz explained.[17] While television itself did not *cause* social change, and people could internalize very different meanings from the same information, TV did facilitate the conditions for the average American to learn about different people, practices, and ideas in simpler, more entertaining, and more ambient fashion than print. One effect highlighted by Meyrowitz was the mainstreaming of "exposure," which "seems to excite us more than the content of the secrets exposed." Through big scandals or milder revelations, television helped make the revelation of deep, dark secrets into an everyday occurrence, drawing public figures closer to the realm of ordinary Americans and vice versa.[18]

In the wake of the cultural tumult of the late 1960s, television's redefinition of reality extended past the nightly news to prime-time entertainment. What Todd Gitlin calls TV's "ability to borrow, transform—and deform—the energy of social and psychological conflict" emerged from TV's vision of itself as the American public sphere, combined with quick-turnaround production schedules and stark competition for viewers.[19] By the early 1980s, TV producers were merging news-derived reality with *stylistic* realism, reappropriating visual tropes and storytelling forms from other programs and formats, to create a hybrid form that Gitlin calls "recombinant culture." NBC's groundbreaking cop drama *Hill Street Blues*, for example, was pitched to network executives as a cross between the pathbreaking series *M*A*S*H*, the 1970s cop sitcom *Barney Miller*, the gritty 1981 crime film *Fort Apache, the Bronx*, and the 1977 vérité documentary *Police Story*. Though *Hill Street* never made it into the top twenty of Nielsen's ratings, its recombinant realism—knotty story lines, disheveled actors, overlapping dialogue, ethnic and racial diversity, roving cameras—made it an instant critics' and Emmy voters' favorite and incredibly influential on a subsequent generation of prime-time policing. The building blocks of documentary reality had become an aesthetic signifier, as easy to deploy as a regional dialect or costume. And they were also a political tool against nosy executives: predicting reality rappers' later arguments, *Hill Street* producers actively deployed the visual and narrative signifiers of truth to insulate themselves from censors. "Producers avail themselves of the claim of realism when censors apply their moralism, when protesters write their letters," Gitlin writes. "In a moral universe supervised by censors, fiction establishes its bona fides by borrowing selectively from fact."[20]

As a recombinant medium with designs on social relevance that came of age in the early 1980s, rap had much in common with television's entertaining realism. First, and most obviously, rap lyrics offered rappers a wide informational bandwidth, with significantly *more words* than their pop, rock, and R&B peers. Though rappers were not *required* to use that affordance for a politicized, quasi-documentary approach—in their moment, reality rappers were joined by clever pop-rappers and Afrocentric eccentrics—rap lyrics offered the unique potential for detailed storytelling and nuanced arguments. These stories and arguments were subsumed by the second advantage of rap as a communication medium: the deeply self-reflexive Black vernacular tradition that had been forged in the private, communal language rituals of African people living in a racist society for multiple generations. "Free of the white person's gaze, black people created their own unique vernacular structures and relished in the double play that these forms bore to white forms," explained Henry Louis Gates Jr. "Repetition and revision are fundamental to black artistic forms, from painting and sculpture to music and language use."[21] What Gates calls "signifying" is also known as "toasting" or "playing the dozens" and is practiced as often in the barbershop and on the street corner as in Black novels, poetry, and the rap recording booth. Riffing on preexisting words, sounds, phrases, and tropes; freely shifting between the literal and the figurative; and making Black social life into a kaleidoscopic array of creativity competition—and vulgarity—Black vernacular expression is a deeply self-reflexive form of serious play. Once the digital sampler was widely adopted by producers in the mid-1980s, the practice expanded dramatically, opening up the history of recorded sound to creative resignification.

Predictably, when the most boundary pushing of these Black signifying practices found their way into the white American mainstream, non-Black cultural eavesdroppers found them fascinating, entertaining, profitable, and, in their rawest forms, prime subject matter for censorship. In 1990, Henry Louis Gates Jr. himself defended the Miami sex rappers 2 Live Crew against such an attempt in court and in the papers, asserting in an opinion piece that their R-rated rhymes were not meant to be taken literally but as part of the deeply self-conscious and often self-parodic Black creative tradition. The best rapper, Gates wrote, is "the one who invents the most extravagant images, the biggest 'lies.'"[22] These excessive recontextualizations were drawn from recent history: the generation of reality rappers who transformed hip-hop and popular culture from 1986 to 1996 came of age amid the peak period of 1970s Black street realism, and their images and lyrics comprised ostentatious riffs on the Blaxploitation screen icons Sweet Sweetback, John Shaft, Youngblood Priest of *Super Fly*, and Goldie from *The Mack*; the smutty street storytelling of Rudy Ray Moore (perhaps best known for his version of "The Signifying Monkey"), Donald Goines, and Iceberg Slim; and the politically infused stand-up comedy of Richard Pryor, who was raised in a Peoria brothel but started his career as a Cosby clone before the Watts rebellion and the assassination of Malcolm X turned him toward more directly confrontational material about race, class, and drugs.

More broadly, the 1970s witnessed the vast expansion of Black television programs: *Good Times*, *Sanford and Son*, *The Jeffersons*, *Soul Train*, and the groundbreaking miniseries *Roots* presented far more nuanced stories and characters than the previous generation's offerings. "Growing up in the 1970s on a staple of black-cast television programs, I rarely considered that the face of television had ever been primarily white," recalled the Black television scholar Christine Acham.[23] When Chuck D told *Spin* that "rap is black America's TV station" the same year that Henry Louis Gates Jr. released his book, he was resignifying his chosen medium to incorporate the practices, tropes, sounds, visuals, and identities of another: that of television journalists, pundits, documentarians, and prime-time producers. But though it was seldom acknowledged, the dialogue went both ways. As a boldly self-reflexive, artful, sophisticated, and often discourteous remix of earlier utterances that was forged in purposeful isolation from whites, African American vernacular communication had developed the theoretical ideas of recombinant culture (a phrase that would soon be dwarfed by "postmodernism") a century before it took over academic discussions and fueled the polyglot "MTV aesthetic" that redefined the look and feel of television programming.

To be sure, reality entertainment was very much *not* what Gil Scott-Heron predicted in his epochal 1971 single "The Revolution Will Not Be Televised," widely regarded as a key text in the development of hip-hop. Perturbed by a TV news story on a political demonstration that cut to a commercial for breakfast cereal, Scott-Heron wrote a powerful poem about the mollifying effects of consumerism. He soon recast the work as a spoken-word recording with minimal accompaniment because "a lot of our school children and a lot of our adults, too . . . do not read comprehensively enough or often enough."[24] Unlike Public Enemy's later metaphorical engagement with TV as a medium for portrayals of Black lives, Scott-Heron cast the tube as the primary facilitator of numbing consumerist apathy:

> You will not be able to plug in, turn on and cop out
> You will not be able to lose yourself on skag
> And skip out for beer during commercials
> Because the revolution will not be televised

Scott-Heron replicates televisual overstimulation to critique it, rattling off a litany of TV references, from commercial jingles to simplistic sitcoms to the formulaic sound bites of the nightly news. He was far from the first public figure to castigate television's lowbrow content—Federal Communications Commission chairman Newton Minow had delivered his iconic "vast wasteland" speech a decade earlier—but Scott-Heron's revolutionary goal was the near opposite of Minow's flinty elitism. If Black Americans continued to waste their time soaking up the white world's hypercapitalist garbage, Scott-Heron argued, the revolution foretold by Malcolm X and ignited by the Black Panthers would be forever deferred.

The fact that Scott-Heron's anti-television provocation did *not* take root in hip-hop's creative mindset is best illustrated by the story of Afrika Bambaataa. After climbing the ranks of the formidable Black Spades to become the rare gang diplomat who could speak equally to each side, the man born Lance Taylor strove to create a more socially conscious civic and cultural organization, partially inspired by a transformative viewing of the 1964 film *Zulu* on TV. Though *Zulu* was narrated from the perspective of British imperialists in South Africa, Taylor, who had renamed himself Bambaataa Aasim after a trip to Africa, chose to focus on the bravery and nobility of the Zulu warriors, who represented a vision of Black Power he'd never seen before. "At that time we was coons, coloreds, negroes, everything degrading. We was busy watching Heckyl and Jeckyl [*sic*], Tarzan—a white guy who is king of the jungle," Bambaataa explained. "To see these Black people fight for their freedom and their land just stuck in my mind. I said when I get older I'm gonna have me a group called the Zulu Nation."[25] To Bambaataa, TV wasn't a consumerist waste product to disavow but a set of raw mass-media materials to resignify. The logic was one of sampling, and Bambaataa was joined by Bronx locals like Clive Campbell (a.k.a. DJ Kool Herc) and Joseph "Grandmaster Flash" Saddler in creating a new cultural form from preexisting cultural commodities. DJs like Bambaataa, Flash, and Herc extracted rhythm "breaks" out of rock, funk, and R&B records; gang members recast street warfare as what a 1984 documentary dubbed the graffiti-waged "style wars"; and the Harlem designer Dapper Dan copy-pasted Gucci and Louis Vuitton logos all over jackets and sweat suits, turning Black neighborhood streets into B-boy runway shows.

When Scott-Heron penned his breakthrough song, it was still possible to imagine a political revolution outside of capitalism (the Black Panthers believed the same thing). But during the 1970s and 1980s, deregulated capitalism implanted itself into everyday life so seamlessly and deeply that the very definition of creativity shifted from the Romantic ideal of individual genius to the artist as clever bricoleur of preexisting styles, commodities, and phrases. Hip-hop's evolution coincided with the rapid growth of corporate brands, which grew from simple visual signifiers of product origin into powerful social forces that drew no distinctions between identity and commodity. In 1984, Michael Jackson rewrote "Billie Jean" to sell Pepsi, for a television ad that hailed its consumers as the "Pepsi generation." Jackson did not actually drink the soda, but that didn't matter because his endorsement, as David Hepworth put it, "was a matter of form, not substance." Jackson insisted that his image be on the screen for only four seconds and that close-up shots of his sequined glove and shoes would fill in. "He had designed himself as a brand," Hepworth observed. "He expected to be similarly recognizable."[26] By the 1990s, the biggest artists were expected to be marketable brands; there was no outside space from which to critique brand culture or capitalism, even for the most independent-minded performers. Just like the "alternative" rockers of the early 1990s who performed with Chuck D, Ice Cube, and Ice-T, reality rappers who staked a claim to cultural authenticity against the mainstream had not somehow transcended the bonds of capitalism but had launched a rival brand. By 1989, Public Enemy cofounder and Def Jam employee Bill Stephney could tell a *Spin* interviewer with no irony that "the revolution *will* be marketed."[27] In a mid-1990s TV ad, the Bronx rapper KRS-One rerecorded "The Revolution Will Not Be Televised" to sell Nike basketball sneakers.

The personification of late-capitalist, multimedia image creation—and reality rappers' initial adversary—was Ronald Reagan. The nation's first recombinant president, Reagan and his advisors pieced together his image from fragments of an imagined American past and delivered it to Americans with a convincing televisual realism. The first president to come of age not as a politician but as an actor and a broadcaster, Reagan made his name in a slew of B movies and, once his Hollywood star started fading, hosted the popular early TV series *General Electric Theater*. Elected governor of California in 1966, Reagan had little grasp of issues and policy, but he did know how to embody a political *image* through television. "Since Reagan was convinced that the camera invariably detects insincerity, his adage about speaking the truth as he saw and felt it applied with special force whenever he appeared on television," wrote his biographer.[28] Presidents had been figuring out how to portray themselves on TV since Eisenhower, but Reagan had been performing for the airwaves since the dawn of the medium. His mastery of televisual politics helped get him elected in 1980, and his staff's savvy at crafting his appearances into taut, visually stimulating packages for the evening news permitted him to weather several scandals and to convincingly allay worries about his declining mental state. On the eve of his 1984 reelection, the *New York Times* remarked that "no matter what is said by the reporters on the evening news, it is the pictures that convey the impression that most Americans get of this presidency."[29] Gil Scott-Heron understood: in a 1984 single, he sang, "We don't need no Re-Ron / We've seen all the Re-Rons before."

Reagan's presidency coincided with, and exploited, the fact that the mass-media representations that reflected the world back to itself—from Hollywood CGI to CNN's satellite-synchronized global news—were growing so impossibly sophisticated that the distinctions between real life and its mediated counterpart seemed to have flipped: the map had grown more detailed than the world it supposedly represented. Jean Baudrillard characterized this surreal scenario as "hyperreality," in which the mediated representation starts to feel *more real* than the world it stands for. Baudrillard has been criticized for the all-encompassing scope of his theories, but by the late 1980s, a significant portion of everyday life was being imagined and lived through the tools and products of electronic media. Reagan's televisual hyperreality coincided with superstar musicians playing concerts to live audiences watching on giant video monitors and with camcorder-wielding Americans convincing themselves that vacations and family gatherings were truly experienced when watched back later on TV.

Reagan's understanding of foreign and domestic affairs seemed to derive less from policy books than from the mass media he constantly consumed. During a 1983 meeting with Democratic leadership about the MX missile, Reagan chose to give an ad hoc review of the film *WarGames*, even telling the chairman of the Joint Chiefs of Staff that he resembled a military leader from the movie.[30] Republican congressional backbencher Newt Gingrich figured out that the best way to get the president's attention was not by requesting an in-person sit-down but by performing on TV for an audience of one. "We got more time with Reagan on C-SPAN than we did with Reagan in his office," he said. "That's a very important reality."[31] The final few years of Reagan's presidency comprised a hyperreal PR battle with the Soviet leader Mikhail Gorbachev to control the narrative about ending the Cold War. Reagan's carefully staged photo ops, slogans, and televised speeches were also a distraction from his frequent tendency to give "mangled and perhaps misleading accounts of his policies or of current events in general." Though Reagan's penchant for what the *New York Times* politely called "debatable assertions of fact" drove reporters crazy, his advisors continued to insist that facts and details were far less interesting to the public than his "larger points."[32]

Reagan's largest point was casting himself as the folksy savior of the American Dream, but Black Americans knew better. While Reagan's foreign policy made for grand diplomatic spectacle, his domestic legacy is marked by a historic increase in the gap between the haves and have-nots, which affected Black communities far more than others, in terms of both policies and their related media representations. Reagan built his domestic agenda upon Richard Nixon's 1968 "law and order" mandate, which sent a coded message to white America that he would end the racial tumult of the late 1960s by waging war on Black urban America. Law-and-order discourse belied a statistical record that showed violent crime declining, but facts didn't matter when faced with the potent reality of "us" (law-abiding whites) versus "them" (the lurking Black criminal threat). Reagan's mythical "war on drugs" ballooned Nixon's reclassification of illegal substances from a public health matter into a criminal spectacle, and his hyperreal "war on crime" redefined police officers from public servants to "crime fighters." As many knew at the time, "drugs" and "crime" were, like Reagan's notorious "welfare queens," code words for urban Black Americans who sought more than their station allowed. Reagan's speechwriters were experts at slyly coded racism, as his key advisor Lee Atwater explained: "You start out in 1954 by saying, 'Nigger, nigger, nigger.' By 1968 you can't say 'nigger'—that hurts you. Backfires. So you say stuff like forced busing, states' rights and all that stuff. You're getting so abstract now [that] you're talking about cutting taxes.... [S]aying, 'We want to cut this' ... is much more abstract than even the busing thing, and a hell of a lot more abstract than 'Nigger, nigger.' "[33] Republican "dog whistling" language enabled them to vilify as burdensome, wasteful "big government" the desires of Black leaders and most Democrats to strengthen the welfare state, impose racial preferences on government contracts and private-sector employment, and institute affirmative action in college admissions. To the more outspoken New Right, those goals were simply "reverse racism."

By recasting crime as the top domestic problem, Reagan roped Black men into a starring role as the nation's lurking criminal menace. As explained by the sociologist Herman Gray, while the 1980s phenomenon

The Cosby Show portrayed a fully assimilated, largely apolitical vision of upper-middle-class Black life, the evening news was redefining whites from victimizer to victimized, while Blackness was constructed "along a continuum ranging from menace on one end to immorality on the other, with irresponsibility located somewhere in the middle."[34] Once viewed as an unprofitable loss leader guiding viewers toward prime time, local TV news broadcasts were transformed into technologically sophisticated profit-making machines in the late 1970s by adopting satellite-equipped news vans, ever-smaller cameras, and inexpensive, durable three-quarter-inch videotape. With most metropolitan markets having two or three stations competing for the same audience, the tools of commercial television—ratings books, market research, and high-end graphics generators—came to local affiliates. As nightly newscasts were renamed "Eyewitness News" and "Action News," and colorful graphics reading "LIVE," "ON THE SCENE," and "BREAKING" helped reporters transport viewers live to some dramatic event, the boring world of government meetings and policy debates gave way to the sensationalistic, ratings-grabbing world of crime. Viewers were pinned to their couches each evening by hyperreal lawbreakers who weren't Hollywood creations but members of their local communities, and Black citizens bore the brunt of this tantalizing fear: one 1990 study concluded that crime-obsessed local TV news was likely "contributing to the metamorphosis of white racism."[35] Similarly, a 1995 study into the "perceived realism" of *Cops* and its successors—a slightly more polished version of nightly news telecasts—concluded that reality TV crime incited more arousal and aggression than fictional crime shows and appealed to viewers who were "likely to enjoy the capture and punishment of criminal suspects who are often members of racial minorities."[36]

At the tail end of Reagan's presidency, a crop of young Black cultural entrepreneurs emerged to forcefully counterprogram his conservative, law-and-order revolution with a harsh reality of their own. Far more than rhyme notebooks and street-corner ciphers, reality rappers were artists of the recording booth, digital sampler, and mixing desk, their extravagant truths realized only in the unpredictable contexts of late-capitalist circulation: music videos, interviews, liner notes, publicity photographs, magazine profiles, and op-eds. They served as discursive foils to the pro-police programs *Cops* and *America's Most Wanted*;

they slipped into the role of talk show hosts who compellingly illustrated the ills and joys of Black lives in America; they delved into the tawdry sensationalism of sex, money, and murder that was the stock-in-trade of evening tabloids; and they issued album-length political programs about everything from Black self-sufficiency to the relevance of the First Amendment. And when they purposefully crossed the boundaries of good taste by sinking into anti-Semitic or misogynistic muck, or refused to draw boundaries around real and performative violence or political action, reality rappers became the quintessential *subjects* of tabloid culture, generating nonstop headlines about their on- and off-record actions and antics. Cutting across their various on- and off-record roles—dead-eyed killer, street reporter, free speech advocate, barbershop bullshitter, talk show host, nationalist world builder, plain-talking pundit, sensitive thug, minority entrepreneur—reality rappers were expert provocateurs, stoking postmodern moral panics out of law-and-order paranoia and trolling the racial dog whistles of the New Right's "family values" discourse. Like TV producers, journalists, and ordinary Americans seeking their fifteen minutes of fame, rappers negotiated the social, cultural, technological, and industrial shifts that coalesced during the late 1980s and early 1990s to wage a sensationalistic, hyperrealistic, and populist struggle with the powers that be over the representation of Black lives in America. In the process, they helped establish a precedent that holds fast deep into the next century: what we know as reality is comprehensible only after being forged in the crucible of mass-mediated popular culture.

CHAPTER 1

PEACE IS A DREAM, REALITY IS A KNIFE

The December 4, 1986, issue of *Rolling Stone* was a landmark: for the first time, a rap group made the cover. The accomplishment was one of numerous firsts on Run-DMC's résumé. Their current LP, *Raising Hell*, was the most critically acclaimed rap album yet and was on its way to becoming the first of the genre to sell double platinum, following their first two LPs, which were the first in the rap world to sell, respectively, gold and platinum. Run-DMC were the first street rappers to earn regular airplay on MTV, and *Hell*'s smash single, "Walk This Way," a rerecording of Aerosmith's mid-1970s hit cut with the band itself, earned them crossover airplay on rock and Top 40 stations. When their tour manager, Lyor Cohen, brought a brand rep to a concert to watch as thousands of fans waved their Superstars in the air to *Hell*'s first single, "My Adidas," the trio became the first rap group to ink a million-dollar sponsorship deal. Run-DMC's status as the lone hip-hop act playing the 1985 charity spectacular Live Aid mirrored their status as rap's preeminent diplomats to the rest of the music world. But the tone of their *Rolling Stone* profile was less celebratory than apprehensive, devoted less to the group's series of firsts than to their newfound affiliation with real-life criminality. "As its fame has increased, the trio has consistently been associated with violence," the writer noted. "To much of white America, rap means mayhem and bloodletting."[1]

Run-DMC had acquired this unwelcome association a few months earlier at the Long Beach Arena, at the fifty-sixth of sixty-four stops on the group's nationwide Raising Hell arena tour with LL Cool J and Whodini. During LL's opening set, local gang members in the crowd started throwing signs and snatching chains. While Whodini performed their hit single "Friends," the violence accelerated: gang members began flashing red and blue colors and breaking legs off of chairs to use as weapons against their sworn enemies. The venue's security guards started ripping off their own shirts to avoid identification. While local DJ Greg Mack took the stage to encourage calm, a person was thrown over a balcony and landed on the stage behind him. All the while, Run-DMC were sequestered in their dressing room, armed with whatever they could get their hands on to protect themselves. By the time police cleared the arena, the trio were at their hotel, watching the aftermath on the TV news.

The next morning, the press was calling it a riot: two hundred to three hundred gang members caused forty-two injuries from beatings, a few stabbings, and a gunshot wound. When officials at the Los Angeles Palladium canceled Run-DMC's concert scheduled for the next evening, the trio shifted into face-saving public-relations mode. "Those kids have nothing to do with Run-D.M.C. They're scumbags and roaches and they would have hit me in the head, too," said Joe Simmons, a.k.a. Run. He added that they wouldn't play Los Angeles again "until police and the authorities take sterner measures to protect Run-D.M.C. fans from local gangs," which "stand for everything that rap is against."[2] To the *Washington Post*, Jam Master Jay simply quoted "It's Tricky" to defend the group's reputation:

> We are not thugs
> We don't use drugs
> But you assume
> On your own
> They offer coke
> And lots of dope
> But we just leave it alone

The story had already gotten away from them. Journalists quickly noted that the Long Beach violence was not a one-off occurrence but part of a trend that worsened as the tour progressed. Police arrested eighteen outside of the July 21 Madison Square Garden stop and twenty-seven following the Pittsburgh show a week later, leading that city's public safety director to opine that "the lyrics in the songs are provocative and pornographic. They incite violence."[3] Officials in Providence, Rhode Island, canceled the group's August 28 concert, and promoters in Philadelphia moved a rap concert completely unrelated to the group from a high school football stadium to the Spectrum arena in response to a neighborhood outcry. Because rap was still a novelty to much of the country, the focus soon swelled to include the entire culture. A week after Long Beach, a *Los Angeles Times* article titled "Can Rap Survive Gang War?" featured a lede that could have been written about the hysterical reaction to the rise of rock and roll in the 1950s: "Rap groups are being accused of inciting hostility and a bad attitude in young music fans." The story featured a quote from Tipper Gore, who was happy to bring rap into her public battle against what she had dubbed "porn rock." "Angry, disillusioned, unloved kids unite behind heavy-metal or rap music, and the music says it's OK to beat people up," Gore said.[4] But later that month, a spokeswoman for the Parents Music Resource Center revealed that Gore's comment was based on scant evidence. "None of us have had a chance to see Run-D.M.C. live in concert, [and] there's nothing in the lyrics that is really explicit or would incite kids to violence," she said.[5] Run-DMC's résumé had added another first: they were the first rappers to be scapegoated by the national press for inciting violence.

Four years earlier, Grandmaster Flash and the Furious Five codified hip-hop as the medium of realist tabloid reportage with "The Message," a stark and funky track born from a scan of their devastated Bronx neighborhood at the peak of a demoralizing economic recession. "Broken glass everywhere / People pissin' on the stairs, you know they just don't care," observes Melvin "Melle Mel" Glover in bold headline argot to open the track. Later, Ed "Duke Bootee" Fletcher chips in his own editorial: "Got a bum education, double-digit inflation / Can't take the train to the job, there's a strike at the station." The song's multiple refrains comprise a devastating reflection on the toll of ghetto life:

> Don't push me 'cause I'm close to the edge
> I'm trying not to lose my head
> It's like a jungle sometimes
> It makes me wonder how I keep from goin' under

Three years after "Rapper's Delight" introduced the world to hip-hop, "The Message" reached no. 62 on *Billboard*'s pop chart, and *Rolling Stone* called it "the most detailed and devastating report from underclass America since Bob Dylan decried the lonesome death of Hattie Carroll—or...since Marvin Gaye took a long look around and wondered what was going on."[6] Not everyone in the Furious Five was a fan. After hearing Duke's lyrics, Flash argued that "people don't wanna take their problems to the disco" and opted out.[7] The rest of the group were persuaded by Sylvia Robinson, the founder of Sugar Hill Records and a music industry veteran whose A&R skills had made "Rapper's Delight" a hit. With a strong sense that a soul-style "message song" would resonate broadly, Robinson produced "The Message" herself, down to determining the order that the rappers appeared on the track. She was proven right.

In the wake of "The Message," every aspiring rapper needed their own socially conscious anthem, or what were commonly called "reality rhymes." The next year, a trio of young men from working-class Hollis, Queens, staked their claim to street reportage. The group that would become Run-DMC was put together by Russell Simmons, a former Seven Immortals gangbanger and party promoter who also managed the breakout hip-hop star Kurtis Blow. Simmons's little brother Joe roped in his friend Darryl McDaniels, who brought notebooks filled with rhymes. Joe and Darryl's first collaboration, "It's Like That," was not as nuanced and vivid as "The Message," but the duo rapped with headline force:

> Unemployment at a record high
> People coming, people going, people born to die
> Don't ask me, because I don't know why
> But it's like that, and that's the way it is

It is not unimaginable that "It's Like That" was resignifying "And that's the way it is," the familiar sign-off that CBS News' Walter Cronkite had uttered for the final time in March 1981, less than two months after Ronald Reagan's inauguration. The phrase maintains its circular logic, but Run-DMC invest it with a resigned undercurrent born of a young Black man's sense that little could be done to change the world apart from spreading the ugly truth. Even more than "The Message," Run-DMC recast hip-hop as a space to reimagine a journalistic perspective, while breaking its sonic signature down to its rudiments. "It's Like That" sounded nothing like disco or the electro-funk of "The Message." Instead, the verses were backed with the starkest and most unforgiving hip-hop beat yet, built by an Oberheim DMX drum machine, a few synthesizer stabs, and feverish bars about the sad state of the world. This was not music to dance to. It was the new gold standard for hip-hop hardness and realism, reflected in the group's look, based in the "stickup kid" style of fresh Adidas Superstars, black fedoras, leather coats, and gold chains: much more accessible to the average Black kid than the elaborate Parliament-Funkadelic-style getups of the Furious Five. Run-DMC's visual image was reflected in the track's B side, "Sucker M.C.'s." Now with DJ Jason "Jam Master Jay" Mizell on the turntables, "Sucker M.C.'s" issued a breaking news alert to their fellow rappers: raise your game or step aside. The "It's Like That" / "Sucker M.C.'s" single was a seismic shift in hip-hop, almost single-handedly cleaving the music and culture from its party-rocking past and laying the foundation for hip-hop's big takeover with a mix of savvy street reportage and hyperstylish toughness.

At the time, Southern California's fledgling hip-hop scene was a nonentity on the national stage. The Bloods and the Crips had received more national press than any rapper from the area. By the time they went to battle inside the Long Beach Arena, the gangs were on their way to becoming the latest avatars for the mythic, ever-encroaching Black criminality that had saturated national discourse over the previous five years. They first came to national attention via Ed Bradley's Emmy-winning 1981 CBS News documentary, *Murder, Teenage Style*. "Just what is it in our society that produces children who shoot to kill for no apparent reason?" Bradley asked at the end of the broadcast. "Guns are not the issue as much as the fundamental social problems we may no longer want to face. But if we don't, what does our future hold?" Responses to the fundamental social problems were in short supply, but media coverage was not: by 1985, stories about the Los Angeles "teen warlords" who were violently expanding their murderous, crack-dealing empires across the

American west were regularly making national news. Many reporters characterized the violence for oblivious readers using pop-culture comparisons; gang-glutted South Los Angeles, one wrote, was an area where "the knives and chains of *West Side Story* have given way to Uzi submachine guns."[8]

Though Run-DMC intended to set a positive example for young Black men, they lost control over the meaning of their work once it hit the mainstream. In Long Beach, their tough image, hard rhymes, and appealing style were filtered through worldviews dominated by a ferocious, zero-sum street rivalry. According to an eighteen-year-old Bloods member interviewed by *Rolling Stone*, the Long Beach concert was less a site for musical enjoyment than a stylish backdrop for settling external antagonisms:

> We don't get along outside, so we're not going to get along inside. Some go to get a kick out of Run-D.M.C.'s music, but most of the guys just go there to fight. I did. We knew other gang bangers would be there. [Run-DMC's] music is up to date. We like their rhymin'. It's hip, it says something to me, and I like their clothes—it's B-boy style to the highest degree. So gangs want to see them, and when you put all these groups together, you're lookin' for trouble.[9]

Popular-music fandom has always been defined by rituals of consumerist communion. Buying records, hanging up posters, and watching music videos are preparation for the one-of-a-kind experience of seeing one's idols perform live while surrounded by thousands of fellow disciples. The 1985 Live Aid benefit and the litany of charity spectacles that followed it offered proof of rock's power to unite people from all walks of life for a good cause. But incidents like the one at the Long Beach Arena exposed the privileged underpinnings of rock's self-aggrandizing self-image. Run-DMC were the first pop superstars to represent the generation of young Black Americans who had been abandoned by society-wide deindustrialization and mass incarceration, left to shape their identities and acquire status not through family ties or social institutions but a fusion of street life and the dreamworld of consumerism. As Long Beach revealed, the rituals of music fandom not only can expose preexisting cultural antagonisms among marginalized populations but can lay a foundation for them to explode.

With the success of *Raising Hell* meeting the controversy of Long Beach, Run-DMC had reached a familiar crossroads for rock stars. In *Rolling Stone*'s phrasing, they had to "decide how to be pop and streetwise at the same time."[10] But while white rock stars could easily merge outlaw allure with a transcendent, unifying message, Run-DMC faced the burden of double representation known to Black musicians: they had to translate a "street" reality into a consumable pop product while also playing the role of racial diplomat to the mainstream. Within the group, there was a strong sense that they could not win: either they watered down their music for a pop audience and alienated their Black fan base, or they doubled down on street toughness and imperiled their standing among the lucrative white mainstream. "Walk This Way" had made Run-DMC a household name, but they resented having to constantly perform a cover of a decade-old song written by a white rock band trying to sound like a Black funk band. And while their lyrics embraced the kind of nonviolence and antidrug language that fit with the "Just Say No" era of personal responsibility, Russell Simmons worried that their success was making them soft. "I look at them and say, 'Stop being a pussy,'" Simmons told *Rolling Stone*. "Let's hope a year from now people don't think they're suckers."[11] Run went so far as to tell the interviewer that he hoped the group's next album flopped so the group could shed the "crossover" stigma. "You have to do what's real," he told the interviewer. What exactly "real" meant, to Run and the group's fans, was anyone's guess.

The issue was larger than Run-DMC, extending to the roles and responsibilities of Black public figures after five years of Reaganism. A few minutes of the October 18, 1986, episode of *Saturday Night Live* provide a snapshot of where Run-DMC fit in the landscape of Black popular culture. That evening's guest host was Malcolm-Jamal Warner, the teen heartthrob who played Theo Huxtable on *The Cosby Show*, the nation's number one sitcom. To introduce Run-DMC as the episode's musical guest, Warner handed the mic to the upstart independent film director Spike Lee, who was fresh off a Cannes screening of his debut feature, *She's Gotta Have It*. Before introducing the group, Lee, reprising his motormouthed Mars Blackmon character, defended rap from its numerous critics: "Lately, the media has been doggin' rap music, sayin' it incites violence, riots. Well, if you go to rock concerts, those are wild, they be illin', throwin' people off balconies, tossin' cherry bombs, but that never makes the papers. But what you have to understand is that rap music is the music of inner-city Black youth." While Lee is talking, the shot cuts back and forth to Run-DMC roughing up *SNL* producer Lorne Michaels backstage for the crime of scuffing their sneakers. In ultra-dry *SNL* fashion, they were disproving Lee's defense while he offered it. "And if any riots across America next ten seconds [it] won't be because of my next guest," Lee continues. "My homeboys, from Hollis, Queens . . . Run-DMC!" The group leave Michaels in a heap on the floor, kick him one last time, and jog to the stage to perform "Walk This Way."

This brief skit outlined the often uneasy coexistence of what Todd Boyd later called the "three phases of contemporary Black male expression" that were struggling for charismatic authority during the post–civil rights moment. The evening's host, Warner, was linked to Bill Cosby, whom Boyd characterizes as a bourgeois "race man" devoted to a politics of racial uplift rooted in Dr. King's assimilationist civil rights movement. Though Warner was portrayed as a hip young Black man (in his opening monologue, he showed a hopelessly square Dana Carvey how to dance), on *The Cosby Show*'s 1986–1987 third season, he was featured in story lines based around Count Basie, the Tuskegee Airmen, and the 1963 March on Washington. Spike Lee represented what Boyd called the "new Black aesthetic" of the post–civil rights era, espousing a more confrontational nationalist politics drawn from Malcolm X and a degree from Atlanta's historically Black Morehouse College. And then there was Run-DMC: on one hand, they were squeaky-clean teen idols who performed at Live Aid and ended *Raising Hell* with "Proud to Be Black," which name-dropped Harriet Tubman, Martin Luther King Jr., and Malcolm X; on the other hand, they were performing a matter of weeks after Bloods and Crips had gone to war at one of their concerts, leading the news media to cast them as the earliest avatars of what Boyd called the "nigga" phase of postindustrial, hyperreal Black politics, which derived not from the pulpit, protest march, or university but from the street.[12]

Run-DMC were in the center of hip-hop's first moral panic, a media frenzy that linked the still-emerging world of rap music with the past half decade's overwrought paranoia about the Black violence of the "inner cities." Developed by sociologists in the early 1970s,[13] the moral panic concept explains how news media, law enforcement, and the justice system do not merely report, monitor, and punish acts of social deviance and crime but work together to create the *very meaning* of crime. The process is cyclical: overwrought press coverage of a supposed societal scourge feeds into an intensified police response, which draws more press attention to the next instance. Locals grow worried about events being held in their neighborhoods, and local politicians and judges promise to crack down on the menace—which, in many cases, doesn't actually exist anywhere save the legal and media networks that brought it into being. At root, moral panics are promotional schemes for the status quo, reaffirming the righteous roles of the press and law enforcement. They're often spurred by what sociologists call "moral entrepreneurs," those public figures, like Tipper Gore, who gain fame by steering public discourse in a particular direction.[14] With all these parts in place, moral panics can quickly crystallize a new reality for anyone who buys into their message: kids are running wild, society is crumbling, crime is rampant. By vanquishing the threat, the press and the police collaborate to reestablish the status quo. Black popular music had faced moral panics throughout the twentieth century: cops raided jazz clubs with photographers in tow during Prohibition and clamped down on DJ Alan Freed's racially mixed "Moondog" dances during the early days of rock and roll. It didn't matter that Long Beach was three thousand miles away from Run-DMC's hometown of Hollis, Queens, or that the trio were closer to Theo Huxtable than any stickup kid: the press and the police had plenty of precedent to link the first superstar rap group with the growing scourge of Black gang violence.

Yet while moral panics can and do torpedo fortunes quickly, with the right amount of media savvy, a performer can flip legal controversy and public notoriety into free promotion and the appearance of outlaw authenticity. This is a primary legacy of British punk, for instance, where the Sex Pistols and others engineered their own controversy from the outset, relying on a voracious British tabloid press to give them as much gratis publicity as they could use. While Run-DMC were very much *not* cast in this mold, one of their biggest Los Angeles fans was. Tracy Marrow, known around LA as the rapper/promoter/hustler Ice-T, was blown away by Run-DMC's performance at the LA Memorial Sports Arena three months before Long Beach. "I was trying to rap, but I didn't realize it could be arena level," he later said. "Up to that point, rap was something you did at house parties, garages, and basements. . . . [T]hat night I went home and wrote."[15] More important than Ice-T's creativity and ambition was his deep understanding of how the modern media system functioned. Where Run-DMC fought tooth and nail against the racist moral panic that had been foisted upon them, Ice-T deputized himself as rap's tabloid reporter from the front lines of the Los Angeles gang crisis. A year after the Long Beach incident, Run-DMC had ceded their spot at the leading edge of street rap to the gang-derived, violent realism of Ice-T, rap's first one-man moral panic.

Fourteen years before Long Beach, the Crips first entered the media spotlight after a Los Angeles concert. Certain that the young attendees of a 1972 *Soul Train*–sponsored showcase featuring Wilson Pickett, Curtis Mayfield, and War would be dressed in their most fashionable attire, a couple dozen members of the fledgling gang waited for the Palladium to empty. After sixteen-year-old attendee Robert Ballou and four of his friends crossed the street, they were accosted by gang members intent on stealing their leather jackets. A tackle on the Los Angeles High football team, Ballou fought back but was outnumbered and beaten to death in broad daylight, his body left in the parking lot of a nearby gas station. Though Ballou's story drew attention to the burgeoning problem of Los Angeles gang violence, cops and reporters alike remained unsure about what actually determined gang membership. The day before the killing, the *Los Angeles Times* ran a story titled "Black Youth Gangs: Is Threat Overstated?," which opened with a conversation between a Los Angeles Police Department officer assigned to South Central's Seventy-Seventh Street Division and a young man under arrest:

> "Are you a Crip?" the policeman asked.
> "Yeah man, I'm a Crip."
> "What's a Crip."
> "I don't know."[16]

By the end of the year, the police and the press had united to give the Crips a distinct identity. "Gang Violence Linked to Desire for Notoriety," an

LA Times headline blared. The article included a detailed map noting the "operating areas" of the major gangs monitored by the LAPD's Seventy-Seventh Street Division: the West and East Side Crips, the Athens Park gang, the Piru gang, and several others. Police had constructed a profile of the average gang member that the story printed verbatim, while noting that the cops were using those profiles to stop suspicious cars, monitor local high schools, and photograph groups of young Black men gathered in public. "There is no question that street gang violence has surpassed the stage of mere talk and rumor," the reporter wrote. "The realities are inescapable."[17]

Though they surfaced in the early 1970s, Black street gangs had been a fact of life in South Los Angeles for decades. They were one of the many social and cultural effects of the Second Great Migration, the period from the 1940s to the late 1960s when millions of Black Americans escaped the horrifying conditions of the Jim Crow South to seek well-paying, unionized, blue-collar jobs in the North and West, a couple decades after millions of others had done the same. Yet as they moved into cities like Watts, South Central, and Compton, Black citizens encountered just as much violent resistance from white homeowners, realtors, and police, who saw them less as fellow citizens than as infiltrators. The LAPD might have had a sterling national reputation thanks to the popular NBC program *Dragnet*, the first police procedural, which was executive produced by Chief Bill Parker. But to young Black men in Los Angeles, the LAPD were a vicious gang, ready to deliver a beating at a second's notice to anyone found in the wrong (white) neighborhood. Black citizens were also terrorized by white street gangs with names like the Spook Hunters, who roamed the streets with the same mindset; one of these young white vigilantes was Daryl Gates, who would grow up to be Parker's protégé and who recalled in his memoir that he and his friends would spend Friday nights hunting down Black individuals who wandered into Highland Park.[18] In response, Black youth formed geographically rooted social clubs that offered strength in numbers, with names like Dartanians, Gladiators, Blood Alley, Haciendas, Slausons, and Businessmen. These early South Central gangs, according to Mike Davis, were "the architects of social space in new and usually hostile settings… 'cool worlds' of urban socialization for poor young newcomers from rural Texas, Louisiana and Mississippi."[19]

By the early 1960s, the Slausons had become the largest such organization, and their most feared branch, the Renegades, was led by Alprentice "Bunchy" Carter, a charismatic and handsome local legend known as the "Mayor of the Ghetto." When Carter was sentenced to a four-year bid in Soledad State Prison for his role in an armed bank robbery, he met the activist and intellectual Eldridge Cleaver, who was doing a stint for assault with intent. Cleaver inspired Carter to join the Black Panthers upon his release, and within months, Carter became one of the revolutionary organization's most effective recruiters, credited with drawing hundreds of wayward Black men and women off the streets and into an organization with a liberationist political platform. Yet as the Panthers' popularity swelled with each of the organization's media-tailored demonstrations, they were increasingly monitored, infiltrated, and even killed by J. Edgar Hoover's FBI, under the auspices of the COINTELPRO operation. In a November 1968 memo to field officers, Hoover strove to foment the growing discord between the revolution-minded Panthers and the culturally focused US organization:

> A serious struggle is taking place between the Black Panther Party [BPP] and the US organization. The struggle has reached such a proportion that it is taking on the aura of gang warfare with attendant threats of murder and reprisals. In order to fully capitalize upon BPP and US differences as well as exploit all avenues of creating further dissension in the ranks of the BPP, recipient offices are instructed to submit imaginative and hard-hitting counterintelligence measures aimed at crippling the BPP.[20]

Less than two months later, at a heated meeting about the future of the University of California, Los Angeles's Black studies program, Carter was shot and killed. Though the FBI's role in fomenting this tragedy would not be known for several years, Carter's death, and those of other charismatic Panther leaders targeted by federal agents, would effectively neutralize the group within a few years.

Raymond Washington and Stanley "Tookie" Williams stepped into the breach. A member of the Baby Avenues gang, Washington idolized Carter and had developed a similar knack for block-by-block civic organizing. Unlike the Panthers, however, Washington and his fearsome associate Williams loathed armed violence, preferring to instill fear in their foes through hand-to-hand combat. The two men federated South Los Angeles's disparate local gangs into the Crips, whose regional enemies— the Brims of South Central, the Watts Haciendas, and the Pirus in Compton, among others—eventually congealed into the Bloods, named after the epithet that Black soldiers gave one another in Vietnam. After Washington was killed in a drive-by and Williams was sent to San Quentin, the nature of LA gangbanging shifted along with the socioeconomic landscape. As social programs were defunded, well-paying jobs were automated and outsourced, and drugs and guns started flowing into Black neighborhoods, gangbanging shifted into a violent form of late capitalism, a color-coded, Black-on-Black war over local turf and market share waged by street soldiers with no aims at achieving political or structural power. Like competing businesses, subfactions sprouted up left and right, named after blocks and streets and intersections. To Davis, the Crips' and the Bloods' dead-eyed nihilism was "unknown in the days of the Slausons and anathema to everything that the Panthers had stood for."[21] They could still provide a sense of social cohesion for young Black men, but these gangs' primary functions were criminal: dealing crack, committing petty larceny, and murdering each another, interpreting a mention in the LA Times Metro section as a macabre endorsement of their exploits and a dose of notoriety. In his 1993 autobiography, the legendary Crip Sanyika Shakur (formerly Kody "Monster" Scott) cited the early 1980s as the moment that the rivalry started to resemble the Cold War between the United States and the USSR, an arms race with no point other than to cow the opposition into inaction. "Our war, like most gang wars, was not fought for territory or any specific goal other than the destruction of individuals," he wrote. "The idea was to drop enough bodies, cause enough terror and suffering so that they'd come to their senses and realize that we were the wrong set to fuck with."[22]

Even more than a decade after their formation, actual gang membership evaded simple definition to outsiders. Bloods and Crips had no discernible politics, spoke a coded language, covered their faces with blue and red bandanas, and signaled to one another with cryptic hand gestures and inscrutable graffiti tags. And in South Los Angeles, they were so widespread that simply living on a block made one an affiliate member. A sociologist coined the term "gang colonization" to describe the fact that it was "nearly impossible to have a social life without the influence of the gang."[23] Sanyika Shakur claimed that the only gang experts are gang members themselves, which leaves significant room for interpretation. "It's easy to persuade the general public of your 'righteousness' when you control major media," explained Shakur. "But those of us who control nothing are in the precarious position of having someone guess what our position is. This leaves quite a large gap for misinformation."[24] That gap was filled by the LAPD and the *LA Times*: the police were granted the authority to manage socioeconomic problems of crime, violence, and drugs, which meant ignoring the realities of racism, segregation, and poverty in lieu of surveilling, harassing, and arresting anyone who fit the gangbanger profile. And the *LA Times* "naturalized police rhetoric and logic by often reporting in terms constructed by the police," according to one researcher, which essentially justified police action as the only solution to the gang problem.[25] Where law enforcement and journalism failed, popular culture stepped in, casting the Bloods and the Crips as the latest spectacular subculture to transfix the nation.

After his parents died in the early 1970s, a teenaged Tracy Marrow moved from New Jersey to live with an aunt in South Los Angeles. Though he resided in a comfortably middle-class Black neighborhood, Marrow became affiliated with the Hoover Street Crips because of his girlfriend's home address. Marrow did not participate in any of the most violent gangbanging activities—he was no soldier—but he was considered an "affiliate" member who committed petty crimes and relied on the group for his social life. After transferring to the Crip-controlled Crenshaw High School, Marrow became much more deeply immersed in the lifestyle and started writing and performing oral poems about the violent, macho, turf-obsessed activities he witnessed on a daily basis. What he did not see, he filled in with his imagination, copying what he heard on the bawdy, R-rated comedy albums of Dolemite, the alter-ego of the singer and comedian Rudy Ray Moore, whose routines updated traditional African American barroom poems and badman toasts. Before "Rapper's Delight" introduced the world to hip-hop, Marrow was reciting what he called "Crip rhymes":

> Strollin' through the city in the middle of the night
> Niggas on my left and niggas on my right

Yo I cr-cr-cr-cripped every nigga I see
If you bad enough come fuck with me[26]

After graduating from Crenshaw High School, having a child, and seeing few opportunities, Marrow spent four years in the army, stationed as far away as Missouri. When he returned to South Central in the early 1980s, he found a city transformed. The Crips and the Bloods had dramatically expanded their territory and upgraded their weaponry, and Marrow's hustler friends were raking in thousands of dollars a week by robbing jewelry stores.

While Marrow dove into the criminal world with abandon, South Central's club scene was taking off, thanks in large part to Rodger Clayton's mobile DJ and promotions crew, Uncle Jamm's Army, the network of dance parties and concerts that helped introduce hip-hop to Los Angeles. This was where Tracy Marrow became Ice-T, hosting hip-hop nights at the local club Radio, a gig that earned him a brief spot in the 1984 pop-lock exploitation flick *Breakin'*. A year later, he merged emceeing and street journalism as the de facto host of the LA hip-hop documentary *Breakin' 'N' Enterin'*, rapping most of his on-camera narration:

Now a hip-hop club is not a disco
It's a record-cuttin', cold-crushin' rappin' show
Like New York's Roxy or L.A.'s Radio
DJs keep you at a peak and on the go[27]

T released a few singles on local indie labels with names befitting the sound of LA's rap scene: Techno Hop Records and Electrobeat Records. The 1985 track "Killers" was his first foray into social commentary, bemoaning the thirst for violence shared by everyone from newly recruited police officers to PTSD-suffering veterans and domestic violence perpetrators.

Yet it was the B side to the 1986 single "Dog'n the Wax" that transformed Ice-T's career and established West Coast rap on the national scene. Instead of the brash boasts of the single's A side, "6 in the Mornin'" merged Run-DMC's hard-core minimalism with a densely packed narrative style closer to a Blaxploitation screenplay or the Black pulp fiction of the crime novelist Donald Goines. While Run-DMC used their

Adidas sneakers as a continuity device linking their Queens corners to the Live Aid stage, T used the footwear brand as a scene-setting narrative detail, opening his story in medias res: "Six in the mornin', police at my door / Fresh Adidas squeak across the bathroom floor." From there, T's character feverishly darts through a number of criminal activities, from the mundane (shooting dice on the sidewalk) to the spectacular (a citywide car chase). After serving a several-year prison bid, he falls back into the game and winds up having to flee LA for New York, where he's embraced as a hero.

The primary inspiration for "6" was the 1985 underground hit "P.S.K. (What Does It Mean?)," independently released by the Philadelphia rapper Schoolly D. Though separated by thousands of miles, Schoolly and T were kindred spirits: in an October 1986 *Spin* interview, Schoolly described his quasi-journalistic songwriting method: "All I do in my rhymes is see something over here and report it over there."[28] T adapted Schoolly's eerily calm vocal style, intonation, and cadence and boiled the cavernous production of "P.S.K." down to its drum-machine rudiments. What he left out, however, were the kinds of specific details that Schoolly left in. "P.S.K.""s titular abbreviation, as was noted in virtually every piece written about the single, stood for Park Side Killers, the gang that patrolled the neighborhood near Fifty-Second Street and Parkside in West Philadelphia, where Schoolly grew up. T's rationale for eliding too many LA gang–specific references on "6" derived in part from basic marketing. "I'm not going to alienate my fans by claiming a certain area. I'll represent the whole West Coast player life," he explained.[29] Yet in the clubs, roller rinks, and high school gymnasiums that served as South Los Angeles's rap scene, T was forced to negotiate the realities of gang life just like everyone else. While signing autographs after performing at a high school in 1986, T was chased off the premises by a Crips crew—a descendant of the group he came up with—for the crime of wearing red in a blue neighborhood.[30]

The detail that most directly connects "6 in the Mornin'" to the realities of South Central street life appears in the song's fourth verse, when T's character hits the streets again after seven years behind bars. Upon his release, he finds a dystopian landscape where "the batter rams rolling, rocks are the thing / Life has no meaning and money is king." The battering ram was the most dystopian symbol of the media-savvy war on drugs being waged by Daryl Gates, who had become LAPD chief in 1978. For decades, the LAPD had been the nation's most highly publicized and emulated police force, and Gates, who was mentored by Chief Parker, used moral entrepreneurship to promote his vision of militaristic law enforcement. Most incredibly, he outfitted a V-100 Commando armored personnel carrier with a fourteen-foot ramming pole to take down the heavily fortified "rock houses" that crack dealers had reportedly established in the city's suburbs. In February 1985, Gates called the press to cover the tank's first suburban deployment, and in full view of newspaper reporters and television cameras, he christened the vehicle and then rode inside while it smashed through the front of a Pacoima home. The sensationalistic visuals belied the raid's paltry haul: cops netted less than 0.1 grams of cocaine, and, according to the *LA Times*, "the only occupants of the home were two women and three children, two of whom were eating ice cream."[31] An LA cop with a publicist's mind, Gates was far less interested in the batter ram's law enforcement efficacy than in its iconography: the "drug war" made terrifyingly literal.

The batter ram's iconography was not lost on Black residents of South Los Angeles. The most compelling coverage of its deployment came from the local DJ Toddy Tee, who wrote and recorded "Batterram" after seeing one smash through a home on television. In the song's first verse, Toddy calls out Los Angeles mayor Tom Bradley, Chief Gates, and President Reagan. "It seems to me that you've created a myth," he raps.

> I done seen it on the news and at the show
> And now it's interrupted on the stereo
> The citizens all say it's the talk of the town
> It has hydraulic lifts that go up and down

Toddy aims the second verse straight at Mayor Bradley: "I got a couple complaints about the LAPD," he opens, before crafting a dramatization that echoed the *LA Times* story of the batter ram's first deployment: He and his children are watching cartoons on television when someone knocks on the door, trying to score rock cocaine. When Tee directs him elsewhere, the man reveals himself as Chief Gates, whom Toddy recalls not for his law enforcement credentials but from seeing him on Channel 7. Convinced of his own authority, the Gates character hops in the tank, fires it up, and drives it through Toddy's home. Elsewhere on the tape, Toddy revoiced recent rap and R&B singles to reflect life in South Central: Rockwell's hit "Somebody's Watching Me" became "The Cops Are Watching Me," UTFO's "Roxanne, Roxanne" was reinvented as "Rockman, Rockman," and Toddy even expressed his admiration for Ice-T by rapping over the "Killers" beat on "Toddy Tee Rocks." The tape was a smash hit in the swap meet and live show networks where Toddy earned his living, and the KDAY DJ Greg Mack had him rerecord "Batterram" for the radio. The new single—with higher production quality, less cursing, and the character of Gates replaced with an anonymous cop—suffused Black Los Angeles throughout 1985.[32]

Though Ice-T admired Toddy, he based his performance persona on the man who had established himself as the preeminent chronicler of Black street life more than a decade earlier. After twenty years working as a pimp on the South Side of Chicago and several stints behind bars, Robert Beck moved to South Central Los Angeles in the early 1960s. A few years later, when many Black Americans felt newly empowered to express themselves in the wake of the Watts rebellion and Malcolm X's assassination, Beck adopted the nom de plume Iceberg Slim and published *Pimp: The Story of My Life*. Adopting a persona emboldened Beck to stake his claim as the foremost raconteur of pimpdom. "It was the pseudonym that authenticated the author's claim to the street. Slim had written Beck out of his life and replaced him with his own mythos," one critic explained.[33] Beck was charismatic and intelligent (his bio noted that he entered Chicago's criminal underground after dropping out of the Tuskegee Institute), and his embellished realism offered a tantalizing yet scholarly glimpse into a seamy urban subculture, even including a glossary deciphering the book's terminology. By the mid-1970s, Beck was a minor star, having sold more than three million books, drawing large audiences to his speaking engagements, and even releasing an album titled *Reflections* on which he translated his thoughts into loose, rhyming verse. Though his writing documented an unglamorous life, it was a life ruled by powerful Black men, and the Iceberg Slim books were passed around like religious texts among South Central's young hustlers and gangbangers. "I went everywhere with his books, idolizing him," T later said. "I'd memorized entire sections and could spit them at will. The Crips back in South Central used to constantly say, 'Yo, kick some more of that shit by Ice, T.'"[34]

In Slim's mold, Ice-T saw himself not just as a Crip affiliate turned hip-hop impresario but as a participant-observer of 1980s LA street life, with a keen ability to translate experience into realist entertainment and a canny knack for self-promotion. "There's so many hustlers and players in the world, but who knows their name?" he reasoned. "If I want to go down in the books, I can't just live the game, I have to document the game." Indeed, though he came up in LA's dance club scene, his music was undanceable by design: "When you listen to my music, don't listen to it like a rap record. Listen to it like me telling you stories over music. But it's not meant to dance to. We intentionally used beats that you couldn't dance to, because you're supposed to sit back and listen to me kick game. That's what all my records are about."[35] T started calling his blend of fictionalized autobiography and street reportage "reality rap."

After Ice-T forged a connection to New York rap royalty through the DJ and producer Afrika Islam, a part of Afrika Bambaataa's Zulu Nation, "6 in the Mornin'" blew up on the East Coast, and T was signed to Sire Records by Seymour Stein, the legendary A&R executive credited with discovering Talking Heads, the Ramones, and Madonna. Like a lot of rock executives, Stein was curious about hip-hop but hesitant to invest in an unproven form. Yet in T's lyrics, Stein heard rich storytelling and echoes of crime-themed calypso music. In his memoir, Stein recalls having T to his office and playing him Mighty Sparrow's 1956 single "Jean and Dinah," about "the troubled prostitution market after Trinidadian independence," and Lord Kitchener's 1978 hit "Sugar Bum Bum," an ode to a woman's ample posterior.[36] Ice-T's desire to serve as a documentarian of Los Angeles Black street culture echoed the calypso and reggae performers who formed a significant part of hip-hop's foundation. Calypso icon the Mighty Duke answered the titular question on his song "What Is Calypso" with "an editorial of the life we living," and the toasting star Big Youth adopted the nickname "Human Gleaner," after Jamaica's oldest newspaper, the *Daily Gleaner*.[37] Before Bob Marley's outlaw reggae anthem "I Shot the Sheriff" came Toots Hibbert, who themed his breakthrough 1968 single "54-46 (That's My Number)" to his trumped-up arrest and sung in character as a corrupt cop: "Get your hands in the air, sir / And you will get no hurt, mister."

Sire released Ice-T's debut LP *Rhyme Pays* in summer 1987, and the album's packaging featured two novel elements: palm trees in the cover photograph (specifically requested by T to distinguish his album from the New York hip-hop world) and a "parental advisory" warning sticker about the "explicit lyrics" contained within. *Rhyme Pays* wasn't the only ultraviolent rap album released that year—Boogie Down Productions' *Criminal Minded* also came out in 1987—but while BDP's album was released by the indie B-Boy, Sire's releases were distributed by the corporate powerhouse Warner Bros., and the label wanted to placate Tipper Gore and the Parents Music Resource Center, who were very active on Capitol Hill. With the universal rectangular sticker design still years in the future, T and Sire decided upon a vertical cylindrical shape that tapered at one end, with a flat bottom. Some saw a bullet, others a condom. "It can be taken either way," Ice-T told the *LA Times*. "It all depends on whether your mind is turned to sex or violence." It was T's first moment as a tongue-in-cheek free-speech advocate, and he was correct in assuming that the sticker would function more as a promotional ploy than a deterrent. "That tells the kids that's something in there they shouldn't hear," he quipped. "Naturally they can't wait to hear it. That sticker helps sell records."[38] Without radio support, *Rhyme Pays* sold well, moving three hundred thousand copies in its first year.

While *Rhyme*'s stickering gambit was T's first playful intervention into the expanding discourse on corporate censorship, a song on the album's B side provided the blueprint for reality rap. Far beyond the realist street tales of "6 in the Mornin'," "Squeeze the Trigger" drew from the nonstop violence of the evening news. Instead of a chorus, T's verses are interrupted by a fictional news anchor solemnly intoning ledes like "Police still have no leads for the apprehension of the South Side Slayer; death toll stands at ten" and "Three killed in an execution-style murder; film at eleven." In the second verse, T introduces his new persona, the straight-talking political pundit and media commentator reporting straight from gang-glutted South Central:

> Murder, intrigue, somebody must bleed
> *Miami Vice* is small time, LA's the big league

From the Rollin 60s to the Nickerson G
Pueblos, Grape Street, this is what I see
The Jungle, the 30s, the VNG
Life in LA ain't no cup of tea

Like a correspondent reporting from a war zone, T reels off gang names and territories: the Rollin 60s Crips controlled much of the west side of South Central, while the Grape Street Crips ruled Watts. The Nickerson Gardens housing projects (the largest government housing project west of the Mississippi), the Baldwin Village "Jungle," and the Van Ness Gangsters were all Blood affiliated. In his *Village Voice* review of *Rhyme Pays*, Robert Christgau was persuaded of T's bona fides: "His sexploitations and true crime tales are detailed and harrowing enough to convince anybody he was there. Wish I was sure he'll never go back."[39]

The trip that "Squeeze the Trigger" took through the sensationalist media looking glass didn't stop at Blood and Crip reportage but extended to op-ed punditry on post–Long Beach fears of rap concert criminality. In an interstitial spoken bit, T reads off a series of mocked-up headlines in news anchor drag, highlighting the false cause/effect correlation between rap concerts and gang violence. "Violence erupts at a Los Angeles hip-hop concert. Rap music is blamed for violence." "Violence breaks out at a nuclear peace rally. Peace is blamed for violence." As the track concludes, the music drops out, leaving T's voice alone, still with a newscaster's delivery: "Los Angeles rapper Ice-T's records banned because of his blatant use of reality."

Though he was reacting to events from August 1986, T's judgments resonated in the summer of 1987, as Run-DMC embarked on its Together Forever tour with the Beastie Boys. In a press conference before the start of the tour, Run-DMC announced that the group had paid a half-million dollars to outfit each venue with metal detectors and security personnel. As local reporters around the country were quick to note, the fact that the tour's crowds would be racially mixed—both groups were platinum sellers, and the Beasties drew a significant white suburban crowd—had stirred up local decision makers more than the usual rap concert. In Seattle, officials canceled and relocated the performance a week before it was scheduled to happen, worried about "potential 'rumbles' after the concert involving teenagers from different races."

On the night of the show, Seattle's NBC affiliate devoted significant air-time to the controversy, cutting between a live aerial shot of the theater's entrance (complete with police patrolling on horseback), a recap of the Long Beach violence, a report from the tour's violence-free previous stop in Portland, and interviews with prospective attendees, many of whom didn't understand what the big deal was. The next day, the *Seattle Times* noted that "the hysteria that preceded last night's rap concert at the Paramount was a lot more bizarre than anything that happened on stage."[40]

On January 30, 1988, twenty-seven-year-old Karen Toshima was celebrating a job promotion in Westwood, a popular nightlife and shopping area near the University of California, Los Angeles. Several members of the Rollin 60s Crips were also hanging out in the area, and when they spotted a rival gang member, they opened fire on him, hitting Toshima in the head with cross fire. She died the next day. To city officials, the killing was a political nightmare; the gang violence that they could previously claim was contained in the Black parts of Los Angeles had spilled into the rest of the city. Immediately, with the city council's financial and political support, Chief Gates instituted Operation Hammer, a dramatic acceleration of his already Draconian antigang tactics, which he had derisively titled CRASH (Community Resources against Street Hoodlums). The Bloods and the Crips, or anyone who looked like they might be a member, had officially become the LAPD's most high-priority targets. To Assemblywoman Maxine Waters, the reaction was further evidence of the city's institutional racism. "A problem is not a problem until it hits the white community," she said.[41]

Several years earlier, Gates had developed CRASH as a zero-tolerance variation of the "community policing" model, permitting LAPD officers to forge local relationships with gang members while collecting intelligence on their operations. But when he was charged with developing a security plan for the 1984 Olympic Games, Gates dramatically accelerated the unit's interventionist tactics. He traveled to Sarajevo to study the Yugoslavian capital's security plan for that year's Winter Olympics, where the city's police chief there simply told him, "Arrest everybody." Gates did just that, making "gang sweeps" a key part of the city's pre-Olympics security preparation. Any young Black men who fit the LAPD's profile—often, merely a group hanging out in public, perhaps wearing blue or red to avoid local retribution from gang members—were subject to harassment and arrest. Long after the Olympics left town, gang sweeps remained a core part of the LAPD's tool kit. Gates liked them because they were a spectacular display of force that provided raw meat for a local media that was eager for crime stories with clear good and bad stakes and gaudy arrest numbers. He defended the tactics as a form of proactive policing that could be drawn from dystopian science fiction: "We went after crime before it occurred," he explained. "Our people went out every single night trying to stop crime before it happened, trying to take people off the street that they believed were involved in crime."[42]

On April 8 and 9, 1988, CRASH conducted its biggest gang sweep yet, and the press rode shotgun. "Police Call Gang Sweep a Success; 1,453 Are Arrested," blared the *LA Times* headline. More than 200 South Central residents were arrested for drug-related felonies, and nearly 600 for misdemeanors, some as paltry as littering or blocking a sidewalk. Of the arrested, 794 were identified as gang members, determined by cross-referencing their state ID information with data gathered from previous sweeps. Processing the arrestees was a big enough issue that the police had to use the LA Coliseum as an ad hoc staging area for booking—and, for many, immediate release, but with an arrest record, making it easier to haul them in again in the future. It was yet another massive public relations coup for Gates, who, naturally, had notified the press in advance. Yet while they justified their actions with eye-catching numbers that evoked video game high scores, LAPD spokespeople found it hard to assess the success of their operation apart from circular logic. "The way the gangs are organized, we have no way of telling if the leaders were picked up," one officer noted. "The fact that we didn't have a lot of criminal activity in the south end over the weekend is encouraging. Crime is on hold."[43]

The next weekend, in a humble police office that looked like a replica *Hill Street Blues* set, a commanding officer briefed a roomful of CRASH officers about their next operation. They were prepping to conduct a gang sweep as a forceful response to a deadly drive-by shooting: a Crip had taken out a Blood the night before. "Get inventive; find some probable cause," the CO told his men before they headed out. "Get both gangs off the street, at least for a night or two." The sweep netted dozens of

Bloods and Crips, who were made to assume the positions that television news had seared into the public consciousness during the tough-on-crime 1980s: a young Black man with hands bound behind his back, thrown over the hood of a police car; a line of young Black men kneeling in front of a brick wall, fingers laced behind their heads. This scenario wasn't pulled from the nightly news but was screened in multiplexes across the country during the first few minutes of *Colors*. Released nationwide on April 15, 1988, less than a week after Gates's massive gang sweeps, *Colors* was the rare major motion picture to reflect real-life law and order with the pro-police immediacy of a local news report. From its opening epigraph, *Colors* positioned CRASH and the LA sheriff's OSS (Operation Safe Streets) operations as outmanned underdogs facing an abstracted enemy. "The combined anti-gang force numbers 250 men and women. In the greater Los Angeles area there are over 600 street gangs with almost 70,000 members," reads the epigraph, lending it the authoritative veneer of a news documentary. "Last year there were 387 gang-related killings."

Though the film's original screenplay set the action in Chicago and followed two cops battling a drug ring smuggling contraband in cough syrup, its director, Dennis Hopper, had a different idea. Hopper had recently returned to Southern California, and when he signed on to direct the then untitled film, he insisted that it shift to what he saw every night on the news. "Make it cocaine, make it real . . . make it about the gangs in Los Angeles," he told producer Robert Solo.[44] Hopper was familiar with edgy cinematic realism: three decades earlier, he had debuted in film as one of James Dean's friends in *Rebel without a Cause*, and fourteen years later, he helped usher in the New Hollywood era with the iconic, mostly improvised countercultural biker film *Easy Rider*. For *Colors*, Hopper recruited Haskell Wexler, the celebrated hyperrealist cinematographer of the 1969 quasi documentary *Medium Cool*, to shoot on location in Watts, San Pedro, and East LA. During preproduction, Hopper consulted with gang experts from the area, cast dozens of actual Bloods and Crips in background roles, and, according to local documentary filmmakers, actually recreated some of their footage (including the film's opening drive-by shooting sequence) for the film.

Hopper's quest for realism stopped at the mise-en-scène. In the world of *Colors*, gangs are not a symptom of larger social and economic issues but a civic cancer infecting LA's social fabric, giving two white cops a shared enemy to unite against and overcome their personal differences. Danny McGavin (Sean Penn), the smirking young Daryl Gates in training, is assigned to the wizened, soon-to-retire Bob Hodges (Robert Duvall), who shows him that the best way to battle the gangs is not through force but relationship building. But apart from one scene in which Latino gangbanger Bird (Gerardo Mejía) delivers a soliloquy to a police intervention officer about gangs as surrogate families,[45] Colors' gangbangers are portrayed as either silent sociopaths or standard-fare street criminals, present to lend ripped-from-the-headlines realism to a standard-fare buddy-cop film. Critics were not kind: "Hopper's faux documentary approach fails to provide either the information that a true documentary might or the satisfactions of a fully realized drama," wrote the *Washington Post*, while the *Los Angeles Times* claimed that Hopper had turned the Bloods and the Crips "into Rebels Without a Context by doing nothing to sketch in the social and economic pressures that lead kids to see gangs as the only brotherhood in a bleak and hopeless world."[46]

Though LA locals and film critics decried Colors' lack of cinematic verisimilitude, ahead of its release, police and the press alike were sufficiently convinced that its theatricalized violence would incite a real-world counterpart, with Run-DMC's Long Beach violence and Karen Toshima's killing still recent memories. Enter the moral entrepreneurs: the volunteer crime-prevention organization the Guardian Angels picketed Penn's and Hopper's homes; the president of the California Gang Investigators Association said, "I wouldn't be the least bit surprised if a shooting erupted in a movie theater"; and an LA County sheriff suggested that the film would send a message that "you can be a movie star if you're a gang member."[47] The day of Colors' release, Dan Rather informed *CBS Evening News* viewers that "Los Angeles police deployed extra patrols today, and theaters added security" out of "fears the movie's make-believe violence may trigger more killing." When a nineteen-year-old was shot to death outside a Stockton, California, theater during the second week of the film's release, the local police chief was quick to blame the film first. "The suspects saw the movie and they saw the victims outside. It makes sense to me that the shooting was related to the movie," he told reporters,[48] drawing the same sort of causal connection between representational violence and real-world tragedy that Ice-T had dismissed in "Squeeze the Trigger."

In a way, *Colors'* producer, Robert Solo, had predicted the film's moral panic, having initially pitched *Colors* as an update to the 1955 youth-in-crisis film *Blackboard Jungle*. Famously, *Jungle*'s use of Bill Haley and His Comets' "Rock around the Clock" over its opening credits generated press hysteria when groups of white teenagers caused small-scale havoc at a number of screenings. *Jungle* was the first bit of proof, critics asserted, that the new youth craze of rock and roll could actually incite teens to riot. Yet the connection between "Rock around the Clock" and *Jungle* has grown blurry over time. The movie's disorderly characters cannot hear the song as it blares over the opening credits; only the viewing audience can. Moreover, "Clock" is the only instance of rock and roll in the movie: in one scene, rowdy teens beat up a teacher to the strains of the Stan Kenton Orchestra. In the original 1954 novel adapted for the film, the students are acolytes of the pop crooners Joni James and Julius La Rosa, whose music would seem laughably out-of-date in the post–Elvis Presley world of teen rebellion into which *Jungle* was released just a year later. Though director Richard Brooks found Haley's 45 rpm single in the record collection of actor Glenn Ford's son and added it to the opening credits at the last minute, *Jungle* is otherwise a product of the pre-rock-and-roll world.

What *Blackboard Jungle* was to rock and roll's overturning the reign of adult pop and hot jazz, *Colors'* soundtrack was to LA Black music's transition from electro-R&B to hip-hop. When Hopper was devising *Colors* in 1987, rap was still on the fringe, and Rick James's funk-pop track "Everywhere I Go (Colors)" was the film's original theme song. While James's song was not nearly as dated as Haley made Stan Kenton and Joni James sound in 1955, it was incredibly tame compared to the city's rap kingpin Ice-T. Sire's parent label, Warner Bros., was releasing the soundtrack, and Hopper not only was convinced to use "Squeeze the Trigger" to soundtrack the film's climactic moment but hired T to record *Colors'* theme song. The resulting track is stark and minimalist, its primary melodic element the squelching, low-frequency Moog line that Afrika Islam winds around a spare landscape of Roland 808 cracks, record scratches, and gunshot sound effects. Lyrically, T switches guises from "Trigger"; he's not a reporter here but a Blood/Crip composite, condensing gang war into pragmatic nihilism: "My life is violent, but violence is life / Peace is a dream, reality is a knife." Instead of repping his Crip-affiliate bona fides, T adopts a participant-observer's perspective, underscoring the rivalry's existential pointlessness and his own performative violent streak: "Red or blue, Cuz or Blood, it just don't matter / Sucka dive for your life when my shotgun scatters." In the film, the song appears after the film's opening CRASH sweep nets the Crip suspect Rocket (Don Cheadle), and he struts through the Seventy-Seventh Street Division police station while T's voice takes over the soundtrack: "I am a nightmare walkin', psychopath talkin' / King of my jungle, just a gangster stalkin'." As the song plays, audible only to the viewers, the camera tracks down the cellblock through mingling gang members who throw their sets at the camera. The sequence concludes with a stylized confrontation between the gangs, separated by prison bars, something that would never happen in an actual lockup. For a moment, the film's gritty cop-drama realism turns into a wide-screen music video.

Though T's rhymes were dark, he was no radical. At the end of the official "Colors" music video, which earned airplay on the newly launched *Yo! MTV Raps* and BET's *Rap City*, he turns to the camera and pleads, "Yo, please stop, 'cause I want y'all to live." Sincerely arguing for the elimination of the warfare he had been personifying a few seconds earlier was an awkward fit, recalling Iceberg Slim seeking to have it both ways in the preface to *Pimp*: "The account of my brutality and cunning as a pimp will fill many of you with revulsion, however, if one intelligent, valuable young man or woman can be saved from the destructive slime; then the displeasure I have given will be outweighed by that individual's use of his potential in a socially constructive manner."[49] Unlike Run-DMC, who rued the fact that the Crips and the Bloods had dragged them into the middle of a moral panic, T was carving out a new rap niche. In an echo of Tipper Gore arguing against the immorality of "porn rock" by promoting vulgar records to unaware parents (Gore was often photographed holding up the album covers she was decrying, like a spokesmodel), Ice-T enacted gang violence on "Colors" in order to effectively argue for peace.

"Colors" was a minor hit, reaching no. 70 on the *Billboard* 100 and launching Ice-T's career as a chronicler of, and an advisor to, LA gang culture. By the end of 1988, he had testified about Los Angeles gang violence in front of the Congressional Black Caucus, gone on a speaking tour to Southern California schools, and appeared on Phil Donahue's syndicated daytime talk show. In September, T released his second album, *Power*, promoted by a music video for the single "High Rollers" that opens with him being interviewed for a fictional public affairs show. "Ice, street violence and youth crime is at an all-time high. Can you tell me what you think is responsible for it?" asks the host. He replies, "Well I think the real problem is the justice system. The youth of today see so much corruption going on in government, and so many officials getting off, just because they have a lot of money. They feel that if they have a lot of money, they'll be above the law. Actually, they're just on a quest to become high rollers."

T's take on how powerful people skirt legal entanglements again demonstrates immorality in order to decry it. The music video mixes *Lifestyles of the Rich and Famous*–style footage of gated entryways, BMWs, and scantily clad models with actual news clips of Daryl Gates's forces battling crime in the streets, complete with mocked-up chyron text reading "SWAT ROCKHOUSE RAID" and "LAPD BATTERING RAM." The link between the two scenarios is tentative and seemingly designed to mirror the lesson he imparts in the final verse, after four verses sketching the titular character: "You'll never get caught 'cause you got nerves of ice / And you're much smarter than those crooks on *Miami Vice* . . . right?" T's attempts at clarification were not illuminating: "I'm aiming at the kid who might go out and shoot somebody," he told a reporter. "Once I got him to pick up this album, if he listens to it, it says, 'Yo, don't do this.'"[50]

Similar contradictions between gaudy style and serious substance were bedeviling the broadcast journalism world. "Television has discovered 'reality.' Or at least the dark side of reality," intoned *Nightline* anchor Ted Koppel to open a June 1988 episode. "When music and visuals come before content and ideas, you're grasping the philosophy of tabloid TV," said Koppel, using language that could have equally critiqued "High Rollers." Koppel, of course, had a personal stake in distancing *Nightline* from its sensationalistic competition: news-adjacent reality television posed a clear threat to the superiority of the networks' centrist, officially sourced public affairs programming. One of the most derided of the new tabloid programs was *West 57th*, CBS's attempt to reinvent *60 Minutes* with an MTV-era flair. Called a "yuppie documentary" by *Rolling Stone*,[51] *West 57th* aimed to simultaneously shock and appease the thirtysomething boomer demographic, interweaving stories on death row inmates, the porn industry, and PCP with profiles of Billy Joel, John Mellencamp, and Deadheads. While the *Washington Post* loved the show's flashy graphics and stylistic innovations, the *New York Times* called it "a supermarket tabloid set to music," and the *Los Angeles Times* dubbed it "the *Flashdance* of TV news." Former CBS News president Fred Friendly was the most vicious, calling *West 57th*'s pilot episode "the saddest day in the history of broadcast journalism."[52]

The Bloods and the Crips were a perfect fit for *West 57th*'s edgy template, and a segment from the May 7, 1988, episode—less than a month after *Colors* hit theaters and a few months before *Power* hit stores—situated the gangs in the center of Reagan-era drug-war hysteria. Though numerous researchers had shown that LA gang members were, at best, not much more than street-level cogs in a much larger multinational cocaine empire, the *West 57th* correspondent frames them as "High Roller"–style entrepreneurs franchising operations around the country. "Thanks to cocaine, LA's so-called homeboys have become entrepreneurs extraordinaire," the correspondent warns. "What began as a disorganized crime network has quickly mushroomed into one of the most successful businesses in America." The package features a repentant, imprisoned former gangbanger ruing his life choices, includes plenty of squad car ride-along footage showing sheriff's deputies rounding up low-level street dealers, and, like *Colors*, leaves no doubt about the real stars: "Tonight in Los Angeles, like every other Saturday night, there are some two hundred cops working the streets, patrolling the neighborhoods, trying somehow to keep the gangs under control." The package ends with a freeze-frame of a tableau that was nearing iconic status: two police officers surround a young Black man who has his hands on his head and his legs spread wide.

Less flashy than *West 57th*, CBS's other newsmagazine innovation, *48 Hours*, explained its gimmick in its name. Each week, a large team of producers, reporters, and videographers would dive into a story for two consecutive days, blending the urgency of the nightly news with the gravitas of *60 Minutes*. The program made its heavily hyped debut in 1986 with "48 Hours on Crack Street," a prime-time special devoted to New York City's swelling drug problem that eschewed deep engagement with social problems for stunts like sending correspondents undercover to buy from corner dealers. The same month as *West 57th*'s Bloods and Crips exposé, CBS aired "48 Hours on Gang Street," set in South Los Angeles and hosted by Dan Rather. "What you're about to see is a crime story, but it's also a human story, set in a scary America many of us don't know," Rather said in his introduction. Where *West 57th* painted the gangs as a nationally expanding criminal empire, "Gang Street" sealed them within South Central's boundaries. The episode opens with a Gates-style gang sweep, endorsing a punitive approach to a socioeconomic and public health issue. As Hopper had done in *Colors*, *48 Hours* portrayed gang life as a localized pathogen reduced to a series of recognizable characters playing social roles they'd soon outgrow. The correspondent, Bernard Goldberg, portrays gang membership as a simple matter of code-switching, showing Bloods member "Dusty Loco" throwing up his set on the street, then sitting at his mother's kitchen table as Bruce, a high school student hoping to get a college scholarship. The segment's illuminating peek into the mundane life of a gang member is undercut by Goldberg's oversimplification: "Dr. Jekyll, meet Mr. Hyde," he says with a knowing paternalistic flair. The other segments focus on antigang efforts: a Black preacher patrolling the Watts streets while chanting, "Up with hope, down with dope," and the victims' advocate Norma Johnson, described as "a battlefield nurse of the gang wars," who professes little sympathy for the gang members. "There's a certain mentality that exists amongst that group of people which, to me, I can't even equate it to being an animal. They are mutations," she told the reporter.

While *West 57th* exuded a mild paranoia about Black gangs infiltrating the rest of the nation, *48 Hours* reanimated the legacy of the 1965 Moynihan Report, which had been wielded after the 1965 Watts rebellion to blame what the report's advocates perceived as the broken Black families who left a (mostly white) police force to stem the tide of violence. The *LA Times* described the *48 Hours* episode in terms that could equally be applied to *Colors*: "a slice-of-life portrait . . . [that] does not spend much time analyzing the roots of the problem or what should be done to deal with it." For its Los Angeles airing, KCBS followed the broadcast with a two-hour in-studio discussion with community leaders, law enforcement personnel, and the city's district attorney. "Images are what television does well. But it's very difficult for television news to put those images into perspective," said the station's news director. "People need a framework for understanding the violent images; otherwise, they're just filled with anxiety."[53] Outside the city limits, "Gang Street" was regarded quite differently, winning a 1989 Emmy Award for Outstanding Coverage of a Continuing News Story in a News Magazine.

By the end of the year, the Bloods and the Crips had been turned into a set of stylistic signifiers, helping launch a national rap career, plot a film, and draw viewers to two upstart reality TV programs. But with few exceptions, the young Black men on the streets of South Los Angeles remained a silent scourge, cast as interchangeable Black criminal avatars of Reaganist law-and-order paranoia. Neither reporters nor rappers let the young men speak for themselves, but the year's most nuanced portrait of a gang member's worldview was crafted by Léon Bing, a former fashion model who, coincidentally enough, circulated in the same celebrity networks as Dennis Hopper in the 1960s, sharing an LSD trip with him and posing for his fashion photographs.[54] While Hopper's countercultural ethos had hardened into a centrist affinity for state power, Bing developed curiosity and empathy for LA's marginalized warriors. Her profile of an eighteen-year-old Crip ran in *LA Weekly* a month after *Colors* hit theaters, revealing a thoughtful young man trapped in a toxic feud whose origins were a mystery to him. "These kids are desperately bored," Bing observed, locating a characteristic that no film, rapper, or sensationalistic journalist would ever think to highlight. "They seem to be seeking the clarity of a warrior in battle. Through violence and death they are seeking to feel alive."[55]

The shadow of the Bloods and the Crips hovered over Run-DMC's performance at LA's Greek Theatre on June 29, 1988. It was the night before "Gang Street" aired on CBS, and metal detectors lined the venue's entryways. Almost two years after the release of *Raising Hell*, the trio were touring behind their fourth LP, *Tougher Than Leather*, which had been delayed while the group sued their label, Profile Records, for nonpayment of royalties. In their absence, the rap landscape evolved quickly. In his review of that evening's concert, *LA Times* reporter Robert Hilburn opined that "It's Like That" seemed "ancient and flat."[56] He was not alone: the *Rolling Stone* review of *Leather* opined, "It seems as if Run-D.M.C. has let the likes of Public Enemy and Ice-T take over the more militant and politically aware hip-hop turf," while *Billboard* columnist Nelson George, who had been tracking hip-hop for a decade, surmised that Run-DMC's image, "once the height of B-boy style, now looks a little old-fashioned."[57] A far greater disaster than the *Tougher Than Leather* album was the Blaxploitation-themed, long-delayed film of the same name, essentially an R-rated jukebox musical. It was savaged by critics: the opening line of one review called it "vile, vicious, despicable, stupid, sexist, racist and horrendously made" before reaching its first period.[58] Run-DMC, the group whose first single split rap into old and new schools, whose third LP was rap's first album-length achievement, and who had weathered rap's first nationwide moral panic, were yesterday's news. Though *Leather* reached the *Billboard* Top 10, sold more than a million copies, and featured some of the group's best rapping and production to date, to most critics it felt worlds apart from rap's emergent engagement with contemporary realities. It was the first Run-DMC album to underachieve its predecessor, commercially and critically. They wouldn't release another album for another two and a half years.

Run-DMC's two opening acts that summer night at the Greek Theatre signaled the two divergent directions in which rap was headed. First was the pop-rap upstart duo DJ Jazzy Jeff and the Fresh Prince, whose single "Parents Just Don't Understand," complete with an extroverted Technicolor music video, peaked at no. 12 on the *Billboard* Hot 100 two months later and would go on to win the first Grammy Award for Best Rap Performance in early 1989. Then there was Public Enemy, the Def Jam–signed, Malcolm X–inspired nationalists whose second album, *It Takes a Nation of Millions to Hold Us Back*, released that week, was already being hailed as one of the year's best albums. As rappers Chuck D and Flavor Flav erupted into their set, they were surrounded by background performers, dubbed the Security of the First World, whose look was inspired not by street gangs but by the Black Panthers. They took to the Greek Theatre stage that night brandishing realistic fake Uzis.

CHAPTER 2

DON'T QUOTE ME, BOY, 'CAUSE I AIN'T SAID SHIT

▼

For a few minutes in late March 1989, it looked like Long Beach might happen again. Ice-T was headlining at the Celebrity Theatre in Anaheim that evening, but the crowd was most excited for the act that preceded him onstage. That was N.W.A, Niggaz Wit Attitudes, who invested T's hard-core street rap with richer production and even more salacious and violent lyrics. Their LP *Straight Outta Compton* had sold half a million copies in just six weeks with little to no radio support, good enough for a no. 41 ranking on *Billboard*'s album chart. During N.W.A's set, a fight broke out in the audience, causing what Robert Hilburn called "a chill of tension" to sweep through the venue. "Rap music, already widely linked in the public mind to gang violence, came within a heartbeat of another bad mark," he wrote. But the hubbub was quickly quieted by Ice Cube, the nineteen-year-old responsible for writing most of N.W.A's lyrics, who grabbed the mic and assailed the audience: "This ain't *Colors*.... You didn't come to see a fight, you came to see a concert." Less than a year after *Colors*' release, it was a punch line to South Central citizens like Cube, in part because the film was a naïve, misguided transfiguration of their day-to-day reality and in part because N.W.A saw what they were doing onstage and on record as far more compellingly real. Where *Colors* portrayed the cops' perspective on Black lives in South Los Angeles, N.W.A were getting crowds to chant, "Fuck tha police," and to rap along with the casual violence in the lyrics of street hits like

"Dopeman" and "Boyz-n-the-Hood." "The group maintains its records are documentaries that reflect the reality of the street world in places like Compton, where they grew up," Hilburn explained. The fans he interviewed for his story agreed. "They tell it the way it really is," one said. "They talk about real life . . . not that fantasy stuff," another concurred. A third saw N.W.A's music as a wake-up call for a serious issue: "I think it's good they talk about gang problems the way they do because it forces people to think about the problems." Cube himself offered some context in an interview. "If I grew up in Beverly Hills, I'd be writing about different things. Our music's not shocking to people who know that world. It's reality. . . . Sometimes the truth hurts."[1]

Two weeks earlier, the pilot episode of *Cops* had staked a very different claim to the uncomfortable truths of American law and order. Like *Dragnet* gone cinema verité, *Cops*' one-hour pilot episode sent a team of videographers to follow officers from the Broward County, Florida, sheriff's department; there was no shooting script and no actors, just police officers performing their duties. A tantalizing warning appeared before the opening credits: "Due to the graphic nature of this program, viewer discretion is advised." The pilot episode's action veered from the mundane to the spectacular, cutting from living room conversations between officers and their spouses to those same officers conducting dramatic drug raids set to a generic rock soundtrack. At one point, officers pull a bloated corpse out of a river. Later, Broward County sheriff Nick Navarro relaxes in bed, watching the news with his wife. "With the addition of *Cops*," one reviewer noted, "Fox has made it tough to look at any other cop series again with a straight face, especially the one with those two well-dressed, sports car–driving hunks down the beach in Miami. *Cops* has the substance. Who cares about the style?"[2] But style was exactly what *Cops* did best; it just happened to be the kind of style that cleverly disguised its own creation. *Cops*' shaky camerawork and tense editing generated a sense that viewers were eavesdropping on police work, which both made for intense action sequences and fostered an intimate connection with the officers. Fox wasn't in enough households yet for any of its shows to make a national dent in the ratings—the pilot ranked seventeth, appropriately ranking between that week's episodes of *West 57th* and Fox's youth-oriented cop show *21 Jump Street*—but returns in key cities were very encouraging, and the show's novelty factor made for at least one minor celebrity. Lori Canada, one of the pilot's featured officers, earned coverage in *USA Today*, in *People* magazine, and on *Entertainment Tonight*. "Everywhere I go, people recognize me. It's unbelievable," she told a reporter.[3]

Not all observers were as enthusiastic. Beyond its novel facade, many noticed, *Cops* was not much more than a lengthy advertisement for the police, while many of those shown in handcuffs, often without their faces blurred, were unable to defend themselves. "What's disturbing about *Cops* is not the images of its protagonists but the odor of exploitation that seeps from too many scenes," wrote a *Newsweek* critic. "The camera begins panning to the faces of those caught in drug sweeps and prostitute roundups, its lens tends to act as a kind of electronic jury. . . . [I]n the eyes of viewers, conditioned by the arresting denouements of *Miami Vice*, the mere click of the handcuffs may be enough to establish guilt."[4] The *New York Times* was less restrained, plainly calling the pilot episode racist: "The dominant image is hammered home again and again: the overwhelmingly white troops of police are the good guys; the bad guys are overwhelmingly black." Describing a scene in which an officer catches a white drug buyer in a Black neighborhood, warning him, "Don't you know what happens over here to white boys like you?" the critic sighs: "The racism is so casual, so taken for granted, that the only response might well be despair."[5]

With *Cops* generating so much buzz, the music video for *Straight Outta Compton*'s title track felt like reality counterprogramming. N.W.A's depiction of police/citizen conflict, delivered to MTV the same month as *Cops'* premiere, strove for the same level of discursive authority about Reaganist law and order, but from the opposite ideological perspective. Where *Cops* advised viewer discretion at the start of each episode, Dr. Dre warned "Straight Outta Compton" viewers that "you are now about to witness the strength of street knowledge." The video was shot not in *Cops'* vérité style but with a visual realism that could trace its lineage back through 1970s cop shows and urban noir action films like *The French Connection*. The cops are clearly the bad guys, arresting N.W.A for what could be characterized only as sartorial crimes. Dave Marsh called the video "docudrama footage of a gang sweep in which the L.A. police violently round up street kids . . . just for wearing dookie ropes and beepers."[6] The mode of identification is flipped from *Cops* too: while each member of "the gang called Niggaz With Attitudes" gets a separate introduction, the police remain anonymous stereotypes, hidden behind mirror shades and fake mustaches, like the nameless "criminals" on Fox. Even though the "Compton" cops prevail in the end, taking N.W.A into custody at gunpoint and throwing them into a paddy wagon, MTV's Standards and Practices department deemed "Compton" too provocative, and the network never aired the video.

On the other hand, the catchy, righteous, and relatively nonviolent "Express Yourself" was welcomed by MTV. Dre's track flipped the impossibly optimistic 1970 funk tune of the same name, which had been taken to no. 12 on the Hot 100 by Charles Wright and the Watts 103rd Street Rhythm Band, a collective named after the symbolic heart of Black Los Angeles. But while the original single was a celebration of the "Black is beautiful" ethos of the early 1970s, N.W.A's take on the phrase nearly two decades later was more urgent. Dr. Dre's first two bars, "I'm expressing with my full capability / Now they got me in correctional facilities," articulated communicative repression amid renewed fears of censorship, fittingly evidenced by MTV's decision to lock up "Straight Outta Compton" and throw away the key. The video drills the same idea home, opening with a sepia-toned recreation of slaves toiling in cotton fields while monitored by a horse-mounted master armed with a whip, a power dynamic later flipped in the streets of Compton, when N.W.A lead a group of young Black men to accost a horse-mounted police officer. Dre delivers his verses from opposite ends of the power spectrum: behind bars and while serving as the first Black president (after surviving a Kennedy-style assassination attempt). Like the "Compton" video, however, there is no confusion about who holds the ultimate power when Dre is electrocuted by the same actor who portrayed the slave master and police officer.

The fact that "Express Yourself" was a hit with no cursing did not contradict N.W.A's claims to being hounded by authorities for speaking the R-rated truth; the single was less a demonstration of reality rap than the group's PG-rated explainer. The song's lyrics, penned by Cube, comprise a thorough clarification of vulgarity and reality:

> Some musicians cuss at home
> But scared to use profanity when up on the microphone
> Yeah, they want reality, but you won't hear none
> They rather exaggerate a little fiction

Deploying free speech to convey ugly truths was only part of the picture. N.W.A were also arguing that the increasingly knotty lyrical mythologies crafted by the rising crop of New York stars were an inauthentic representation of Black life in America. When Dre raps, "Some drop science, well I'm droppin' English," he is taking aim at the influence of Five Percent theology, an independent offshoot of the Nation of Islam with a lexicon of terminology that introduced "cipher," "word is bond," and "dropping science" into hip-hop vernacular. Adherents included two of the era's best rappers, Rakim and Big Daddy Kane, who pioneered a dexterous and fast-paced rhyme style that wove Five Percent doctrine into hip-hop's worldview. But for N.W.A, Five Percenters obscured more than they revealed: "Blame it on Ice Cube / Because he said it gets funky / When you got a subject and a predicate." In the place of obscurantist Five Percenter mysticism, N.W.A argued for plainspoken, Compton-based rap journalism.

After "Express Yourself," N.W.A were welcomed to MTV by Fab 5 Freddy, the avuncular host of the network's breakout hit *Yo! MTV Raps*, who flew to Compton to grant the group a starring role in an episode. The network could have it both ways: a full episode with the country's edgiest and most compelling rap group cast not as anticop crusaders but as safe-for-the-mainstream tour guides of their hometown. The episode's first segment positioned them at the "Welcome to Compton" sign on Alameda Street, before moving three miles north to the Compton Swap Meet on Long Beach Boulevard, where MC Ren introduced the video for Ice-T's "High Rollers." To conclude the show, they strolled down the Venice Boardwalk, where they too conveniently ran into the rising teen pop-rap group the Boys, who hailed from nearby Carson. N.W.A's political edge did bleed through the facade, however: while the group were being driven toward Venice in the back of a flatbed truck, Freddy prompts Cube to introduce the antiviolence charity single "Self-Destruction," a signal from the nascent East Coast rap industry that it was united in opposition to real-world violence. Less a social activist than a media critic, Cube took Freddy's prompt as an opportunity to distinguish his city from its most recent Hollywood representation. "After people saw *Colors* they thought LA's just all violence. That's not true," he told viewers. He finished with an admonition: "When a brother kills a brother man, the only people that's happy is the other man."

Cube's commentary revealed the inspiration of Chuck D, the leader of Public Enemy and hip-hop's most outspoken organic intellectual. Released a few months before *Straight Outta Compton*, PE's second album, *It Takes a Nation of Millions to Hold Us Back*, dramatically expanded rap's rhetorical bandwidth, updating the fiery pro-Black rhetoric of Malcolm X and Huey Newton to address the effects of Reaganism on Black Americans. The dizzying, sample-heavy production of the group's production team, known as the Bomb Squad, significantly raised the stakes for rap productions (Dre himself was an acolyte), reactivating a potent strain of Black Power via soul, funk, and R&B samples from the heady late 1960s. Though N.W.A was a going concern before PE's *It Takes a Nation, Straight Outta Compton* would not have sounded remotely the same without Public Enemy's inspiration. Chuck claimed that he gave one of his first copies of *Nation* to Dre and Eazy-E during a 1988 tour stop, and one critic has astutely noted that the Bomb Squad's sample of James Brown's "Funky Drummer" appears in the same spot in the second verse of "Fuck tha Police" as it does in PE's single "Bring the Noise."[7] Where N.W.A were using rap as a rhetorical Molotov cocktail in the national discussion on race in the late age of Reagan, Public Enemy sought to resurrect the peak era of Black political empowerment.

In the fall of 1988, rappers and reality TV producers were joined in the national discussion about race and criminality by Republican presidential candidate George H. W. Bush. As the election heated up, Bush's campaign approved an external advertisement that linked Democratic presidential candidate Michael Dukakis with Willie Horton, a dark-skinned Black murderer and convicted rapist. Titled "Weekend Passes," the ad blamed a Dukakis-instituted Massachusetts furlough program for Horton's raping a white woman while on temporary release. The ad ran for a full month, and though it generated no shortage of outrage for its clearly racist intent, it never mentioned race at all, permitting Bush to engage in the kind of plausibly deniable racism that his predecessor, Reagan, had mastered. Bush renounced all responsibility for the ad's racism while benefitting from it, and Dukakis's campaign never recovered. Horton provided the ideal Reagan-to-Bush transitional image, signaling in the crassest terms possible that no media tactic was too morally repulsive if it could help ensure the continuity of the Reagan agenda.

Willie Horton compressed into a single image the exact sort of racial paranoia that Public Enemy was battling, N.W.A was satirizing, and *Cops*—along with its innovative reality predecessor, *America's Most Wanted*, which debuted in 1988—was exploiting. By aligning with law-and-order ideology, Fox had positioned itself at the forefront of a new wave of television: *Cops* provided a pseudodocumentary, behind-the-scenes access to everyday police work, and *Most Wanted* pioneered reality TV as vicarious participation by turning vigilante crime fighting into an interactive, multimedia armchair sport. While *Cops* and *Most Wanted* used cutting-edge media technologies to generate empathy for law enforcement, N.W.A earned themselves the ire of federal and local officials alike by bringing racist police brutality to the forefront of the national conversation. Meanwhile, Public Enemy became political pariahs after a group member's anti-Semitic rantings made national news, and they became bona fide superstars thanks to "Fight the Power," their incendiary contribution to Spike Lee's critically acclaimed 1989 film *Do the Right Thing*. The reality era had begun, on wax and on Fox.

In April 1986, the veteran TV journalist Geraldo Rivera hosted *The Mystery of Al Capone's Vaults*, a heavily hyped live two-hour spectacular that held out the tantalizing promise of revealing new information about the country's most notorious gangster. After a significant buildup, which included a segment in which Rivera brandished a period-specific Thompson submachine gun, the vault was shown, live via satellite, to be empty. Rivera apologized on air and was ridiculed for weeks afterward, but he had accomplished his goal: somewhere between thirty and forty million viewers had tuned in to see the syndicated special. What was terrible journalism made for remarkable television entertainment. "There are probably producers all over Hollywood looking for clones of Al Capone's vaults right now," said NBC programming chief Brandon Tartikoff four days later. "It did very well."[8]

For more than a decade, Rivera had made his name as a crusading journalist who frequently made himself the center of his stories. His highlights were impressive, including a Peabody Award for his exposé on patient neglect at a school for disabled children, but at the same time, Rivera was also a constant tabloid presence, thanks to his reputed philandering, drug use, and multiple high-profile divorces. His eccentricities and love of the spotlight often bled into his reporting. In a *20/20* package from 1985, he dressed up as the subway shooter Bernard Goetz, in a staged recreation of Goetz's wounding of four Black teenagers. Rivera's love of scandal triggered his exit from *20/20* in late 1985 after executives shelved his exposé that linked Marilyn Monroe with the Kennedy family. In the meantime, Rivera had developed a strong interest in how local law enforcement was waging President Reagan's war on drugs. After seeing a 1983 syndicated television documentary titled *Cocaine Blues*, in which documentary cameras tagged along with a vice squad and captured a drug raid as it happened, Rivera reached out to one of the producers, an industry veteran named John Langley, to inquire about the possibility of staging such a spectacle live via satellite.

The result was the syndicated special *American Vice: The Doping of a Nation*, which aired nationally on December 2, 1986, less than eight months after the Capone vault disaster. "What you're about to see is not a made-for-TV movie, or a police drama," Rivera tells viewers in the show's opening moments, while standing in front of a suburban home. "This is real life." As he finishes, the camera zooms out to show yellow-jacketed SWAT officers storming past Rivera and rushing into the house, guns drawn. "You'll experience this world as it's happening," Rivera promises. "Get any closer to it, and you'd be busted." In a unique hybrid of multiple nonfiction formats, Rivera hosted the program in front of a studio audience while cutting to preedited packages about drug enforcement efforts like a studio-bound news anchor. In the show's most unprecedented component, Rivera narrated live-via-satellite footage of actual drug raids being conducted in cities around the country. It was high-concept TV journalism, but the perspective was remarkably one-sided. The engineers of Reagan's drug war, as well as the sheriff's departments roped into participation, could not have hoped for a more energetic promotional reel. And, of course, Rivera was front and center: as the studio host and, for one pretaped hidden-camera bust, on site, playing the role of the buyer. When the cops rushed in, the mark was asked a *Candid Camera*–style question: "Did you know you just sold a kilo of cocaine to Geraldo Rivera?"

American Vice was high-concept gimmickry that rushed past journalistic ethics in its quest for the most sensational footage. While Fort Lauderdale police busted into the home of a man suspected of dealing cocaine, Rivera narrated the action live from the studio. "One thing I want to make very clear here, we're not showing this guy's face because he's just a suspect," Rivera noted, at the exact moment that the camera operator panned over to reveal the unblurred face of a woman holding an infant. Uncertain of how to resolve that contradiction, the broadcast cuts back to Rivera, who explains, "It's live television, we have no control over it, it's risky business." As with *Capone's Vaults*, journalists were both deeply critical and gobsmacked. The *Los Angeles Times* called the show's satellite gimmick "a bizarre extension of the live TV fraud that local TV stations daily put over on the public in their newscasts . . . whose only purpose is to convey false excitement to viewers."[9] The fallout was legal too. A woman shown live during a Houston raid was not the drug dealer Rivera had assumed but an innocent housepainter. She filed a $30 million lawsuit against Rivera, claiming libel, defamation, invasion of privacy, and emotional distress. The case was eventually settled out of court, but Rivera's fortunes only continued to rise. *American Vice* was a debacle, but it was also the fifth-highest-rated syndicated special in American TV history. Less than a year later, Tribune debuted Rivera's syndicated talk show, simply titled *Geraldo*. Riding high on his own success, *American Vice* producer John Langley put together a demo reel from the show and sent it to executives at the newly launched Fox.

In the video for "We Want Eazy," the third single from Eazy-E's 1988 debut, *Eazy-Duz-It*, the diminutive Los Angeles rapper demonstrates his own skillful use of satellite technology. The video opens with Eazy getting busted by a cop, apparently for the crime of walking down the street as himself, rendering him unavailable for that evening's concert. Miraculously, Eazy and his cellmates (one of whom is played by Ice Cube) plan an outlandish jailhouse escape, courtesy of a satellite-equipped video rig that they somehow discover in their cell. Cut back to the concert, and while Dr. Dre and MC Ren are hyping the live crowd, Eazy suddenly appears on a large video monitor above the stage, with the graphic "Live from Compton Jail" noting his whereabouts. As Eazy delivers his verses like an on-location reporter, the crowd goes wild, but Eazy is unsatisfied with his virtual appearance. The video climaxes with Eazy transcending the medium, and the space-time continuum, entirely. Taking a running leap, he sprints out of the cell and lands on the stage to a rousing ovation. Eazy's celebrity could not be contained by his criminality.

Before there was N.W.A, there was Eazy-E. Like Ice-T, Eazy was far from a virtuosic rapper but was a clever entrepreneur who translated his street bona fides into a new form of reality-rooted pop stardom. A few years earlier, five-foot-four Eric Wright developed a signature look while dealing crack in loose affiliation with the Kelly Park Crips. He drove around town in a candy-red Suzuki Samurai, clad in a stylish Compton uniform that merged prison garb with street style: a white T-shirt under a thick, dark-colored Dickies jacket, baggy jeans, dark sunglasses, and a baseball cap. His street game was inextricable from his desire for fame. A voracious consumer of the *Los Angeles Times*, by the mid-1980s Wright was seeking a way out of the street and into the celebrity spotlight: specifically, the notoriety that sensationalistic, realistic stories of Black street life could generate. In early promotional photos, while his groupmates/producers were mean mugging or brandishing weapons, Eazy was often shown reading his own press in newspapers and rap magazines.

While Wright was working his way off the streets, he met Andre Young, who grew up in the same part of Compton and was making a name for himself as Dr. Dre, the DJ star of Lonzo Williams's R&B and hip-hop group, World Class Wreckin' Cru. A competitor to Uncle Jamm's Army, the Cru's home base was the nightclub Eve's After Dark, but they had also toured with Rick James and released two albums on Epic Records. Nonetheless, Dre had been angling for a way into harder-edged street music ever since Williams booked Run-DMC's first Los Angeles concert in 1983, and he found a like-minded striver in O'Shea Jackson, an intelligent and wisecracking teenage rapper and lyricist dubbed Ice Cube by his older brother. Jackson was bused to a charter school in the mostly white San Fernando Valley, a daily commute that introduced him to the stark realities of racial inequality and gave him the kind of outsider perspective necessary to turn his South Central life into a caricature, leading to "Boyz-n-the-Hood," a hard track about the sensationalistically violent exploits of a young Black gangster. Wright and Dre failed to get a New York group called H.B.O. to record the song—the lyrics were too LA specific—and with Cube tied up with another group called C.I.A. (Criminals in Action), Dre suggested Wright record the vocals. Reluctant to be anything other than a Berry Gordy figure for the group, Wright was coaxed into the booth and recited Cube's lyrics with the kind of blunt, unadorned phrasing that underscored its casual violence. The single would be released under his newly acquired recording moniker: Eazy-E.

Like Ice-T, the nascent N.W.A were relating vivid tales of Compton street life through the lens of crime reporting. At the end of the second verse of "Boyz," Eazy's character catches a freebase addict trying to steal his car stereo. The climax of this brief interaction is not retribution or jail time but press coverage:

> Chased him up the streets to call a truce
> The silly cluckhead pulls out a deuce-deuce
> Little did he know I had a loaded twelve-gauge
> One sucka dead, *LA Times* front page

To Eazy and Cube, criminal exploits were as much about earning public notoriety as street credibility. At the end of the chorus, Eazy dips back into journalistic vernacular:

> 'Cause the boyz n the hood are always hard
> You come talkin' that trash, we'll pull your card
> Knowin' nothin' in life, but to be legit
> Don't quote me, boy, 'cause I ain't said shit

That last line is crucial: Eazy wants the world to know his story, but on *his* terms alone. Within "I ain't said shit" are two journalistic riffs that are crucial to understanding a song that David Toop described as "a tabloid report from the crime beat fed through a paper shredder."[10] At once, the line means "this stuff happens every day" (it may be newsworthy to you, but not to us) and "you didn't hear this from me" (keep my name out of the story). "Boyz" is the third and final piece of the formative triumvirate of reality rap. Eazy's rhyme cadence was clearly indebted to Ice-T's on "6 in the Mornin'," which itself was a riff on Schoolly D's "P.S.K." Like Schoolly, who translated the titular acronym into a series of hip-hop references, Eazy was aiming toward a larger audience while staying evasive with actual details. Ice-T called his records "reality rap," but those and "Boyz" could just as easily have been called "tabloid rap."

Once Eazy, Cube, and Dre joined with MC Ren and DJ Yella to form N.W.A, they still made party songs (roughly half of *Straight Outta Compton* was cut for the club), but the more harrowing and undanceable stuff was what drew them the most attention. When asked to account for the vulgar and violent content of their music, they replied with a common refrain: they were street reporters and should receive the same latitude as objective journalists. "We're not on the good side of violence, we're not on the bad, we're in the middle," said Dre.[11] When asked about the group's negative influence on their young listeners, Eazy retorted, "Would you ask a news reporter if he's promoting gang violence because he's doing the news?"[12] Cube told an early interviewer, "We deal with reality, plus we say what kids want to hear," stressing truth and entertainment equally, before asserting, "We talk about things that the news don't go real deep into."[13] But a song like "Boyz-n-the-Hood" made critics like Toop pause: "The problem with N.W.A.'s projection of themselves as objective reporters was that their music . . . was exhilarating stuff," he wrote. "Should crime reporting make your heart pound?" Toop compared N.W.A to true-crime predecessors like Truman Capote's *In Cold Blood* and Jules Dassin's *The Naked City*, but the outrageous tabloid journalism of Geraldo Rivera was a better comparison. In either sense, Toop's conclusion is relevant: "The dividing line between news as information and the thrill of voyeurism has always been fragile."[14]

Chuck D was the most voracious consumer of Public Enemy's own press, a fixation that began in April 1987, when he read the *Village Voice* critic John Leland's review of the group's debut album, *Yo! Bum Rush the Show*. The review was titled "Noise Annoys," a nod to the 1978 Buzzcocks single and also an acknowledgment of Leland's central complaint, the "migraine tone that runs through the center of [the single] 'Public Enemy #1'." A sound that off-putting, Leland wrote, enabled him to finally understand his wife's complaints that rap music conveys only "a hatred of white people."[15] To Chuck, Leland's jab was plainly racist. Black music had been dismissed as "noise" by generations of intolerant whites, and PE leaned in to the insult by demonstrating the complexity, artfulness, and rhetorical force of Black music through his own press vehicle. "Bring the Noise" opened with a loop of Malcolm X intoning "too Black . . . too strong," before erupting into a sound storm of samples, scratches, and Chuck's variable-speed rhymes—a different cadence for each verse—and concluding with a dismissal of Leland and his ilk: "A magazine or two is dissin' me and dissin' you."

Though music critics were in Chuck's sights on "Bring the Noise," he also used the track to assail the other gatekeeping institution that could limit the circulation of rap: the bourgeois world of rap-averse Black radio programmers. A February 1988 article penned by PE's "Director of Enemy Relations," Harry Allen, for the *Black Radio Exclusive* trade journal laid into a complacent, R&B-heavy media landscape that failed to accurately represent the most pressing issues for Black America. "There's no hard information in these formats," he wrote. "Where's the news about our lives in this country?"[16] On "Noise," the complaint was translated into a furious, verse-ending dare: "Radio stations I question their Blackness / They call themselves Black, but we'll see if they'll play this." It all adds up to a sonic and political revolution: between Chuck's broadsides against ignorant critics and out-of-touch radio, "Noise" is rap's first recursive single, its lyrics feverishly arguing for the means of its own existence. Leland, for one, was sold. "On 'Bring the Noise,' they all but attack me by name," he wrote in the February 1988 *Spin*. "But that single sounds right now like one of the best things I've ever heard."[17]

A few months later, PE included "Noise" as the second track on *It Takes a Nation of Millions to Hold Us Back*, the most critically acclaimed album of that year and one of the most consequential albums in the history of popular music. Condensing the past half century of Black nationalist thought and pro-Black pop into a nonstop hour of furious, funky Black noise, *Nation* was rap's first political concept album. "P.E. wants to reconvene the black power movement with hip hop as the medium," Greg Tate wrote in the *Village Voice*.[18] Nearly half a century earlier, Black jazz musicians had developed the complex musical patterns of bebop in part to resist incorporation into the white mainstream. The Bomb Squad updated this tactic for the electronic age, undergirding the frantic pace of Chuck's words with an impossibly intricate layering of Black cultural artifacts. Unlike many classic rock concept albums of the past, PE's opus didn't use literature, cinema, or opera as the inspiration, but television. "It was sort of like, well, can we make our album work like a TV show?" Chuck explained.[19] The Bomb Squad eliminated "dead air" between songs by densely interweaving soul and funk samples with bits from Black Power–era speeches, and Chuck's lyrics cut through the storm with a dizzying amalgam of political aphorisms and constantly shifting rhyme cadences. "I turned into a schizophrenic rapper, because of people's attention spans being so short," he explained. "I figured I'd rap the same way people paid attention, giving five seconds to one thought, 10 seconds to another thought, and seven seconds to another thought."[20]

Public Enemy's first widely disseminated music video,[21] for the single "Night of the Living Baseheads," enacted Chuck's claim that rap was "Black America's TV station" by playfully reimagining the group as "PETV." The song itself is a mordant conceptual piece about the crack epidemic, but as the rap scholar Tricia Rose has elaborated, the video parodies Black Entertainment Television (BET), which, she notes, "professes dedication to Black programming but fails to address Black outrage and working-class Black social issues."[22] Coanchor Sherelle Winters, representing the bourgeois Black news "establishment," is bedeviled by the excitable PE hype man Flavor Flav, who represents the street-level "real truth." In a sly exposé of the white cocaine users who were safe from the drug war, field correspondent MC Lyte busts in with her camera crew on Wall Street executives doing lines of blow on a conference table. Chuck himself files his rapped report in front of a shuttered Audubon Ballroom, the legendary Washington Heights venue in Manhattan where Malcolm X was assassinated in 1965. Rose astutely characterizes the ballroom scene as the video's "philosophical point of departure"; a once-iconic symbol of African American self-worth and cultural reproduction had been replaced, she explains, with "today's primary communication mechanism—television."[23]

Several years earlier, Public Enemy coalesced out of Long Island's mobile DJ scene, whose most popular act in the late 1970s was Hank Boxley's Spectrum City. In the wake of "Rapper's Delight," Boxley sought out a rapper to front his operation. He happened upon an Adelphi University design student, Carlton Ridenhour, whose booming baritone was the perfect tool to get the dance floor's attention. Changing his name to MC Chuckie D, Ridenhour started drawing cartoons that portrayed Spectrum City as intergalactic, antiracist superheroes and designing flyers for their concerts. At Adelphi's campus radio station, WBAU, Ridenhour met program director Bill Stephney, who gave Spectrum City its own Saturday night rap show starting in 1982. Soon, the manic performer William Drayton, who called himself DJ Flavor, was in the studio along with them. While their extracurricular work was wrapped up in the nascent rap scene, Ridenhour, Stephney, and Harold McGregor (a friend from Ridenhour's animation class) immersed themselves in

African American history and music. Together, Jeff Chang writes, the crew's lengthy discussions were part "advanced rap seminar," part Harlem Renaissance.[24] After he graduated, Stephney became one of Def Jam's first full-time employees and convinced Chuck, who had cut a few demos with Boxley, to take a meeting with Rick Rubin, who signed him on the spot after hearing his demos. Now it was time to devise an image.

Chuck initially wanted to call the group the New Black Panthers, a direct nod to the radical organization founded in Oakland in 1966 by college students Bobby Seale and Huey Newton. In the wake of the Watts uprising and the assassination of Malcolm X, Seale and Newton were impatient with the civil rights movement's nonviolent stance and believed that true Black liberation could never be achieved without upending the deeply racist American infrastructure, starting with the police. The Black Panthers were many things—a political party, an anticolonialist movement, a node in an international network of revolutionaries, a community organization that organized children's breakfast programs, and a paramilitary operation sworn to "police the police"—but cutting across all their activities, they were a media organization. They published their own newspaper, the *Black Panther*, which featured philosophical opinion pieces from Newton and Seale, the party's ten-point platform, and the vividly drawn editorial cartoons and logos of Emory Douglas. The stories that they didn't publish themselves, the Panthers staged for the mainstream press. Instead of nonviolent sit-ins, the Panthers armed themselves with pistols and rifles and monitored local police for incidents of racist brutality, knowing that the image of armed Black civilians marching in lockstep behind the cops would generate instant press, which would serve as valuable free publicity to swell their ranks.

The Panthers coalesced at a moment when many observers were fretting about the infiltration of journalism by the ever-expanding world of public relations, creating a surplus of what the sociologist Daniel Boorstin dubbed "pseudo-events" in a widely read 1962 book. The pseudo-event, Boorstin explained, was created to be reported, and it borrowed the format of the newsworthy event—press conferences, press releases, photo ops—to disguise PR as straight news. While Boorstin lamented that pseudo-events were presented in the same format and given the same serious attention as spontaneous, "real" events, newspaper editors and TV news producers gobbled them up, knowing that their subscribers and viewers would go elsewhere if they weren't given a continuous stream of news—or at least news-esque items. Public figures, corporations, and even universities hired entire staffs devoted to conjuring and transmitting the right combination of sloganistic words and compelling visuals to generate the right kind of promotional news coverage, the rise of what Boorstin, predicting the later rise of brand culture, ruefully called "the image." A contrived replica of reality that predicted hyperreality, the image could be much more compelling and dramatic than the real thing, especially on TV. "What happens on television will overshadow what happens off television," Boorstin wrote.[25]

The Black Panthers were already legitimate journalists in their own right, but they savvily used pseudo-events to transmit a powerful image of young Black revolutionaries standing up to oppressive state forces. When in 1967 a California assemblyman introduced a bill outlawing the open carrying of firearms, thirty armed Panthers marched onto the Sacramento capitol lawn, causing the news photographers covering Governor Ronald Reagan's photo op with local schoolchildren to flock toward them. Some reporters followed the Panthers into the chambers where the bill was being debated, while others stuck around outside to document Seale reading from the party's platform. The Panthers failed to meaningfully influence legislation that day (Reagan swiftly signed the open-carry ban into law), but the Panthers' larger point was to disseminate their message and image through the press. "Ninety percent of the reason we carried guns in the first place was educational," Newton told the *New York Times Magazine* about the Sacramento stunt. "We made black people aware that they have the right to carry guns."[26] The lead photograph of that article, commissioned by the journalist Eldridge Cleaver, the Panthers' minister of information, showed Newton, the group's minister of defense, sitting in a high-backed wicker chair, holding a spear in one hand and a rifle in the other. It was a potent image with a clear point: Black Americans' situation was the same as those in the so-called Third World who were forced to live under violent colonialist power, and the only way to fight back was to take up arms. At the time, Newton had accomplished little compared to the predecessors whose photos decked out the article—Malcolm X, Mao Zedong, W. E. B. Du Bois, and Marcus Garvey—but there was no question that Newton's *image* had become just as potent.

The nation's most media-savvy federal lawman viewed the charismatic Black revolutionaries as a grave threat to American law and order. Through the COINTELPRO operation, FBI director J. Edgar Hoover infiltrated the Panthers' ranks and spread disinformation to discredit its leaders, while federal agents staged raids on Panther offices across the country for a variety of ultrathin rationales. The same month that the prominent Chicago activist Fred Hampton was murdered during an early morning raid while he lay unarmed in bed, Daryl Gates, steadily working his way up the Los Angeles Police Department ranks, used the Panthers to debut a paramilitary force he'd designed in large part to counter Black street resistance: the SWAT team. In the final days of the 1960s, four hundred of Gates's men surrounded the Black Panthers' Los Angeles offices in South Central, exchanging fire for three hours while news cameras rolled. "Practically, logistically, and tactically, the raid was an utter disaster," summarizes Radley Balko in his book on the militarization of American police. "But in terms of public relations, it was an enormous success."[27] While Gates's stock rose and other departments took notice of the SWAT idea, the Panthers were surveilled and harassed into effective exile; both Cleaver and the Panther adjunct Stokely Carmichael left the country, while Newton, arrested after a firefight with a San Francisco police officer, sat in jail until 1972.

By the mid-1980s, the situation for young Black men in America had scarcely improved since the Panthers' heyday. In the months leading up to the recording of Public Enemy's breakthrough 1987 single "Rebel without a Pause," a Black man was murdered by a gang of white men in Howard Beach, Queens; the officers who had killed a sixty-six-year-old mentally ill Black woman named Eleanor Bumpers and the twenty-five-year-old Black graffiti writer Michael Stewart were acquitted; and the saga of "subway vigilante" Bernie Goetz absorbed an outsize amount of press attention.[28] Chuck D's design for Public Enemy's logo reflected his view of how many young Black men were feeling at the time: like a faceless Black silhouette framed by a rifle scope. But PE's image reflected plenty of Panthers-style aggression too. To round out the group, Chuck brought in his longtime friend Richard Griffin, renamed Professor Griff, to lead the Security of the First World. Part security detail and part backup dancers, the S1Ws marched in lockstep during the group's live shows while clad in military gear and brandishing realistic fake Uzis. Based on Cleaver's precedent, Chuck gave Griff the title "Minister of Information," while McGregor changed his name to Harry Allen and became the group's "Media Assassin," sending out periodic newsletters and publishing the occasional article. Stephney became PE's behind-the-scenes political svengali and their early industry "in" through his post-Adelphi job at Def Jam.

With a mix of media savvy and righteous political fury, Chuck and Def Jam forced their way into the public sphere. Through his tenure as a DJ at Adelphi's WBAU radio station, Chuck had a front-row seat to hip-hop's ascent, and he watched with deep resentment as Run-DMC were engulfed by a media-fueled controversy that the trio had no role in fostering. Chuck was resolute that the same thing would never happen to Public Enemy. "I felt I could be a person who, if the media wanted to fuck with me, could fuck with them just as much, because I would deal with the media at a higher level," he claimed. "Reporters could ask me questions in front of the camera, and I'd be able to turn it around without having a publicist speak for me."[29] In the run-up to PE's first album, Def Jam's in-house polemicist Bill Adler and independent publicist Leyla Turkkan pushed Chuck in front of any microphone or tape recorder around. Chang estimates that "Chuck D had probably done more interviews than any other rapper to that point."[30] Chuck drew little distinction between interviews and lyrics, politics and promotion: on the singles "Rebel without a Pause," "Don't Believe the Hype," and "Bring the Noise," he presented a feverish pro-Black message with the concision of the best Madison Avenue sloganeering.

Like the Panthers, Public Enemy played multiple roles: they were critically acclaimed rap stars whose music was distributed by a major corporation *and* a performative political organization that believed popular music could effect radical political change for Black Americans. Without a real precedent for the group's potent image, the press often saw no alternative but to hold Chuck and the rest of the group to the standards of truth required of journalists, politicians, and civil rights leaders. In the same September 1988 *Spin* interview where Chuck called rap "Black America's TV station," John Leland, the critic whose review had spawned "Bring the Noise" a bit more than a year earlier, pressed Chuck to clarify the statements he made during PE's concerts and on their recordings. Did he really think his phone was being bugged by the

FBI? "It's happened to most black leaders. It's no secret. The FBI does get involved with somebody even a slight bit outspoken." Did he really believe that the Klan were waiting outside Public Enemy concerts, ready to shut them down? "No. But at the same time, I was letting people be aware that these forces exist." Was he okay with manipulating facts to make those points? "Uh huh."[31]

Where the name Public Enemy resignified a law enforcement term to sound an alarm for a generation of Black men targeted by police and citizens alike, Fox's *America's Most Wanted* transformed the FBI's Ten Most Wanted Fugitives list into a dramatic, interactive alert system for would-be vigilantes. Developed by the Fox executive Stephen Chao, who possessed a Harvard MBA and a résumé that included a stint at the *National Enquirer*, *Wanted* was developed to exploit Americans' overinflated perspective on the prevalence of violent crime and to give them the opportunity to help stanch the spread. Chao hired Michael Linder, a Los Angeles TV newsmagazine veteran who had helped launch *Entertainment Tonight* in 1981, to produce. Before meeting Chao, Linder relished the capacity of TV news cameras to provide live, late-breaking coverage of the most sensationalistic crime stories, but what he *really* wanted to show was what happened *before* the police tape was unrolled around the scene. The only way to achieve that goal, he decided, was to work with detectives and federal agents to recreate violent crimes: to show American TV viewers a full, officially sanctioned, *real* view of American violence. The opportunity to participate in capturing the perpetrators by dialing a 1-800 number with tips closed the circle, making *Wanted* a self-contained loop of criminal justice as entertainment. The reenactments overdramatized an American sickness, and the telephone tip line provided a cure.

Though relatively few viewers would actually phone in valid tips, *Wanted's* primary draw was what Linder called the "very hot, gritty, sort of new realism" of the crime reenactments.[32] Dispensing with a documentary or news-style visual approach, Linder settled on a reenactment aesthetic that one of the show's freelance producers described as "Killer Rock Videos."[33] This aesthetic extended to *Wanted's* MTV-style opening credit sequence, directed by the video artist Gretchen Bender, who was also responsible for the fast-paced, information-age-themed video for New Order's "Bizarre Love Triangle." To reassert its realism, Linder staged *Wanted* in Washington, DC, instead of in Fox's Los Angeles studios, part of a novel format that remixed preexisting forms of nonfiction TV into a hybrid novelty. With officers stationed at desks surrounded by photos of suspects hanging on walls, the stage set merged the iconography of the newsroom with the TV police station, and the banks of operators taking viewer calls stirred in the iconography of a 911 dispatch center and a live telethon.

From this set, host John Walsh introduced the reenactments like a stern, paternalistic MTV VJ. *Wanted*'s choice of host added an emotional appeal and tabloid patina to its edgy stylistic innovations. After auditioning politicians, actors, and broadcast journalists, producers settled on a combination of the three with Walsh. The Florida real estate developer had made himself into a national advocate for missing and exploited children after his son was kidnapped and murdered in 1981 by a killer who remained at large. Fewer than two years after the tragedy, Walsh transformed his family's real-life tragedy into a novel televisual hybrid: the made-for-TV movie, or "trauma drama." Like 1983's *M.A.D.D.*, about teen drunk driving, and 1984's *The Burning Bed*, about spousal abuse, *Adam*, which aired in October 1983, turned an incident of domestic terror into edge-of-your-seat prime-time fodder, combining "the ideology of the cop show with the reality claims of the news," as one critic put it.[34] At their core, trauma dramas were Reaganist propaganda, showing the individual resilience of traumatized families who take matters into their own hands in the face of government impotence. A key scene in *Adam* finds Daniel J. Travanti, the *Hill Street Blues* star, playing Walsh at the end of his rope: "The FBI can locate your stolen truck but not your stolen child?"

With its opening disclaimer that "the names of the principal characters and government officials depicted have *not* been changed," and the real Walshes coming on screen at its conclusion to promote a missing children hotline, *Adam* established *America's Most Wanted*'s ideological framework: to stop violent criminals' threat to the sanctity of the American family, citizens had to volunteer to help their government. Opening an episode from December 1989, Walsh works squarely in this rhetorical mode, segueing between holiday idyll and sheer paranoia: "Washington has been trimmed in snow all week long, a perfect prelude to the holiday season. A time when families gather, and people remember the familiar face of a friend. Tonight, we'll show you a new face. It's one we hope you won't forget, because it's the face of a killer on the run." That killer was James Donald King, a once-promising young Black man from North Carolina who, at some point, became an alcoholic, a wayward father, and a murderer. Like many other *Wanted* reenactments, King's path to criminality is left tacit; his crimes were not triggered by larger sociological factors but arose purely from his fractured psychology. "At some point, something snapped, and James Donald King became a vicious man," a detective explains during the segment. The melodramatic reenactments of King's youth give way to sensationalistic portrayals of his crimes, cut with the taut energy of an R-rated movie trailer. Then, the viewers are deputized: Walsh shows a variety of real-life photos and King's prison identification card and describes his habits and physical appearance. Like every profile, King's ended with a prompt noting the show's hotline: 1-800-CRIME-89.

Though civil liberties advocates warned about *Wanted*'s capacity to taint juries, and cultural critics bemoaned the tastelessness of its reenactments, *Wanted* was incredibly successful as both entertainment and law enforcement adjunct. Within days, viewers helped capture the very first fugitive profiled on the show in 1988, and dozens more met the same crowdsourced fate over the next few years. Fox executives relished the fact that *Wanted* became the first Fox program to win its time slot against the big three networks, and Linder claimed that FBI agents were bombarding him with requests to help with their caseloads. Chao admitted that the show's producers "actually scared ourselves" with *Wanted*'s success at converting prime-time TV into one of the nation's most effective crime-fighting platforms. No one had ever "flexed the muscles of television like this before," he boasted.[35]

On September 10, 1988, rap fans filed into Long Island's Nassau Coliseum for a stop on the hip-hop package tour called Jam '88, featuring Eric B. and Rakim, Kool Moe Dee, and Doug E. Fresh, among others. One of those fans, nineteen-year-old Bronx native Julio Fuentes, would not leave the venue alive. Despite a significant security presence at the entrance, Fuentes was one of several concertgoers attacked by a group that had smuggled knives and other weapons into the arena, intent on robbing others for their jewelry. The assailants attacked more than a dozen people, but when Fuentes fought back, he was tackled and stabbed in the heart. Nearly two years after Run-DMC, and rap as a whole, became linked to Southern California gang violence after the Long Beach Arena show, rap was back in the national spotlight for all the wrong reasons. The Nassau Coliseum banned all future rap concerts pending an investigation, and journalists were quick to draw connections between the violence and the music. "The violence Saturday was the latest in a wave that seems to follow rap performances almost as closely as the... fans decked in gold rope chains, expensive sneakers and nylon track suits," wrote a *New York Times* reporter in a front-page story. "Although artists and promoters of rap music...have tried to discourage the violence, it persists."[36]

Worried that their music and culture would be overtaken by crime paranoia, several members of the East Coast rap industry immediately set out to squelch the latest round of controversy. The response was spearheaded by the *Billboard* columnist Nelson George, the Jive/RCA executive Ann Carli, and KRS-One, the leader of the militant Bronx group Boogie Down Productions, whose DJ, Scott La Rock, was himself murdered while trying to mediate a dispute. The ad hoc coalition named their movement after a Boogie Down Productions song title, "Stop the Violence," and recruited a handful of rap's elite—Kool Moe Dee, Public Enemy, MC Lyte, Stetsasonic, and Heavy D, among others—to contribute verses to rap's first charity song, "Self Destruction." Despite its name, Stop the Violence was less a social or political movement than a calculated PR strategy to change the press narrative around rap.[37] In a short book released to accompany the recording, George blamed the national media for reporting the Nassau killing "as if the music itself had inspired its young listeners to carve each other up" and asserted that it was time for rappers "to define the problem and defend themselves."[38] The single was released on January 15, 1989, Martin Luther King Jr.'s birthday, and a month later, Stop the Violence and a group of high school students marched through Harlem carrying a coffin to stage a press conference at the Apollo Theater. They partnered with the first major hip-hop magazine, *Word Up!*, to sponsor an essay contest and donated the single's profits to the National Urban League, a veteran civil rights organization.

"Self Destruction" was well-timed, to be sure; its release coincided with hip-hop's official recognition by the record industry. That February, DJ Jazzy Jeff and the Fresh Prince were awarded the first Grammy for Best Rap Performance (when the producers announced that the award presentation would not be televised, several nominees boycotted the event), and in March, *Billboard* unveiled its inaugural Hot Rap Singles chart, which was topped by "Self Destruction" for its first several weeks. While the song was a diplomatic success, signaling that rappers could effectively self-police, the movement's actual message placed part of the blame on Black communities themselves. In its lyrics, along with the interviews conducted by its contributors, the phrase "Black-on-Black crime" appeared constantly, and not as the subject of dispute. "Black-on-Black crime was way before our time," rapped Stetsasonic's MC Delite in the song's second verse, a statement that echoed George's primary rationale for the Stop the Violence Movement: "for the rappers to raise public awareness of black-on-black crime and point out its real causes and social costs."[39] Though it had no social scientific backing, the social reality created by the idea of "Black-on-Black crime" was every bit as potent as the law-and-order world of *Cops* and *America's Most Wanted*: Black people were killing *themselves*, and the Black entertainment world needed to help everyday people and law enforcement create a safer world.

Most commonly associated with conservative politicians and columnists, the Black-on-Black crime idea erupted into public consciousness during the early years of the Reagan administration as a tactic to cast Black Americans as the root cause of the crime in their communities, to rhetorically isolate crime from the numerous socioeconomic factors that contribute to its spread, and, consciously or not, to let racist police off the hook.[40] Yet the notion was not limited to the New Right or even whites: in August 1979, *Ebony* magazine devoted its entire issue to a discussion of Black-on-Black crime, which the magazine's publisher claimed "has reached a critical level that threatens our existence as a people."[41] In his brief remarks at the Apollo Theater press conference, National Urban League vice president Frank Lomax III explained, "In the six minutes that it takes these rap artists on the song to express their collective disdain for black-on-black crime, two African-Americans will have become victims. So, if you have not already been victimized, chances are you or someone very close to you will."[42] To battle the press narrative of hip-hop as a violent subculture, Stop the Violence adopted the conservative language of respectability politics in lieu of a broader attack on infrastructural racism—which, in all fairness, would be much harder to link to a concert killing, let alone turn into a pop music slogan.

KRS-One made a logical spokesman for the effort. Like Public Enemy and Ice-T, he boldly negotiated the fine line between embracing the aesthetics of armed violence and advocating for peace (T was tabbed to participate in "Self Destruction," but his *Power* promotional duties disallowed it). For the cover image of Boogie Down Productions' 1988 album *By All Means Necessary*, KRS recreated Malcolm X's famous *Esquire* magazine pose, peering out an apartment window while holding a gun—though substituting an Uzi for X's long rifle. Like his peers, KRS believed that rappers could draw in wayward Black youth with outsize representations of street toughness and criminality, then teach them positive life lessons once they had their attention. His thesis statement is presented most clearly in "My Philosophy," the music video of which opens with a group of young Black children watching KRS on a living room television. He presents himself as a street-wizened educator—"In four seconds, a teacher will begin to speak," he announces—who is providing lessons not only about the world but about the value of hip-hop as pedagogy. "It's not about a salary / It's all about reality," he intones in one of the song's most memorable couplets.

That same line appears in another, very different single that appeared in the inaugural *Billboard* Hot Rap Singles chart topped by "Self Destruction." Checking in at no. 12 that week, two spots below "High Rollers" and four above "We Want Eazy," was "Gangsta Gangsta," a single from *Straight Outta Compton* that sharpened the "Boyz-n-the-Hood" archetype into a nihilistic antihero. "Since I was a youth, I smoked weed out / Now I'm the mothafucka that you read about," raps Ice Cube, reveling in the notoriety earned by doing exactly what Stop the Violence was preaching *against*. (To emphasize the group's fixation on the frenzy of renown, Dr. Dre is shown on the cover of the "Gangsta" twelve-inch single reading the *Los Angeles Times*.) When Dre scratches "It's not about a salary / It's all about reality" into the "Gangsta" chorus, the sentiment takes on an almost parodic meaning in the context of a song whose most memorable line is "Life ain't nothin' but bitches and money." To N.W.A, not only could salary and reality coexist, but the latter was the prerequisite for the former. An overblown parody of Black-on-Black violence and a reversed-perspective take on *America's Most Wanted*'s fugitive profiles, "Gangsta" gleefully asserts from its first moments that, yes, young Black men are trying to kill you, and themselves. The song opens with a brief dramatization of an exasperated citizen reacting to the sound of police sirens. "I wonder who they fucked up today?" As it happens, the gangstas are waiting for him outside: Eazy yells, "You, motherfucker!" followed by the sound of semiautomatic gunfire and Dre's voice, declaring that they "got him."

In a June 1988 interview, KRS tried to fine-tune his reality: "I'm not saying so much 'fuck the police' as 'let's grow up more.'" A few months later on *Straight Outta Compton*, N.W.A simply said, "Fuck tha police." At the exact moment that the Stop the Violence Movement sought a détente with the powers that be by stressing Black responsibility, "Fuck tha Police" pointed the finger and the firearm at the *actual* criminals on the other coast: Daryl Gates's LAPD. Where KRS and Chuck D were making high-concept hip-hop for adults, "Fuck tha Police" was spurred by the resentment of getting caught in an act of juvenile delinquency. Eazy and Dre were busted shooting paintball guns at passing cars on the Harbor Freeway and were humiliated by LA highway patrolmen, who forced them to lie prone on the street while cars zoomed by. Yet the song was no less radical for its vulgar and adolescent flavor of agitprop: like the best protest chants and pop songs, simply uttering the titular catchphrase generated its own visceral thrill. The title was such a violation of public propriety that the song would never be played on the radio, and even the specter of N.W.A recreating the performance live in arenas or amphitheaters was enough to generate condemnation from local authorities. Still, pumping out of cars and boom boxes, or secretly enjoyed through the mobile privacy afforded by the Walkman, "Fuck tha Police" turned N.W.A into hip-hop's first bona fide countercultural icons and recast Compton as what Joshua Clover called "the national stage for the drama of the African-American underclass."[43] As close to an actual weapon as popular recordings get, "Fuck tha Police" single-handedly injected rap music into the blossoming culture wars that "Stop the Violence" was trying to defuse. It is not an understatement to suggest that "Fuck tha Police" is the most truly transgressive American song, dangerous enough to earn a letter from the FBI.

For all of its historical importance and revolutionary force, "Fuck tha Police" is also a funny song and, in its arrangement and production, a groundbreaking one. When put to tape in 1988, hip-hop producers were just beginning to embrace the possibilities of the digital sampler (with the Bomb Squad leading the way) and to explore song and album arrangements that incorporated nonmusical elements. This was the dawn of the moment when, Jeff Weiss explains, "rap albums could suddenly be more than song collections. They could be game shows, panoramic films, or self-aware parody."[44] The same autumn as *Straight Outta Compton*'s release, Compton's own King Tee incorporated the first humorous skit on a rap album: a brief game of the dozens in the middle of his aptly titled debut LP, *Act a Fool*. "Fuck tha Police" went far beyond the skit format, borrowing from two popular reality TV formats. Before MC Ren and Eazy deliver their verses, Dre inserts dramatizations of the acts of police malfeasance (an unwarranted traffic stop for Ren, a domestic raid for Eazy) to riff on *America's Most Wanted*'s crime reenactments from the opposite perspective, with just as much creative license and shock factor. While N.W.A were no strangers to using the courtroom as a stage for their storytelling (the final verse of "Boyz-n-the-Hood" chronicled a shoot-out during a trial), the structure of "Fuck tha Police" played like a riff on the proto-reality-TV syndicated sensation *The People's Court*. That show's small-claims cases were litigated according to California statutes, but everything else was fully staged: like hired actors, the litigants earned scale; all monetary judgments were paid by the show; and each case was recapped by an announcer (played by producer Doug Llewelyn, who oversaw Geraldo Rivera's failed foray into Al Capone's vault). *The People's Court* reimagined the judicial system as a small-stakes game show, and N.W.A's own courtroom revenge fantasy was just slightly less artificial and just as entertaining. It's easy to imagine the credits rolling as Judge Dre declares the nameless police officer "guilty of being a redneck, white bread, chickenshit motherfucker."

N.W.A portraying the cops as an occupying, racist force receiving an imagined comeuppance was counterprogramming not only for *Cops* and *America's Most Wanted* but for the procop reality that the LAPD had been sponsoring for decades. The rise of what many now call "copaganda" was pioneered at the dawn of television by *Dragnet*, which aired on NBC for nearly three hundred episodes between December 1951 and August 1959. The first TV police procedural, *Dragnet* merged the realist conventions of documentaries, 1950s social realist films, radio crime dramas, and film noir into twenty-two-minute vignettes drawn from actual case files. The show was executive produced by LAPD chief Bill Parker—Daryl Gates's mentor—and served as weekly prime-time propaganda for Parker's militaristic expectations of officer discipline, factory-floor-style efficiency, new technologies, and the belief that police were the "thin blue line" separating peaceful society from rampant crime. *Dragnet*'s Sgt. Joe Friday (Jack Webb) had no internal life and few off-the-clock experiences; his entire existence was as an avatar for effective police work, which was the show's true star. Webb's oft-stated desire for the raw facts of a case could have doubled as a maxim for journalists, and the police work portrayed on *Dragnet* was, likewise, an objective process of impartially evaluating information. Based on *Dragnet*'s template, J. Edgar Hoover oversaw the creation of *The F.B.I.*, which aired 241 episodes from 1965 to 1974 (it was the nation's tenth most popular show for the 1970–1971 season), with the foremost federal officer exerting veto power over scripts, casting, and even advertising until his 1972 death. The 1970s were a boom time for cop shows shot on location in Los Angeles. In 1975 and 1976 alone, fifteen LA-based police shows aired in prime time on the three networks. One of the shows, produced by Aaron Spelling of *The Mod Squad* and *Starsky and Hutch*, was called *S.W.A.T.*

Black Los Angelenos knew full well that prime-time policing had little to do with their day-to-day reality in what Mike Davis called the "carceral city," where Black citizens were redlined into specific neighborhoods, deprived of employment and social services, and surveilled constantly by the police. In this landscape, N.W.A crafted its image at the intersection of three different definitions of "profiling": the criminal profiles projected onto them by the LAPD, the street fashions they pioneered by "styling and profiling" in public, and the magazine and newspaper stories that shaped the group's image for mass audiences by combining the first two phenomena. Late capitalism made it a circular path: when N.W.A blew up in 1989, their everyday gear—dark jeans, T-shirts, Raiders and LA Kings paraphernalia, locs (sunglasses), gold chains, pagers—became subcultural fashion, which the LAPD included in its profiles used to harass, detain, and arrest young Black men, alongside the blue and red bandanas of the Bloods and the Crips. One of the primary charges Cube issues against the officer on trial in "Fuck tha Police," after all, is a crime that hadn't yet been introduced into common conversation—racial profiling:

> Fuckin' with me 'cause I'm a teenager
> With a little bit of gold and a pager
> Searchin' my car, lookin' for the product
> Thinkin' every nigga is sellin' narcotics

In N.W.A's universe, the cops themselves are profiled too: they're not much more than the sum total of their costumes and props. Ren issues a dare:

> Pullin' out a silly club, so you stand
> With a fake-ass badge and a gun in your hand
> But take off the gun so you can see what's up
> And we'll go at it, punk, and I'ma fuck you up!

For Eazy, it's a similar scenario: "Without a gun and a badge, what do you got? / A sucker in a uniform waiting to get shot."

To N.W.A, as for Gates and Reagan, law-and-order culture was inextricable from its mediated performance. Their flipped script is best captured in the first major magazine profile written about the group, by the LA Weekly reporter Jonathan Gold. In the story, Gold relates an anecdote about the group's preparation for a photo shoot, during which they obsess over the verisimilitude of a bag of guns that Eazy emptied onto the ground to use as props. Ice Cube notes that Public Enemy's S1Ws use only plastic guns, while he is holding the real thing. Even for a photo shoot, there was no more authentic accessory than a *real gun*: the symbolic object that ties the three definitions of "profile" together. The affective connection between the "point and shoot" technologies, cameras and guns, was crucial to N.W.A's public profile—Eazy points a pistol at the camera on the cover of *Straight Outta Compton*—and it was not lost on Gold, who onomatopoeically recreates the photo op for his readership: "Click. Click-click. Click. (The photographer shoots back.)"[45]

Law enforcement officials first developed profiling tactics at international airports during the "skyjacking" scare of the 1970s and modified them to fit the image of the drug smuggler in the 1980s. Though police profiling is not codified in law enforcement training manuals—departments are careful not to publicize any techniques that might violate the Fourth Amendment's prohibition of unreasonable searches and seizures—police officers have wide latitude to stop, if not detain, citizens who meet particular criteria. Profiling creates a legal reality with dire consequences: once they cast citizens in the role of criminals, cops can search them based on the tacit intimidation of their uniform. One of the key figures in the development of profiling was the media-savvy Broward County, Florida, sheriff Nick Navarro, whose officers were accompanied by John Langley's crew on one of *American Vice*'s live-via-satellite drug busts. Sworn in as Broward County sheriff in 1985, Navarro quickly implemented controversial profiling tactics on south Florida public transportation, authorizing swarms of plainclothes officers to board trains and buses, asking "suspicious" passengers for tickets, IDs, and permission to search their bags. Theoretically, any passenger could refuse the request. In reality, very few did. "You're sitting on a bus, in a cramped space, when an officer with a gun sticking out of his belt asks if he can look through your luggage," explained one Broward County judge. "Do you really think the average person believes he can say no?"[46] In his autobiography, Navarro claimed that his officers limited their searches to "selected individuals who seemed to fit our profile" but neglected to elaborate on what exactly that profile comprised.[47] In 1987 and 1988, Florida judges heard three different cases involving Navarro's profiling methods, leading one judge to issue a damning condemnation. "This is not Hitler's Berlin, nor Stalin's Moscow, nor is it white supremacist South Africa," read the decision.[48] Though citizens of underprivileged, drug-ravaged communities saw him as Florida's own Daryl Gates, Navarro (like Gates) was widely popular, a dutiful soldier in Reagan's war on drugs who earned 63 percent of the vote in his 1988 reelection campaign.

Given his previous work with Langley on *American Vice*, Navarro's department was a perfect choice for the pilot episode of *Cops*, which Langley pitched to Stephen Chao when the executive was fresh off selling his Fox bosses on *America's Most Wanted*. Like Chao, Langley had moved from academia to entertainment (he dropped out of a PhD program to try his hand in Hollywood) and wanted to merge his intellectual side with the new world of edgy nonfiction fare. As Dennis Hopper had shown with *Colors*, Langley's 1960s-honed antiauthoritarianism had softened into an affinity for the agents of state authority. "I'm a child of the '60s. If you would've told me that I was going to do a show about cops, I would've said, 'What am I going to call it? Pigs?'" he told an interviewer. "I just happened to get in an arena that was dramatic and started doing documentary films about it that became so-called reality television," he added. To sell Chao on what would become *Cops*, Langley took Chao on a shoot, where his skeleton crew was following a group of Navarro's police officers on an airport drug bust. "So we're standing, literally, at a little food court watching them stop the suspect. Now they start asking questions.... Steve [asks], 'why are you wasting my time? That guy's innocent. Why are they bothering him?' And I said, 'I'll bet you $100 he's carrying drugs.'"[49] As it happened, the man had already been profiled as a drug courier, and Langley's cameras captured his dramatic struggle with the officers after he resisted being taken into custody, along with his booking process and phone call. According to Langley, that demonstration sold Chao on his novel idea, and the edited sequence was included in the pilot episode of *Cops*.

Navarro, dubbed the "show-biz sheriff" by the *Orlando Sentinel* and "Nick at Night" for his frequent appearances on the evening news, was the perfect choice to star in the hour-long pilot. The Cuban-born sheriff drew few distinctions between police work that was good for his community and that which would increase his public profile. Navarro kept an autographed photo of Al Pacino over his desk—a memento from advising the actor for his role as the Cuban cocaine titan Tony Montana in the 1983 film *Scarface*—and even auditioned for the role of the recurring villain character Calderone in the popular 1980s cop show *Miami Vice*. Navarro's decision to send local officers to infiltrate international smuggling efforts on the Bahamian islands of Bimini was lightly fictionalized by Robert Coram for his 1988 novel *Narcs*, and from 1989 to 1991, Navarro's undercover officers posed as crack dealers outside area high schools with a product that Navarro's department *had cooked themselves*, using confiscated cocaine: the cops were acting as their own prop department.[50] In 1986, Navarro implemented a heavily hyped countywide drug sweep that he named Operation Crackdown. Like Gates's LAPD gang sweeps, Navarro's Crackdown was much less effective as a crime deterrent (only 17 out of 294 arrestees were convicted and sentenced) than as a massive pseudo-event designed as a spectacular display of force.[51]

Though Langley was an outspoken proponent of the "fly on the wall" documentary, the *Cops* pilot is anything but a passive view of police work, building up to a five-and-a-half-minute music video–style portrayal of Operation Crackdown no. 3. Set to up-tempo instrumental rock music, the montage opens as Navarro puts on a headset and enters a helicopter, while an unidentified man slaps a "SHERIFF" badge on his all-black tactical gear, and officers walk to their cars armed with crowbars and sledgehammers. As a lower-third graphic reads "8:47 AM CRACKHOUSE WARRANT," a van door flies open and officers spill out, running toward a suburban home and smashing its windows before slamming the hammer into the front door. After looking over a table full of confiscated guns and holding up a bag of drugs for the cameras, Navarro walks by a row of handcuffed Black suspects sitting in the driveway (none of whose faces are blurred) and declares, "Everyone here goes to jail. Everyone here. Book them all." Then, a staged bust: filmed from a distance, a Black man walks up to a car, ostensibly to buy drugs, and is greeted by the overwhelming sight of four squad cars peeling up to the scene. One officer walks toward the unarmed man, gun drawn, screaming. A few seconds later, a handcuffed woman wails in pain while being pushed into the back of a police cruiser, while a female officer mocks her cries and slams the door. The sequence ends with a visual that could have been drawn from any number of TV police procedurals: an unidentified officer watches the ten o'clock news coverage of the crackdown. It's just another day at the office.

Cops did not bother with results—the visual spectacle of law and order was all Langley was after—but local newspapers reported them the next morning: Operation Crackdown resulted in 188 arrests for drug-related offenses, five abandoned houses demolished, dozens of abandoned cars towed, and a grand total of ten guns and small amounts of crack and marijuana seized. The *Fort Lauderdale News / Sun-Sentinel* noted the presence of Langley's team on one raid: "Dozens of reporters and photographers from local newspapers and television stations— even a crew hoping to sell a documentary—paraded behind deputies." The story noted details left out of *Cops*: one of the arrestees was a former Pompano Beach police officer, and the two largest Broward County police departments declined to participate. Fort Lauderdale's chief of police cited the complications of adding a media presence to street-level operations, mentioning that his department had rebuffed multiple offers from Geraldo Rivera, while the Hollywood, Florida, police chief simply called Navarro a "media mogul."[52] Meanwhile, Operation Crackdown's nearly two hundred arrestees glutted the North Broward detention complex, forcing Navarro to erect a temporary tent city on a nearby basketball court to accommodate the overflow.[53]

Three months after the *Cops* pilot aired, N.W.A embarked on its first post–"Fuck tha Police" national tour. As they would learn as they traveled from city to city, the song had become more than a musical phenomenon. To a significant number of moral entrepreneurs, it represented a bona fide threat to the established social order. Everywhere they stopped, they were greeted by moral panics of various sizes. N.W.A's scheduled June 18 performance at Cincinnati's Riverfront Coliseum is a case study of the media hype and fearmongering that followed them through the Midwest. Most locals were unaware of the group's music, and to a significant extent, the figures who were protesting N.W.A's appearance in Cincinnati were also promoting it. Eight days out, members of the local Baptist Ministers' Conference read the group's lyrics aloud at a press conference, announcing, "That garbage is not going to go in Cincinnati," while members of the Macedonia Baptist Church reported that they had not heard of N.W.A until their pastor brought a copy of the lyrics to a Bible study.[54] Two days before the concert, a group of citizens read and discussed N.W.A lyrics on a local cable-access show, and the *Cincinnati Enquirer* ran an editorial asserting that N.W.A's music represented not protest but a "descent into savagery."[55] Mayor Charles Luken said that he wanted the group to stay out of the city, and the day before the concert, city councilman (and Bengals linebacker) Reggie Williams staged a press conference with Ice Cube and MC Ren, not to support their music but to generically assert their First Amendment right to perform it. "The music itself is real," Ren told the gathered reporters. "We're speaking through it."[56]

That Sunday evening, a crowd of around 6,400 filed into the venue, greeted by a doubled security contingent provided by the Cincinnati Police Department, which stationed sixty-three more officers around the downtown area. "They're here just because the music is geared toward young blacks," one attendee told a reporter afterward. N.W.A agreed not to perform "Fuck tha Police," as they did in numerous other cities, and the concert went off without any violence. The city got in the last word, however, issuing the trio and their opening act, the Oakland rapper Too $hort, $114 citations for disorderly conduct for the crime of uttering "four-letter words" to the crowd. Apparently, the performers had violated an obscenity statute that confused the venue owner. "We never agreed to require the band to conform to FCC lyrics," he said. Local judge Harry McIlwain rejected N.W.A's motion to overturn the charges on First Amendment grounds. "I hold the city of Cincinnati responsible for allowing the concert and I hold mothers and fathers responsible for allowing their children to go there," McIlwain stated in his decision (which was overturned on appeal).[57] Whether the localized hysteria arose out of legitimate fear or opportunism, it was undoubtedly productive for N.W.A, who earned heaps of free publicity merely for showing up.

A few months later, the rest of the country learned just how dangerous American conservative activists and federal law enforcement thought N.W.A were. At an anti-censorship rally in October, rock critic Dave Marsh and activist Phyllis Pollack revealed the existence of the letter sent to Priority Records by the FBI agent and *America's Most Wanted* consultant Milt Ahlerich. "My intent was that those representatives for the licensing, distribution and publishing of the record should have the benefit of knowing the facts of police violence," Ahlerich explained to reporters, adding that he had not listened to the song itself but had been sent lyrics by other law enforcement officials. Further reporting revealed a sub-rosa communications network that authorities had installed to oppose "Fuck tha Police," countering the song with a two-fronted censorship attack that merged obscenity statutes with incitement claims. Faxing the song's lyrics from city to city (and, likely, to Ahlerich), public officials had alerted ministers, police organizations, judges, and local media outlets to N.W.A's impending arrival. At some stops, the trio were actually profiled about their gang connections. At the end of their Detroit concert, the group launched into "Fuck tha Police," causing police stationed around Joe Louis Arena to rush the stage.

On October 10, Marsh and Pollack published their findings in the *Village Voice*, highlighting a chilling precedent being set by a network of moral entrepreneurs. They cited an article from the June issue of Focus on the Family's *Citizen* (the publication of the far-right organization founded by Reverend James C. Dobson) that urged readers to "alert local police to the dangers they may face in the wake of this record release." At the time, Dobson was most well-known for claiming that serial killer Ted Bundy's actions came as a result of his pornography addiction and for campaigning to remove the teaching of evolution from classrooms. Marsh and Pollack also noted that the Parents Music Resource Center's Susan Baker (wife of Treasury secretary James Baker) sat on Focus on the Family's board of directors, and they observed that Jennifer Norwood, the spokeswoman for Tipper Gore's organization, was quoted in the same *Citizen* issue as saying, "We want music critics and organizations like Focus on the Family to disseminate this information to their constituencies."[58] The Parents Music Resource Center's position in the mainstream of American politics, the authors argued, was sanitizing the intolerant zealotry of figures like Dobson and raising significant concerns about the mounting pressures on the record industry to adopt a content-labeling system. The conservative war against reality rap was ready to explode.

The day after N.W.A's Cincinnati concert, Public Enemy were faced with a different controversy, spawned not by a performance or a recording but by an interview that the group's minister of information had given to a reporter. In a late May conversation with David Mills for the *Washington Times*, the newspaper founded in 1982 by the cultish "Moonie" movement leader Sun Myung Moon, Professor Griff had made a series of baldly anti-Semitic comments. "The Jews are wicked," Griff told Mills, amid various other conspiracy theories. "And we can prove this."[59] This was not the first time that Griff's appalling views had appeared in print. John Leland's *Spin* profile from September 1988 opened with an extended quotation (originally from the UK music magazine *Melody Maker*) that ended with Griff saying, "If the Palestinians took up arms, went into Israel, and killed all the Jews, it'd be alright." But Mills was in his own way as savvy a self-publicist as Chuck D, and he avidly promoted his interview to *Rolling Stone* and *Spin*. Harry Allen leaked to Chuck that the *Village Voice*, where Allen was a freelancer, was publishing an excerpt on June 20. On June 19, like a politician distancing himself from a controversial cabinet member, Chuck issued a press release announcing that he was stripping Professor Griff of his title as PE's minister of information. Chuck was far from conciliatory, referring to an "emotional lynch mob" mentality that was besetting the group. The story quickly became national news and posed the first significant test of Chuck's PR skills in avoiding a Run-DMC-style crisis. He failed. Two days later, he issued a second announcement: Griff had been fired from the group. The next day, Chuck told Kurt Loder on *MTV News* that Public Enemy was breaking up.

Public Enemy's implosion was a hyperreal chapter in the long relationship between American Jews and African Americans. Jews had played a significant role in the civil rights movement, from their cofounding the NAACP in 1909 through their well-documented participation in the marches and voting-rights actions of the 1950s and 1960s. While the rise of the Black Power movement "opened the door for Jews, as well as other ethnic, racial, and gender groups, to embrace identity politics for their own communal benefit,"[60] the relationship between Black and Jewish Americans was often strained, particularly in the urban North. In his autobiography, Martin Luther King Jr. offered a nuanced impression of the relationship between Jews and an individual he termed the "urban Negro": "On the one hand, he is associated with Jews as some of his most committed and generous partners in the civil rights struggle. On the other hand, he meets them daily as some of his most direct exploiters in the ghetto as slum landlords and gouging shopkeepers."[61] The relationship was further complicated by the rise of the Nation of Islam, founded in Detroit in 1930 by Wallace Fard Muhammad to "teach the downtrodden and defenseless Black people a thorough knowledge of God and of themselves, and to put them on the road to self-independence with a superior culture and higher civilization than they had previously experienced."[62] The Nation of Islam grew significantly under the stewardship of Elijah Muhammad, who ran the organization until his death in 1975. Anti-Semitic remarks litter the speeches delivered by Nation of Islam leaders, like one from Minister Jeremiah X, who claimed that "Jews are the Negro's worst enemies among whites." After Elijah Muhammad's death, Louis Farrakhan, a former calypso singer who had become the Nation of Islam's national representative in 1967, took over with a new media-savvy message of Black separatism and self-reliance.

Farrakhan came to national attention as a key surrogate to Jesse Jackson's 1984 presidential candidacy, though their political ideologies—Jackson an assimilationist civil rights veteran and Christian, Farrakhan a radical, isolationist Muslim conservative—could not have been more different. Jewish groups were enraged when the Black *Washington Post* reporter Milton Coleman printed some off-the-cuff remarks of Jackson's that referred to New York City as "Hymietown." When Farrakhan called the creation of Israel an "outlaw act" in the midst of the campaign, Jackson quickly distanced himself. Unbowed, Farrakhan used his new platform to broaden his popularity with Black Americans and to double down on his notoriety with everyone else. He steered the Nation toward active support of Black-owned businesses and Black-driven social reforms. His drive to clean up crack houses mirrored the self-reliance ideology of "Self Destruction," and his relaunch of the Nation's newspaper (formerly *Muhammad Speaks*) as the *Final Call* reflected a long history of powerful Black nationalist journalism, from Marcus Garvey's *Negro World* through the *Black Panther*.

Farrakhan also continued to exploit Black Americans' distrust of a mainstream, white-run media that had long mis- and underrepresented them. During a notorious 1985 appearance on *The Phil Donahue Show*, Farrakhan defended a recording of a speech in which he referred to Judaism as "a gutter religion," claiming that the white media had twisted his words. Farrakhan offered a similar explanation for the press's report that he had called for Milton Coleman's death, which many reporters present during the supposed utterance had confirmed as a mischaracterization.[63] He also defended Jackson's "Hymietown" remark, claiming that "Reverend Jackson was speaking in slang and off the record."[64] Whites were outraged by Farrakhan, but to a significant number of Black Americans, he was the perfect no-nonsense leader to step into the breach of a fractured civil rights leadership. While Elijah Muhammad had turned Wallace Fard Muhammad's theories into a worldview, Farrakhan translated them into a powerful mass-media image. His speeches to Black audiences drew the attendance of a pop concert, he understood the power of television more than any of his predecessors, and his followers looked upon him as the kind of plainspoken savior who could outduel the white devils while the world watched.

Professor Griff introduced Farrakhan to Public Enemy, and Chuck's support for the Nation of Islam was evident on the *Yo! Bum Rush the Show* album track "Rightstarter (Message to a Black Man)," coming out in full force on "Bring the Noise," when he rapped, "Farrakhan's a prophet and I think you ought to listen to / What he can say to you, what you ought to do is follow for now." If Farrakhan couldn't affiliate with mainstream Black politicians, Public Enemy provided a politicized entertainment platform to spread his message. Yet while Chuck's fusion of the Nation of Islam's interior-looking mythologies with the revolutionary politics of the Black Panthers made for exhilarating pop rhetoric, it did not lend itself to the coherent ideological perspective that critics and journalists sought. That tentative fit came to a head on the final track of *It Takes a Nation of Millions to Hold Us Back*. In the second verse of "Party for Your Right to Fight," Chuck rightly notes that the FBI played a significant role in debilitating the Black Panthers and extends that fact to the two other most prominent Black leaders, both of whom were under federal surveillance:

> J. Edgar Hoover, and he coulda proved to you
> He had King and X set up
> Also the party with Newton, Cleaver and Seale
> He ended, so get up

The last verse of "Party" delves into Nation of Islam mythology that resonated with many adherents but read like ahistorical fantasy to others:

> For the original Black Asiatic man
> Cream of the earth and was here first
> And some devils prevent this from being known
> But you check out the books they own
> Even Masons they know it
> But refuse to show it, yo
> But it's proven and fact

Chuck's fusion of the Panthers' righteous political energy and the Nation of Islam's abstruse mysticism was one stumbling block. Another was the deeply conservative, often hateful perspective that Farrakhan endorsed, including misogyny, homophobia, and anti-Semitism. "To know P.E. is to love the agitprop (and artful noise) and to worry over the whack retarded philosophy they espouse," Greg Tate wrote. "Since P.E. show sound reasoning when they focus on racism as a tool of the U.S.

power structure, they should be intelligent enough to realize that dehumanizing gays, women, and Jews isn't going to set black people free."[65]

To the *Village Voice* reporter R. J. Smith, whose article broke the Griff scandal, Farrakhan's influence was obvious, but the writer was sympathetic toward Public Enemy's political position. "Think back to 1984. A black man calls Judaism a 'gutter religion,' and suddenly everybody wants a piece of his associate," Smith wrote. "From many quarters… demands were made that [Jesse Jackson] disassociate himself from Minister Farrakhan. Chuck D. calls similar demands to oust Griff 'divide and conquer.'"[66] For Chuck, the problem was less the repugnance of Griff's comments—which, critics noted, were not reflected in PE's recordings at all—than the news media's reaction to them. Like Farrakhan with Milton Coleman four years earlier, Chuck blamed the press for intervening where they had no business. Smith's *Village Voice* follow-up story quoted a phone call from Chuck in which he issued a threat: "Any shit comes down on me, it's coming down on you."[67] Griff's statements exposed the schism within Public Enemy, chronicled in the September 1989 *Spin* article by John Leland. Griff had already been chafing at his reduced role, especially when it came to using Public Enemy's fame to spread the Nation of Islam's message. "Griff was supposed to be the Minister of Information," Hank Shocklee told Leland, "but he wasn't allowed to do interviews."[68] In public, Chuck blamed the white press, while in private, Leland revealed, he believed Griff had sabotaged Public Enemy out of jealousy. Either way, the resulting spectacle was orders of magnitude larger than the one that had surrounded Run-DMC; the first time that many Americans heard of Public Enemy was in press accounts of Griff's anti-Semitism, a massive failure of Chuck's ostensible gift for hip-hop public relations. Leland wondered, as did millions of fans, if the controversy "may mean the end of the most innovative and influential group of the late Eighties," the final moments of the group who "changed the way hip hop sounds, the way it is made, what it does."[69]

Chuck had another reason to remove Public Enemy from the spotlight. Jewish groups were threatening protests against *Do the Right Thing*, Spike Lee's highly anticipated film that opened two weeks after the Griff debacle broke and that prominently featured "Fight the Power," the group's most rousing single to date. "Power" was *Do the Right Thing*'s leitmotif, blasting out of the boom box of local hardhead Radio Raheem

(Bill Nunn), who patrols his Bedford-Stuyvesant block while sporting matching "LOVE" and "HATE" four-finger rings. After the character Buggin' Out (Giancarlo Esposito) forcefully confronts pizzeria owner Sal (Danny Aiello) about the uniformly white photographs hanging on the wall of his restaurant, Sal destroys Raheem's PE-pumping boom box with a baseball bat, symbolically annihilating the powerful pro-Black message it was blasting into the air and leading Raheem to violently confront Sal. When the white police show up, they only inflame the situation more, eventually choking Raheem to death, leading Mookie (Spike Lee) to spark the fiery riot that concludes the film. The finale of *Do the Right Thing*, the most discussed film of a tumultuous year, was sparked by an argument over Black representation in popular culture, which Chuck extended in "Fight the Power":

> Elvis was a hero to most, but he never meant shit to me
> He's straight out racist, that sucker was simple and plain
> Mother fuck him and John Wayne

The song's Lee-directed music video opens with newsreel footage from the March on Washington, which Chuck calls "nonsense," countering that "young Black America" was rolling up Black Panther–style, with "seminars, press conferences, and straight-up rallies." The future of the American civil rights movement, it seemed, was destined to be a pitched battle over cultural representation in the mass media, with Public Enemy (and Spike Lee) leading the charge . . . if Public Enemy was still even a group, that is.

In the introduction to the book that accompanied *Do the Right Thing*, Lee confessed that he had been disappointed by Run-DMC's *Tougher Than Leather* the year prior because of both its Blaxploitation framework, a genre Lee disdained, and the fact that it was directed by Def Jam's Rick Rubin, "a white man with no film experience." Lee notes the powerful and politically relevant work being done by the Black filmmakers Robert Townsend, Keenen Ivory Wayans, Melvin Van Peebles, and Julie Dash and offers a word of inspiration to Black film students to continue the filmmaking revolution.[70] Though *Do the Right Thing* did not bear many visual markers of documentary realism, Lee embeds the story in the same hypercurrent intersections of race, violence, and politics that were inspiring Public Enemy. At one point, Lee's character, Mookie, walks by a brick wall on which is spray-painted "TAWANA TOLD THE TRUTH!" referencing Tawana Brawley's recanted 1987 rape allegation against four white men, and as Sal's Pizzeria burns and the police and firefighters arrive, the crowd chants "Howard Beach" in reference to the murder of Michael Griffith, which, Lee noted, was the event that spurred him to make the film in the first place.

For some white critics, however, the film's timely, violent realism was likely to trigger among its Black viewing public the same reaction that had ended the film. In *New York* magazine, David Denby opined that "the end of this movie is a shambles, and if some audiences go wild, [Lee is] partly responsible," and the political columnist Joe Klein suggested that "if Lee does hook large black audiences . . . [and] they react violently—which can't be ruled out—the candidate with the most to lose will be [the Black mayoral candidate] David Dinkins."[71] Lee did not disagree that the film had an electoral point. The film's loquacious radio DJ, Mister Señor Love Daddy (Samuel L. Jackson), uses the airwaves to urge the neighborhood's Black residents to vote, and Raheem and Buggin' Out are shown standing next to "Dump Koch" graffiti in a brief scene. "We had this plan because the film came out in August and that fall was the Democratic primary," Lee recalled. "And Dinkins won."[72]

As the long, hot summer of 1989 wound down, the world of reality television was entrenching itself in the mass-media firmament. The crime dramatizations of *America's Most Wanted* were continuing to bear fruit: the *Arizona Daily Star* reported that murder suspect John Patrick Eastlack had been captured two nights after his profile aired: the sixty-sixth capture in the show's year and a half on the air, out of a total of 179 fugitives.[73] In an interview later that month for an article about the rise of "crime time" television, Michael Linder called *Wanted* "the birth of a new era and a new wave of journalism," spurred by citizens who "want to better understand and help the police." The story revealed that *eighteen* new real-life cop shows were in various stages of network production at the moment.[74] Though *Cops* lost that year's Best Informational Series Emmy Award to PBS's *Nature*, the program's nomination alone signaled its immediate acceptance by the medium's standard-bearers, offering no solace to numerous critics worried about the creeping tabloidization of prime time. "How do shows such as the slime-ball syndicated *A Current Affair*, NBC's semi-loathsome *Unsolved Mysteries*, the puffball syndicated *Entertainment Tonight* and the real-life cops-and-crum-bum *Cops* from Fox get nominated along with the sublime *Nature* on PBS?" asked an incredulous critic for the *Hartford Courant*.[75]

Any doubts that the national conversation about race and crime would transpire in a form other than the hyperreal fictions of electronic media were put to rest by President George H. W. Bush. On September 5, he commandeered the prime-time airwaves to deliver an address about "the greatest domestic threat facing our nation today": crack cocaine. To drive the point home, Bush held up a bag of the drug that had been purchased in Lafayette Park, across the street from the White House itself. The stagecraft was drawn straight from the media-relations playbooks of Nick Navarro and Daryl Gates, fueled by the same overheated media paranoia that the toxin spawned by the Black inner city was making a beeline for the white suburbs. The day after the broadcast, newspaper reporters pointed out the obvious: no one sold drugs at that park, because its proximity to the White House meant it was always crawling with police. Instead, agents of the Drug Enforcement Administration had lured a suspected dealer, a senior at nearby Spingarn High School with no prior record, to the park, where they paid him $2,400 for three ounces of crack. It was later revealed that the young man initially had no idea where, or what, the White House was. When he was informed, he replied, "Oh, you mean where Reagan lives."[76] Bush himself regarded the ruse as stagecraft worthy of his predecessor, if not an episode of *Wanted*. "I mean, the man was caught selling drugs in front of the White House. I think it can happen in any neighborhood, and I think that's what it dramatized."[77]

CHAPTER 3

GET ME THE HELL AWAY FROM THIS TV

▼

In December 1989, Ice-T appeared on *The Oprah Winfrey Show* to defend the lyrics of (and promote) his new album, *The Iceberg / Freedom of Speech...Just Watch What You Say*. The episode addressed the impact that explicit rock and rap lyrics were having on the minds of innocent children, and a song from *Iceberg* joined songs from Eazy-E and N.W.A, Guns N' Roses' "One in a Million," and Professor Griff's interview among the topics of discussion. T was joined on the panel by the ex–Dead Kennedys front man and outspoken free speech advocate Jello Biafra, whose alarmist, Orwellian spoken-word diatribes opened and closed *Iceberg*. Also on the dais were Nelson George, Rabbi Abraham Cooper from the Simon Wiesenthal Center, and the conservative Black columnist Juan Williams. Sitting next to T was Tipper Gore, who was targeted on *Iceberg*'s penultimate track, "Freedom of Speech":

> Yo Tip, what's the matter? You ain't gettin' no dick?
> You're bitchin' about rock 'n' roll, that's censorship, dumb bitch
> The Constitution says we all got a right to speak
> Say what we want Tip, your argument is weak

After the success of *Rhyme Pays* and *Power*, Ice-T had taken on the role of free speech crusader, with his anti-censorship bromides arguing for First Amendment protection, while his casual misogyny demonstrated the breadth of its coverage. In the second verse of the same song, T files another report:

> Let me tell you about down south
> Where a motherfucker might as well not even have a mouth
> Columbus, Georgia, said they'd lock me up
> If I got on the stage in my show and said "fuck"

He was referencing the "anti-lewdness" ordinance that officials had enacted after a March 1987 Beastie Boys show that featured the white rap trio performing alongside a huge inflatable penis. Subsequent Black performers, including LL Cool J and Bobby Brown, were actually arrested for violating the decree, which felt to T and fans of rap and R&B much more like a law against Black music than one trying to maintain any kind of social order.

Gore and T did not interact much on *Oprah* that day, though Gore did reiterate the argument from her 1987 book *Raising PG Kids in an X-Rated Society*: record companies were marketing "porn rock" directly to children, and it was time for parents to take a stand against a venal industry. The savviest rhetorical move by Gore's Parents Music Resource Center (PMRC) was reframing a censorship issue as one of consumer protection. On Oprah's stage, Gore reframed the sexism and violence of rap lyrics into a question aimed at the host's core audience of anxious parents: Is it possible that your kids are listening to this toxic music in their Walkman headphones? In Gore's view, music wasn't cultural but was more like an unregulated chemical that if consumed by innocent children would have immediate detrimental effects on their mental health. The argument was even more potent with rap music, where a poison from the Black ghetto was threatening the God-fearing suburban American family. Rap might as well have been crack, and to Gore, the record labels were packing the pipe. That argument was working too: by late 1989, legislation to ban or restrict the sale of obscene recordings, the PMRC's project since 1985, was pending in nineteen states. As Gore's movement gained steam, antiregulation conservatives bit their tongues. After all, supporting the moral crusade of a woman who called herself "a liberal Democrat" made them appear bipartisan. As was his wont, Ice-T cared about warning stickers only to the extent that they offered him a new blank slate for creative expression. On *Iceberg*'s penultimate track, he explains what he learned from *Rhyme Pays*: "Hey PMRC, you stupid fuckin' assholes / The sticker on the record is what makes 'em sell gold."

For *Iceberg*'s sticker, T one-upped the *Rhyme Pays* bullet/condom warning with a much larger label. In all caps, it read "ICE-T X RATED" across the top, and in smaller type below, "SOME MATERIAL MAY BE X-TRA HYPE AND INAPPROPRIATE FOR SQUARES AND SUCKERS." The striking cover illustration below it depicted a jacked-up "gangsta" archetype in a sideways Raiders hat, with a shotgun forced in his mouth and handguns jammed in each ear. Together, they issued a macho dare to the consumer that mirrored T's sexist insults toward Gore: Listen up, unless you're scared. The only way that such a macho form of cultural expression as rap could make its way to Oprah's deeply feminized broadcast space was by someone like Gore opening the door, and Winfrey adapted one of the PMRC's savviest tactics to open the episode, separating a few of Ice-T's lyrics from their cultural and musical contexts and presenting them as the embodiment of their own guilt. A passage from "The Iceberg" was exhibit A:

> Evil E was out coolin' with a freak one night
> Fucked the bitch with a flashlight
> Pulled it out and left the batteries in
> So he could get a charge when he begin

Later in the same verse, T calls himself "a 1989-type Dolemite," contextualizing those lines in a lineage of parodic, R-rated African American cultural expression not meant to be taken literally but to be appreciated for the degree to which it transgresses acceptability and believability. But Oprah's stage preferred rhetorical combat to nuanced discussion, and Juan Williams calling T's music "a malevolent, evil influence" on young people led T straight into the literalist trap. "It doesn't say he raped her. As far as you know, the girl might have liked it," he replied, unconvincingly. His performance as a talk show pundit in the "High Rollers" video was far more persuasive.

Daytime talk was dominated not by masculinist logic but by what one critic called "a serial association of testimonials," in which participants, primarily women, filtered the issues of the day through the lens of their personal experiences.[1] "I'm a woman, and I don't see the humor in sticking flashlights up women, any more than you would see the humor in someone singing about stringing a Black man up by the neck," one audience member argued later in the show. T gamely deflected his response to his wife, Darlene Ortiz, the model who had posed on the covers of his first two albums and who was sitting in Oprah's audience. "She's from Mars!" Ortiz responded. Referencing the hyperbole in T's lyrics, Ortiz asked, "Who's gonna take that kind of stuff serious?" Hands shot up across the audience. Oprah pivoted to a young woman sitting near Ortiz who self-identified as Black. "I have young brothers at home that listen to this stuff. And it changes their personality, I don't care what you say," the woman said. The audience broke into applause. "If that is the case," Ortiz responded, "then are you gonna start rating the news every night? If you're talking about the realism, then you'd better stop your kids from watching the news." The other woman was unbowed. "I don't see how you can sit here, putting down women like that. It really just ticks me off." Ortiz interrupted her: "He's not putting down women. When he calls a bitch a 'bitch,' that means that she's a bitch. When he says 'bitch,' I don't turn around." The other woman was not convinced. "The point is, that these young kids out here listening to it...they're not mature enough to see it that clearly." The audience erupted in applause, and Oprah sent the show to a commercial break. As the camera zoomed out and the theme music swelled, the women continued arguing. Even though it lasted only a few moments, the back-and-forth was one of the rare, if not only, times that two women of color could speak to one another—and to a national audience—about how rap lyrics portrayed women.

By late 1989, American popular culture was reinventing itself in the image of daytime talk. After taking her Chicago show national in 1986, Oprah quickly surpassed her mentor Phil Donahue in audience share, spurring a ratings battle that roped in upstarts Geraldo Rivera and Sally Jessy Raphael. For millions of Americans who had become alienated from the distant, dry informational content of the daily newspaper and who sought to understand large, important issues—especially women's experiences—through the scrim of individual identity, daytime talk was a revelation. These shows translated American democratic participation into a domestic TV spectacle by situating their hosts—most often known just by their first names—amid audiences of regular people, while discussing the kind of intimate topics that were otherwise limited to living rooms or bedrooms. Once the ratings race took off, the content grew increasingly salacious, with hosts and producers fervently competing to book the most controversial and tempestuous guests.

At the same time that reality rap was emerging out of Los Angeles, civil rights discourse was being transformed in the image of the combative talk show. In early 1988, the boisterous, chain-smoking, guest-insulting conservative Morton Downey Jr. became an icon of abrasive talk show "confrontainment," known for loudly insulting his guests, railing against "pablum-puking liberals," and even going toe to toe with "Rowdy" Roddy Piper at WrestleMania V. That summer, Downey hosted a live episode at the Apollo Theater featuring a debate between the conservative civil rights activist Roy Innis and the liberal Al Sharpton, which erupted into a heated argument that ended with Innis shoving Sharpton backward off his chair. After the incident, the two offered to settle their beef publicly in the boxing ring for charity. Sharpton said he hoped Don King could organize a match. "The best part is that we will be giving a very positive lesson to young black people in this city about conflict resolution," said Innis, before clarifying, "but not on the street with guns and knives."[2] Three months later, Innis exploded again on Geraldo Rivera's set, this time at a twenty-year-old white supremacist whom Rivera seated next to him on an episode devoted to "hate-mongers." When the guest called Innis an "Uncle Tom," Innis lunged at him, triggering a studio-wide brawl that left Rivera with a broken nose and the highest ratings of his career.

Predictably, old-guard journalists and critics viewed daytime talk shows as a transgression of taste and decorum, in large part because Oprah, Phil, and Geraldo threatened their institutional identity as journalists and their hold on the national conversation. In a November 1988 column, the Washington Post TV critic Tom Shales described daytime talk shows in the same way that Tipper Gore talked about violent rap music: as an environmental contaminant. "Talk Rot infests the airwaves and pollutes the atmosphere," Shales declaimed.[3] A couple weeks before that, Newsweek ran a cover story titled "Trash TV," with a close-up photo of Geraldo Rivera's broken nose. "Battled by dwindling audience shares and the encroachments of cable and home video, the television industry is fervently embracing a radical survival tactic: anything goes as long as it gets an audience," the story read. "Shock 'em to attention. Hammer their ideological hot buttons. Inflame their libidos. Deliver a visceral rush by playing to their most primitive fascinations."[4] While daytime talk shows triggered the journalistic establishment's lowbrow-taste alarms, they represented something entirely different for millions of others. "The truth is that the fringy, emotional matters brought up on Oprah [and] Donahue . . . are almost always related in some way to deep cultural and structural problems in our society," wrote the cultural critic Elayne Rapping in 1991. "The people on these shows are an emotional vanguard, blowing the lid off the idea that America is anything like the place that Ronald Reagan pretended to live in."[5]

For those versed in journalistic history, the explosion of daytime talk was less an out-of-nowhere phenomenon than a spectacular return of the long-repressed tabloid energies that helped forge modern journalism itself in the late nineteenth century. Long before such news was shunted off to supermarket tabloids during the industry's professionalization period, Joseph Pulitzer's *New York World* was as well known for fusing populism, pugilism, sensationalism, and consumerism as it was for codifying the modern techniques of objective investigative reporting and for forcefully asserting the right of a free press. Under Pulitzer's leadership, the *New York World* became more than a simple way to transmit the news of the day, emerging as a broad medium that, in its accommodation of politics, entertainment, sports, gossip, Wall Street, and much more, foreshadowed the rise of radio and television decades later. Like the talk show hosts who would arise in his image a century later, Pulitzer knew that his "yellow journalism" was guaranteed to rope in hundreds of thousands of readers, if only to rubberneck at the tawdry content, where a grisly description of a beheading could run opposite an etiquette column. Jane Shattuc has drawn direct comparisons between the peak of turn-of-the-twentieth-century tabloid journalism and the talk shows that popped up nearly a century later, both of which "present stories of ageless fascination: sex, violence, crime, and tragedy" to audiences who "feel repressed by day-to-day conformity and economic limitations."[6]

Ice-T's appearance on *Oprah* to discuss his First Amendment–themed album was the perfect preface for 1990, the year that the New Right's cultural and political influence crested, triggering a series of heated national debates about popular art, taste, and obscenity. The March 19 issue of *Newsweek* fanned the argument with a cover titled "Rap Rage" and a feature package asserting that rap's "attitude" was infecting the minds of the young. Jerry Adler wrote that the "first important cultural development in America in 25 years that the baby-boom generation didn't pioneer" was also the "culture of American males frozen in various stages of adolescence." He went on to castigate "their streetwise music, their ugly macho boasting and joking about anyone who hangs out on a different block—cops, other races, women and homosexuals."[7] Though Adler's story contained kernels of truth, especially about rappers' one-dimensional portrayals of women and their use of homosexuality as a signal of weakness, it was widely, and rightly, mocked for unconsciously reviving the race-related fears surrounding earlier generations' music. "The story is really a reflection of white parents who are freaked out that their kids are all into rap," Ice-T told the *Los Angeles Times*.[8]

Indeed, it was no coincidence that the *Newsweek* cover featured the LA rapper Tone Loc, a Crip affiliate who had crossed over in 1989 with the hit singles "Wild Thing" and "Funky Cold Medina" and whose debut album reached no. 1. Though Loc was far from controversial, he was a useful avatar for a story about ghetto poison infiltrating the suburbs and a key representative of hip-hop's bifurcation into its pop and punk moments. While MC Hammer and Vanilla Ice took a mainstream-friendly version of the music to the top of the charts, Kid 'n Play's teen-friendly *House Party* rocked multiplexes, and Will Smith took the Fresh Prince to NBC prime time, Public Enemy's third album triggered the kinds of fringe debates over racial authenticity native to daytime talk, Ice Cube's debut solo album was reprimanded for sexist violence, and the raunchy south Florida rappers 2 Live Crew became pungent free speech avatars. Closing the tabloid circle, one of the Crew's primary antagonists was more familiar to *Cops* viewers than to rap fans: Broward County sheriff Nick Navarro. The year that hip-hop went mainstream, it cleaved into numerous factions: reality, pop, Afrocentric. As often as reality rappers warred with conservative moral entrepreneurs, they fought with other rappers.

Public Enemy rang in 1990 with a New Year's Eve concert at the Manhattan club the World. According to the *Village Voice* critic Robert

Christgau, close to half of the group's eighty-minute set was given over to speechifying. Professor Griff, who had been invited back into the group once the controversy over his anti-Semitic comments waned, opened the show with a plug for his forthcoming solo album, *Pawns in the Game*, warning the crowd that "the U.S. government got some shit comin' for both black people and white people," which Christgau interpreted as "an AIDS plot, apparently."[9] Most notably, the group had a new song to perform, "Welcome to the Terrordome," which had been released as a twelve-inch single four days earlier and was described by Chuck from the stage as "a black male correspondent's view of how we looked at 1989." He added, "I don't look at Ted Koppel. . . . I'm not going to look at 1989 like the *New York Times* is gonna look at it. . . . I'm looking at 1989 like a brother on the motherfuckin' block."[10] Equal parts PR campaign, op-ed column, and conspiracy tract, "Terrordome" allowed Chuck to comment on a recent spate of white-on-Black violence, with the Bomb Squad's trademark sirens sounding less like an external warning and more like the low throb of a migraine. Like reading from a year-end news ticker, Chuck notes the August murder of Yusuf Hawkins by white men in Bensonhurst, Brooklyn, and an uprising in Virginia Beach the same month, instigated by intolerant police against participants in Greekfest, a Black fraternity gathering hosted by the tourist-friendly town.

Chuck reserved the track's most incendiary comments for the Griff furor, much of which had been led by the outspoken moral entrepreneur Rabbi Abraham Cooper. While he had played nice with Cooper on television, touring the Holocaust Museum for news cameras and gently sparring for Jane Pauley on the *Today* show, Chuck offered a very different message on his own media turf. "Told a Rab, get off the rag," he bellows, reframing the dispute as a matter of personal martyrdom:

> Crucifixion ain't no fiction
> So-called chosen, frozen
> Apology made to whoever pleases
> Still they got me like Jesus

Cooper was ready; a day after "Terrordome" was released, he issued a press release decrying the lyrics. A month later, *NBC Nightly News* ran a four-and-a-half-minute segment devoted to the group. "Public Enemy didn't come to mainstream attention until recently, when one member of the group made explicitly anti-Semitic remarks," the correspondent Bill Schechner explained. "There was a furor, the group apologized," he added, before cutting to a still image of PE with the offending "Terrordome" lines. The story concluded with some free promotion. While PE's "Don't Believe the Hype" played in the background, Schechner informed viewers that "Public Enemy is at work on its next record. It will undoubtedly be crafted carefully, listened to closely. It's called *Fear of a Black Planet.*" With that kind of free national publicity, it was not a stretch to believe that Chuck D had conceived the hype as a promotional tactic.

A follow-up as unabashed in its pro-Black politics as *It Takes a Nation of Millions to Hold Us Back, Fear of a Black Planet* further legitimized Public Enemy to rock critics, who saw the group as rap's first transcendent political icons. "Public Enemy has never aimed for anything less than a comprehensive view of contemporary black America," wrote Alan Light in a four-star *Rolling Stone* review.[11] "Much like Bob Dylan in '60s rock and Bob Marley in reggae, Chuck D has elevated rap artistry and ambition, and given the music a critical credibility that once seemed beyond its grasp," Robert Hilburn wrote in the *Los Angeles Times.*[12] In the *Chicago Tribune*, Greg Kot cited a similar canon: "What Bob Dylan did for rock in the '60s, what George Clinton did for funk and Bob Marley did for reggae in the '70s, Public Enemy's Chuck D has done for rap: given it legitimacy and authority far beyond its core following."[13] Tom Moon declared in the *Philadelphia Inquirer* that *Fear* was "the first true rap concept album, the first salvo to be fully focused from start to finish."[14] At the *Village Voice*, Robert Christgau proclaimed, "Not even in the heyday of . . . the Clash has any group come so close to the elusive and perhaps ridiculous '60s rock ideal of raising political consciousness with music."[15] Like the Clash in the late 1970s, PE were "the only band that matters" at the dawn of the 1990s, achieving near-universal praise wholly on their own political and cultural terms and despite, or because of, their near-constant proximity to controversy. The majority of rap criticism was still the domain of middle-aged white rock fans, which a short story on *Fear* in the April issue of the Black-run, youth-aimed *Word Up!* magazine viewed as a necessary evil. "P.E. is still committed to its pro-Black cause. Working within the system, contradictory as that may seem, is sometimes the best way to make sure that things get done."[16]

The influences of Louis Farrakhan and the Nation of Islam were tamped down on *Fear*, but the album's new guiding spirit proved just as controversial, leading the *Entertainment Weekly* critic Greg Sandow to take the unusual step of appending a postscript to his review. "After I'd written this review, Harry Allen, who describes himself as Public Enemy's 'director of enemy relations,' sent me an astonishing 1970 tract that, he says, 'should be seen as some of the inspiration for *Fear of a Black Planet*.'" Sandow did not view *Fear* as a racist album on its face, but, he stressed, if the group's support for the author of this tract was honest, then "a miserable new chapter now may have opened in the Public Enemy story.... I emphatically withdraw my support."[17] The tract Sandow was referring to was a fifteen-page pamphlet titled "The Cress Theory of Color-Confrontation and Racism (White Supremacy)," published in 1970 by the Black psychiatrist Frances Cress Welsing. Welsing was the most prominent exponent of the "melanists," a fringe group of African American psychologists and psychiatrists who eschewed empirical research in lieu of "a diverse collection of literature on Egypt and the New Age."[18] Welsing theorized what she called "pigment envy," the idea that white aggression against people of color around the world arose from a "profound sense of numerical inadequacy and color inferiority in their confrontations with the majority of the world's people—all of whom possessed varying degrees of color-producing capacity."[19] In essence, Welsing was giving the imprimatur of academia to the Nation of Islam's notion that the devil Yakub had developed the races to pave the way for the lighter skinned to dominate the darker skinned. Though Howard University denied Welsing tenure in 1975, she remained very active on the collegiate speaking circuit and was especially popular with Black audiences. While *Fear* was flying off record store shelves, Welsing was named one of *Essence* magazine's "Legends in Our Time."

Phil Donahue had recently devoted a full hour of his show to Welsing's race theories. Sitting across a table from the host, Welsing calmly explained her theory of "pigment envy" while audience members reacted with a mixture of disbelief and laughter. Yet when she noted the irony in the fact that the American stereotype of the ideal man is "tall, dark, and handsome," the camera cut to Black audience members smiling and applauding at the connection. For many Black observers, the fact that Welsing's claims were far outside the boundaries of academic ortho- doxy was a feature, not a bug. A tactic that Donahue shared with Public Enemy, after all, was gaining an audience's attention with outrageous claims in order to spark a deeper conversation about the important issue lying underneath. "I don't think we've asked enough questions about this thing called racism, which has, in my opinion, the capacity to bring us down as a nation," Donahue admitted at the start of the hour. Chuck himself expressed a similar sentiment in NBC's January 1990 story on "Terrordome" and *Fear*: "If anything, the lesson I've learned is to ask more questions." What Sandow resisted in both Welsing and Public Enemy in his *Entertainment Weekly* postscript was the same thing that establishment journalists resisted in daytime talk shows: the ideas of a fringe ideologue that appealed not to logic or science but to deeper emo- tional truths.

Welsing's work circulated in the far outer orbit of Afrocentrism, a school of thought that positioned Black American culture in its African historical context instead of within a Eurocentric framework. As a move- ment, Afrocentrism's most recent predecessors were the black identity movements of the 1960s, like Maulana Ron Karenga's cultural nation- alist US organization, whose members learned Swahili and introduced the Kwanzaa holiday; as well as political leaders like Stokley Carmichael and the Black Panthers, who asserted common anticolonialist cause with freedom-seeking groups around the world. Afrocentrism had es- tablished itself on college campuses with the 1987 publication of *The Afrocentric Idea*, by Molefi Kete Asante, chair of Temple University's African American studies program. Echoing critiques of white-focused journalistic "objectivity," Asante opened his book by critiquing the social sciences as "a kind of collective subjectivity of European culture."[20] As Afrocentric curricula proliferated through college campuses and K–12 education (350 "Afrocentric academies" were educating fifty thousand children by 1991), a newly potent sense of racial pride stressed continu- ity with an African past, coinciding with Jesse Jackson's 1988 call for "African American" to replace "Black" as the default racial nomencla- ture. The rise of Afrocentrism coincided with and buttressed the broader 1980s fight against the South African apartheid regime as well. Inspired by the civil rights gains of the 1960s and by Jackson's 1984 presidential campaign, campus activists and political representatives exerted significant economic and political pressure on the country, resulting in the February 1990 release from prison of Nelson Mandela after nearly three decades behind bars.

Not coincidentally, 1990 was the tipping point for Afrocentrism to permeate the rap landscape. It was the breakthrough year for the Native Tongues collective—the Jungle Brothers, De La Soul, A Tribe Called Quest, Queen Latifah, and the London expat Monie Love—who boldly embraced their African roots with red, black, and green Africa medallions, brightly colored kente cloth, and a focus on the unifying connection between New York City and the motherland. It was the year that Five Percenter philosophy surfaced in rap as well, courtesy of the debut albums from X Clan, Poor Righteous Teachers, and Brand Nubian, which built entire sonic universes around the Five Percenters' vibrant cosmology and cryptic lexicon. Floating above it all was *Fear of a Black Planet*, an opus of tabloid Afrocentrism and the year's preeminent concept album of any genre. Chuck D's thesis is laid out on *Fear*'s title track: "What is pure? Who is pure? / Is it European? I ain't sure." While those bars evoke a fairly mainstream spin on Afrocentrism's political reorientation of academic objectivity, a robotic voice then squeaks out a program interruption that edges closer to the melanist fringes of the belief system:

> Excuse us for the news
> You might not be amused
> But did you know white comes from Black
> No need to be confused

On "Pollywanacraka," Chuck expands this notion to support interracial dating, breaking with the Nation of Islam's doctrine outlawing "race mixing" and aligning with Welsing's view that white pigment envy would have no choice but to wane in a world dominated by such variegated skin tones.

Though both were contained within the album's shortest track, Chuck's views on AIDS and homosexuality, again borrowed from Welsing, garnered an excess of attention for *Fear*. On the short interstitial track "Meet the G That Killed Me," Chuck riffs on Welsing's long-professed claim that homosexuality was projected onto Black men by whites who were insecure in their genetic weakness.[21] The track opens with a sample of Welsing's voice, in full conspiracy-theory mode: "Every Black person who says that they're a leader needs to pen blazing questions about HIV," a virus that she believes was developed to counteract declining white birthrates.[22] The G in the song title, Chuck later explained, "could have been a guy, a girl, a germ [or] the government."[23] Much clearer are Chuck's opinions on homosexuality, which he raises in the opening lines:

> Man to man
> I don't know if they can
> From what I know
> The parts don't fit

It's easy to imagine Chuck, who later unsuccessfully developed and pitched his own *Larry King Live*–style talk show, arguing this position to a daytime talk audience and parrying arguments from a fervently opposed studio audience.

Fear is at its strongest when Chuck breaks from Welsing and returns to the more tangible topics that had long vexed Black Americans: organized religion, police corruption, infrastructural racism, and bootstrapped Black self-empowerment. The album's most ingenious tracks exposed the ways that racial bias was not always overt but was deeply ingrained in American institutions. *Fear*'s biggest hit was "911 Is a Joke," a protest song about emergency services deprioritizing Black communities in favor of white neighborhoods. With mischievous glee, Flavor Flav laments those who died waiting for "latecomers with the late-coming stretcher," while the video mutates the crack-addicted zombies of "Night of the Living Baseheads" into corpses turning the sidewalks into an urban cemetery. A staple of *Yo! MTV Raps*, BET's *Rap City*, and Black radio throughout the summer of 1990, "911 Is a Joke" counterprogrammed the latest reality TV sensation, *Rescue 911*, which had debuted the year before. Like *America's Most Wanted*, *Rescue* used dramatic, often violent reenactments of real emergency calls to valorize the everyday emergency dispatchers and hyperalert citizens who protect American families from the mortal dangers of modern life. One critic claimed that the show, which aired at 8:00 p.m. on CBS, "is guaranteed to frighten half to death any young child who sees it,"[24] which contrasts with Flavor's inspiration for his "911" lyrics, which he based on a memory from seventh grade. He called 911 after he witnessed a boy being stabbed, but when the ambulance didn't arrive quickly enough, the boy died from his injuries on the way to the hospital.[25]

The second of *Fear*'s three exposés of American infrastructural racism, the video for "Brother's Gonna Work It Out" demonstrates how Black civic activism can be extinguished by a single white authority figure. The song's high-concept music video is a flipped-perspective reenactment of the previous summer's Labor Day weekend Greekfest uprising. The incident was spurred by police overreaction to a group of revelers who had taken over a Virginia Beach hotel parking lot on Labor Day weekend, with *Do the Right Thing* still in theaters, chanting "Fight the power," "Fuck the police," and "Black power."[26] Police changed into riot gear and confronted the crowd, many of whom had been harassed by police earlier in the day. The brief melee resulted in some property destruction and a handful of minor injuries—translated by the press into "racially tinged violence and looting by youths."[27] In the "Brother's Gonna Work It Out" video, PE imaginatively flip the events of Greekfest into a parable of Black citizen journalism through a fictional reenactment of a group of idealistic young Black students armed with Polaroid cameras and notepads documenting numerous incidents of police brutality at the event. The reenactments are peppered with actual news footage of handcuffed young Black people and rampaging police as well as the fictionalized in-person interviews conducted by the new PE member Sister Souljah, posing as a PETV journalist. As the video concludes, the students hand over their evidence to a white official at the city council office, only to have him toss the material into a trash can the second they leave. The video concludes as it opens: with Chuck and Flavor pulled over on the side of the road, with a trigger-happy white southern policeman menacingly reaching for his sidearm.

The final part of *Fear*'s triptych of race, media, and politics, "Burn Hollywood Burn" was the most scathing indictment of the film industry's racism since Robert Townsend's 1987 satire *Hollywood Shuffle* and was an extension of Chuck and Flav storming the gates of the white star system on "Fight the Power." Seeking solace from fearmongering coverage of gang violence on the nightly news—"Get me the hell away from this TV / All these news and views are beneath me"—Chuck discovers a more garish and overt racism at the local cineplex. On his guest verse, Big Daddy Kane chastises the film industry's decades-long insistence on casting Black actors in demeaning roles as "butlers and maids, slaves and hos," accompanied in the video by the cartoonishly racist footage itself. Fresh from his split with N.W.A over a financial dispute the previous December, Ice Cube cameos on "Burn Hollywood Burn," and while his brief verse stops well short of representing the depth of his knowledge on the political economy of Black filmic representation—he missed an opportunity to take another swipe at *Colors*—the East-West mind meld between the thirty-year-old Chuck and the twenty-year-old Cube heralded a much richer collaboration to come.

If Louis Farrakhan proved anything during his March 1990 appearance on *The Phil Donahue Show*, it was his ability to remain serenely calm while sending white audience members into fits. In a comment about affirmative action, a woman yelled at the Nation of Islam leader, "I am so sick and tired of this chip that you're carrying on your shoulder. We have bent over backwards; we have done backflips to make you feel equal!" After the applause died down, Farrakhan replied to the woman in a tranquil voice, the opposite tone of the fire-and-brimstone invective he delivered to his all-Black audiences. "I realize that this is an irritant to white people because you really don't understand," he placidly intoned. "And it's not really your fault." As Farrakhan sat alone on the stage, the permanently harried Donahue jogged around the audience with a handheld microphone, trying to accommodate as many respondents as possible. Farrakhan ably parried any accusation that came his way, at times with historically grounded logic about American white supremacy, like when he cited the post-Watts Kerner Commission report that laid the blame for the uprising at the feet of white America, which was buried by the Lyndon Johnson administration. At other times, Farrakhan pulled from his quiver of conspiracy theories and claimed that the news media always distorted his recorded words. More than anything, Farrakhan's simple insistence on the continued existence of infrastructural racism drove audience members crazy. Later in the episode, a young woman took the mic: "I was raised to be equal to anyone. Listening to you, you are so prejudiced, I just can't believe it. I am shocked! You're scaring me!" The crowd burst into applause. Farrakhan sat and smiled.

Ice Cube was watching. In his rented Manhattan apartment, he and his Lench Mob posse took in the televisual spectacle while on a break from recording his first solo album, *AmeriKKKa's Most Wanted*, with Public Enemy and the Bomb Squad, who had just finished tracking *Fear of a Black Planet* in the same studio. A *Rolling Stone* reporter was there to write a feature on Cube, whose split with N.W.A and alliance with PE had made his forthcoming solo debut one of the year's most anticipated albums. While Farrakhan held forth on *Donahue*, "Cube [was] frozen," the reporter notes. After the episode concluded, the rapper started pacing around the apartment and thinking aloud:

> Reverend Farrakhan say that white people owe us liabilities for the shit they put us through 400 years ago. But them muthafuckas ain't giving up no ass. I can see it now. 'Gimme my forty acres and a mule.' Yo. Right. You got to take the booty. You got to get your own. Help your muthafuckin' self. If you at home and you ain't got no car, do not wait for a muthafucka to pick you up. You find your way there. You know what I'm sayin'?[28]

Released five weeks after *Fear*, *AmeriKKKa's Most Wanted* merged the spirit of late-1960s political radicalism with Farrakhan's virtuosic capacity to get under white America's skin, sharpening Cube's gangsta archetype into what he called "the nigga you love to hate." In the first verse of the song of that name, Cube swiftly dispatches opportunistic crossover artists ("suckers who went pop") and assails Afrocentrism ("Put 'em overseas, they be beggin' to come back") while establishing his new persona:

> Kickin' shit called street knowledge
> Why more niggas in the pen than in college?
> Because of that line, I might be your cellmate
> That's from the nigga you love to hate

In four bars, Cube relocates "street knowledge" from the introduction of "Straight Outta Compton" to a salient observation on the mass incarceration of Black men and an acknowledgment of rap censorship. It was a bold new chapter in the career of the rapper who spent the previous summer being profiled, passively threatened by the FBI, and chased out of venues by police, all for the crime of threatening to perform a song.

Cube initially wanted Dr. Dre to produce *AmeriKKKa's Most Wanted*, but Eazy squelched that notion after Cube's unceremonious split from N.W.A. Cube had been talking to Chuck—at this point, hip-hop's wise elder statesman—about how best to handle the N.W.A split, and when the subject of his new album came up, Chuck recommended working with Sam Sever, who had coproduced 3rd Bass's innovative and funny 1989 Def Jam debut, *The Cactus Album*, with the Bomb Squad. When Cube showed up at the Def Jam offices, Sever wasn't available, but Chuck D happened to be there, leading to Cube slipping his verse into "Burn Hollywood Burn" at the last minute and the idea of a larger collaboration quickly taking shape. The alliance was inspired; despite a ten-year age gap, they shared an affinity for high-concept rap that suffused the revolutionary Black politics of the late 1960s with the rapidly expanding world of 1990s electronic mass media. Barely out of his teens, Cube brought his wisecracking sexist vulgarity with him to New York, but Chuck had no doubt that he would mature as they worked together. "We knew it had to be the best of both worlds," Chuck later explained. "He had to deliver the gangsta thing. . . . You don't gotta become conscious overnight, but you also have to grow. And I definitely think he did that."[29]

Cube's maturation is evident in the skit that opens *AmeriKKKa's Most Wanted*, in which the rapper is executed in an electric chair, while a sample of Julian Bond's narration from the landmark PBS civil rights documentary *Eyes on the Prize* merges into the sizzling soundscape: "Was America willing to maintain order, no matter what the cost?" It was clear that under Chuck D's mentorship, Cube's musical approach had bloomed into a full-fledged boob-tube phantasmagoria, what David Toop called "television structured music, influenced as much by tabloid news dramatizations as by the fragmentation of TV narrative by over-frequent commercial breaks."[30] The production team of Cube, Sir Jinx, and the Bomb Squad were inspired by *3 Feet High and Rising*, on which the Long Island trio De La Soul and producer Prince Paul (who also worked on *The Cactus Album*) incorporated a running game-show skit and enough '70s samples and pop culture references to suggest an entire worldview shaped by TV's flickering images. Cube disses Arsenio Hall and *Soul Train* and compares a musty drug house to *Good Times* before the police storm in the front door in a *Cops* homage. In an interview promoting the album for the rap TV show *Pump It Up*, Cube told host Dee Barnes that he was "much more than just a reporter" but thought of his creative process as a cyborg-like extension of TV technology. Pointing at his temples, he explained, "This is my VCR. I just like, go through the streets and live, and kinda observe." The minute-long skit "The Drive-By" shows Cube's mental VCR in action: after a staged reenactment of the titular crime, humorously soundtracked by Young MC's pop-rap hit "Bust a Move," the voice of Tom Brokaw takes over: "Outside the South Central area, few cared about the violence, because it didn't affect them." Sampled from the news anchor's introduction to the August 1989 NBC documentary *Gangs, Cops, and Drugs*, the sound bite segues into "Rollin' Wit the Lench Mob," *AmeriKKKa*'s parodic equivalent of a fearmongering news segment on violent Black gang life.

As the album's title makes plain, Cube was one of millions of viewers of *America's Most Wanted*, which a few months later would be named the most violent prime-time show by a TV monitoring group, who noted that the Fox reality phenomenon averaged fifty-three "violent acts per hour."[31] On the album's title track, Cube flipped *Wanted*'s script: after robbing a suburbanite's home at gunpoint, he sits down to watch TV, only to see his own face on the screen, being profiled by John Walsh. He concludes with a salient statement on the racial cartography of policing that Walsh would never utter:

> I think back when I was robbin' my own kind
> The police didn't pay it no mind
> But when I start robbin' the white folks
> Now I'm in the pen with the soap-on-a-rope
> I said it before, and I'll still taught it
> Every motherfucker with a color is most wanted

"AmeriKKKa's Most Wanted" metaphorically mirrors Cube's own travails from the previous year, where his on-record exploits on "Fuck tha Police" were translated into a suspicion of real-world criminality.

If N.W.A had remained an underground sensation popular only with Black audiences, the powers that be would have left him alone. But once the group crossed over to white audiences, they became dangerous.

AmeriKKKa was well-received by critics, finishing fifth in the *Village Voice*'s year-end critics' poll, two spots behind *Fear of a Black Planet*. But the album was far from uncontroversial. Several reviewers noted the album's sexist lyrics: in the *LA Times*, Robert Hilburn counted eighty-two instances of the word "bitch," and none of them, he noted, were used "in an ironic or humorous sense."[32] While that point is debatable, Cube's brief flash of morbid fantasizing on "You Can't Fade Me" is much harder to swallow. When a woman tells Cube's character that she's pregnant with his child, he immediately wonders if he should "kick the bitch in the tummy" and jokes that he's "in the closet looking for the hanger." In an interview for the *Village Voice*, Greg Tate admitted that he "couldn't even get past that track on the album." Cube replied that "everybody has fantasies," comparing the song to someone who imagines robbing a bank while standing in line waiting for a teller. "You think that shit but you'll never carry it out," he said. "But you put this on wax and people think you're for real."[33] Greg Kot speculated that the reason *AmeriKKKa* sold so well—half a million copies in its first ten days—was because of its shock value: "Its harsh language plainly appeals to youths' taste for illicit thrills the same way that graphic horror films and raunchy MTV videos do."[34]

Kot could have added *Geraldo* as well. Attempting to out-outrageous Phil and Oprah, Rivera had reinvented his crusading journalism as a series of garish exposés into the most disreputable corners of human behavior. In late 1988, Rivera hosted a two-hour special titled "Devil Worship: Exposing Satan's Underground" that triggered countless condemnatory reviews and advertiser blowback for its detailed accounts of the skinning of human babies and other vile acts. A primary fixation of Rivera's was the sexual exploitation of young girls. During one 1989 ratings period, Rivera's episode titles included "Teen Prostitutes," "Girls Who Can't Say 'No!'," "Campus Rape," "Illicit, Illegal, Immoral: Selling of Forbidden Desires," and "Parents of Slain Prostitutes."[35] Unlike Ice Cube, whose fantastic realism hit much harder because it was narrated from rap's autobiographical viewpoint, Rivera could defend his equally sordid content through the framework of a dispassionate journalistic investigation. Regardless, by late 1989, a full 25 percent of the 194 stations that carried Rivera's program received complaints about viewers' children seeing "Kiddie Porn Underground" on the living room television. In early 1990, Rivera pledged to clean up his act. "I'm out of the freak show business," he said.

On June 13, 1990, Rivera's stage provided the perfect venue for not quite a freak show but certainly the biggest public controversy that rap had yet faced. On that episode, Luther Campbell of the Miami rap group 2 Live Crew sparred with Broward County sheriff Nick Navarro, whose deputies had arrested Campbell three days earlier on obscenity charges. Nearly four years earlier, Navarro had starred in Rivera's *American Vice* spectacular, but that morning Rivera played interrogator, asking Navarro if he didn't have "bigger fish to fry" than arresting rappers, given south Florida's drug crisis and "murder at record levels." Navarro replied that his police force was more than capable of arresting and prosecuting Black men for obscenity charges *and* drug charges. "This past Friday our organized crime division in Broward County arrested 160 people for sale of crack cocaine," he bragged. Rivera then turned to Campbell with a different set of statistics, informing the rapper that the 2 Live Crew's album *As Nasty as They Wanna Be* contained "87 references to oral sex and 116 mentions of male and female genitalia." Did the group simply not have better things to rap about? Campbell, as perfect a tabloid figure for the rap world as Navarro was for the police, countered that the 2 Live Crew were unfairly targeted because of their race. The core issue, he countered, was simple: "whether or not an adult should be able to listen to the 2 Live Crew."

Campbell's sudden notoriety was certainly a unique twist for a group that over the past few years had become the South's most popular and notorious rappers. The 2 Live Crew (DJ Mr. Mixx, Brother Marquis, and Fresh Kid Ice) had formed six years earlier on the March Air Reserve Base in Riverside, California, about an hour east of Compton. They released their first single through Macola Records, the same indie operation that distributed the early Ice-T, N.W.A, and Eazy-E records. After hearing the Crew's up-tempo, bass-heavy tracks, Luther Campbell—a well-known party promoter and DJ in the Black-populated Liberty City community of Miami—convinced them to move to south Florida.

Campbell soon joined the group in impresario mode, like Eazy-E, rapping and releasing the records on his independently owned Luke Records (originally Luke Skyywalker Records). Though Campbell was as intelligent and politically aware as Ice-T, Chuck D, and Ice Cube, the 2 Live Crew had no ambitions toward reportage or political commentary. Theirs was music for the club and the trunk: songs like "We Want Some Pussy" and "Move Somethin'" were promoted with album cover photographs of scantily clad women and performed live with shows that resembled a boisterous strip club. Their salacious image and constant touring translated to strong sales, especially in the South: their first two LPs both made the *Billboard* album charts in 1987 and 1988.

Yet in an increasingly conservative cultural climate, the 2 Live Crew's popularity led to increased scrutiny, especially in the reactionary Deep South. On July 29, 1988, a retailer sold both of their albums to an undercover police officer in Alexander City, Alabama, and was arrested on a misdemeanor charge of selling obscene material. In his memoir, Campbell cites that day as the moment that "the legal war against hip-hop started."[36] Back in Florida later that year, the far-right attorney and moral entrepreneur Jack Thompson raised the stakes. With a vendetta against vulgar popular culture, Thompson called himself "Batman," a nod to the superhero vigilante whom he described as "a lone activist who helped authorities do a job that they seemed unable to accomplish on their own."[37] By late 1989, as the 2 Live Crew's third album, *Nasty as They Wanna Be*, was rising up the album charts and its single "Me So Horny" was crossing over to Top 40 stations, Thompson faxed the album's lyrics to Florida governor Bob Martinez. With 1990 an election year, Martinez called for an obscenity and racketeering investigation into the 2 Live Crew's recordings. While the state's prosecutor declined to investigate, the challenge was accepted by Nick Navarro, never one to shrink from a moralistic publicity opportunity. Navarro ordered one of his deputies to purchase *Nasty* from a local retailer, transcribe its lyrics, and file an affidavit. A sympathetic local judge issued an order finding probable cause for *Nasty*'s obscenity on March 9. It was the smallest of legal margins, but Navarro's intimidation tactics had worked: Broward County retailers started removing *Nasty* from their shelves. At a press conference, Campbell defended his group's music: "We write about what happens in everyday life. If they don't like what we sing about, then change what we see in society."[38]

The case went to US district court in mid-May. Because the question was obscenity, arguments relied on the *Miller* test, derived from the Supreme Court's 1973 decision in *Miller v. California*, which established a three-part guide: Did the work appeal to prurient interests in a way that violated community standards? Did it depict sexual conduct in a patently offensive way? Did it lack serious artistic or political value? The 2 Live Crew's defense brought in a stack of lurid materials that were purchased in Broward County, from Eddie Murphy and Andrew Dice Clay records to pornographic magazines and tapes, to illustrate the breadth of "community standards." They called *Miami New Times* music critic Greg Baker, who explained the history of hip-hop and characterized *Nasty* as "important music" and "good music,"[39] and called a Columbia University professor to situate the album within African American history and culture. But in a June 6 decision, Judge Jose A. Gonzales Jr. characterized the recording as "an appeal to 'dirty' thoughts and the loins, not to the intellect and the mind." For the first time in history, a popular recording had been deemed legally obscene.[40] In a news conference outside the courthouse, Campbell blasted the ruling, calling it "toilet paper" and arguing that "the judge doesn't understand our culture." Jack Thompson was elated, proclaiming that "children will no longer be mentally molested by Luther Campbell."[41]

Navarro was now unleashed to send his deputies after the 2 Live Crew and any record store that dared sell the year-old album *As Nasty as They Wanna Be*, which was climbing back up the *Billboard* charts due to the controversy. Two days after Gonzales's decision, Charles Freeman, the Black owner of the Broward County store E-C Records, spoke out. "I don't plan on stopping at all," he told the *South Florida Sun-Sentinel*. "I'm going to jail sooner or later if it comes to it."[42] Navarro sent an undercover officer to purchase a copy of *Nasty* from E-C the same day that Freeman's interview hit newsstands. Once the transaction was completed, six deputies rushed into the store and arrested Freeman in front of the news cameras that Navarro had alerted. That same night, a defiant 2 Live Crew played a concert on Navarro's turf at Club Futura in Hollywood, Florida. In the audience were two of Navarro's plainclothes officers, armed with a tape recorder. The show started with a Campbell-led chant denouncing Martinez and Navarro and otherwise proceeded as every other 2 Live Crew show did, with the group pulling women onto the stage, simulating sex with them, and occasionally pouring water over their scantily clad bodies. After the show concluded, Navarro's officers arrested Campbell and his group in the parking lot, again in full view of the news media.

That summer's most heated public performance was now fully cast, and the conservative war against rap now became a full media spectacle. Campbell spent much of the next few weeks duking it out with Navarro and Thompson across the news and reality TV spectrum. The same week of his *Geraldo* appearance, Campbell appeared on MTV's *The Week in Rock* while Thompson hit *CBS This Morning* and *Crossfire*. The two squared off on *Donahue*'s stage (the 2 Live Crew's second appearance in three months), when Thompson, staring at Campbell, asserted "the causal nexus between what you do and the mental molestation of children and the physical molestation of women." Campbell vociferously responded, telling Thompson, "You're out of your mind," and claiming that he was purposefully conflating the 2 Live Crew's music with unrelated song lyrics from a different group. In the third person, Thompson retorted, "The only problem with Jack Thompson is he's a Christian concerned about women and children." Thompson was drawing from the same well of Reaganist moral vigilantism as John Walsh and Tipper Gore but taking the argument a step further than the previous year's threats against N.W.A. In this newly potent strain of antirap discourse, discourteous Black popular music posed a direct threat to the American family and was thus unprotected by the First Amendment, and if the government would not act, these moral entrepreneurs would take their fight directly to the American people. The logic was strained but potent, mixing two legal arguments that could be made to work together to circumvent the First Amendment and ban rap: obscenity and incitement. The idea seems ludicrous on its face—that music describing graphic sex would directly inspire its listeners to commit acts of sexual violence themselves—but the conservative columnist George Will made the argument that summer in *Newsweek*, tied into the media furor around the April gang rape of the Central Park jogger: "Where can you get the idea that sexual violence against women is fun? From a music store, through Walkman earphones, from boom boxes blaring forth the rap lyrics of 2 Live Crew."[43]

To Campbell, the obscenity/incitement controversy boiled down to the simple fact that "black guys talking about sex" was "the single biggest taboo you could be breaking."[44] Indeed, comments like George Will's echoed centuries of whites acting on their fears about rampaging Black male sexuality. The handful of 2 Live Crew defenders who spoke up publicly in the group's defense (as Campbell noted, a lot of his hip-hop peers stayed silent) argued that a full understanding of *As Nasty as They Wanna Be* requires a much deeper appreciation of African American culture. In a *New York Times* editorial, Henry Louis Gates Jr. explained the 2 Live Crew's music as "a parodic exaggeration of the age-old stereotypes of the oversexed black female and male." Extrapolating from the argument of his 1988 book, *The Signifying Monkey*, Gates continued: "For anyone fluent in black cultural codes," the Crew's "exuberant use of hyperbole" mitigated "a too literal-minded hearing of the lyrics."[45] The group's sexism was indeed troubling, Gates stressed, but he added that the group's "defiant rejection of euphemism" was controversial only because, unlike the 1970s comedy albums by Rudy Ray Moore and Redd Foxx that inspired it, *Nasty* was not niched into "race music" categories but had reached the mainstream: white ears. In a *Los Angeles Times* opinion piece a week later, Gates was joined by no less than Ice Cube, who expanded on his own, similar argument from *AmeriKKKa's Most Wanted*. "2 Live Crew has been around since the mid-'80s, but as long as black kids were buying their records, nobody said a thing about obscenity," he wrote. "As soon as white kids in the suburbs started buying them . . . now suddenly we've got a controversy. That hypocrisy makes me mad."[46]

The 2 Live Crew were unavoidable during much of 1990, which was working wonders for the group's record sales. Every appearance on *Donahue* or *Nightline* or in a *Newsweek* or a *Time* feature was invaluable free promotion. To capitalize on their First Amendment notoriety, the 2 Live Crew issued their own op-ed that July 4 in the form of the album *Banned in the U.S.A.* The fact that *Banned* became the first album to be sold with the "Parental Advisory: Explicit Lyrics" sticker that the recording industry had agreed upon earlier that year didn't scare away Atlantic Records, which signed an agreement with Luke Records to distribute *Banned* through its vast network of retailers: a clear acknowledgment of the commercial value of notoriety. Like a scandalous, low-budget version of a Public Enemy LP, *Banned* alternated between the vulgar sex raps that were the 2 Live Crew's brand and a series of short interstitial "news flashes" addressing and satirizing the controversy that had engulfed them, including direct shots at Thompson, Navarro, and Martinez. Though the group's music could not be more different from Public Enemy's, it did have one advantage: economic independence. "Chuck D used to say that hip-hop was black America's CNN," Campbell later wrote. "He's right except for one thing: White people own CNN ... [and] white corporate money controlled his voice."[47] Campbell's anti-censorship battles had established him not just as rap's most prominent First Amendment spokesperson but also as a fiercely independent and wildly successful Black businessman. It was enough to convince Professor Griff to release his 1990 debut solo album, *Pawns in the Game*, on Campbell's label.

With the summer's hubbub dying down, the trials started that October, and E-C Records owner Charles Freeman was up first. Freeman's lawyers successfully convinced the judge to stop prosecutors from giving the jury a transcript of *Nasty*'s lyrics, arguing that excising the words from their musical context misrepresented the reality they brought to life. Freeman's lawyers also brought two music critics as witnesses. Greg Baker of the *Miami New Times* argued that *Nasty* "reflects a ghetto culture" and then sparred with a prosecutor who recited 2 Live Crew lyrics and asked Baker if they were funny. "Not the way you say it, but the way they say it," Baker countered. Also testifying was John Leland, who had moved to *Newsday* from *Spin*. Leland offered a brief history of hip-hop and characterized the 2 Live Crew's music as "exaggeration" and "comedy." After three days of testimony, the all-white jury, which reporters characterized as being drawn from the middle and upper-middle classes, deliberated for two hours before finding Freeman guilty. To observers, the verdict was the predictable outcome of a jury that did not come close to comprising Freeman's peers and had no interest in understanding the culture from which the music emerged. Outside the courtroom, Freeman fervently objected. "It's unfair. . . . They don't know where E-C Records was; they don't know nothing about the goddamn ghetto."[48]

Eleven days after Freeman's conviction, the 2 Live Crew's trial began in earnest, after the group's attorneys successfully convened a jury that more accurately represented the community that produced the music. One of the prosecution's key pieces of evidence, a recording made at the

Hollywood show, had been rendered nearly inaudible due to crowd noise and static on the tape. When a judge disallowed a written transcript of the lyrics to be submitted, a Broward County detective reenacted and narrated the night's events from the stand for upward of three hours, while playing five- to ten-second snippets of the garbled recording. When segments of the actual *Nasty* recording were played in the courtroom, jurors started laughing out loud, which was a positive sign for Campbell. "That's what this music is about," he told reporters. "They're supposed to be laughing."[49] Henry Louis Gates Jr. testified to much the same effect, arguing that *Nasty*'s vulgarity was as "real" as the content of a satirical sitcom: "Was Archie Bunker put on television so people could learn how to become racist? No. It was put on television so you could laugh at a racist, ignorant man."[50] On October 20, the 2 Live Crew were acquitted of obscenity charges. One juror, a middle school assistant principal, said she "took the whole thing as a comedy." Freeman, sitting in the courtroom spectators' section, applauded the verdict. "They did the right thing. Justice. Finally."[51]

Throughout the 2 Live Crew spectacle, the group's opponents, from Navarro and Thompson all the way to Vice President Dan Quayle, asserted that the case was not about censorship but about protecting the vulnerable by regulating obscenity. But censorship is not always a matter of simply banning something outright; it can take many subtler forms. The example of the Houston trio the Geto Boys later that fall, for instance, might be called "supply-chain censorship." While the 2 Live Crew were garnering headlines through the summer of 1990, the Geto Boys were preparing to reissue *Grip It! On That Other Level*, their second album, which had sold half a million copies on the Houston indie label Rap-A-Lot. The group's gory, realistic sensationalism—inspired by Ice-T and N.W.A and reflecting lives lived in their crime-and-drug-plagued Fifth Ward neighborhood—fit perfectly on Rick Rubin's new Def American roster, which had already released Slayer's thrash metal opus *Reign in Blood* and Andrew Dice Clay's 1989 comedy album, *Dice*, a plainly sexist and profane recording that Campbell often used as a racial point of comparison during the 2 Live Crew's obscenity spectacle.

With true-crime lyrics, savvy media critiques, and gory misogyny, *Grip It!*, retitled *The Geto Boys* for its Def American reissue, was a dark, tabloid-rap masterpiece. "Scarface" is the origin story of its titular protagonist, the cocaine-dealing rapper born Brad Jordan, while "Trigga Happy Nigga" and "Gangsta of Love" translate the Fifth Ward's street reality to record with even more shocking detail than Ice-T or N.W.A. Yet no track was more extreme than "Mind of a Lunatic," on which group member Bushwick Bill raps about raping and murdering a woman before having sex with her corpse, and Scarface slits the throat of his girlfriend and her grandmother and then engages in a bloody shoot-out with the police. Then, "all of a sudden, shit got silent," Scarface raps. "I remember wakin' up in an asylum / Bein' treated like a troubled kid / My shirt was all bloody, and both of my wrists was slit." He was rapping from experience: as a young man, Jordan had been diagnosed with bipolar disorder and, after attempting suicide for a second time, spent two years of his teens in and out of the mental health facilities of Houston hospitals. While *Grip It!* sold well with no controversy on Rap-A-Lot, Rubin's Def American was distributed by the major label Geffen, which contracted its CD-pressing duties to the Digital Audio Disc Corporation in Terre Haute, Indiana. After listening to *The Geto Boys*, the Indiana company refused to duplicate the album and then severed its relationship with Def American. The *New York Times* speculated that Geffen "added the album to its August release schedule and then began listening to it."[52] When approached about the ostensible hypocrisy of Geffen releasing a Dice Clay album and rebuffing the Geto Boys, a spokesperson adopted the same defense that had helped get the 2 Live Crew off: "He's dealing with situations that scare—or offend—people in a humorous light. The Geto Boys record isn't funny."[53]

The Geto Boys' morbid crime fantasies were matched by their savvy media punditry. On "Talkin' Loud Ain't Sayin' Nothin'," Bill addresses the hypocrisy of media-fueled controversy over violent content: "You don't want your kids to hear songs of this nature / But you take 'em to the movies to watch Schwarzenegger." And on "No Sell Out," cut for the Def American release, the group's resident political hardhead Willie D stakes a space in a more provincial battle, claiming that Professor Griff's ouster was label mandated ("CBS was just looking for a reason / To get him out, and that was all they needed") while questioning the Blackness of David Mills, the light-skinned Black reporter whose *Washington Times* interview triggered the PE media avalanche: "Lock him up for impersonating a Black man," D suggests. With his group in the crosshairs, Bushwick Bill defended his group's music with a rationale that echoed N.W.A's: "This is the reality I've seen on the news and around me growing up," Bill told the *Los Angeles Times*. "When I turn on the TV there's always someone getting raped, someone getting killed." Coining a phrase that perfectly encapsulates tabloid culture, Bill added, "There is no line between reality and exploitation."[54]

After some wrangling, the album was released in August with distribution from Warner (which, ironically, owned Geffen) but, in a seeming compromise, without listing the distributor's name on the packaging and adding a Def American disclaimer that the label and distributor "do not condone or endorse the content of this recording, which they find violent, sexist, racist and indecent." In a recap of the debacle, the *New York Times* pop critic Jon Pareles offered the first mainstream critical elaboration of "gangster" rap's negotiation of multiple realistic storytelling genres. "For all its first-person machismo," Pareles explained, the music "is not a simple or naive narrative form, and it's certainly not autobiography." Instead, it "falls somewhere between the brute titillation of action movies and the sober titillation of tabloid television," mixing "storytelling, mock-documentaries, political lessons, irony and self-promotion in unpredictable proportions." Like N.W.A, Ice-T, and Ice Cube, the Geto Boys were young Black men using music to relate unapologetically violent, realistic, sexually violent, and misogynistic tales that presented a composite, yet limited, worldview shared by many others. "The world it describes is terrifying, and gangster rap distills that terror, not just as exploitation but as exorcism," Pareles wrote. "But if it weren't scary, it would be a lie."[55]

The 2 Live Crew and Geto Boys cases were textbook examples of the obscenity-as-incitement argument for artistic censorship, which moral entrepreneurs backed with post hoc rationalizations about protecting young people and women. Yet during the entire debate about *As Nasty as They Wanna Be* and *The Geto Boys*, the voices of women, especially the Black women portrayed in the music and silently performing on the 2 Live Crew's stages, were muted. Black women could count on strong matriarchal roles on television and in film, but in most rap music they were reduced to one-dimensional sex objects, if not the recipients of sexual violence. As Tricia Rose recalls, female rappers like Salt-N-Pepa, Yo-Yo, MC Lyte, and Queen Latifah were put in a tough position when responding to the 2 Live Crew case, used as "a political baton to beat male rappers over the head, rather than being affirmed as women who could open up public dialogue to interrogate sexism and its effects on young black women." When asked to take a stance on the sexism that pervaded the music of their male peers, women rappers evaded forth-right condemnation by defending male rappers' freedom of speech and addressing censorship rather than sexism.[56] In a July 1990 *New York Times* editorial, Michele Wallace shed some light on this double bind: "There is a widespread perception in the black community that public criticism of black men constitutes collaborating with a racist society."[57]

In a 1991 essay for the *Boston Review*, the Black feminist scholar Kimberlé Crenshaw explained the nuances of a Black feminist reaction to the 2 Live Crew. "My immediate response... was ambivalence," she wrote. "I wanted to stand together with the brothers against a racist at-tack, but I wanted to stand against a frightening explosion of violent im-agery directed at women like me." The key word in Crenshaw's essay is "intersection," which she uses to describe the uniquely fraught subject position of Black women within the larger political economy of Black popular representation. "My sharp internal division," she wrote, "is characteristic of my experience as a black woman living at the intersec-tion of racial and sexual subordination."[58] Social categorizations of race and gender are inherently interdependent and overlapping, Crenshaw explained, and an attempt to isolate them from one another—through the simplistic frames of the courtroom and news media—obscures more than it reveals. "The debate over 2 Live Crew illustrates how race and gender politics continue to marginalize black women, rendering us vir-tually voiceless," she added. Though Crenshaw agreed with Gates that the Crew had been singled out for their race and that their music re-flected a Black cultural worldview, she parted ways with his argument that the music was hyperbolic and parodic enough to make him "bust out laughing." Crenshaw found nothing funny about the 2 Live Crew using women's bodies as punch lines.

Crenshaw also took issue with the *Miller v. California* obscenity test's obsession with "prurience" and its exclusion of material deemed "political":

Against an historical backdrop that prominently features the image of the black male as social outlaw, gangsta rap might be read as a subversive form of opposition that aims to challenge social convention precisely by becoming the very social outlaw that society has proscribed. For this reason, their lyrics might even be read as political, *and if they are political they are not obscene*. So long, then, as prurience remains an obsession of First Amendment argument, and violent imagery is seen as distinct from sexuality, rap artists may actually be able to strengthen their legal shield by heightening the level of violence in their lyrics.[59]

The "social outlaw" convention, to Crenshaw, is what permitted the more expressly political N.W.A, Ice Cube, and the Geto Boys to avoid the same level of legal scrutiny suffered by the comparatively apolitical 2 Live Crew. Indeed, to reality rappers, armed violence against a racist power structure provided a rhetorical shield for depictions of sexual or emotional violence perpetrated against women. During the same Ice Cube interview in which Greg Tate expressed his revulsion at "You Can't Fade Me," Tate coaxed the rapper into explaining that greedy women—before even the police—were the primary cause of the Black man's troubles. "A girl you want to get with can make you do damn near anything," Cube explained. "All the crime shit, dope, gangs, all that's over material shit to get women. Nothing more, nothing less."[60] Cube demonstrated this viewpoint in a duet with his protégé Yo-Yo titled "It's a Man's World," the one time on *AmeriKKKa's Most Wanted* when a Black woman's voice pierced Cube's misogynistic armor. But while Yo-Yo delivered a strong verse, the fact remained that she was performing on Cube's stage, playing a diminished feminist role in which the provision of sex was the woman's primary contribution. Cube frames the pair's dialogue in the first verse, "Women, they're good for nothing, no maybe one thing / To serve needs to my ding-a-ling," leaving Yo-Yo with a one-dimensional response: "Without us your hand would be your best friend." The track is included to allow Cube a performative out: he provides a platform for a woman to respond to his sexist lyrics, but in the end, they both end up poking fun at his misogyny, on his terms.

It was likely not coincidental that the first two Public Enemy albums— deeply influenced by the masculinist, if not outright sexist, Nation of

Islam—contained the group's most misogynistic songs. While Chuck D's lyrics were a far sight from the sexualized violence of Ice Cube or the Geto Boys, "Sophisticated Bitch" portrayed women as moneygrubbing connivers, while on "She Watch Channel Zero?!" they were shallow consumerists believing the fantasy world of soap operas as real life. *Fear of a Black Planet*'s "Revolutionary Generation" marked a noted improvement, giving a Mary McLeod Bethune sample ("The true worth of a race must be measured by the character of its womanhood") the same spotlight that Malcolm X received on other PE tracks. In true self-referential fashion, Chuck casts blame on centuries of white supremacy:

> Beat us, mated us
> Made us attack our woman in black
> So I said "Sophisticated B"
> Don't be one!

Compared to Cube's clear resentment of female authority, Chuck's advocacy for the radical rapper and activist Sister Souljah was quietly revolutionary. Yet in the soul tradition of James Brown's "It's a Man's Man's Man's World," "Revolutionary Generation" still situated a Black woman's agency as an appendage to a Black man's movement: "It takes a man to take a stand / Understand it takes a woman to make a stronger man."

Black women seeking to speak out on their unique representational burdens could not even find a regular space on daytime talk shows. Even Oprah Winfrey, the most talked-about figure on television (and one of its wealthiest stars), was in the process of pivoting her show away from discussions of infrastructural inequities and toward more New Agey, consumer-friendly themes of personal resilience. In 1990, the most prominent nonmainstream Black woman to appear on daytime talk shows was Shahrazad Ali, a Nation of Islam–affiliated author and canny self-promoter whose book *The Blackman's Guide to Understanding the Blackwoman* advocated the occasionally violent suppression of Black women by Black men. In appearances on *Sally*, *Donahue*, and *Geraldo*, Ali sent audiences into spasms by simply quoting from her book. "If she ignores the authority and superiority of the Blackman, there is a penalty," Ali wrote. "When she crosses this line and becomes viciously insulting it is time for the Blackman to soundly slap her in the mouth."[61]

Black public figures roundly condemned Ali's book as a privately issued vanity project that got swept up into putatively "serious" discussion. Yet as with reality rappers and talk show hosts themselves, it was exactly *because* of its shocking contents, counterintuitive approach toward sexual power relationships, and thin veneer of intellectualism that Ali was granted a public stage.

Within this cultural context, it could be hard to remember Black women's formative contributions to rap's ascendance only a few years earlier, let alone the more recent fact that N.W.A's first national tour came as the opener for Salt-N-Pepa. The 1990 breakthrough single and music video from Queen Latifah, "Ladies First," aimed to rectify this imbalance, portraying the rapper as an Afrocentric militant leading a small brigade of other Black women musicians while a Malcolm X quote ("There are going to be some changes made here") threads through the track. As Tricia Rose observes, "Ladies First" creates a self-sustaining universe of Black womanhood that declines to chastise Black men in lieu of reasserting Black women's historical roles in political activism and freedom movements.[62] Yet Latifah was much more the exception than the rule: from the world of label A&R though the scarce opportunities for airplay on radio and television, rap was guided by a profoundly masculinist mindset. As Rose reveals, casual sexism even extended to the most well-respected and widely read critics. In a late 1989 column celebrating the tenth birthday of rap as a recorded medium, *Billboard*'s Nelson George fretted over the music's increasing commercialization and dilution. "The farther the control of rap gets from its street corner constituency and the more corporations grasp it," he wrote, "the more vulnerable it becomes to cultural emasculation." Rose expressed tongue-in-cheek astonishment: "Corporate meddling not only dilutes cultural forms, but also it reduced strapping, testosterone-packed men into women! Could we imagine anything worse?"[63] For Rose, as for many other women hip-hop fans and performers, the only thing worse than blatant, unapologetic hip-hop misogyny was the same ideas quietly forming a commonsense understanding of rap as a man's domain.

While the 2 Live Crew, Ice Cube, and Public Enemy were generating headlines and critical acclaim, Compton and South Central became the record industry's latest hot spot. Ruthless Records released Above the Law's 1990 debut, *Livin' Like Hustlers*, whose lead single, "Murder Rap," sampled Chuck D's voice and replicated Public Enemy's call to arms by sampling the keening synthesized siren from Quincy Jones's *Ironside* theme. That summer, Run-DMC's label, Profile Records, signed the rapper and producer DJ Quik, who was affiliated with the Tree Top Piru set and financed by Funky Enough Records, run by a budding rap entrepreneur and Blood affiliate named Suge Knight. On his first single, "Born and Raised in Compton," Quik pitched himself as "a young brother who's up on reality." The industry gold rush was epitomized by *It's a Compton Thang*, the debut album from Compton's Most Wanted. While the group's name and album title suggested a cynical executive-suite mandate to exploit market demand, Compton's Most Wanted proved a strong addition to the growing ranks of reality rappers on "One Time Gaffled Em Up." A detail-rich, day-in-the-life account of living under constant police surveillance in Compton, "Gaffled" is rapped with gravitas by MC Eiht, a nineteen-year-old Tragniew Park Crip. Shot on location in Compton, the song's video crosscuts shots of young Black men kneeling with their fingers laced behind their heads with the kind of footage of everyday Compton landmarks that would soon become iconographic: a Compton Boulevard street sign and the words "Compton Blue City" painted on the wall of a local high school.

Gang-affiliated reality rap was diversifying too. The year 1990 saw Island Records' dance imprint, 4th and B'Way, release the debut LP from the Samoan American rappers and instrumentalists Boo-Yaa T.R.I.B.E., a sextet of hulking West Side Piru brothers who learned to play in their father's church band and named their own group after the sound of a shotgun blast. "This ain't a game, straight up reality / Made by the streets, done by insanity," they claimed on "Once Upon a Drive By." That same year, Virgin released the debut LP from the Chicano rapper and self-proclaimed "Aztec warrior" Kid Frost—a veteran of the early 1980s LA break-dancing scene that spawned Ice-T—whose single "La Raza" brought Spanglish rhymes and cholo street culture to the viewers of *Yo! MTV Raps*. With so much marketplace competition, it was little wonder that N.W.A would use "Real Niggaz," from their stopgap August EP *100 Miles and Runnin'*, to reassert their reality rap dominion.

On the song's spoken intro, Above the Law's Laylaw chastises "clone ass N.W.A bitin' ass motherfuckin' everywhere man / Non-reality seein', non-reality feelin' / Non-reality livin' ass motherfuckers."

That summer, a brief flash of social responsibility sliced through the violent realism. The charity single "We're All in the Same Gang" was spearheaded by Michael Concepcion, a thirty-three-year-old Crip OG who became an antiviolence advocate after being paralyzed from the waist down in a gang-related shooting. Produced by Dr. Dre, distributed by Warner, and mixing verses by N.W.A and Ice-T with the crossover stars MC Hammer, Digital Underground, Young MC, and Tone Loc, "Same Gang" was a key part of LA mayor Tom Bradley's antigang "Peace Weekend," with its profits benefitting Representative Maxine Waters's Project Build organization. A sequel of sorts to "Self Destruction," "Same Gang" debuted in June on *The Arsenio Hall Show*. Its video, shot on location in the Nickerson Gardens housing project, aired in regular rotation on MTV and BET through the fall, and the single spent four months on the Hot 100. The effort was well-intentioned, but less than two years after "Self Destruction," the "Same Gang" message was more muddled: Jonathan Gold noticed that "the rappers turn back-flips to elide the essential peacemaking function of the song."[64] Tone Loc recalls his gangbanging days with an ambivalence bordering on nostalgia, Above the Law introduce themselves as pimps, and Dre and Ren take pains to buffer themselves from accusations of social conscience: "Yo, we're not here to preach / Because we're not ministers." In the final verse, Eazy-E adopts a similarly libertarian position on the problem of gang violence: "I'm not tryin' to tell ya what to do / You have your own freedom of choice who to listen to." Like "Self Destruction," "Same Gang" preached the gospel of individual responsibility in the face of infrastructural failures. It worked well as a charity spectacle and fundraiser, but any anti-crime lesson was overshadowed by its participants actively denying their status as role models.

While "Same Gang" struck a wary balance between exploitation and erasure, *America's Most Wanted* was portraying the Bloods and the Crips as murderous criminal franchises spreading their operations across the country. John Walsh delivered his opening remarks for the show's July 15 episode in front of the Watts Towers: "What was once LA's problem is exploding in neighborhoods across America. The new foot soldiers in this gang war are being recruited to sell crack in more than sixty-five US cities. Cities like Wichita." This segment's suspect was Sedrick Scott, "part of an expansion project by the Rolling 20 Crips from their Los Angeles headquarters" into the American Midwest. The story started in September 1989, when fourteen-year-old Charlie Green started selling crack for Scott—who, as a diminutive man outfitted with a Jheri curl, a ballcap, and black locs (sunglasses), looked strikingly similar to Eazy-E. But when Green tried to escape, Scott tracked him down and tortured him in an abandoned warehouse, beating him bloody, forcing him to play Russian roulette, and burning him with a hot iron. Though Scott was convicted of aggravated assault and kidnapping, Walsh notes, he escaped eight days later, and it was time for Fox viewers to go to work capturing America's most wanted Crip. "He doesn't wear colors, and he doesn't use drugs," Walsh noted, while Scott's mug shot and information appeared onscreen. Eleven days after his profile aired, Sedrick Scott was captured after a tip located him in Los Angeles. The young actor playing Green, a sixteen-year-old South Central native named Tyrin Turner, gave a compelling performance in the nearly ten-minute reenactment, segueing from mumbling teenage naïveté to howls of pain and sputtering exhaustion. Judging by the summer's entertainment slate, the two most effective ways to stop the Bloods and the Crips were leveraging the realist charisma of the West Coast's most popular rappers or using sensationalistic televisual realism to send Fox viewers on the hunt.

Rap became pop culture in 1990, and the thematic concerns first voiced by reality rappers started resonating throughout the entertainment landscape. Helmed by the Black director Reginald Hudlin, Kid 'n Play's R-rated comedy *House Party* was a surprise hit, earning $26 million on a $2 million budget. Though the film's message was simple—high school kids throw a huge party—the film's villains were not parents or a school principal but the two racist white cops harassing the teens throughout the film. That fall, NBC's *The Fresh Prince of Bel-Air* brought rap's debates about hip-hop realness and racial authenticity to prime-time TV audiences, via the bickering between West Philly–raised homeboy Will Smith and his fully assimilated cousin Carlton Banks. First-season episodes featured Don Cheadle playing Smith's gangsta friend Ice Tray, Will reading *The Autobiography of Malcolm X* for a school project, Will and

Carlton being pulled over by a white officer and accused of stealing their own car, and Will betting Carlton that he cannot survive seventy-two hours living in his friend Jazz's Compton neighborhood. That same fall saw the Fox debut of *In Living Color*, an innovative sketch comedy show cast in hip-hop's image. Created by Keenan Ivory Wayans, whose low-budget 1988 film *I'm Gonna Git You Sucka* skewered the outlaw machismo of Blaxploitation films, *Color* allowed Black comedians to validate Black culture and politics through parody, as *Saturday Night Live* had been doing for a decade and a half. First-season *Color* sketches sent up many of the figures, programs, and topics well known to fans of reality rap and reality TV: Louis Farrakhan, MC Hammer, Arsenio Hall, Andrew Dice Clay, *People's Court*, Luther Campbell, Oprah Winfrey, and Spike Lee. Musical guests included KRS-One, Queen Latifah, and Public Enemy, who were introduced by Ice Cube. Where *The Arsenio Hall Show* reinvented the late-night talk show for the hip-hop generation, *In Living Color* was "hip-hop sketch comedy," and, combined, these two groundbreaking programs signaled that Fox executives were intent on positioning the young network as not just a space for Reaganist law-and-order reality shows but as something close to the opposite.

Four years after Run-DMC set the stage for rap's mainstream emergence by striking a tenuous balance between street toughness and mass appeal, the music was splintering into genre factions—gangsta/reality, Afrocentrism, dance-pop—and being divided into visual and sonic tropes capable of being freely reappropriated. The primary site tracking hip-hop's expansion, or dilution, into the mainstream of American pop music was the *Source*, started by two white rap aficionados and Harvard undergraduates as a tip sheet to advertise their college radio show. In 1990, the *Source* moved operations to New York City and expanded into a full-fledged magazine complete with advertisements for hip-hop record labels and clothing brands like Cross Colours. The January/February 1990 issue established the publication's authoritative voice on hip-hop, christening the previous ten years as "the rap music decade: 1980 to 1990." As Jeff Chang explains, there might have been better, more carefully copyedited writing in the *Village Voice* and *Spin*, but the *Source* "spoke to its readers in its own voice, reflected their concerns and controversies, fed their needs. Most importantly, it captured hip-hop's *attitude*."[65] Regular features not only tracked and reviewed new rap singles and albums but kept an eye on how hip-hop was being covered in the rest of the news media. In the summer 1990 issue, with Ice Cube on the cover and a fairly negative review of *Fear of a Black Planet* inside, J. Sultan pointed out what happens "when new-jack sucker music critics . . . try to review rap records," chastising an error-riddled review of a new Eric B. and Rakim album in the *Daily News*.[66] The *Source*'s writers and editors kept careful tabs on the 2 Live Crew spectacle throughout the year as well, publishing a detailed time line of the complex legal wrangling and including a tear-out postcard to mail to elected officials that read in part, "It is shocking that the government is succumbing to the values of the religious right rather than the community that has created and enjoyed rap music for the past fifteen years." The magazine editorial staff knew its heroes and enemies: the January 1991 issue named Luther Campbell "Hip-Hop's Man of the Year" and featured an editorial by Public Enemy's Bill Stephney that labeled Bell Biv DeVoe (BBD) one of "the worst threat[s] rap music has faced thus far."[67] Made up of three ex-members of the squeaky-clean Black boy band New Edition, BBD recorded a handful of songs from their debut album *Poison* with the Bomb Squad—around the same time that the production team was making *AmeriKKKa's Most Wanted* and *Fear of a Black Planet*—and described their hybrid format in promotional copy and the video for "Poison" as "mentally hip-hop, smoothed out on the R&B tip with a pop feel appeal to it." Proudly reciting their genre signifiers like an inventive fusion chef lists off ingredients, BBD signaled a future for Stephney and many of the *Source*'s readers in which hip-hop was not a cultural force but another musical component, mixed in for demographic targeting.

On November 3, 1990, critics and fans manning hip-hop's ideological front lines had a new enemy when Vanilla Ice's "Ice Ice Baby" became the first rap song to top *Billboard*'s Hot 100 chart. That same day, the white rapper's debut album, *To the Extreme*, topped *Billboard*'s album chart, replacing *Please Hammer Don't Hurt 'Em*, the second LP from Ice's erstwhile tour mate MC Hammer, which had held the spot for the previous twenty-one weeks. *To the Extreme* would hold the top spot until March 1991, two months after the Recording Industry Association of America certified that the album, like Hammer's, had sold seven million copies. Though the Oakland-born Hammer was begrudgingly accepted by many in the rap establishment, the twenty-two-year-old Vanilla Ice, born Robert Van Winkle, was held at arm's length, to put it lightly. In large part, Van Winkle created his own obstacles, by attempting to prove his street credibility instead of accepting his fate as rap's Pat Boone. Not only had he borrowed the title and lyrical hook of "Ice Ice Baby" from a Black fraternity chant and his performance moniker from Ice-T and Ice Cube, but Van Winkle's press biography boldly asserted his hardscrabble childhood on the streets of Miami, the multiple stabbings he sustained in a 1986 gang fight, and the fact that he attended the same Miami high school as Luther Campbell. Though reporters quickly revealed that these claims were fictionalized, the rapper remained steadfast, claiming, like everyone from Chuck D to Eazy-E, that the press was twisting his words.

Writers at the *Source* were armed for combat. "To those folks who think of themselves as guardians of 'real' hip-hop culture," wrote Dan Charnas in the *Source*, Vanilla Ice "sounded like rap's death knell."[68] In a *New York Times* editorial, *Source* editor James Bernard zeroed in on a telltale couplet from "Ice Ice Baby" as evidence of Vanilla's unexamined privilege: "Police on the scene, you know what I mean / They passed me up, confronted all the dope fiends." While reality rappers "document the real tensions between black youth and police," Bernard wrote, "Vanilla Ice, clean-cut and white, never has to worry about being a suspect."[69] Even the normally reverential interviewer Arsenio Hall took the star to task during a February appearance. After the rapper brought out Flavor Flav for an embrace before the interview started, Hall asked, "Is that why you brought him out, to show you have a Black supporter?" During the combative interview, Hall's questions frequently veered into cross-examination. When Ice claimed he'd never said anything bad about MC Hammer, his former tour mate and a frequent *Arsenio* guest, Hall was indignant: "That's not true! I have an audiotape!" Hall's audience, audibly made up of screaming young people, loudly booed. They didn't want a *Donahue* interview; they wanted to watch Vanilla Ice dance.

The phrase "keeping it real" was not yet in common use at the end of 1990, but the notion was quickly spreading through a rap world threatened with pop assimilation. Rap was more popular than ever, and its best artists were expanding the possibilities of the form. In the wake of the 2 Live Crew controversy, hip-hop was also more contentious than ever. While reality rap had triggered questions about rap's epistemology

(Was it really *true?*), its pop-crossover moment generated heated debates about its ontological realness (Was it even *rap?*). While Vanilla Ice, MC Hammer, and Kid 'n Play were turning rap into danceable, kid-friendly fare, street rappers doubled down on their claims to represent the ugly truths of Black life in America, spurring numerous debates that would come to dominate the discourse: subcultural authenticity versus pop trend-chasing, Black versus white, underground versus commercial, hard versus soft, streets versus suburbs, and old-school heads versus the new jacks.[70] Threading throughout these debates were questions that rappers and rap critics were now being regularly, and unfairly, forced to confront: What were the social effects of this music on the young people it was marketed toward? Should rappers, or their record labels, assume a greater level of responsibility?

A bit more than a year after his *Washington Times* interview with Professor Griff, David Mills tackled the issue in his cover story for the December 1990 issue of the *Source*. Titled "The Gangsta Rapper: Violent Hero or Negative Role Model?," Mills's essay landed firmly on the latter half of its provocative title, which ran atop a photo of Eazy-E pointing a gun at the camera. Mills believed that rappers' desire to make money from their art negated their claims to represent the truth of Black lives in American cities. Actual "street reporters" were not concerned with personal profit, Mills argued, but strictly with conveying the truth, no matter how unfashionable. "Gangster rap isn't about the reality of underclass America," Mills contended, "it's about shock value. Show business." The fact that gangsta rap was very profitable for its creators fed Mills's belief that rappers' mercenary capitalism would lead to a health crisis. Using the music-as-toxin language of the Parents Music Resource Center, Jack Thompson, and Nick Navarro, Mills wondered "whether, like radiation exposure, it'll be years before we really know the consequences of our nasty little entertainments."[71]

To make his argument, Mills compared gangsta/reality rap not to tabloid television but to violent cinema. Nineteen-ninety, after all, was when *Goodfellas*, the outlandish and viscerally violent enlargement of an ex-gangster's autobiography, ranked among the year's biggest films. Mills drew a bright line between violent rap music and violent cinema, based in their audiences' respective expectations: "When Americans indulge our fascination with gangsters at the movies, we demand that our sense of right and wrong be satisfied by the fadeout, that evil people meet a just demise. In gangster rap, right and wrong are irrelevant."[72] Mills follows this with a moral challenge—to rappers, not Martin Scorsese: "If these rappers were dedicated to 'reality,' how come they never deal with the results of the gunshots they throw into the mix?"[73] Mills begs the reality question in the essay, accepting a moral and an aesthetic distinction between the narrative conventions of violent realism in cinema and rap music: "No one thinks that Martin Scorsese . . . or Robert De Niro . . . are actual gangsters, or endorse gangsterism. Yet the all-important element of 'authenticity' in hardcore street hip-hop relies upon the indistinguishability of rapper and role." Here, Mills offers a pass to cinema, which is predicated on audiences' suspension of disbelief, while assuming that rap listeners cannot make a similar epistemological leap past the lyrics' first-person perspectives. Inconsistencies notwithstanding, Mills's article provided a framework for excusing Hollywood and condemning rappers that was taken up as common sense, putting reality rappers in a tough bind. If listeners couldn't tell the difference between rapper and role, that meant the music was *too real*. But if rappers also failed to show the consequences of the violent acts they portrayed, they were somehow not being *real enough*.

CHAPTER 4

I'M GONNA TREAT YOU LIKE KING!

▼

At 12:45 a.m. on Sunday, March 3, 1991, a Los Angeles plumber, George Holliday, was awoken by the sound of helicopters overhead. Seeing a scene transpiring outside, he instinctively grabbed his newly purchased Sony Handycam, stepped out onto his balcony, and started shooting. A group of several officers were violently hitting a man with batons and zapping him with their Tasers. Two other residents of Holliday's apartment complex got their camcorders out as well—it was the hot technological trend in early 1991—but they lacked Holliday's second-floor vantage point. The violent scene dispersed, and Holliday went back to bed. A few hours later, he used the same camera to record one of his employees running in the Los Angeles Marathon, but he remained disturbed about the brutality he'd witnessed. Sunday night, Holliday called the Foothill Police Station, but no one there seemed interested in the footage. The same went for CNN's Los Angeles bureau. On Monday, Holliday took the tape to local TV station KTLA. Producers were shocked at what they saw and screened it at the Los Angeles Police Department headquarters, where officers expressed the same reaction. The motorist's name, Holliday learned, was Rodney King. He was Black, and the officers who brutalized him on video were all white. The footage aired for the first time that night on KTLA's newscast and, because of a licensing agreement, was simultaneously transmitted via satellite to CNN's Atlanta bureau. On Tuesday night, the eighty-one-second clip that showed King's body receiving fifty-six baton blows and several Taser shocks ran on all three national newscasts. It would air thousands more times in numerous informational and entertainment contexts over the coming year and a half.

Without the videotape, the King beating would have likely led to an Internal Affairs investigation by the LAPD, with King's injuries weighed against the fact that a Black ex-convict had led the officers on an eight-mile chase and was intoxicated and behaving strangely at the scene of the encounter. Like countless other Black victims of police abuse, Rodney King would have been part of an LAPD database entry, his name forgotten by everyone except his friends and family, who knew the truth. But George Holliday changed all that. Like a far more expensive scientific instrument, his $1,000 Sony Handycam revealed a hidden pathogen, always lurking just out of sight, that the *Los Angeles Times* or KTLA or CNN had never disclosed so clearly. There was no denying the repulsive truth of the King video, regardless of one's political position. President George H. W. Bush said the video "sickened" him, the archconservative pundit George Will referred to the actions as a "police riot," and even Daryl Gates called the actions "a very, *very* extreme use of force—extreme for any police department in America."[1] In an April poll of registered Los Angeles County voters, 81 percent of respondents believed the officers were guilty. It appeared for all intents and purposes that, after centuries of Black men being surveilled by the state—slave patrols, lynching, Jim Crow, mass incarceration—the ultimate 1990s surveillance technology, the video camera, had effectively indicted that same authority.

A few months after King's beating, a Black man named Malice Green was beaten to death by Detroit police officers. As John Fiske has observed, while Green's death mattered intensely in its own regard, it "counted for less" than Rodney King's beating because it wasn't rendered legible to television discourse with anywhere near the same potency as the violence against King.[2] Because it was videotaped, King's beating became what Fiske calls a "media event," a symptom of an electronic mediascape that, by 1991, was suffusing every aspect of American lives, to the degree that "we can no longer work with the idea that the 'real' is more important, significant, or even 'true' than the representation."[3] Media events like the King tape are far more than merely recorded representations of events; once they enter the circuits of a technologically sophisticated, capital-intensive media environment, they become *hyper-real*. As the video of King's brutalization was played and replayed thousands of times on television, and "Rodney King" became a symbol for racist police brutality in Los Angeles, the video also became raw material for edgy creative expression, digitized and morphed into what John Caldwell characterizes both as "an anchor for journalistic discourse and as a cutting-edge component in newsroom interior design and station marketing flash."[4]

George Holliday's video footage of the worst day of Rodney King's life was a news commodity, understood not just in terms of its informational content but also its aesthetics. The shakiness and blurry focus of Holliday's video only bolstered its perceived truth value. "It was low in clarity but high in authenticity," Fiske explains. "The 'lowness' of its technology indexed the 'lowness' of the social position from and for which it spoke."[5] In this sense, it was the opposite of the 1990 federal sting operation that caught Washington, DC, mayor Marion Barry smoking crack on a hidden camera video, which many saw as a GOP targeting operation to tie the nation's most prominent Black mayor, one beloved by his majority-Black constituency, directly to the drug war, using Geraldo Rivera's *American Vice* playbook.[6] As with the Barry video, the King tape was contextualized with a blend of moral outrage and morbid voyeurism—evoked by Dan Rather in his introduction to CBS News' first story on George Holliday's video as "a new chapter in the saga of police brutality"—because neither the police nor the motorist *knew* they were being videotaped. For years, news directors had been promoting citizen-reporter initiatives in the hope of capturing the kind of spontaneous events that a professional news crew could never scramble quickly enough to get. The benefits of camcorder journalism worked both ways: citizens could achieve the rare thrill of contributing to national news discourse, and news producers could acquire incredible footage for a small fee (KTLA paid Holliday $500).

In this landscape, it made no sense anymore to compare the putative authenticity of reality rap to *Goodfellas*. The King video had instantly recast the national discourse on racist policing in the image of N.W.A's mock trial on "Fuck tha Police," combined with the intense reality effects of amateur videography. Nonetheless, MC Ren's reaction was to shrug: "It ain't nothin' new to me. It's just nobody never captured it on a videotape like homeboy did." As was his wont, Eazy-E acknowledged N.W.A's public validation, while trying to capitalize on King's own fame. "We were criticized a lot when we first released that song, but I guess now after what happened to Rodney King, people might look differently on the situation," he told the *Los Angeles Times*, noting that he had offered King a guest spot on a charity remake of "Fuck tha Police" (the collaboration never materialized).[7] Also stirred by the video was Lyndah McCaskill, half of the new female reality rap duo Bytches with Problems (BWP), who had released their debut album in February. "For years rappers have been talking about police brutality and no one has taken heed of it, or justice has never been done," McCaskill told an interviewer. "So now that it's been taped, it's been caught in the act and visualized, it's in black and white ... we truly hope people don't just forget about it a week later."[8] BWP were deeply inspired by N.W.A, and McCaskill had written her own experience with police brutality into a song called "Wanted," which references N.W.A in its first moments: "I can't help but agree with Eazy-E / Why the police always fucking with me?" Likewise, the imagery of the music video plays into the new storytelling possibilities offered by the Rodney King media event: interspersed with camcorder-shot footage of police in riot gear brutalizing protesters is a sequence in which two men with a camcorder videotape the police brutalizing BWP, but their footage is confiscated by the authorities, just like at the end of Public Enemy's "Brother's Gonna Work It Out." Edited into the video, however, are a few seconds of Holliday's video, showing Laurence Powell violently striking King with his baton. Though Holliday was initially reluctant to license the footage, he consented after viewing the completed BWP video, convinced that it "delivers the message to the public that law enforcement must respect individual rights in order to get the respect it deserves."[9] In return, BWP's record label (Russell Simmons's Rush Associated Labels) donated $1,500 to Holliday's new anti-police-brutality nonprofit.

As March turned into April, the focus shifted to Daryl Gates, for whom the video was a galling aberration and an all-too-human violation of clearly defined police protocols. LAPD officers were required to use billy clubs and Tasers, he noted, because they had been banned from using choke holds years earlier after more than a dozen suspects had died from the tactic, the vast majority of them Black. One of those was twenty-year-old James Mincey Jr., whose 1982 killing was strikingly similar to the King incident: after leading officers on a brief chase, Mincey was arrested by Foothill Division officers, one of whom put him in a carotid choke hold that deprived his brain of oxygen. He died two weeks later. That same year, Gates told the *Los Angeles Times* that "in some blacks when [the choke hold] is applied, the veins and arteries do not open as fast as they do in normal people."[10] Previous incidents in which LAPD officers killed Black Los Angeles residents resurfaced nationally, like the 1979 case of Eula Love, a thirty-nine-year-old Watts woman who was brandishing a butcher knife and arguing with two men from the gas company over an unpaid bill. Two minutes after LAPD officers arrived, Love was dead, shot eight times at close range. Gates claimed that his officers had reacted in self-defense, but there was no video evidence. Twelve years later, after King's LAPD assailants had been indicted, a second piece of technological evidence bolstered the racism charge against them. The press received a transcript of a message sent by officer Laurence Powell to another officer through his mobile digital terminal, referring to a group of Black citizens from earlier that night as "right out of *Gorillas in the Mist*." It was later revealed that the category "NHI" was used by Los Angeles public officials, from the police up through the judicial system, to refer to cases involving charges against young Black men. The acronym stood for "no humans involved."[11] The proof was overwhelming: in order to effectively patrol Black neighborhoods, authorities had convinced themselves that Black citizens were something less than human.

The Rodney King video was the quintessential media artifact of the first wave of reality entertainment, a pivot point in the representation of American law and order, and a reality rap validation. Those vicious eighty-one seconds verified the street reportage of N.W.A and Ice Cube and cast the growing faction of reality rappers not merely as angry young Black men but as street prophets. The tape had the gritty, voyeuristic appeal of a bombshell *A Current Affair* story and was infinitely more *real* than any of *Cops'* pro-police vérité entertainment: if the same footage had leaked from a *Cops* edit bay labeled "DESTROY," it would have been just as believable as it was coming from a white plumber's camcorder. To the extent that a Rodney King–themed *Donahue* episode from April 1991 could serve as evidence of the national mood, the country was fed up with the police too. When a cop called in to the show to defend his fellow officers for bravely putting their lives on the line, Donahue cut him off. "Oh, come on. You whine more than any other people I've ever heard in my life. If you don't wanna do this work, then get outta the uniform." The audience erupted in applause. More broadly, the lo-res King spectacle kicked off a year in which the mass-mediated visions of Black lives in the "inner city" and in the suburbs alike went blockbuster, with three million-selling, highly controversial albums and two feature films starring Ice-T and Ice Cube, the latter helmed by a self-proclaimed "hip-hop director." Reality rap was both bigger and realer than ever.

On March 16, *Saturday Night Live*'s "Weekend Update" host Dennis Miller cracked a joke about the violence that had erupted at the premiere of Ice-T's new film. The LAPD "decried *New Jack City* as a violent, exploitative film," Miller reported. "And you know, folks, I'm thinking if anyone knows what a violent, exploitative film looks like this week, it's gotta be the LAPD." Miller was riffing on the events of the previous weekend, when, as the *LA Times* reported, "hundreds of youths went on a rampage" at *New Jack City*'s Westwood Village premiere.[12] Because many more tickets were sold than there were seats available, hundreds of young people who had waited hours for entry only to be turned away at the door expended their energy by looting stores, fighting on the sidewalks, and vandalizing cars. The *LA Times* article cited "strained" racial tensions in the wake of the King video's release as a contributing factor, and the location of the dustup compounded the issue: Westwood Village was where the UCLA student Karen Toshima had been gunned down in gang cross fire three years earlier. In an interview with *Rolling Stone*, Ice-T summarized the situation better than most news anchors: "In L.A., you got gangs, and gangs live in territory. You create a magnet that draws them across territory lines to one place, you're going to have drama. They're not used to looking each other in the face."[13] In the *Village Voice*, Nelson George dug a bit deeper: "These outbreaks are not caused by rappers or movies, but by the same crushing sociological forces that incubate all forms of black-on-black violence," and the violence was further fueled by the lack of "large-scale social events for black youth."[14] Furthermore, though many observers were keen to link the film's portrayal of violence with the minor flare-ups at its premiere, they overlooked the fact that those young people were agitated because they had *not* seen the film.

Ice-T was initially reticent to portray a cop in his first major film role, which, not coincidentally, was being released by Sire's parent company, Warner Bros. But once he read the *New Jack City* script, he realized that the dreadlocked, Africa-medallion-wearing Scotty Appleton gave him a chance to mirror his on-record persona. As the film's coscreenwriter Barry Michael Cooper later surmised, Ice-T "saw the gangster *in* the cop."[15] Like T with his lyrics, Cooper envisioned *New Jack City* as a composite of scenarios and characters he had witnessed growing up as a young street reporter. "I used to carry a little reporter's notebook with me," Cooper recalled. "I would just watch people and take notes."[16] In 1985, Cooper penned one of the earliest crack crisis exposés for *Spin*, "Crack, a Tiffany Drug at Woolworth Prices," and two of his 1987 stories for the *Village Voice* ushered the phrase "new jack" into common parlance: "Teddy Riley's New Jack Swing: Harlem Gangsters Raise a Genius" chronicled the rising producer's innovative fusion of hip hop swagger into R&B, and "Kids Killing Kids: New Jack City Eats Its Young" exposed the country to the crack war zone of urban Detroit, where the new jack was the "calculated novice who enjoys killing you, aside from making a name for himself."[17] The latter story earned Cooper a trip to Hollywood to meet with producer Quincy Jones to discuss reworking "Nicky," a screenplay about the outlandish 1970s Harlem kingpin Nicky Barnes that would become *New Jack City*.

Far from the insulated and apolitical world of *Colors*, *New Jack City* was Hollywood's first attempt to tackle the urban scourge of the 1980s crack epidemic. Director Mario Van Peebles's father, Melvin, had spurred the Blaxploitation film cycle with 1971's *Sweet Sweetback's Baadasssss Song*, and Mario styled *New Jack City* as an update of the gritty crime dramas of that era. Opening in 1986 before jumping to the present day, *New Jack City* linked the Reagan era's hyperindividualistic wealth accumulation to the existentially damaging war on drugs. "You gotta rob to get rich in the Reagan era," proclaims crack kingpin Nino Brown (Wesley Snipes). "Times like these, people wanna get high. Real high, and real fast." Brown is a multidimensional character, portrayed as a pragmatic villain with a grasp of the picture beyond the projects. "Ain't no Uzis made in Harlem," Brown crows from the witness stand during the film's climax. "Not one of us in here owns a poppy field. . . . This is big business. This is the American way." Though Brown escapes with a light sentence, he is murdered by a local elderly man outside the courtroom as vigilante justice for poisoning the city. Before the credits roll, Van Peebles fills the screen with a warning, linking the fictional *New Jack City* to the reality of America's drug war: "Although this is a fictional story, there are Nino Browns in every major city in America. If we don't confront the problem realistically—without empty slogans and promises—then drugs will continue to destroy our country."

Cooper's influence on *New Jack City* extended to the soundtrack, which was full of the emergent genre that had been dubbed new jack swing: Teddy Riley's trio Guy, Heavy D, Johnny Gill, Keith Sweat, and Color Me Badd. But the film's theme song was written and performed by its costar, which required Ice-T to switch roles, in a sense. In the video for "New Jack Hustler (Nino's Theme)," T plays a Nino-esque figure in his preferred context: barking to the press from behind banks of press conference microphones. The image transfixes a young Black kid, who gazes with glazed-over eyes at his TV screen. Where *New Jack City* warned its viewers of future Nino Browns, the "New Jack Hustler" video ends with the word "HUSTLER" plastered over a freeze-frame of the young man, as if cautioning its audience against the mass media's role in creating future Ice-Ts, not Nino Browns. Reflecting his successful transition to the big screen, T dispensed with pro-free-speech diatribes on his fourth album, May 1991's *O.G. Original Gangster*, in lieu of a career retrospective. The album opens with a short medley that simply lists the songs that made T's reputation, while the title track chronicles his shift from party rap to reality rap:

When I wrote about parties
It didn't fit
"6 in the Mornin'"
That was the real shit

A few years earlier, Ice-T's participation on the *Colors* soundtrack had served as a pivotal moment in another Black director's cinematic radicalization. When producer Robert Solo screened *Colors* at the University of Southern California in 1988, a student named John Singleton took him to task during the Q&A. The film was marketed as a realistic portrayal of Black LA gangs, Singleton asserted, but its story revolved around the lives of two white LAPD officers. When Solo countered that Ice-T had written the film's theme song, Singleton shouted, "Well, Ice-T didn't write the fucking script!"[18] Having grown up in a South Central that was much closer to what N.W.A portrayed than what *Colors* showed, Singleton was determined to properly incorporate the lessons of hip-hop into his story—the *real* story—of Black lives in South Central. To Singleton, *Straight Outta Compton* and *Eazy-Duz-It* were cinematic in their own right. "If you didn't grow up in Los Angeles, it looked like cowboys and Indians, but . . . these guys were talking about shit that I seen," he said.[19] He named his screenplay *Boyz n the Hood* and doggedly sought to get it into Ice Cube's hands by navigating reality rap's musical, televisual, and ideological networks. He first pitched Cube while interning at *The Arsenio Hall Show* in 1989. An irritated Cube ignored Singleton's request, having shown up to discuss with Arsenio the host's reluctance to book N.W.A on his show. Later that year, Singleton rekindled the conversation at the Nation of Islam's "Save the Black Family" rally in Los Angeles and was similarly rebuffed. The next year, with his screenplay nearly finished, Singleton pitched Cube at a January 1990 Public Enemy concert in Hollywood. Finally, Cube entertained the enthusiastic twenty-two-year-old's entreaty, and the two discussed the film after the show in the parking lot, continuing the conversation as Cube gave Singleton a ride back to his University of Southern California dorm room, playing a rough mix of *AmeriKKKa's Most Wanted* while Singleton described his vision for *Boyz n the Hood*. "We're just two kids talking about our dreams," Singleton recalled.[20]

Boyz n the Hood was released in July 1991, and Cube played Doughboy, a character based on one of Singleton's childhood friends. Cube's performance is especially resonant for what it lacks: the intelligence and bravado of his records is melted into the dreary demeanor of a young man grown old before his time. Cube saw the recently paroled, jobless, and hopeless character as a vision of what he could have been. "I would still be like Doughboy if I wasn't making records," he told the *Source*.[21] In the film's final scene, after Doughboy's brother Ricky (Morris Chestnut) was murdered in a drive-by shooting, Doughboy expresses to Tre (Cuba Gooding Jr.) a melancholic and exhausted version of the media-saturated sentiments that Cube barked about on record: "Turned on the TV this morning. Had this shit on about livin' in a violent world. Showed all these foreign places, where foreigners live and all. Started thinking, man. Either they don't know, don't show, or don't care about what's goin' on in the hood." While shooting the film, Cube released the single "Dead Homiez," his closest-yet attempt at a sorrowful soul-style lament, set at a funeral for a senselessly murdered friend. His tone is solemn, but his observations, as always, are sharp: in the *Source*, Ras Baraka noted that both "Homiez" and *Boyz* were themed to "the senseless killing of Black boys."[22] Singleton likewise saw *Boyz* as a filmic extension of hip-hop culture: "Nobody's rapping, but it's a hip-hop film because it has the political as well as the cultural aesthetic that rings true."[23] And because he shot the film on location in South Central, Singleton was forced to confront the reality of gang warfare he'd grown up with. Though the Crips and the Bloods are only a tacit presence in the film, identified mainly through the presence of reds and blues in its art direction, a local Blood leader told Singleton that shooting near Baldwin Hills, a gang territory known as the "Jungle," could lead to trouble for Cube if a young kid looking to earn his stripes decided to take aim at the star. Singleton relocated his shoot to avoid his star getting shot.[24]

The South Central suburbs of Singleton's film were revelatory for audiences, not just because they provided a feature-length introduction to the previously invisible neighborhoods that had birthed N.W.A's lead songwriter, but because they showed a Los Angeles that was not a mythic coastal utopia or gloomy noir cityscape, but a superficially serene war zone born from decades of de jure segregation. What the *New York Times* called "a disconcertingly gritty peek into a facet of life to which virtually no white audiences have been privy" was as voyeuristically shocking, in its way, as the Rodney King video.[25] Cube opined that "white people who see this movie will better understand why black Americans behave like they do."[26] But as Singleton ensures in the film's opening text, any understanding was conditioned by a framing of the city as an open-air venue for Black-on-Black crime: "One out of every twenty-one Black American males will be murdered in their lifetime. Most will die at the hands of another Black male." Singleton mostly elides the role of the police in actively delimiting the possibilities for young Black men, save for one particularly chilling scene. While driving away from a gathering that has just been shot up by gang members, Tre has reached his emotional limit, telling Ricky that he's leaving the city. In a sequence that seems drawn straight from Cube's "Black police showing out for the white cop" line from "Fuck tha Police," Tre is pulled over, thrown over the hood of his car, and then threatened by an overaggressive Black cop, who puts a gun to Tre's throat while accusing him of being a gang member. In an interview with the *LA Times*, Singleton shed light on this moment: "I can't change white cops. But I think I can change the minds of some Black cops. They shouldn't care more about doughnuts and coffee than they care about the people in their community."[27]

Boyz n the Hood's focus on Black-on-Black crime braids into the film's subdued but potent theme of Black nationalism, primarily visible through the character of Tre's father, Furious Styles (Laurence Fishburne), whom Doughboy jokingly calls "Malcolm Farrakhan." Like Nation of Islam doctrine, *Boyz* asserts that men are primarily responsible for Black achievement, and the film opens with Tre's exasperated mother (Angela Bassett) sending him to live with his father. Cube told the *Source* that *Boyz* demonstrates "how a man can teach his son to be a man and a woman really can't do that."[28] While the film's two tragic figures, Ricky and Doughboy, are sons of a single mother, the relationship between Furious and Tre is the emotional core of *Boyz*. Some of the film's most intimate scenes involve Furious trying to instill responsibility and self-reliance in his son. Like Singleton's real-life father, Furious is a real-estate agent, and in the film's lone scene that looks outward to the larger forces pinning Black families into neglected communities, he gives an ad hoc lecture to Tre and Ricky, and a gathered group of locals, about the damaging impact of gentrification efforts being undertaken by an unnamed "they." "What we need to do is we need to keep everything in our neighborhood, *everything*, Black. Black-owned with Black money," Furious advocates. When an elderly man blames declining property values on the young Black people selling crack on street corners, Furious zooms outward, echoing Nino Brown at the end of *New Jack City*: "How you think the crack rock gets into the country? We don't own any planes. We don't own no ships." Then, he segues into his own media critique: "I know every time you turn on the TV that's what you see—Black people sellin' the rock, pushin' the rock—but that wasn't a problem as long as it was here. It wasn't a problem until it was in Iowa, and it showed up on Wall Street, where there are hardly any Black people." To his captive audience, Furious concludes by asking why Black neighborhoods have gun and liquor stores on every corner. "They want us to kill ourselves," he explains.

Though the violence in *Boyz n the Hood* is far from gratuitous, Columbia arranged preview screenings of the film for Los Angeles gang counselors and the LAPD's antigang CRASH unit. According to the *LA Times*, these audiences deemed *Boyz* a film with a strong antiviolence message, but the news media was quick to blare the fact that thirty injuries and a single death were reported during the film's opening weekend. True to form, the deaths were blamed on the effects of an occasionally violent film, not the social and economic circumstances of the film's target audience, or the "magnet" effect that Ice-T described for *New Jack City*. True to his hip-hop nature, Singleton aggressively dismissed the media hype, accusing the press of "lying in wait" for violence. In fact, the *New York Times* had done just that, posting a reporter at the three-screen, 420-seat theater in Baldwin Hills, on the outskirts of South Central, where Singleton himself lived. "All weekend, long orderly lines of young black people waited to get into the theater, then quietly absorbed its message of the value of family, school and hope," the story read, with no shortage of condescension. The theater's owner offered an explanation rooted in the same kind of civic pride that Furious tried to instill in Tre in the film. "We live in this community. We hire the local kids. Maybe the gangs respect this. They walk in here and take off their hats. This is neutral territory."[29]

Despite the media-stoked controversy, *Boyz n the Hood* was a critical and commercial sensation. It earned a twenty-minute standing ovation at the Cannes Film Festival and received a significant boost after Roger Ebert dubbed it "not simply a brilliant directorial debut, but an American film of enormous importance." Singleton would go on to earn Oscar nominations for Best Original Screenplay and Best Director, becoming the youngest-ever nominee for the latter award. Like *New Jack City*, *Boyz* was incredibly profitable. While Van Peebles's film earned six times its budget at the box office, Singleton turned his film's $6.5 million budget into $57.5 million in receipts. What industry observers were calling the "Singleton Thing" proved to Hollywood studios what hip-hop had taught the record industry and Fox had verified for television: the

Black youth market was very lucrative. By the end of 1991, a total of nineteen Black-directed films had been released in American theaters, more than the 1980s' entire total.

The area where John Singleton shot *Boyz n the Hood* was about twenty-five miles southwest of Los Angeles's Foothills region, where Rodney King was beaten by the Los Angeles Police Department a few feet from his white Hyundai while LAPD helicopters illuminated the scene. At an April 1991 fundraiser also attended by George Holliday, Daryl Gates morbidly joked about the cinematic tone of the King video. "As a guy who never goes to the movies and loves home movies, that was a lousy movie," Gates said. "If it wasn't for our helicopter, the lighting would have been terrible."[30] Gates's tactless comment echoes a shot from the first act of *Boyz*—set in 1984, the year of Reagan's reelection and Gates's first gang sweeps—that shows student drawings hanging on a classroom wall, one of which depicts an LAPD helicopter shining a bright spotlight on a red car below. Though *Boyz* did not reference Rodney King, Singleton is careful to highlight the omnipresent whir of overhead surveillance, monitoring South Central's car culture. As dream hampton noted in the *Source*, Singleton's use of "the militaristic sounds of police helicopters patrolling the neighborhood" and the periodic "loud flash of inspective outside light" served as "a painful reminder that our communities are under siege by the government's police."[31] The LAPD's oppressive observation from above is a conspicuous chapter in the American annals of Black surveillance. "Surveillance is nothing new to black folks. It is the fact of antiblackness," writes Simone Browne.[32] Hundreds of feet below the helicopters, much of the film's action took place in cars: Furious having a formative chat with young Tre, Ricky gunned down in a drive-by shooting, Tre being threatened next to his Volkswagen, Doughboy cruising down Crenshaw Boulevard.

The tension between automotive freedom and constant surveillance structures the video for "Steady Mobbin'," the first single from Ice Cube's second LP, *Death Certificate*, which debuted while *Boyz n the Hood* was still in theaters. It opens in the morning, as Cube leaves his suburban home to join his compatriots in the 1962 Chevy Impala idling in the driveway. Before getting in, Cube stops for a second to watch a young Black man laid out prone in front of his own car on the curb directly in front of Cube's home. Off camera, the cop yells, "I'm gonna treat you like King!" to which a man replies, "What King?" "Like Martin Luther King, like Rodney King, like all those Kings from Africa!" the cop angrily replies. One of Cube's compatriots gets out of the car and settles the dispute off camera (for MTV, the sound of gunfire was replaced with the honking of a car horn). Then, they go for a cruise. In a much lighter fashion than *Boyz n the Hood* or "Straight Outta Compton," Cube's drive through South Central maps his political and social realities. He cruises past representatives from opposite ends of the Black-enterprise spectrum—Nation of Islam members hawking bean pies and copies of the *Final Call* and a man selling bootleg MC Hammer T-shirts—and then past a sawed-off-shotgun-wielding Korean grocery owner chasing a Black thief out of his store. The video's action is the mundane stuff of life in the hood: two men boxing on a street corner to impress women, Cube scooping up Sir Jinx on Ruthelen Street, stopping by his mother's house to relieve himself, hitting the Crenshaw strip, stealing another man's woman, and taking her to a motel, where he promptly falls asleep on the bed while his car stereo is stolen in the parking lot. But as the video concludes, it revisits off-camera police violence, when Cube is awakened by a clamor outside and drearily walks to the motel window. As the music cuts out, Cube's expression changes to one of confusion as the same King-themed exchange from the opening of the video reappears outside the motel. Even typical South Central days, "Steady Mobbin'" shows, are structured by a never-ending cycle of police brutality.

Cube slotted "Steady Mobbin'" on side A of *Death Certificate*, the hour-long concept album he released in November 1991. The album was a reality rap manifesto, complete with a cover photo as political cartoon, depicting the rapper standing next to Uncle Sam's lifeless body lying in a morgue. The album was divided into the "Death" side and the "Life" side, a divergence mirrored in a liner-note photo showing Cube reading an issue of the Nation of Islam newspaper the *Final Call*—with the full-page headline "Unite or Perish!"—backed by his Lench Mob cronies on one side and Nation of Islam members on the other. A portion of that photo's caption reads, "The best place for a young Black male or female is the Nation of Islam," reflecting Cube's earnest solutions to the Black community's problems contained on the "Life" side. The "Death" side, however, more closely resembles *AmeriKKKa's Most*

Wanted's trip through the television dial. "My Summer Vacation" is a national report on gang franchising in St. Louis, flipping the perspective of tabloid TV with a begrudging respect for gangs' nationwide entrepreneurship efforts. "The Lifestyles of the Poor and Unfortunate" satirizes the wealth-obsessed 1980s reality TV staple *Lifestyles of the Rich and Famous* (Ice-T tackled the idea from a different perspective on the *O.G.* album cut "Lifestyles of the Rich and Infamous"), followed by two R-rated, sitcom-style takes on the Black class divide (the raunchy, sexist "Givin' Up the Nappy Dug Out") and the necessity of safe sex in the AIDS era (the hilarious "Look Who's Burnin'"). The side's most striking moment is "A Bird in the Hand," the richest distillation yet of Cube's persona as the scholarly "street knowledge" shit talker. Over a magisterial track that sounds like a hip-hop national anthem, Cube portrays a young Black man in George H. W. Bush's America who finds himself faced with the dead-end choice of working at McDonald's or putting a kilo (known as a "bird") on the street. "We don't want a drug push," Cube concludes, "but a bird in the hand is worth more than a Bush."

The "Death" side ends with "Alive on Arrival," a detailed account of infrastructural failings that finds Cube bleeding from a drive-by shooting in a hospital waiting room, while being profiled as a gang member by aggressive police: "Yo, I didn't do a thing / Don't wanna go out like my man Rodney King," he pleads. The cops leave Cube's character to languish in the waiting room, measuring his time in the number of episodes of *M*A*S*H* he watches on the TV. He dies at the end of the track, and his eulogy is a minute-long speech by Khalid Abdul Muhammad, the Nation of Islam's second most popular public figure after Louis Farrakhan. The "Death" side's concluding half hour of bad behavior, according to Muhammad, provided evidence that Black people had been "brainwashed with the white man's mind." The "Life" side aimed to rectify this problem, primarily through violent acts of separatism and racial reeducation. A second short Muhammad speech sets the scene: "Before we can make a way for the peacemaker, we must kill, and get rid of, the peace breaker." Per the Nation of Islam's teachings, and recalling Furious's speech from *Boyz n the Hood*, the bulk of Cube's venom is aimed at the Black community itself. "Color Blind" assails Black-on-Black gang violence, while "Us" aligns "dope dealers" with the police, "'cause ya kill us." The most exhaustive expression of Cube's full-blown Nation of Islam militancy comes in the video for "True to the Game," where an armed, masked Cube takes three hostages who are bringing down the race: a suburban Black man married to a white woman, an MC Hammer–style pop rapper, and a Carlton Banks–ish corporate striver who laughs off his white colleagues' racism. One by one, Cube binds and blindfolds them and drives them to an unidentified warehouse, where he ties them to chairs . . . so Muhammad, who plays himself in the video, can lecture them.

Cube's broadsides against insufficiently Black Americans were drowned out in the press by the forty-seven-second track titled "Black Korea," a rhetorical Molotov cocktail thrown into the deeply strained relationship between Korean American store owners and Black communities. For years, Black South Central and Compton residents had deeply resented the proliferation of merchants who didn't financially support the local communities and who eyed their Black customers with suspicion. It was no coincidence that Singleton had Furious stage his gentrification lecture in front of a billboard advertising "Seoul to Seoul Realty" in *Boyz n the Hood*. But in the wake of the South Central shooting death of fifteen-year-old Latasha Harlins by the Korean grocery store owner Soon Ja Du less than two weeks after the Rodney King beating, Cube was not in the mood to lecture. In a tragic mirror of the King beating, Du shot Harlins in the head from behind after a brief flare-up over a purportedly stolen bottle of orange juice, and it was clearly captured on the store's surveillance camera. Though District Attorney Ira Reiner withheld the footage from the media to ensure an unbiased jury in Du's trial, depriving Harlins's killing from the national outrage that greeted King's beating, the evidence was enough for a jury to convict Du of voluntary manslaughter. Though the conviction carried a maximum sentence of sixteen years in prison, Judge Joyce Karlin gave Du a mere five years' probation, explaining that "this is not a time for revenge." Cube exacted rhetorical revenge on "Black Korea," calling Korean American merchants "chop-suey ass," "Oriental, one-penny-countin' motherfuckers," and, in the space of two bars, shifting from a nationwide boycott to a threat to "burn your store right down to a crisp." For good measure, he samples the *Do the Right Thing* scene where Radio Raheem argues with Asian American convenience store merchants over the proper kind of replacement batteries for his boom box.

Cube's anti-Korean bigotry was matched on *Death Certificate*'s final song, the withering anti-N.W.A diss track "No Vaseline," with even more hate speech. While Cube excoriates his former group mates with numerous variations on homophobic slurs, he singles out Ruthless Records co-owner Jerry Heller, with baldly anti-Semitic language, as "the Jew" who "broke up [the] crew" and, even more startlingly, as a "devil" to eliminate with "a bullet in his temple." Combined with the "Korea" blowback, Cube's "Vaseline" slurs overwhelmed media coverage of *Death Certificate*. The Simon Wiesenthal Center called for a nationwide boycott of the album, while Priority Records' European distributor, Island Records, removed "Vaseline" and "Black Korea" from copies there. The *Village Voice*'s Robert Christgau called Cube "a straight-up racist, simple and plain"; *Rolling Stone* claimed that "if there is a recipe for social revolution in *Death Certificate*, it's hard to hear it amid the bigotry"; and the *New York Times* compared Cube's lyrics to the speeches of ex-Klan leader David Duke.[33] In a rare editorial, *Billboard* condemned the album as "the rankest sort of racism and hatemongering" that "crosses the line that divides art from the advocacy of crime."[34] The backlash intensified after Cube enthusiastically promoted the book *The Secret Relationship between Blacks and Jews* at a late October press conference. An anti-Semitic conspiracy tract disguised as historical research, the book was written by the Nation of Islam's "Historical Research Department" and proffered the ahistorical argument that Jews played a foundational, though disguised, organizational role in the transatlantic slave trade. Cube had become Professor Griff and Chuck D simultaneously: espousing hateful conspiracy theories, claiming the press twisted his words, and refusing to apologize, all of which combined to make *Death Certificate* the most controversial album in hip-hop history.

Cube did have his defenders. *Source* editor James Bernard called *Billboard* "too dainty and thin-skinned to hear the anger and rage and frustration that many people are forced to deal with every day."[35] In *Newsweek*, Jon Leland called out the *Billboard* editorial for neglecting to discuss Cube's tirades against other Black people (Timothy White responded that he "couldn't make out the other lyrics").[36] In a nationally syndicated column, Greg Kot warned against dismissing Cube as merely a hateful opportunist, claiming he spoke for "disenfranchised Blacks, a segment of society that rarely is spoken about on the 10 o'clock news or in the halls of Congress," and framing the album's hard-line message within a worldview emboldened by the revelations of the Rodney King video.[37] In the world of popular music, sales numbers are the ultimate validation, and *Death Certificate* debuted at no. 2 on the *Billboard* 200, outselling MC Hammer's massively hyped *2 Legit 2 Quit* in its first week. Though Cube was well aware that *Death Certificate* was being purchased en masse by non-Black listeners, he was forthright in his dismissal of their opinions. "I don't care what the white community thinks about the record," he told the *LA Times*. "I'm talking directly to my black brothers and sisters."[38] The separatist ideologies of the Nation of Islam had facilitated a turning point in popular music: a million-selling Black superstar could now use the white-run mass media to direct a message to a Black audience. For non-Black audiences, the result was simultaneously voyeuristic and journalistic, like hearing the recording of Farrakhan calling Judaism a "gutter religion" to a gathering of Black people. But unlike Farrakhan's teachings, Ice Cube's rhetoric did not have to be exposed. He had turned the Nation's incendiary rhetoric into one of the most popular albums of the year.

Cube had company with his freshly sworn enemies: five months before *Death Certificate*, the long-awaited second album from N.W.A, *Niggaz4Life*, debuted at no. 2 on the *Billboard* 200, the highest first-week entry for any album since Michael Jackson's *Bad* debuted at no. 1 in 1987. In its second week of release, it overtook Paula Abdul's *Spellbound* to claim the no. 1 spot. Where *Billboard*'s editorial staff excoriated Cube, its decision to reconfigure how it measured album sales by merging its time-tested system with a startup known as SoundScan greatly benefitted N.W.A. Instead of ranking albums based on retailer self-reports, which industry insiders had known for decades were inaccurate and easily rigged, SoundScan counted the actual number of units sold by scanning bar codes at checkout counters. Of course, even SoundScan was far from a foolproof metric itself: participation in the system was voluntary, and without the participation of large chains such as Tower Records and many independent stores, it accounted for only about 40 percent of retail sales at launch. Yet, like Nielsen ratings for television, *Billboard* charts had long been the record industry's secular religion, an agreed-upon hallucination of scientific accuracy that allowed the business to ascertain consumer demand and mitigate risk. SoundScan's role in *Niggaz4Life*'s chart-topping achievement marked an interesting symmetry to N.W.A's own remarkable run. A group who used rap as a medium to illuminate the scourge of police brutality in Black Los Angeles had themselves just been revealed as the nation's most popular group by another technological innovation. The record industry couldn't hold N.W.A, or reality rap, at arm's length anymore. The number one album in the nation had the word "nigga" in its title.

More than any other rap album released that year, *Niggaz4Life* certainly *sounded* like a blockbuster. A quantum leap in Dre's production, the music was sonically richer than any rap record before it, an apt reflection of the group's newly extravagant image as Prohibition-era gangsters in the "Appetite for Destruction" video. But the political edge of their music was blunted without Ice Cube's lyrical contributions. While the MC Ren–penned title track was a keen interrogation (and justification) of the word "nigga," it amounted to the album's only sustained moment of reflection, and even it ends with Eazy slipping into an ad hoc remix of an old Dr. Pepper TV ad jingle: "Wouldn't you like to be a nigga too?" The group's righteous anger had devolved into mere hedonism, and violent misogyny dwarfed any other ideas. The album's rampant sexism was especially prominent on its second half: titles such as "One Less Bitch," "Findum, Fuckum and Flee," and "To Kill a Hooker" showed a group seemingly emboldened by the 2 Live Crew's obscenity exoneration and daring the moral entrepreneurs to give them even more publicity. In a special editorial devoted to the album, *Rolling Stone* lamented the group's moral decline. While *Straight Outta Compton* had chronicled, "in searing detail, the daily horrors of life in South Central L.A." and had posed "a moral and political challenge to anyone who encounters it," the group's follow-up "is all attitude and . . . little point."[39] At the *Source*, however, Jon Shecter had a different take. "*Niggaz4Life* contains harmful, hurtful words. It is unnecessarily violent, and it is sexist to a disgusting degree," he wrote, before situating the album within the newly established context of reality rap. "But understand that *Niggaz4Life* is *real* hip-hop. Not Hammer, not [Vanilla] Ice, this is the sound of rap music from the streets, created and performed by talented artists who refuse to sell out."[40]

Where *Straight Outta Compton* aimed to erase the boundaries between on-record and real-life violence, the *Niggaz4Life* press cycle witnessed the members of N.W.A committing and embracing actual violence against women to match the over-the-top musical representations. Before the album's release, it was revealed that Dre had violently attacked the TV rap journalist Dee Barnes during Bytches with Problems' album release party, in retaliation for an Ice Cube diss toward N.W.A that had been included in a recent episode of her show *Pump It Up*. Barnes filed a lawsuit against Dre and N.W.A, and the *LA Times* published her account of the evening: "He picked me up by my hair and my ear and smashed my face and body into the wall....Next thing I know, I'm down on the ground and he's kicking me in the ribs and stamping on my fingers. I ran into the women's bathroom to hide, but he burst through the door and started bashing me in the back of the head."[41] Instead of denying the charges or apologizing to Barnes, N.W.A unapologetically confirmed Dre's actions. "She deserved it," Ren told *Rolling Stone*, followed by Dre's casual dismissal: "It ain't no big thing—I just threw her through a door." In the September 1991 *Spin*, they were even more overt: "He grabbed the bitch by the little hair that she had," Eazy crowed. "Threw the bitch to the bathroom door. Pow!! She hit her head. He just start stompin' on the bitch....She was fucked up worse than Rodney King!"[42] Barnes offered her own evaluation of N.W.A's violent streak to *Rolling Stone*: "Their whole philosophy has been that they're just...reporting how it is on the streets. But they've started believing this whole fantasy, getting caught up in their press....They think they're living their songs."[43]

N.W.A might have moved on from its "Fuck tha Police" days, but the anti-LAPD discourse was taken up by 1991's biggest Hollywood action blockbuster. In *Terminator 2: Judgment Day*, Arnold Schwarzenegger reprised his role as the futuristic cyborg bounty hunter T-800, battling the more sophisticated T-1000 (Robert Patrick) that was sent from the future to eliminate the future resistance leader John (Edward Furlong). Yet for most of the T-1000's screen time, Patrick adopts the guise of an LAPD officer, all the better to permit a ruthless, single-minded killing machine to move through Los Angeles unnoticed. The T-1000 was not even granted a smidgeon of personality, looking more like an expensive CGI version of the anonymous white cops from the "Straight Outta Compton" video. According to *Terminator 2* director James Cameron, this was no coincidence. "Cops think [of] all non-cops as less than they are, stupid, weak, and evil," he explained. "They dehumanize the people they are sworn to protect and desensitize themselves in order to do that job."[44] Cameron shot much of the movie on location around Los Angeles, including a scene at a saloon only a few hundred yards from the site of the Rodney King beating. In fact, on the same camcorder he had used to capture those consequential eighty-one seconds of brutality, George Holliday shot footage of Cameron, Schwarzenegger, and crew during production. "That, to me, is the most amazing irony considering that the LAPD are strongly represented in *Terminator 2* as being a dehumanized force," Cameron reiterated.[45] The technological villain in both *Terminator* movies was Skynet, a government-created artificial intelligence system designed for protection but which turned rogue and started attacking humans. In *Terminator 2*, Cameron mirrored Skynet in the LAPD.

Politically engaged reality rap does make an appearance in *Terminator 2*, symbolically at least. Throughout the film, the T-1000's quarry is future rebel leader and current moody teenager John Connor, who spends the entirety of the film wearing a Public Enemy T-shirt. Though the rifle-scope logo that Chuck D had designed five years earlier was not visible, the group's white-on-black stenciled name made the perfect image to recirculate as a signifier of antiauthoritarian rebellion in 1991. "I knew who the group was, but it was more that the symbol made sense," explained the film's costume designer.[46] *Source* editor James Bernard opened the magazine's October issue by using PE's *T2* appearance to critique the political economy of Black filmmaking. Why was it acceptable to sample Public Enemy's pro-Black iconography for a blockbuster action film, Bernard asks, but not to provide Black filmmakers the same kind of support given to mavericks like Cameron? Bernard specifically cites the botched rollout by the Samuel Goldwyn Company of Charles Burnett's 1990 film *To Sleep with Anger*, the story of a Black middle-class family in Los Angeles's historic Sugar Hill district that, despite starring Danny Glover, was poorly marketed by the studio and had the misfortune of being released a year before, not after, *Boyz n the Hood*. "Sometimes I wish we had our own Arnold android to protect the Hip-Hop Nation against these Hollywood and music biz 'terminators,'" observed Bernard. "But maybe we should get our *own* black leather, motorcycles and sawed-offs to have these fascists hauled off."[47]

To an even greater degree than any reality rapper short of Ice-T, who played the inaugural alt-rock festival Lollapalooza with his band Body Count in the summer of 1991, Public Enemy's music and image had crossed over to white audiences. PE's rerecording of "Bring the Noise" with the thrash-metal band Anthrax, featuring bassist Scott Ian rapping the song's entire third verse, was an MTV and radio hit, and the two groups embarked on a joint tour that followed PE's jaunt with the goth Sisters of Mercy and the political postpunk Gang of Four earlier that year. By 1991, Columbia Records estimated that a full 40 percent of Public Enemy's audience was white. Despite that reality, Public Enemy's fourth album, *Apocalypse 91 . . . The Enemy Strikes Black*, did not kowtow to white listeners but, like *Death Certificate* a month later, spoke to Black audiences while permitting white eavesdroppers. Chuck was a fan of Cube's programmatic second LP. "His album is a warning," Chuck told the *LA Times*. "The Black community is a car out of control, heading toward a wall at 85 miles per hour. . . . It's scaring people. That's good. That's the way it should be."[48] Like Cube on "True to the Game," Chuck's lessons on *Apocalypse* were directed at the Black community's role in its own future. "We, the black race, have double agents in our ranks who are contributing to the genocide," Chuck told *Melody Maker* of the album's title. "In order for us to get our shit in order, we've gotta get those motherfuckers."[49] Throughout the album, Chuck and Flav seek to cleanse Black America of its most profitable toxins: on "Nighttrain," it's "the sellout" drug pusher who "deal the keys from Key Largo," and on "1 Million Bottlebags," it's malt liquor companies who target Black neighborhoods, while on "Shut 'Em Down," PE argue that Black-focused companies like Nike should "give up the dough to my town." While not quite the blockbuster that *Death Certificate* would be, *Apocalypse* debuted at no. 4 on the *Billboard* 200, was certified platinum in November, and ranked second in the year-end Pazz & Jop critics' poll (*Death Certificate* ranked sixteenth, and Ice-T's *O.G.* was no. 12).

Apocalypse also demonstrated that PE were still obsessed with the news media. On "A Letter to the New York Post," the issue was Flavor Flav's own newfound notoriety: he had recently served a thirty-day sentence for assaulting his then girlfriend. The group's response was predictable: attack the messengers. Chuck calls the *New York Post* "America's oldest continuously published daily piece of bullshit," and Flav questions *Jet* magazine's news-gathering ethics for running the same story

("Should have checked with me before you wrote it / Got it from another source and quote it"), without denying the facts of the story. Yet they were much more effective when they used their own platform to intervene in news discourse. On Martin Luther King Jr.'s birthday in January 1992, the group debuted its explosive single "By the Time I Get to Arizona" with a press conference that doubled as the announcement of their new "Black awareness program." Public Enemy's starkest statement on (and stoking of) a current media controversy yet, "Arizona" was inspired by a late 1990 ballot initiative to establish King's birthday as a holiday in the titular state, as every other state apart from New Hampshire had done. When that initiative failed, popular culture took over: two weeks after the Rodney King video went national, NFL owners voted to move the 1993 Super Bowl out of Phoenix. The resulting media tumult inspired Chuck to pick up the pen, and the camera. The "Arizona" video opens with a dramatization of former Arizona governor Evan Mecham asserting in 1987 that the state would not recognize the holiday, while Sister Souljah commands heavily armed PE mercenaries to arm themselves and head west. Upon arrival, they blow up the governor, poison a state senator, and gun down various other officials. Rounded out with a guest appearance by Ice-T, "Arizona" generated the kind of national publicity through controversy that Chuck desired. MTV showed the video a few times before withdrawing it, and Chuck himself appeared on *Nightline* to debate the Black columnist Clarence Page on the issue. Like many other commentators, Page noted the irony that the "Arizona" video portrayed "the exact opposite of the message that Martin Luther King died for." Chuck's response was unequivocal: if King had survived after taking a bullet, his tactics would have changed. Arizona voters approved a ballot proposal for the holiday in November 1992, but it was increasingly clear that the era of King's nonviolent resistance had long passed.

CHAPTER 5

WHO GOT THE CAMERA?

▼

Rodney King never testified on his own behalf during the 1992 trial of his four Los Angeles Police Department attackers. Instead, George Holliday's video footage took the stand for him. To tens of millions of Americans, including Daryl Gates, the video provided ample proof for the jury to find the officers guilty. But a year later, the most consequential viewers of King's beating were ten whites, an Asian American, and a Latina drawn from the conservative, mostly white Los Angeles suburb of Simi Valley, where a judge had moved the officers' trial out of a concern for "fairness," even though the new venue fell squarely within Los Angeles's vast media market. During jury selection, the defense eliminated any prospective jurors who expressed negative reactions to the clip as biased, leaving the final verdict in the hands of those who either did not share the general population's horror at Holliday's footage or doubted that the video told the full story of the incident. The reality of a captured event is never embedded in the pixels of a videotape, the nation learned, but in the specific contexts of that tape's viewing, if not manipulation. The defense digitally cross-examined Holliday's footage, slowing it down and blowing it up to desensitize the jurors to its horrors and create an entirely new evidentiary artifact. The defense convinced the jurors that King was not a victim but a subdued attacker, a belligerent Black man driven to unpredictable violence by the powerful substances coursing through his body. In a *Los Angeles Times* opinion piece, Ice Cube placed the remixed King footage in the broader representational economy of race:

> America looks at Black men in two ways. You have the nice Black man, like a Bill Cosby, and you have the bad Black man . . . the person you see going to jail at night on the news. . . . If Rodney King was seen as a good Black, then the officers would have been found guilty, but all through the trial, they kept saying that he was a monster . . . a wild animal . . . plus he had a past criminal record. To the jurors, he was a bad Black so anything done to him was justified.[1]

The LAPD's defense team had effectively transformed Rodney King from a victim of police brutality into the Black bogeyman of local news paranoia—the new Willie Horton.

On April 29, 1992, with the nation glued to their television screens, Judge Stanley Weisberg read the jury's decision: all four officers had been acquitted. Within hours, the streets filled with angry citizens, vociferously airing their disgust at a plain miscarriage of justice. John Singleton heard the verdict on his car radio and immediately drove to Simi Valley. As the hundreds of TV outlets crowded into the courthouse parking lot waited for the exonerated officers to exit the building, a Fox 11 anchor asked Singleton to characterize his "initial emotional reaction." He paused and then replied, "If I said that, then there'd probably be an explosion," adding, "There's a lotta things in LA that are gonna happen . . . probably in the next couple months, that people are gonna have to remember why they happened." The on-the-ground response to the verdict initially assumed many forms, from peaceful street protests to vociferous gatherings at churches and community centers to the willful looting and destruction of city-owned buildings and private businesses. Multiple constituencies participated, from fed-up Black citizens to the area's significant Latino population (arrested in comparable numbers to Black individuals) to disenfranchised whites and the LGBT community, who took to the streets in solidarity, carrying signs that read "Queers of All Colors Unite." But after the LAPD proved unable, or unwilling, to respond, the city erupted into what a special committee of the California Legislature later called "the worst multi-ethnic urban conflict in United States history."

A bit more than a year after the Rodney King video provided seemingly incontrovertible evidence of police brutality, a new form of high-concept realism supplanted more comfortable representations of Black America in the wake of the officers' exoneration. The final episode of *The Cosby Show*, one of the most watched and critically lauded programs in American entertainment history, aired on Thursday night, after the first full day of the Los Angeles uprising. This made for an awkward segue from the KNBC news desk, when, after anchors noted a total of seventeen deaths that day and informed viewers of various uprising-induced closings, a third anchor introduced *The Cosby Show* as "a welcome change of pace" and "a breath of fresh air in a sometimes crazy and chaotic world much like we saw today." The contrast between what was happening on the streets of Los Angeles and the final *Cosby* episode was stark: while the streets of Los Angeles were being taken over by thousands of young Black men who had been locked out of the American Dream, Cliff was preparing for Theo to graduate from NYU and wistfully recalling a moment from the show's first season when he taught his son the value of financial literacy by using Monopoly money. The remarks offered earlier that day by Congresswoman Maxine Waters, who was a year younger than Cosby and represented a district that included South Central, described another world entirely: "Young Black males in my district are feeling at this moment, if they could not get a conviction with the Rodney King video available to the jurors, that there can be no justice in America."[2]

Though it was catalyzed by the King verdict, the rebellion was overdetermined by numerous other factors—overpolicing, mass incarceration, economic devastation—that were impossible to understand and portray from a single journalistic perspective. "In an event as massive as this, to be present at one street corner does not make you a reliable source," explained Norman Klein. "Nor does it give you enough background to discuss long-term causes, the subtleties of a particular street, its normalcies, its survival. Panic was the story that made this a ratings bonanza."[3] Thanks to nonstop television coverage, it became a dramatic, high-tech television blockbuster sequel to the Rodney King video. The racialized crime panic of local television news coverage became a weeklong national television spectacle, with endless shots of dramatic building fires and interchangeable ethnic locals—"hooligans" and "thugs"—smashing windows and looting stores. When it was over, the uprising was reduced to statistics that, like Daryl Gates's gang sweeps, disguised more than they revealed: more than sixty deaths and over two thousand injuries, over twelve thousand arrests, and property damage totaling upward of $1 billion. But the attempts to define what the event *meant* lasted much longer: for more than a year, everyone from national politicians to reality rappers and sitcom and TV drama producers would attempt to give the seismic event some semblance of narrative.

An uncredited executive producer of the Los Angeles rebellion was Daryl Gates, who had assumed that King's assaulters would be convicted and had woefully underprepared his officers for a response. It was a remarkable contradiction of what he'd been building toward for the past three decades. A field commander during the 1965 Watts rebellion, Gates had witnessed firsthand the inability of the LAPD to deal with what he called, in his favored military parlance, "guerrilla warfare." The Watts rebellion was catalyzed, but not caused, by the fraught and violent interaction between a Black motorist, Marquette Frye, and the California Highway Patrol officers who pulled Frye and his brother over on suspicion of drunken driving a block from Frye's home on Wednesday, August 11, 1965. When an officer hit the resistant Frye with his nightstick, Frye's mother came to his aid and was quickly pinned to the hood of a patrol car, triggering an angry response from the gathering crowd of onlookers, who would square off against a phalanx of officers from the department's notorious Seventy-Seventh Street Division for the next several hours. Not only had Black citizens been chafing under the yoke of Chief Bill Parker's racist "thin blue line" approach to policing for years, but they were uniquely aware of the story of Beverly Tate, a twenty-two-year-old Black woman who had been arrested and raped by an LAPD officer a few weeks earlier. While Tate died of "mysterious causes" three months later (while five months pregnant), her assailant was quietly fired but never tried for his crime. Tate's story was prominent in the Black press, including two mentions in *Jet* magazine, but was presented in the *LA Times* only as an anonymous legal issue and a collection of rumors.[4] The rapidly spreading word of the previous night's battle became intertwined with Tate's tragedy and numerous examples of suppressed incidents of LAPD brutality. Local gang members and other Black youths strategized in the Jordan Downs projects, while community leaders met to plan a different kind of response. The ensuing Black rebellion lasted until the following Tuesday, August 17, claiming thirty-four lives (including two police who were killed by friendly fire), injuring a thousand others, and burning numerous buildings to the ground.

The epistemological gap between Black Watts's knowledge and white Los Angeles's ignorance was exposed by press coverage of the uprising, immediately labeled the Watts riot, with all the connotations, Mike Davis and Jon Weiner explain, of "mob violence, mindless destruction, and the absence of any moral restraint."[5] The term that took hold in the Black community was "rebellion," which, Davis and Weiner observe, highlights the uprising's ideological infrastructure: "The uprising did have explicit grievances (police abuse, mercantile exploitation, unemployment, and so on); articulate voices (usually ignored by the media); clear, if informal codes of behavior (homes and Black-owned businesses, for instance were off limits to looting or arson); and an emotionally infused but *rational* strategy (the destruction of white-owned property as a means to force reforms and create a sense of urgency that nonviolent protest had been unable to achieve)."[6] The looting and antipolice violence that characterized the rebellion emerged not simply from Frye's interaction with the police but from what Davis and Weiner dub "the economic flytrap that snared the lives and hopes of Black youth" in the city.[7] While Chief Parker's LAPD ignored white-collar and white-neighborhood crimes, they cast a dragnet over Black communities like Watts, arresting young Black men who had already been left out of LA's postwar economic boom for petty crimes in the city's street economy, their arrest records further restricting their chances of earning gainful employment. To the Black youth of Watts, the LAPD were not there to protect and serve, but to surveil, harass, and pummel.

Little of this was visible in the news media's coverage of Watts, which erupted a mere five days after the passage of the Voting Rights Act of 1965. Although the civil rights protests that convinced President Lyndon Johnson to sign the act into law were made for the new medium of television news, the Black rebels of Watts cut the opposite figure. To a news media more used to conversing with police than spending time in local communities, the explosion of Black anger was impossible to parse.

"Reporters struggled to comprehend a threat to their city from the sort of racial conflict that until then had largely been limited to America's southern and northeastern states," one *LA Times* reporter recalled, noting that by the third day of the rebellion, the word "Negro" had become synonymous with "rioter" in the coverage.[8] TV news coverage focused on the most sensationalistic, warlike aspects of the rebellion: visuals of burning cars and stores being looted, paired with a cacophonous soundtrack of radio dispatchers, sirens, and gunfire. By Friday night, when the National Guard had taken over, a memorable shot showed military police looking at a city map unfolded on the hood of a car and lit by a flashlight, looking like in-country grunts negotiating the Vietnamese jungle, a perspective reinforced by their camera-equipped helicopters surveying the smoldering buildings from above.

What was the reality of Watts? It depended upon the source of information. Governor Pat Brown tapped former Central Intelligence Agency director John McCone to investigate the underlying causes, and the resulting report, issued in December 1965 and titled "Violence in the City—An End or a Beginning?," recommended social reforms for Black communities, advocated structural fixes to police departments, and wagged its finger at a sensationalistic media; but it also insisted on "attitudinal training" for Black citizens, refused to acknowledge the LAPD's complicity in the uprising, and concluded that the rebellion was, in the end, a violent uprising spurred by a handful of agitators with no larger political goals. At the same time, an already-existing report proved even more influential on the postrebellion conversation. "The Negro Family: The Case for National Action" had been released in March 1965 by Daniel Patrick Moynihan, a sociologist and an advisor to President Johnson, and it made the case that the Black community's problems arose not from racism but from Black families' own inability to adapt to the social and cultural realities that they encountered after leaving the Jim Crow South. Moynihan's theories played a prominent role in the December 1965 CBS television documentary "Watts: Riot or Revolt?," a widely viewed attempt to define the rebellion, along with the McCone Commission's report, interviews with Chief Parker, and, as Christine Acham dryly observes, "finally, interviews with local African American leaders and residents of Watts."[9] Moynihan's report generated numerous critics, who dismissed the idea that to succeed in America,

Black people simply had to more properly assimilate to white culture. Many of these critics were Black public figures who felt newly empowered to speak about Black lives in the wake of Watts, the February 1965 assassination of Malcolm X, and the October 1965 publication of his best-selling autobiography. "The time when white men, whatever their motives, could tell Negroes what was or was not good for them, is now definitely and decidedly over," Moynihan unsympathetically remarked about the backlash. "An era of bad manners is certainly begun."[10]

While Watts rebuilt, what Moynihan dismissively called "bad manners" was, to Black Los Angeles residents, the next wave of a revolution. Not only did the rebellion help radicalize a generation of young Black men—from Bobby Seale and Huey Newton to the writer Robert Beck (Iceberg Slim), the stand-up comedian Richard Pryor, and countless area gang members and Nation of Islam converts—it spurred a renaissance of Black art in Watts itself. Spurred by the desire to recreate a version of South Central's vibrant jazz scene of the 1940s and 1950s, the pianist Horace Tapscott tapped into the thread of Black nationalism that John Coltrane had recently woven into his music to create the Underground Musicians Association (UGMA), a democratically minded free-jazz consortium with a pronounced focus on jazz's roots in West African music and culture. Along with the UGMA emerged the Watts Writers Workshop (WWW), established by *On the Waterfront* screenwriter Budd Schulberg, who had been stirred to action after watching the Watts rebellion on television: "Like millions of other dazed or complacent Los Angelenos, I was watching an unscheduled 'spectacular,' the damnedest television show ever put on the tube. Into our living rooms raged an element that is usually forbidden on television—life, and its dark, red underbelly, death."[11] In response, Schulberg established the WWW, which, with assistance from some noteworthy writers, including James Baldwin and John Steinbeck, was funded by a grant from the National Endowment for the Arts. A schism quickly emerged between Schulberg's well-intentioned Hollywood liberalism and the more radical artists of the WWW, and out of the workshop's second wave came the Watts Prophets, a trio of poet-musicians who brought the language of the Black streets in dialogue with the long tradition of Black oral poetics. While the growing Black Power movement had started ushering the word "Negro" into the historical dustbin, the Prophets' work pushed the descriptors even further with recordings like "Dem Niggers Ain't Playin'," issued on the album *Rappin' Black in a White World*. "Look at them flames lighting up the sky / Ain't never seen fires shooting up so high," the trio declaims, evoking the smoldering vision of Watts aflame. "It sure looks to me like dem niggers ain't playing."

Twenty years after Watts, Gates told a reporter that if another such uprising occurred, "the Los Angeles Police Department would not allow it to go the way it did before. We would stop it the first night."[12] But during the first two days of the uprising, a constant refrain echoed through TV coverage: Where were the LAPD? All visual evidence showed that Gates's forces had apparently ceded the streets of South Central to its infuriated Black and Latino citizens. Firepower wasn't a problem: Gates had all the authority in the world to meet the rebellion with the massive militarized force he had deployed against the Black Panthers in 1969, against suspected suburban rock houses in 1985, and in the Operation Hammer gang sweeps. But he had also been in the media and political crosshairs for more than a year, starting with Mayor Tom Bradley calling for the chief's resignation weeks after the King footage went national, followed by the damning Christopher Commission report a few months later, which cast in sharp relief the legacy of racist brutality of Gates's tenure. Gates shrank from the opportunity to send his fearsome Metropolitan Division to South Central out of "his weariness of political combat and an unwillingness to be blamed for any police-caused incident," Lou Cannon believes.[13] As South Central erupted, Gates took off for a political fundraiser in Brentwood: fittingly, to speak against the passage of charter amendment F, a Christopher Commission recommendation that would dramatically increase civilian control over police departments. Gates later publicly regretted his decision to leave his post, a decision that Cannon suggests "would have led to a court-martial if the L.A.P.D. were a true military organization."[14] But there was significant suspicion across political lines that Gates's inaction was partially performative: if you don't want to respect the police, he was tacitly saying, knowing his days were numbered, then we'll stand down and show you what total disorder looks like. Either way, Gates's dereliction of duty lost him the support of white Los Angeles, and he retired on June 26, replaced by the Black veteran cop Willie Williams.

Nearly twenty-seven years after Watts, on the evening of April 29, a swarm of helicopters—belonging not to the police, as in *Boyz n the Hood*, but to the news media, redeployed from their usual work of filing traffic reports and tracking high-speed chases—hovered above the intersection of Florence and Normandie in South Central, mere blocks from the setting of *Boyz n the Hood* and the "Steady Mobbin'" video. Hundreds of Black locals had taken to the streets, and a few broke into a liquor store and made off with armloads of booze. Locals who saw their neighbors clearing out stores live on television, with not a cop in sight, left their sofas to join in. Meanwhile, a white truck driver named Reginald Denny was heading through the intersection on his way to drop off a delivery, unaware of the acquittal of Rodney King's assailants. As the helicopter cameras rolled, Denny was dragged from his cab and beaten unconscious by several Black men, live on television. One of them knocked Denny's body limp by throwing a slab of concrete at his head and then looked upward to the helicopter and flashed the sign of the Eight Tray Gangster Crips, like a hunter posing next to his bagged prey. Bloodied and near death, Denny lay unattended in the intersection for several minutes while other men spit on him, emptied his pockets, and threw a bottle at his body. After the cameras had moved on, he was rescued by a group of Black locals who sped to the scene after watching his beating on television. To reporters piecing together a narrative as they went, the Denny beating became a stomach-churning stand-in for the racialized retribution transpiring in South Central and a bit of journalistic "balance" for the King video. Two weeks later, Daryl Gates himself placed the handcuffs on one of Denny's assailants himself, with news cameras in tow. The following November, Denny forgave another of his assaulters on an episode of *The Phil Donahue Show*.

For most of the uprising, television journalists and citizen videographers seemed to dwarf the presence of law enforcement. The weeklong television spectacle of arson and looting cast local TV news reporters as war correspondents, filing reports in front of broken store windows while B-roll footage of burning buildings suggested that the City of Angels had descended into the lawless anarchy of a postapocalyptic action blockbuster. The memory of Latasha Harlins's death still potent, looters and arsonists specifically targeted Korean American businesses, but not without resistance. In one incident shown on live television, Korean Americans stalked a parking lot armed with pistols, while others took sniper positions on their roofs and engaged in a brief firefight with the young rebels seeking to burn them out. The nonstop media coverage suffused daytime talk shows as much as the evening news and CNN, turning the uprising into a national rebellion against racial injustice, triggering smaller iterations in Las Vegas, Denver, Buffalo, Toledo, Seattle, Chicago, and New York City. CNN aired a story on the young Black HBCU students in Atlanta who marched in solidarity and were violently confronted by police, and another on a group of "leftists" in Berlin who unfurled a banner in solidarity with Los Angeles during an anti-Nazi rally. Yet because the Los Angeles rebels had no formalized leadership or specific demands, the most visceral media imagery came to stand for itself. The dominant message of the media coverage, one study concluded, was that "most of the responsibility lay with the rioters because they were lawless, immoral, and greedy people."[15]

As the smoke cleared, a sharper picture of the rebellion started to emerge, courtesy of Los Angeles's networks of local, alternative, and citizen-activist journalists. They pieced together an on-the-ground time line of events, chronicled decades of LAPD malfeasance, and provided a zoomed-out perspective on the vast economic gulf between the city's white haves and Black and brown have-nots. In the *LA Weekly*, Marc Cooper and Greg Goldin offered a nuanced perspective on the alarming imagery:

> What looks to the television cameras like so many mounds of rubble is, in reality, a mosaic of anger over decades of L.A.P.D. brutality, of agony over a court system that sends a black man to jail for shooting a dog while freeing a Korean shopkeeper who shot a black teenager, of frustration over an economy that no longer provides a real living, of discontent with a welfare system that punishes. The growing heap being carted to the city dump contains the recognition by blacks, Latinos and disenfranchised whites that they are not merely discriminated against, they are abandoned, written off as "losers."[16]

The alternative press unpacked a reality that was invisible to the national news media: participants were setting fire to the buildings around them in full knowledge that it wasn't *their* property at all. As portrayed in *Boyz n the Hood* and on *Death Certificate* and *Apocalypse 91*, these businesses were owned not by friendly neighbors but by outside infiltrators who wanted only to exploit the Black community, not enrich it. And the job of the police, they knew, was to protect property rights before seeing to the needs of the citizens themselves. The 1992 rebellion, argued writers in the *LA Weekly*, the *Village Voice*, and numerous other regional publications, was less a cry for the creation of a better world than a firm rejection of the existing one. The violence that commandeered the world's attention for a week was nothing compared to the daily economic and legalistic violence that the state had been waging on Black Los Angeles for decades and that had been ignored by the news media until a massive counterattack rendered it newsworthy.

This perspective was bolstered by the *Source*'s coverage of the rebellion, which reflected the magazine's significant editorial growth over the prior two years into what its cover now proclaimed was "The Magazine of Hip-Hop Music, Culture and Politics." The *Source*'s August 1992 issue featured Oakland's Too $hort on the cover but devoted significant space to coverage of the uprising. "Chuck D's 1988 warning about the media still holds true today," read Chris Wilder's editorial. "Most anything reported about the Black community is coming from an outsider's perspective, which surely means there will be misunderstandings and that leads to misrepresentation."[17] *Source* editor James Bernard flew to South Central immediately after the verdict and filed a lengthy report on what he called "the hip-hop generation's first collective gasp." After Mayor Bradley lifted the curfew, officially ending the rebellion, Bernard took a ride through the city with some local filmmakers and gang members. "I was surprised about how carefully chosen the 'rioters'' targets were," he explained. One of his interlocutors called the looting and arson "surgical strikes." A Jordan Downs projects resident affirmed, "Oh, we knew what businesses we wanted out of the neighborhood." When Bernard noted that the "corporate monster" McDonald's was still standing, he was informed that "they hire a lot of Blacks from the community." A Comfort Inn was left untouched, Bernard was told, because the brand name had made an appearance in an *AmeriKKKa's Most Wanted* track. Bernard's interviewee said with a laugh, "Where else are the fellas gonna take their girls?" Bernard's tour of postrebellion LA led him to the conclusion, absorbed by hip-hop heads across the country, that "the 'riots' were really a very disciplined and spontaneous cry for economic empowerment."[18]

Though the *LA Times* did not reach the same conclusion as Bernard in the *Source*, the uprising did generate an internal reckoning for Los Angeles's paper of record. David Shaw, who had won the 1991 Pulitzer Prize for criticism for his investigation of the news media's coverage of a child molestation case, wrote a five-part series of columns, published in late May, that pinned much of the blame for the rebellion on journalistic malpractice. Titled "The Media and the LAPD: From Coziness to Conflict," Shaw's series scans the twentieth century and finds example after example of the news media acting as a PR machine for an often violent and crooked police department:

> It may be difficult to believe in this era of Rodney G. King and Bill Clinton, of home videos and CNN, of "60 Minutes" and supermarket tabloids, but in terms of muckraking journalism, the press was more lap dog than watchdog in this city in those days, and except for some routine coverage of the most notorious events, it largely ignored or whitewashed much of the crime and corruption—what was really happening behind the scenes—especially in the early years.[19]

Shaw rewinds to the dawn of Hollywood and the pulpy crime novels of Raymond Chandler to examine how Los Angeles was once portrayed as a corrupt, gangster-clotted town, which changed with LAPD chief Bill Parker's tenure. Shaw also delves into the overly friendly relationships between reporters and cops, who regarded one another as professional equals, each institution lending the other a necessary credibility. His biggest indictments came in the contemporary context, assailing the paper's coverage for essentially ignoring swathes of Black Los Angeles. "The *Times* has no bureau or regional section in either South Central Los Angeles or East Los Angeles," he wrote, adding that the paper had few minority reporters and no Black editors in high-level positions (the same went for all of LA's commercial television stations as well). "Editors and news directors who have not lived in such communities often find reports of routine police harassment and excessive force in those areas hard to believe," Shaw concluded.[20]

Daytime talk shows provided another national forum to come to terms with the reality of the rebellion. Phil Donahue convened a combative panel that included District Attorney Ira Reiner, the Reverend Al Sharpton, and Theodore Briseno (via satellite with his attorney), one of the four officers charged in King's beating. The episode's most dramatic moment came when a police spokesman superciliously insisted that it was "time for healing," prompting Sharpton to sharply retort that it was actually time for justice, a moment that resulted in the episode's longest applause break. While Oprah Winfrey shot the two uprising-based episodes of her show in LA, the tenor of her approach was less public affairs debate than New Age emotional therapy for middle-class suburbanites. "Why are Black people so angry?" she asked at the start of the first episode, during which she repeatedly expressed disappointment with the looters. One of her audience members pushed back:

> We come from the streets. We live in hell. We go through the trials and tribulations of all type of things. And when a situation happens like this and people want to get theirs, and they work hard, and they still can't get groceries, and they see the place burning up—what you gonna do?
>
> You gonna go out there and get the food for your family, cause you don't know if that place is going to be standing tomorrow.[21]

Winfrey was not moved. What was most important at this point, she countered, in an echo of the police spokesman on *Donahue*, was not political and economic justice but emotional recovery. "It has been a painful time for this city and for America," she concluded at the end of the second episode. "There's a time for healing. This is our prayer."

The reality rappers who had been chronicling the festering unease between Black citizens and police for years were finally being regarded as journalist-pundits, at least for the moment. "It should now be obvious to all that rappers are reporting real events and not just striking tough-guy poses," wrote Alan Light in *Rolling Stone*.[22] While the uprising was still happening, Ice-T called an *LA Times* reporter from his car phone while driving through South Central. "I'm not saying I told you so, but rappers have been reporting from the front for years. . . . Public Enemy, Ice Cube . . . we were all saying that you have a potentially explosive situation."[23] To *Rolling Stone*, he simply said, "My answer to what happened is 'Refer to album 3, track 5.'"[24] Cube himself questioned the media's framing. "First of all, I don't even call it a riot, I call it an uprising," he told the *LA Times*. "Unfortunately in this country, quiet protest really doesn't work. You can hold your signs. You can march. You can do all those things, but conditions aren't going to change."[25] The Latino rapper B-Real of Cypress Hill told John Leland at *Newsweek* that "we're journalists," citing the group's 1991 song "Pigs," which opened with the sampled voice of a police dispatcher, as the group's musical response to an LAPD officer pushing him onto a parked car. "We've been reporting this," agreed Tupac Shakur, a rising Oakland rapper whose debut album, *2Pacalypse Now*, had been released the previous November. "When you hear Ice Cube or Public Enemy, you know you're not alone. It's like being in Vietnam and seeing another soldier on the battlefield."[26]

The voices and images of reality rappers weren't equally welcomed on *all* cultural battlefields, however. The film *Looters*, for instance, was produced well in advance of the rebellion and scheduled for release in summer 1992, but from its name to its characters, story, and symbolism, it felt eerily like a parable of recent events. Directed by the action-film veteran Walter Hill, *Looters* chronicled the attempts of two white firefighters (Bill Paxton and William Sadler) to loot a cache of buried treasure in a burned-out husk of an East St. Louis building. The efforts of these out-of-towners are violently contested by local crime boss King James (Ice-T) and his consigliere, Savon (Ice Cube). To deepen the film's realism, Hill gave T and Cube free rein to adapt the screenplay to a more representative version of Black street vernacular and had one of King James's associates constantly chronicle everything with a handheld camcorder. Early in the film, Ice-T's King James blends the rapper's on-record punditry with the film's narrative, spoken into the camcorder: "See, the white man makes dope, right? Then he gives it to us. Then he wants to buy it from us, right? Then he puts us in jail when we sell it to him. It don't make no fuckin' sense. Only thing a man's got is his family and his pride. That's all he's got." Recalling that Pauline Kael had called Hill's 1979 cult classic *The Warriors* "visual rock," a *New Yorker* critic characterized the film as "visual rap."[27] But by then, it had been retitled *Trespass* and buried on a Christmas Day release, a concession by Universal Studios that the coincidences in Hill's plot and casting were a bit *too* real.

The May 29 issue of the *Shield*, the Dallas Police Association's monthly newsletter, contained a unique article. On page nine was an article titled "New Rap Song Encourages Killing Police Officers," written on a tip from a fellow officer, whose daughter had brought home the self-titled album from Ice-T's punk-metal side project, Body Count, which contained the track "Cop Killer." More a call to arms than an opinion piece, it read, in part, "I urge you to BOYCOTT any and all Time Warner products and movies until such time as they have recalled this tape."[28] Though the album had been released to little notice in March, and Body Count had performed the song multiple times at the previous year's Lollapalooza festival, it became the most controversial song in America when Texas's largest police union held a press conference on June 10 to decry it. On the track, T plays a character who explodes after a lifetime of harassment, spending about half the song shouting, "Fuck the police," and naming Daryl Gates, the LAPD, and Rodney King. Neither FBI letters, warning stickers, or obscenity lawsuits had worked to stop reality rap, so the police union threatened a boycott of Sire Records' parent company, Time-Warner.

Going after the liberal entertainment industry was the perfect election-year wedge issue, especially for Republican candidate George H. W. Bush, who used Dan Quayle—originally tapped to connect the lifelong moderate with the conservative Christian voting bloc—to assail rap music for the deep problems between Black Americans and the police. In a press statement, Quayle crowed that "Time Warner is making money—a lot of it—off a record that is suggesting it's alright to kill cops." Never one to back down from a challenge, Ice-T, who saw the album's sales skyrocket after calls for a boycott, responded by comparing his lyrics to America's foundational conflict: "Have they forgotten that Paul Revere became a Revolutionary War hero for warning everybody, 'The police are coming, the police are coming?'"[29] But the skirmish quickly exploded into the latest front-page controversy, pitting artistic freedom against claims of Black musical incitement. Along with rap fans, the artistic community, the American Civil Liberties Union, and the National Black Police Association, Ice-T's free speech cause—expertly cleaved from Ice-T's actual music—was supported by Gerald Levin, the president and co-CEO of Time-Warner, who published an op-ed in the *Wall Street Journal* titled "Why We Won't Withdraw 'Cop Killer.'"[30] But the public opposition to "Cop Killer" was rooted in a much more sensationalistic and attention-grabbing argument than arid First Amendment protections, allowing everyone from the 2 Live Crew nemesis Jack

Thompson to President Bush, LAPD chief Willie Williams, disgraced Iran-Contra participant Oliver North, and the National Rifle Association to castigate Time-Warner for effectively endorsing the murder of police officers. Outside of Southern California, the tumult over the song made Rodney King and the LA rebellion feel like distant memories.

A week after *Body Count* arrived in stores, Sister Souljah released her debut album, *360 Degrees of Power*, also to little notice. Much more an activist and orator than a rapper, Souljah had been convinced to record by Chuck D after he watched her speak. In May, during a press-cycle interview with the *Washington Post* reporter David Mills (of the earlier Professor Griff scandal) Souljah was asked to comment on the LA uprising. As in her powerful public oratory, Souljah unapologetically decried racial double standards:

> If black people kill black people every day, why not have a week and kill white people? You understand what I'm saying? In other words, white people, this government and that mayor were well aware of the fact that black people were dying every day in Los Angeles under gang violence. So if you're a gang member and you would normally be killing somebody, why not kill a white person? Do you think that somebody thinks that white people are better, or above dying, when they would kill their own kind?[31]

Of the same nationalist mindset as Chuck D and Ice Cube, Souljah had expressed a sentiment no different than Cube's "AmeriKKKa's Most Wanted": the white American power structure was fine to ignore Black criminality as long as it could be contained within Black communities. But in the heat of a presidential election, the quote provided the perfect platform for Democratic candidate Bill Clinton to speak to Black America out of both sides of his mouth. Despite tapping Tipper's husband, Al Gore, as his running mate, Clinton was not itching for a fight with the entertainment industry. Unlike Bush and Quayle, Clinton and Gore were directly courting the Black vote: a week before the "Cop Killer" press conference, Clinton wore dark sunglasses and took to Arsenio Hall's stage to play "Heartbreak Hotel" on his saxophone. But Clinton was also a centrist, seeking to signal to moderate white voters that he could stand up to powerful Black interest groups. With Sister Souljah, he found his opportunity. Clinton gave a campaign speech to Jesse Jackson's Rainbow Coalition on June 13, the day after Souljah herself had talked to the group. To a quietly astonished crowd, Clinton isolated a specific part of her *Washington Post* interview for rhetorical effect: "If black people kill black people every day, why not have a week and kill white people?" Clinton told the crowd, "If you took the words 'white' and 'black' and reversed them, you might think David Duke was giving that speech."[32] The next day, Souljah held her own press conference, unrepentantly claiming she was being "used as a vehicle, like Willie Horton and various other black victims of racism."[33] Chuck D had taught her how to fight fire with fire in the media, but unlike her mentor with the Griff debacle, Souljah was firmly on the right side of the argument.

A complete unknown on the national scene only a month earlier, Souljah appeared on the cover of *Newsweek* in June and was a subject, along with Ice-T, of John Leland's feature article, "Rap and Race." Citing the bootstrapped, self-sufficiency-themed nationalism of Public Enemy's *Apocalypse 91* and Ice Cube's *Death Certificate*, Leland noted that "one of the contradictions most often overlooked in rap is that it is a radical voice with an often conservative agenda."[34] Yet it was Leland's zeroing in on the core rationale for the explosion of media interest, apart from the election year, that provided the article's most potent claim: Black musicians had taken over popular culture without even pretending to cater to white tastes or politics. As the summer wound on, and hip-hop became the stand-in for substantive discussions on race and policing, the conservative attacks on "Cop Killer" increased. Souljah's *360 Degrees of Power* was incendiary, but her music and message were not going to cross over to white audiences. *Body Count's* punk/metal hybrid, though, "got inside suburbia a little deeper than a normal rap record would," in Ice-T's explanation.[35] On July 21, T appeared on *Arsenio* to a standing ovation and explained how rap lyrics work as performance: "With music, you got a lotta leeway. You rap in the first person, you sing in the first person. In 'Colors' I became a gang member, in 'New Jack Hustler' I play a drug dealer. I ain't none of them. You know? I'm a businessman." That summer, he took his anticop trolling to a new level, appearing on the cover of *Rolling Stone* in a police uniform: only the second rapper to make the magazine's cover since Run-DMC in 1986 (MC Hammer was the other). But T would soon learn that even though Gerald Levin characterized his music as "the CNN of the streets,"[36] it paled in comparison to police associations vowing prosecutions if an officer was killed anywhere the *Body Count* album was available. In July, conservative protesters picketed the corporation's annual shareholder meeting in Beverly Hills. As part of Time-Warner's music division, Ice-T's fight for artistic freedom was running the risk of affecting the financial bottom lines of the corporation's holdings in film, theme parks, and cable TV franchises. In a bizarre moment, the National Rifle Association spokesman Charlton Heston read some of the album's lyrics aloud at a press conference. Signaling that police officers had become an overburdened identity group, Heston compared *Body Count*'s anticop lyrics to homophobia and racism.

Time-Warner was cornered, and on July 28, Ice-T held a press conference to announce that he approved pulling "Cop Killer" from future editions of the *Body Count* album. It was a strange and unprecedented announcement, in light of T's status as one of the country's most prominent First Amendment advocates. Even odder was Ice-T himself taking personal responsibility for the action, out of concern for the safety of Warner Bros. and Sire staffers, who he claimed had received death threats from police officers. "The cops are in a criminal mode," he said.[37] Rap fans were gobsmacked that the rapper who had spent his career going directly after the mass-media powers that be would fold so quickly. The *Source*'s Reginald T. Dennis condensed the reaction into an apocalyptic prediction: "Mark July 28, 1992...as the beginning of the end of rap music." The future of rap would be grim, Dennis added, if conservative special-interest groups could pressure a massive corporation to censor themselves. "If Bush is re-elected this year, you can imagine the stance he will take on these issues," he warned. "If Clinton wins, we can look forward to having Tipper Gore as the Vice-President's wife." If Ice-T's next album was going to be as uncensored as the rapper had promised, Dennis worried, "the only place we will be able to hear it is in his living room."[38] The censors had won: they successfully eradicated a recording from commercial circulation and shifted the national discourse from postrebellion protest to a referendum on hip-hop incitement.

The effects of the month-and-a-half-long "Cop Killer" spectacle rippled outward quickly. The most prominent victim was the militant Oakland rapper Paris, whose second album, *Sleeping with the Enemy*,

was scheduled for release in July on Tommy Boy Records, another Warner subsidiary. Paris was a member of the Nation of Islam who had paid
tribute to the Black Panthers on his December 1990 debut, *The Devil
Made Me Do It*. But *Sleeping with the Enemy* went conceptually and politically beyond its predecessor, its combination of nationalistic fervor
and violent political skits as gripping as any Ice Cube or Public Enemy
album. The song "Bush Killa," a far more realistic assassination fantasy
than "Cop Killer," drew particular attention. The song opened with a
dramatization of President Bush's assassination, a scenario that was realistically photo-illustrated in the liner notes. The album was initially
slated for a summer release date, which was crucial if Paris was to in-
ject his chosen issues into the election discourse. In true Public Enemy
form, he released a flyer titled "Paris vs. George Bush: Whose Record
Is Scarier" to promote the "Bush Killa" single, detailing the president's
record on mass incarceration, unemployment, poverty, and decreasing
life expectancy in Black communities. His aim was clear, but in the wake
of "Cop Killer," Time-Warner wanted nothing to do with it and bought
out his contract. Paris used the money to self-release the album, but not
until the election had ended. *Sleeping with the Enemy* sold well, peaking
at no. 23 on the *Billboard* 200, and the *Los Angeles Times* called it "rivet-
ing melodrama," but postelection success was cold comfort. "I voted for
[Clinton]," Paris told a reporter. "But as far as I'm concerned, the government is guilty until proven innocent."[39]

After a summer of political spectacle, conversations about the uprising returned with the kickoff of the 1992 prime-time TV season, with
the premieres of *Doogie Howser, M.D.*, *L.A. Law*, *Knots Landing*, and
Beverly Hills, 90210 using the events of late April and early May as a dramatic backdrop. They were overshadowed by the sixth-season premiere
of the *Cosby Show* spin-off *A Different World*, however, which devoted
a two-part episode to the rebellion, based around Dwayne Wayne (Ka-
deem Hardison) and Whitley Gilbert (Jasmine Guy) recounting their
Los Angeles honeymoon to their Hillman College friends. Temporarily
separated, the newlyweds hear about the Rodney King verdict and experience the first moments of the unrest in its two most symbolic spaces:
Dwayne is pulled over in a rental car by two white police officers, while
Whitley is in an electronics store, with a wall of televisions in the background. In a state of shock, Whitley meets a woman named Ianta (Sister

Souljah in a cameo appearance) who tells her to "stop worrying about integrating and being accepted, and start thinking about building—for yourself, for our people, so that we can provide a future for our children." Three months after Bill Clinton turned her into a pariah, Souljah took her nationalist oratory to the stage of the most popular Black sitcom. The live studio audience broke into applause.

A few months later, it was Ice Cube's turn to hold forth on the rebellion and his own tumultuous life. Released in November, *The Predator* was not quite a *Death Certificate*–style concept album but was the fullest-yet realization of Cube's intertwined passions: the state of Black lives in America and his own mass-media notoriety. "We Had to Tear This Mothafucka Up" is Cube's dramatization of the uprising, opening with a smash cut: from a sample of Nashville mayor Ben West responding to violence at a 1961 sit-in ("Riots, melees, disturbances of the peace...cannot be permitted") to Tom Brokaw announcing the King verdict ("The jury found that they were all not guilty"). Cube then reels off a litany of grievances and imagined scenarios, from fantasies about murdering the officers to the racial economy of looting and arson ("Don't fuck with the Black-owned stores but hit the Foot Lockers"), while reminding everyone that he told them so on *Death Certificate*: "I told you it would happen and you heard it, read it / But all you could call me was anti-Semitic." *Billboard*'s anti–*Death Certificate* editorial earns a response in the chorus of the album's title track ("Motherfuck *Billboard* and the editor"), and LA County district attorney Ira Reiner, blamed for letting Rodney King's assailants get off, earns a shout-out as well. Cube rhymes "S-I-M-I Valley" with "KKK rally" and flips Laurence Powell's infamous mobile digital terminal message into a rallying call: "Gorillas, gorillas report to the mist." The VCR brain he debuted on *AmeriKKKa's Most Wanted* reappears on the album's three short interstitial segments: "I'm Scared" is a brief montage of Louis Farrakhan's 1990 *Donahue* appearance (Cube raps "Farrakhan for president" on the title track); "Integration" incorporates Malcolm X; and "Fuck 'Em" is a condensed interview that recaps his anti-Semitic, anti-Korean, and sexism accusations (each accuser gets his or her own "Fuck 'Em"). It ends with Cube pivoting back to Los Angeles's racial reckoning: "Anything you wanted to know about the riots was in the records before the riots. All you had to do was go to the Ice Cube library and pick a record." The last thing heard on the album, a seeming nod to Ice-T squeezed in after the final song, is a dramatization of a police murder.

Though less controversial than *Death Certificate*, *The Predator* returned to *AmeriKKKa's Most Wanted*'s vision of Cube as a Black vigilante speaking in the media's own language. He used the album's liner notes to focus his message, sarcastically thanking "America's cops for their systematic and brutal killings of brothers all over the country (most of their stories never made it to the camera)." Accordingly, *The Predator*'s most intelligent and persuasive moment is the album track "Who Got the Camera?," where Cube solidifies the role of citizen videography in the existential power struggle between police and Black men. In a post–Rodney King landscape, Cube's first instinct upon being pulled over and harassed is no longer to reach for a gun:

> If the crowd wasn't around, they would've shot me
> Tried to play me out like my name was Rodney
> Fuckin' police gettin' badder
> Cause if I had a camera, the shit wouldn't matter

As the cops are "tearing up [his] coupe, looking for the chronic," Cube shouts, "Goddamn, nobody got a Panasonic?" The images recorded by George Holliday's Handycam might not have made a difference in the Simi Valley courtroom, but Cube held out hope that pointing and shooting with a Sony was still a viable alternative to the same action with a Smith and Wesson. Cube's imagined retaliatory tactics rarely correspond with the nonviolent ideologies of Martin Luther King's civil rights movement. But on "Camera," he argued that the novel world of consumer videography might offer a productive update of King's marches and sit-ins, crafted as they were for the then-new medium of broadcast television. It might not have convicted Rodney King's assaulters, but the video camera might still usefully function as a weapon of representation.

The South Central filmmaker Matty McDaniel agreed. A key cog in the LA hip-hop scene, McDaniel had used his VHS camcorder to become what Big Daddy Kane later called "the west coast Walter Cronkite."[40] After the King verdict was announced, McDaniel headed to the streets of South Central and chronicled the rebellion, which he edited into a film titled *Birth of a Nation: 4*29*1992*. McDaniel's title, a nod toward

D. W. Griffith's epic and famously racist 1915 Civil War drama, neatly encapsulates the merger of Black nationalist rhetoric and the hard-core violence of reality rap. The opening text establishes the film's ideological aim: "The white dominated media portrayed this as a riot; just a group of lawless hoodlums looking for an excuse to burn and loot. The media was incorrect. Rodney King was a reality check. For the first time Bloods and Crips, Blacks and Mexicans joined together in one justified cause, rebellion! This was The Birth of a Nation." Instead of using documentary tropes to signify reality within rap music, McDaniel does the reverse, positioning hip-hop as the journalistic voice of young Black America. McDaniel's *Birth of a Nation* opens with a string of his own interview clips with Ice-T, N.W.A, KRS-One, Ice Cube, and Chuck D. He edits in a Bryant Gumbel interview from the *Today* show with Sheena Lester from the Black newspaper the *Los Angeles Sentinel*, who argued that Bush should be talking to the real Black leaders: "people like Ice Cube, KRS-One, Sister Souljah, James Bernard, people like that."

Dr. Dre wasn't one of Lester's Black leaders; he was much more an entrepreneur than a political figure. Having split with Eazy and Ruthless earlier that year, he was recording his first solo album during the rebellion. McDaniel had known Dre for years and stopped by the studio to play him some raw footage from the agitated Wednesday evening gathering at the South Central AME Church. While Florence and Normandie was erupting, and the church was packed with concerned locals, dozens of others were out on the sidewalk chanting, "Africans Unite!" and carrying signs opposing charter amendment F. Out of the vociferous crowd, a man wearing a Malcolm X hat and T-shirt cleared a path to McDaniel's camera to make a statement that merged nationalist fervor with gangsta attitude: "If you ain't down for the Africans here in the United States, period point-blank, if you ain't down for the ones that suffered in South Africa from apartheid...you need to step your punk ass to the side and let us brothers...us Africans, step in and start puttin' some foot in that ass!" Another of McDaniel's interviewees connected the verdict to the economic reality of South Central: "That's what they told us today, in other words: 'You still a slave.' No matter how much money you got, you still ain't shit." Dre incorporated those two clips into "The Day the Niggaz Took Over," the rebellion-themed track from his blockbuster December 1992 album *The Chronic*. The album commemorated the rise of a new archetype for Black popular culture, one that had little actual revolutionary politics but a surfeit of stylized Black anger. Four years earlier with N.W.A, Dre and Cube had thrust the word "nigga" into popular discourse, linking "their identity to the 'hood instead of simply to skin color," Robin D. G. Kelley writes, and "acknowledg[ing] the limitations of racial politics—black middle-class reformism as well as black nationalism."[41] Three years after that, while Cube was preaching Farrakhan's gospel, Dre, Ren, and Eazy solidified "nigga" as a lucrative form of rebellious lifestyle branding on *Niggaz4Life*. "The Day the Niggaz Took Over" is the cultural apex of the form, positioning the LA uprising not as the birth of a new nation but as the triumph of reality rap as a form of radical Black consumerism.

The second half of James Bernard's *Source* report from the rebellion focused on the hard work being done toward a truce between the Bloods and the Crips. Attempts at peace had fizzled out in 1980, 1984, and after the Run-DMC flare-up in 1986, but the gangs had signed an armistice on April 26, three days before the Rodney King verdict, brokered by college-educated Watts gang members, with help from NFL hall of famer Jim Brown and Louis Farrakhan, and with language sampled from the 1949 United Nations cease-fire agreement between Egypt and Israel. Bernard observed, "When gang members found themselves throwing bricks alongside their rivals, the oft-repeated question became its own answer: *why are we fighting each other?*" It wasn't anything close to a Farrakhanian nationalism, but it was a start. When the rebellion broke, "everything basically changed right then," a Crip named Li'l V told Bernard. "We knew we had to come together as one. We know that we're a strong nation."[42] A member of the United Negro Improvement Association, the nationalist organization started by Marcus Garvey in the mid-1910s, compared the moment to the post-Watts feeling of banding together for a bigger cause. "There was a lot of Black consciousness and the Black Panther Party came out of it. Same thing with the Crips and Bloods right now."[43] The final page of Bernard's story featured a sidebar with the gang members' plans to revitalize their communities: replace decrepit buildings with community centers and career-counseling facilities; funnel $700 million into the school system; provide low-interest loans to Black entrepreneurs; build new health-care facilities near Black neighborhoods; revamp policing by hiring officers who live in the communities they patrol; and, updating a Black Panther idea that sounded a lot like Ice Cube's "Who Got the Camera?," hire ex–gang members as "patrol buddies" who "will monitor all police activity armed with video cameras to fight potential abuses."[44]

The celebratory mood was registered by the Nation of Islam member and Ice Cube affiliate Kam in the 1993 single and video "Peace Treaty," which depicted former enemies holding barbecues and cruising untouched through one another's turf in tricked-out Impalas. In March 1993 came *Bangin' on Wax*, recorded by actual Bloods and Crips, who rerouted their street-level animosities into electro-funk rap songs designed to boom out of twelve-inch speakers in car trunks. For the first time since they had arrived on the national scene seven years earlier, the red- and blue-clad gang members were permitted to speak for themselves to a mass audience. But the postriot calm was captured most prominently by Dr. Dre's epochal November 1992 single "Nuthin' but a 'G' Thang," which had nothing to do with the Bloods and the Crips. Based on an interpolation of Leon Haywood's sinuous 1975 bedroom R&B jam "I Want'a Do Something Freaky to You" and a supple, keening sine-wave melody that Dre coaxed out of his Minimoog, " 'G' Thang" rebranded reality rap as a chilled-out postrebellion soundtrack. Like Ice Cube's "Steady Mobbin'," the " 'G' Thang" video was based around a single day in Black suburban Los Angeles, a far sight from the desaturated, dilapidated LA of "Straight Outta Compton" and with no reds or blues in sight. The police were no longer a rival gang but a distant danger, and in a symbolic rebuke to the post–Rodney King world of hypercautious Black motorists, Dre and his protégé, the twenty-year-old Long Beach Crip Snoop Doggy Dogg, peacefully cruise through the city in exorbitantly detailed lowriders. The video opens with Dre pulling up to Snoop's home to pick him up for a neighborhood picnic, walking through the front yard and winding through the home of an extended family starting its day. After a day of revelry, the crew caravan to a party at another suburban residence, fueled by forty-ounce bottles of malt liquor and copious amounts of the high-potency weed that gives *The Chronic* its title. As the sun rises, Dre drops Snoop back at home, where he drunkenly stumbles toward the front door.

Reality rap had gone fully suburban and had been rebranded as "G-funk." The video for "Let Me Ride," released in September 1993, was "the next episode" promised by Dre and Snoop in the "'G' Thang" chorus. It starts with Dre sitting on the couch and watching the game show parody skit "The $20 Sack Pyramid," before leaving to cruise around the city. Like "Steady Mobbin'" and "'G' Thang," the "Let Me Ride" video is a documentary of Black car culture in LA, prominently featuring local landmarks like the Crenshaw Car Wash and slowly panning across the Crenshaw and Slauson street signs, as if to establish that intersection as the new symbolic center of Black Los Angeles, replacing Florence and Normandie. Though violence bleeds into Dre's periphery, he drives right past it. "This is the kind of idyllic, Arcadian vision of inner-city Los Angeles that everybody wants to exist," Jonathan Gold wrote of the video in *Rolling Stone*.[45] The video even stages a truce between the two most prominent ex-N.W.A members when Ice Cube walks out of a women's restroom picking his newly grown Afro, looks at the camera, and says, "Damn right, it was a good day."

Cube was referencing the second single from *The Predator*, released in early 1993 as the first reality rap single expressly themed to the *absence* of death and violence. The track is built from the Isley Brothers' lush 1977 Quiet Storm staple "Footsteps in the Dark," and its music video opens on nearly the same note as "'G' Thang," with a tracking shot following a young girl into a ranch-style suburban home, through the interior hallways, to Cube, who, like Snoop, gets up from bed to start his day. "I dunno, but today seems kinda odd," he observes, as he moves through a vision of South Central that looks like a peaceful, dream-sequence vision of *Boyz n the Hood*'s constant fear. Though as in "'G' Thang," the action in "It Was a Good Day" takes place on a single day, calendrical specificity is far less important than condensing the postriot, early-truce feeling of community serenity and Black camaraderie. A dramatic shot of Bloods and Crips burying their comrades dissolves the gang members completely out of the frame, and Cube takes note that the omnipresent sound of the "helicopter lookin' for the murder" had been replaced in the skies over South Central by a congratulatory message on the side of a Goodyear Blimp. In his first national TV appearance four years earlier on *Yo! MTV Raps*, Cube told the country that "after people saw *Colors* they thought L.A.'s just all violence. That's not true." After "Steady Mobbin'," "Good Day" was his second successful attempt at a counternarrative. It would not be his last.

The Predator went multiplatinum and debuted at no. 1 on the *Billboard* chart, higher than *The Chronic*, which peaked at no. 3. Yet it was Dre's apolitical and sonically polished album that would become the cultural icon, an ascent symbolized by a few bars from "Let Me Ride": "No medallions, dreadlocks or Black fists / It's just that gangsta glare with gangsta raps / That gangsta shit makes us gangs of snaps." *The Chronic* heralded the rise of what Jeff Chang called "a guiltless, gentrified gangsta,"[46] a world of lowriders, copious numbers of voiceless "bitches," and thick plumes of weed smoke. Dre's primary on-record enemies were not cops or censors but his industry competition. *The Chronic*'s first seven minutes are its most fearsome, with Dre and Snoop settling scores with three rappers: Luther Campbell, whose 1992 song "Fakin' Like Gangsters" questioned Dre's authenticity; the Bronx rapper Tim Dog, whose "Fuck Compton" ignited an East-West turf war; and Dre's erstwhile group mate Eazy-E. Dre started recording *The Chronic* while extracting himself from his Ruthless contract, and the music video for "Fuck Wit Dre Day (And Everybody's Celebratin')" portrayed his former partner as an incompetent executive serving at the whim of a white boss. Eazy would soon retaliate with "Real Muthaphuckkin' G's," which painted Dre as a studio gangsta, dredging up his glammed-out pre-N.W.A past to assail his credibility. With verbal battles over personal authenticity slowly overtaking reality rappers' diatribes against racist authority, *The Chronic* shared much with MTV's summer 1992 entry into the reality TV landscape: *The Real World*.

Dre's new solo venture floated above the tentative peace on the streets of Compton and South Central, but the creation of its lavish soundscape was funded in part by a Blood affiliate. Four years before *The Chronic*, the LAPD, joined by the Drug Enforcement Administration and Mayor Tom Bradley, announced to the press that they had just dismantled a massive national cocaine ring run by the twenty-seven-year-old South Central native Michael Harris. On the streets of South Central, Harris was "Harry-O," a gregarious figure dubbed "the gang godfather" who invested his cocaine-dealing profits in a limousine dealership and a Beverly Hills hair salon and who could be found chatting up Watts gang members as often as red-carpet celebrities. In the August 1988 bust, agents seized three of Harris's luxury homes, five expensive cars, and a speedboat, claiming to have undone his operation, which extended as far east as Chicago, Detroit, and Shreveport, Louisiana. Yet a twenty-eight-to-life sentence in San Quentin did not end Harris's participation in the entertainment world: he financed the 1988 Broadway play *Checkmates* (starring a young Denzel Washington) to the tune of $770,000, while his wife served as the talent recruiter for his fledgling music label, Death Row Records. Two and a half years later, Harris's attorney, David Kenner, connected him with Suge Knight, the hulking, Blood-affiliated ex–defensive lineman, bouncer, and artist bodyguard who was forcing his way into the rap business with a label called Futureshock Records. It was Knight who had helped secure Dre's release from Ruthless earlier that year, by physically threatening Eazy and Jerry Heller, and now Dre and Knight were trying to launch a new label. With Kenner's assistance, they entered into an agreement with Harris, who contributed $1.5 million in start-up capital, to run Death Row. Dre's success with *The Chronic* helped Death Row secure a five-album deal with Interscope, the two-year-old Warner-distributed label run by industry maven Jimmy Iovine.

Dre had never affiliated with the Bloods or the Crips, but with Knight at Death Row, he had no choice. Truce or not, LA gang life was at the very center of the new label. While gang-affiliated rappers were often hesitant to speak too specifically about the life, Knight brandished his Blood connections proudly, wearing bold red in photos and using Blood slang, like calling Compton "Bompton." The division of labor was deeply problematic. Dre was Death Row's house producer, while Knight simultaneously ran Death Row's daily operations *and* served as the de facto manager for its artists, a conflict of interest that gave Knight an incredible amount of power to dictate not just creative decisions but the careers of Death Row's artists. Meanwhile, Dre's frequent legal run-ins had turned him into rap's latest tabloid figure. While the languid menace of G-funk was dominating radio and MTV, Dre was pleading not guilty to breaking the jaw of a local record producer, facing eighteen months in jail for a dustup with New Orleans police, and staring down a $20 million civil suit filed by Dee Barnes. The wild success of *The Chronic* and the rise of Death Row marked the end of a two-year crucible for reality rap that had certified its believability and commercial viability. Reality rap's truth claims had been validated by citizen-shot camcorder footage, its prescient warnings and simmering rage were widely credited with predicting the nation's largest incident of civil unrest in decades, and its commercial viability was confirmed by SoundScan. Ice-T and Ice Cube had become Hollywood stars playing variations on their album identities, and a South Central–raised "hip-hop director" was the youngest-ever Best Picture nominee. Reality rap had reached the summit of the entertainment industry largely on the rappers' own terms. It was time to wield that power.

CHAPTER 6

STOP BEING POLITE AND START GETTING REAL

▼

While studying at Rutgers University in the late 1980s, Kevin Powell became friends with Sister Souljah, then known as Lisa Williamson. "It was in her kitchen at her apartment on 141st Street and Convent in Harlem that Lisa first told me that Chuck D of Public Enemy...had asked her to become the first female member," Powell recalled. Powell and Williamson organized rallies, marches, and protests around the country. "We were creating what became known as 'hip-hop activism' without even realizing it," Powell wrote.[1] Neither of them were rappers, but their work directly intersected with rap. Williamson was a budding orator, and Powell was a poet and a critic. In the summer of 1990, the Public Enemy media assassin Harry Allen connected Powell with Danyel Smith, an editor at the *San Francisco Weekly*, and his writing career took off from there. Over the next few years, he landed bylines in the *Source*, *LA Weekly*, *Interview* magazine, and *Rolling Stone*, and he coedited a literary collection titled *In the Tradition: An Anthology of Young Black Writers*. Powell's status as one of the country's most promising and outspoken young Black writers brought him to the attention of an MTV producer, who asked him to submit an audition video for an upcoming documentary series titled *The Real World*.

A groundbreaking experiment in nonfiction entertainment, *The Real World* merged the everyday realism of documentary with the overwrought interpersonal drama of daytime soap opera. Cocreator

Mary-Ellis Bunim was an executive producer on *As the World Turns* and *Santa Barbara*, and her partner, Jonathan Murray, had used his University of Missouri journalism degree to work through the TV news ranks. Filtered through MTV's corporate mandate for original programming that appealed to its eighteen-to-twenty-four demographic, Bunim and Murray cast Powell, a female rapper (Boogie Down Productions affiliate Heather B.), two rock musicians, a model, an aspiring dancer, and a designer to live together for three months. MTV covered rent and food costs, freeing the septet to talk and argue, with their interactions shot and edited to reflect the fears, beliefs, and ambitions of young people on the precipice of adulthood. The thirteen-week series, one critic noted, "records its subjects like a documentary, looks like an extended Levi's 501 commercial, sounds like a music-video playlist and plays like a steamy, saucy afternoon soap."[2] Bunim and Murray freely admitted that *The Real World* was a contrivance, and as a line from the credits revealed, the "real" in the title meant not "authentic" but "dramatic" and "unscripted." The tagline could equally have described *Geraldo, Cops*, or reality rap: "Find out what happens when people stop being polite and start getting real."

At first, Powell thought the show would be a boon for his burgeoning career as a public speaker. "I remembered Sister Souljah always getting speech opportunities each time she appeared on television, especially national television," he recalled.[3] As savvy as Chuck D or Ice Cube about Black popular representation, however, Powell was firm regarding the performance of self he would *not* be giving. "I had already thought long and hard about the images of Black folks in popular culture," Powell recalled. "There was no way I was going to go on MTV shufflin' and jivin' and saying and doing things that would embarrass the Black race, or me."[4] All the show's first-season drama grew out of topical arguments between roommates, and most of Powell's camera time was devoted to his attempts to convince the white cast members that they were participating in a system permeated by infrastructural racism. This exploded in a late-season argument with Alabaman housemate Julie Oliver (cast as the naïve white southerner) during an episode shot in May 1992. Oliver had accused Powell of an incident of off-camera violent behavior, and the rest of the cast took her side, citing Powell's earlier emotional outbursts as evidence. On camera, the pair litigated their conflict in an argument that spilled onto the sidewalk in front of the Manhattan loft. When Powell asserted the role of race in Oliver's accusation, she exploded, "Get off the black/white thing! I'm sick of it!" Powell replied by citing recent events: "Look at Los Angeles!...How you gonna say 'get off the black/white thing' when that's the reality? Racism is everywhere, that's my point." Oliver replied, jabbing her finger in his face, "Because of people like *you*, Kevin!" Though he was unable to convince Oliver of his side, Powell's smile throughout the argument signaled that he nonetheless relished the opportunity to make his point. Back in the apartment, they shook hands and agreed to disagree.

More than any reality show before it, *The Real World* was a cultural phenomenon that made its cast instant stars: Powell remembers being mobbed at the MTV Video Music Awards more than some pop icons in attendance. Soon after shooting wrapped, MTV News capitalized on Powell's fame, casting him as the host of a special on postrebellion Los Angeles, with "We're All in the Same Gang" organizer Mike Concepcion and Ice-T as his on-site tour guides. Powell had also been in contact with the editors of the soon-to-be-launched *Vibe* magazine, pitched by Quincy Jones as the *Rolling Stone* of hip-hop. The *Source*, nearing one hundred thousand readers by mid-1992 and running ads from industry titans like Nike and Sega, had proven hip-hop's profitability,[5] and *Vibe*, with a $1 million investment from Time-Warner, wanted to be its up-market competitor. After a successful September 1992 test issue, with a print run of two hundred thousand and ads from Armani and Versace, the magazine's September 1993 debut featured Powell interviewing another heavily hyped newcomer, Snoop Doggy Dogg. After Snoop's star turn on *The Chronic*, his forthcoming debut, *Doggystyle*, was, the article's subheadline noted, the most anticipated debut in hip-hop history. Powell's story outlined Snoop's star image: he grew up in Crip-controlled Long Beach, hit the streets selling drugs immediately after graduating high school, and had been in and out of the penal system ever since. "Snoop, like too few black boys before him, has managed to survive and represents something real, something doable to ghetto youth trapped in inner cities across America," Powell wrote.[6]

Dr. Dre's most promising protégé, Snoop was reality rap's first native son, and his very real legal entanglements made him the personification of everything threatening and *real* about rap. "Snoop's lyrics are his reality," Powell wrote, noting that the rapper never traveled alone and always packed two guns.[7] Yet the issue went to print before Snoop's proximity to real-life gun violence transformed his life and career and conditioned the public's perception of rap music. On August 25, Snoop's bodyguard McKinley Lee shot and killed a man named Philip Woldemariam from the passenger seat of a vehicle that Snoop was driving. Woldemariam was allegedly a member of the Venice Shoreline Crips, and Snoop and his bodyguard claimed the killing was in self-defense. Three months later, Snoop's sudden shift to real-world tabloid notoriety was inextricable from the significant consumer enthusiasm for *Doggystyle*. *The Chronic* had made reality rap into a massive economic and cultural force, and now Snoop turning himself in to authorities on a murder charge appeared to legitimize the threat of violence that underscored the music, just as much as the Rodney King video had proven rappers' claims of police brutality two and a half years earlier. Either in spite of or because of his authentic connection to criminality, the twenty-two-year-old Snoop became rap's next big thing that autumn, his face adorning the covers of the *Source*, *Rolling Stone*, and *Newsweek*. On November 23, *Doggystyle* became the first album to debut at no. 1 on the *Billboard* album chart. Two and a half weeks later, Snoop appeared in front of Los Angeles County Superior Court judge Lance Ito and pleaded innocent to murder.

A few months earlier, Kevin Powell had traveled to Atlanta to report his second *Vibe* cover story on Tupac Shakur, who had an even longer rap sheet than Snoop and an unparalleled family lineage: his mother, stepfather, and multiple family friends were prominent Black Panthers. Yet when Powell met Shakur, it was the *Real World* star's reputation that preceded him. "You my man from that MTV show. I had your back, dog," Powell recounted Tupac saying in the profile that ran in *Vibe*'s February issue. "Yeah, he *is* an angry black man," wrote Powell, who clearly knew what it meant to perform an outsize caricature of outspoken Blackness for entertainment purposes. He described Shakur's music as "a cross between Public Enemy and N.W.A., between Black Power ideology and 'Fuck tha Police' realism," but the article focused far more on Shakur's growing list of nonmusical accomplishments and exploits.[8]

He was a budding movie star who had earned positive reviews for his performances in the Harlem crime drama *Juice* (directed by *Do the Right Thing* cinematographer Ernest Dickerson) and John Singleton's *Boyz n the Hood* follow-up, *Poetic Justice*. In his short time in the spotlight, however, Shakur had also become rap's most scandal-plagued figure, seemingly engineering run-ins with police when the cops themselves didn't instigate them. By the end of 1993, Shakur was involved in numerous high-profile lawsuits and had multiple charges pending against him across the country. More than Snoop, more than Eazy or Cube or Chuck or Ice-T, Tupac Shakur was the embodiment of hip-hop's headfirst dive into tabloid culture.

Snoop's and Shakur's rap personas were very different from one another, but the two shared a wealth of personal charisma and substantial claims to personal authenticity: the stuff of superstardom in any realm. Their emergence signaled that reality rap had itself become a massive industry, in part by congealing into a set of recognizable and marketable tropes (Kevin Powell was cast for *The Real World* because he fit an archetype), which also made it susceptible to parody. In early 1993, the reality rap satire that *In Living Color* had pioneered hit the big screen, courtesy of the indie *Fear of a Black Hat*, which debuted at the Sundance Film Festival in January, and *CB4*, which hit theaters in March, cowritten by *Saturday Night Live* cast member Chris Rock and Nelson George. To George, the timing was perfect:

> To do something like this, you have to have something that's really identifiable to make fun of . . . and the Jheri curls, the Dickies, the guns—that's the image that people think of when they think about rap now. That kind of rap is almost like wrestling—it's larger than life, it's boasting. So once you have something that also attracts so much fire, you can make fun not just of the thing itself, but the people who are shooting at it, too. You've got the right-wing people who hate it who are ripe for parody.[9]

It was more than the fashion and the controversy: like *This Is Spinal Tap* did for heavy metal, *Fear of a Black Hat* and *CB4* drew their humor from positioning gangsta rap as a comically overwrought pose easily exposed by documentary filmmakers. *Fear* was directed by the comedian Rusty Cundieff, who had appeared in Robert Townsend's *Hollywood Shuffle* and Spike Lee's *School Daze* and was inspired to create his film by the ridiculousness of the 2 Live Crew obscenity spectacle. His film's documentarian is sociology PhD student Nina Blackburn (Kasi Lemmons), who seeks to understand the broader forces that have made N.W.H (Niggaz With Hats) so popular and controversial. *Fear of a Black Hat* is less successful at that goal than it is at cleverly skewering reality rap controversy (a Cincinnati concert crowd pulls their *own* guns on the group) and the occasionally awkward fit between vulgarity and politics, as when the titular acronym from "Come Pet the P.U.S.S.Y." stands for "Political Unrest Stabilizes Society, Yes!" A clear fan of the culture, Cundieff shrewdly highlights the connections between video and violence. In one scene, Ice Cold (Cundieff) is pulled over by a gun-wielding security guard, and the incident is captured by a half-dozen amateur videographers and a courtroom sketch artist. In another, Tasty Taste (Larry B. Scott) proves as savvy as Ice Cube about the metaphorical similarities between an Uzi and an auto-focus camcorder. To use either, he says, "you just spray the area."

Fear of a Black Hat had some trouble finding a distributor because producers knew that the more star-studded *CB4* was being shopped around at the same time. Directed by Tamra Davis, whose credits to that point included the music videos for Young MC's "Bust a Move" and Tone Loc's "Wild Thing," *CB4* is loosely structured around documentarian A. White (Chris Elliott) following the titular superstar rap group led by Eazy-E look-alike MC Gusto (Rock), but it quickly turns into a series of flashbacks, tracing Gusto, born Albert Brown, back to a peaceful South Los Angeles suburb—in one scene, Brown watches Ice Cube navigate a similar-looking neighborhood in the "Steady Mobbin'" video. A good kid at heart, Gusto is repentant about building a career by stealing his gangsta identity from an incarcerated local criminal (Charlie Murphy) after a few other hip-hop personas failed to register with the public. His anxiety about the real Gusto's parole and revenge is compounded by a *Source* journalist (Theresa Randle) who threatens to expose the group as frauds and by the public vendetta of a white politician and moral entrepreneur (Phil Hartman) whose son loves CB4. The film's overarching message, however, is a positive one. From its faux Rap Hall of Fame opening credit sequence to a "King of Rock" rap-along mimicking the *Wayne's World* "Bohemian Rhapsody" lip-sync to the newly reunited group performing "Rapper's Delight" at the conclusion, *CB4* was the first major motion picture with a story, not just a soundtrack, rooted in a deep love for hip-hop culture. In its opening minutes, *CB4* features faux-interview cameos from several reality rap superstars gamely parodying their images. Ice Cube claims to have met Gusto at a barbecue, while Eazy-E tells the faux rapper to cut his Jheri curl. Flavor Flav calls them fake, and Ice-T worries that the group's intimidating realness is impinging on his own reality rap territory.

Yet while the first wave of reality rap superstars were willing to toy with their public images, Snoop's and Shakur's crimes did not fall within the realm of discourse or parody but involved real guns and actual criminal charges. They were the "niggaz" who had taken over, and a new round of media hype and interrogation came with them. The November 29 cover of *Newsweek* featured Snoop's smirking face accompanying an article titled "When Is Rap 2 Violent?" Now that gangsta rap had "found a pot of gold in selling images of Black-on-Black crime to mainstream America," wrote John Leland, what exactly *was* the relationship between "capital rhymes and capital crimes"?[10] To answer this question, Leland and some other reporters interviewed some Black high school kids, learning that although young people could easily distinguish between truth and fiction and could skip over the most offensive songs, a number of other groups—Black radio stations, Jesse Jackson's followers, the fan magazine *Rap Sheet*—were threatening boycotts of the music. That summer, the filmmaking twins who directed Shakur's earliest music videos released their first film, *Menace II Society*, which made *Boyz n the Hood* look tame and became inextricable from the tabloid morbidity and political ambivalence of reality rap's new phase. Nurtured by the interwoven networks of journalism and entertainment, reality rap stardom had matured. Powell had brought the Public Enemy–inspired "angry, educated Black man" to MTV, a performance of the self that made him a reality star, which in turn enabled him to craft the images of rap's new dangerous duo. Shakur and Snoop had no problems being "polite": the former charmed audiences as the sensitive-thug postal clerk Lucky in

Poetic Justice, while the latter reenacted the *Home Alone* scream in the "Gin and Juice" video. Their problems emerged when they got too real.

Released in the same furious autumn as Ice Cube's *Death Certificate* and Public Enemy's *Apocalypse 91*, Tupac Shakur's 1991 debut *2Pacalypse Now* was unsparing toward an American power structure designed to neutralize young Black men. On "Trapped," Shakur depicts Black neighborhoods as police hunting grounds, where he "can barely walk the city streets / Without a cop stopping me, searching me, then asking my identity." When his character finally explodes at the end of the song, it does not feel like random violence but the predictable result of living under prison-style surveillance. Like Cube on "A Bird in the Hand," Shakur revealed the ruthless pragmatism created by structural oppression; his gift for burrowing deep into the tortured psyche of a young Black man was equaled that year only by the Geto Boys' elegiac hit "Mind Playing Tricks on Me." The album's most harrowing track is "Brenda's Got a Baby," a soul-rap elegy based on a story Shakur read in a New York tabloid about a twelve-year-old who gives birth to a rapist's child. The music video, shot by the twenty-year-old twins Albert and Allen Hughes, opens with the disclaimer "Based on a True Story" and intercuts Shakur's performance with graphic dramatizations that recalled the sordid aesthetics of *A Current Affair* and *America's Most Wanted*: Brenda giving birth in a public restroom, dropping the child into a dumpster, and resorting to prostitution to make ends meet. Shakur's emotional crescendo is phrased like a tabloid headline: "Prostitute Found Slain." A rap single had never struck such a balance between lurid subject matter and believable empathy, and it registered broadly, peaking at no. 3 on *Billboard*'s Hot Rap Singles chart in May 1992 and airing in high rotation on *Yo! MTV Raps* and BET's *Rap City*. Though "Brenda" jump-started Shakur's solo career, it was an album track, "Soulja's Story," that would prove the most consequential. Shakur begins the song with a mordant spoken-word editorial:

> They cuttin' off welfare
> They think crime is rising now
> You got whites killing Blacks
> Cops killing Blacks, and Blacks killing Blacks

Shit just gonna get worse
They just gonna become souljas

With a docudrama's sense of stagecraft, that introduction previewed a two-part performance, with Shakur playing two roles. In the first verse, he is a street-educated hardhead named Soulja who gets locked up; in the second, Shakur plays Soulja's younger brother, whose lack of alternatives leaves him no choice but to follow in his sibling's criminal footsteps.

Written when Shakur was only twenty, "Soulja" is a preternaturally well-crafted cautionary tale, but the rapper had no control over its subsequent redefinitions. On April 11, 1992, while the trial of Rodney King's Los Angeles Police Department assailants was dominating the national news, nineteen-year-old Ronald Ray Howard was driving a stolen Chevy Blazer down Highway 59, about two hours southwest of Houston, when Texas Department of Public Safety trooper Bill Davidson pulled him over for a missing headlight. Howard, who was on probation for car theft, shot Davidson in the neck with a 9 mm pistol that his mother had bought him at a pawn shop a week earlier, and he was caught later that night after crashing the truck. Davidson died several days later.

The case was strictly local until August, in the wake of the national referendum on Ice-T and Body Count's "Cop Killer"—a spectacle instigated by Texas cops. Knowing that his client's murder charge was an open-and-shut case, Howard's lawyer sought to exploit the antirap election-year climate to earn his client a life sentence instead of the death penalty. As it happened, authorities had recovered some rap tapes from Howard's car, and *2Pacalypse Now*, released by Interscope, which was owned by Time-Warner, was among them. Howard's defense team transcribed a few lines from the first verse of "Soulja's Story":

Only fifteen and got problems
Cops on my tail, so I bail 'til I dodge 'em
They finally pull me over and I laugh
"Remember Rodney King?" and I blast on his punk ass

What fans and critics heard as the terrifying actions of a directionless young Black man hounded by police, Davidson's attorney described as "pages out of a cop-killing manual.... [W]ithout the music riling him up, I do not think that this incident would have occurred."[11] While Texas law enforcement spokesman Ron DeLord addressed Time-Warner with the same language as Tipper Gore and Nick Navarro—"If it's illegal to produce physical pollution, it ought to be illegal to produce mental pollution"[12]—Davidson's widow filed a civil suit against the company for gross negligence in inciting imminent lawless action. She was supported by the Freedom Alliance, a group put together by disgraced Iran-Contra participant and ex-general Oliver North, which had organized the "Cop Killer" boycott a month or so earlier. Vice President Dan Quayle piled on: "There is absolutely no reason for a record like this to be published by a responsible corporation. Today I am suggesting that the Time-Warner subsidiary Interscope Records withdraw this record. It has no place in our society."[13]

Though Shakur was a relative newcomer to the entertainment business, he was no stranger to fighting back against law enforcement, having been born twenty-two years earlier into a prominent lineage of Black political rebellion. When she was pregnant with Tupac, Afeni Shakur stood trial as a member of the so-called Panther Twenty-One, a group of Harlem-based Black Panthers accused of conspiring to blow up several New York department stores. When Tupac was eight, his "aunt" JoAnne Chesimard (later Assata Shakur) escaped from the prison where she was serving a sentence for her role in the death of a New Jersey state trooper, eventually finding political asylum in Cuba. A few years later, when Tupac was studying acting at the Baltimore School for the Arts, federal agents visited him to ask if he had recently seen his Panther stepfather, Mutulu Shakur, whose robbery of a Brink's truck landed him on the FBI's Ten Most Wanted Fugitives list (he was captured in 1986). The year that Chuck D name-checked Assata on Public Enemy's breakthrough single, "Rebel without a Pause" ("Recorded and ordered, supporter of Chesimard"), Tupac moved to Marin City, California, to live with Linda Pratt, the wife of Geronimo Pratt, a Black Panther arrested in 1972 on dubious murder charges (his conviction was vacated in 1997). After scoring a gig as a roadie for Bay Area pop-rap superstars Digital Underground through a connection at a local poetry group, Tupac's undeniable talent soon moved him toward center stage. Around the time he signed a record deal with Interscope, he scored a leading role in *Juice*, released in January 1992.

Dickerson cast Shakur as Bishop, the most hotheaded and ambitious of a group of Harlem friends who turn to crime in an attempt to garner a small amount of power on the streets. In a pivotal scene, the crew watches the 1949 gangster film *White Heat* on TV. While the rest of the group comes in and out of attention, Bishop focuses intensely on the film's fiery conclusion, when, cornered by police, the ruthless criminal Cody Jarrett (James Cagney) fires his gun into a gas storage tank, incinerating himself in a huge, dramatic explosion. Bishop is mesmerized: "If you gotta go out, *that's* how you go out. That motherfucker took his destiny in his own hands." As Bishop is speaking, a live report comes on the news behind him. Blizzard, a man they all know from the neighborhood, was killed in a shoot-out with police after attempting to rob a bar earlier that day. Bishop and his friends had seen the man just before the stickup but had balked at Blizzard's offer to participate. To the rest of the crew, this was cause for relief. For Bishop, it was a sign that they were soft and were not prepared to take their destiny in their own hands.

Bishop's revelation in *Juice* was the perfect introduction to Shakur's single-minded goal as a star: death as an outlaw was better than life as a nobody. Where his inspirations Ice-T, Ice Cube, and Chuck D drew firm distinctions around their on- and off-record personas, Shakur sought to merge his. Allen Hughes remembers him as a funny and charming presence on the sets of his early music videos but claims that Shakur "was never the same" after he saw himself on-screen as Bishop.[14] After *Juice*, Shakur moved from Oakland to Los Angeles and started affiliating with gang members, immersing himself in street culture like a method actor preparing for a role or a reporter gathering material for a story. "He could be with this poet, this pimp, this thug—he could suck everything from each of them and that would be part of him," one friend said.[15] When the 1992 uprising exploded, Shakur was shooting *Poetic Justice* on location in LA and immediately hopped in a car and headed straight for the heart of the action. As another friend recalled, Shakur headed to a record store that was being looted and gleefully signed stolen copies of *2Pacalypse Now* in the parking lot. This was around the time he got "THUG LIFE" tattooed across his stomach, which he said stood for "The Hate U Give Little Infants Fucks Everyone." Like the Black street kids recruited and radicalized by the Black Panthers, "thug" was equivalent in Shakur's universe to the righteous street "soulja" who did what he had to do to survive. Like his peers, Shakur was no fan of "gangsta," and his efforts to create his own parallel brand revealed his understanding of the modern publicity system—and his awareness that "thug" was bound to tweak bourgeois pieties.

The promotional cycle for Shakur's second album, *Strictly 4 My N.I.G.G.A.Z.* . ., released in February 1993, was dominated by the rapper picking fights with anyone who crossed him in the slightest. In March, he was arrested for assault at an *In Living Color* taping after attacking a limousine driver who asked Shakur and his friends to stop smoking marijuana in his car. That same month, after seeing an interview with the Hughes brothers on MTV in which they claimed to have fired him from their forthcoming film *Menace II Society*, Shakur brought a group of Crips to confront the brothers on the set of the video shoot for Spice 1's "Trigga Gots No Heart," the *Menace* soundtrack's lead single. Days later, Shakur gleefully incriminated himself on *Yo! MTV Raps*, while Ed Lover and Dr. Dre tried in vain to stop him. In April, Shakur attacked a fellow rapper with a bat during a Lansing, Michigan, concert (an act for which he would later serve ten days in jail). That October, while in Atlanta to play a concert at a college, Shakur confronted two white men who he said were harassing a Black man. Guns were drawn and shots were fired from both sides; Shakur was unscathed, but he hit one of the men in the abdomen and the other in the buttocks. Charged with two counts of aggravated assault, Shakur was cleared when it was revealed that the two men were intoxicated off-duty police officers who had stolen their weapons from a police evidence locker. Reminiscent of the shoot-out with San Francisco cops that had turned Huey Newton into a Black folk hero in his own time, Shakur had become a secular deity to rap fans and public enemy number one to law enforcement. In 1993, Shakur was mapping a new star territory for rappers as he went: one of the most famous musicians in the country, with a number one album, a hit single ("I Get Around"), and a popular film in theaters, Shakur was simultaneously conducting a miniature crime spree in full public view. As *Rolling Stone* put it that fall, Shakur was known "less for the quality of his music than the controversy it has evoked."[16] A feature profile in the *Source* arrived at a more chilling conclusion: "There are only two places for Black men like Tupac. Jail and Heaven. He's already been to jail."[17]

Introducing his June interview with Shakur, Arsenio Hall said there were "two Tupacs." Actually, there were four: the strident revolutionary, the spirited hedonist, the ally to women, and the brooding poet in deep emotional conflict with his own stardom. All four are in clear evidence on *Strictly 4 My N.I.G.G.A.Z.* . . The single "I Get Around" portrayed Shakur as a jubilant horndog, chasing bikini-clad women around a swimming pool. The single hit no. 11 on the *Billboard* Hot 100 and made him a star. That October came the tonal opposite, "Keep Ya Head Up," which advocated for female self-empowerment and sampled the Five Stairsteps' soul classic "O-o-h Child," which Shakur had first heard on the *Boyz n the Hood* soundtrack.[18] The album's first single, "Holler if Ya Hear Me," was Pac as Chuck D, issuing a siren-laden call to action: "This ain't just a rap song, a Black song / Tellin' all my brothers, get they strap on." On the unapologetic "Soulja's Revenge," Shakur looped the "I remember Rodney King" line from the instantly notorious *2Pacalypse Now* track and concluded the song with the mantra, "Can't find peace on the streets / 'Til the niggas get a piece / Fuck police."

Strictly's most compelling moments found Shakur in the middle of his lothario and rebel extremes, lamenting his celebrity and settling scores publicly. On "Soulja's Revenge," he hits back at the vice president ("What the fuck does Quayle know / What young Black males need?") and later follows Quayle's sampled remark that *2Pacalypse* "has no place in our society" with a snippet from one of his own interviews: "I was raised in this society, so there's no way you can expect me to be a healthy person." On the album's ruminative title track, he admits that "life as a celebrity ain't everything they make it" and confesses, "I'm not violent, I'm petrified and nervous." In the despondent R&B-flavored interlude "Something 2 Die For," Shakur expresses remorse for the accidental death of six-year-old Qa'id Walker, the child killed by the stray bullet at the Marin City festival in 1992: "Young Qa'id, remember that name / Cause all you motherfuckers will go to your grave with that name on your brain / Cause jealousy and recklessness is not something to die for." That last bar demonstrates Shakur's mindset clearly: even when mourning the loss of a six-year-old, he took time out to note that Walker's death was caused not by a cruel twist of fate but by haters who envied the rapper's fame.

His increasing paranoia surfaces in "Point the Finga," Shakur's most direct condemnation of life in the tabloid spotlight:

> As far as jealousy, bein' a celebrity
> No matter who committed the crime, they all yell at me . . .
> Every day I read the paper there's another lie
> They show my picture for the crimes of another guy.

The other guy was Ronald Ray Howard, and during the sentencing phase of his trial, Howard's lawyer tried to prove that Shakur's music had brainwashed his client, playing rap music for two straight days in the courtroom—2Pac, N.W.A, Houston's Geto Boys and their Rap-A-Lot signee, Ganksta N-I-P—on the assumption that simply hearing the music would convince the jury of its inherent danger. Howard's reality on the night of the killing, his attorney argued, had been transformed into a violent Hollywood film, with *2Pacalypse* as the soundtrack: "The music is the background. It's kind of like a movie, and he's the movie. He hears the Uzis and the machine guns."[19] The jury took a different view of rap's social effects and sentenced Howard to death. "Music brings about different kinds of moods. We discussed this in-depth," a juror explained. "But a person is responsible for their own actions. . . . A lot of different things can affect people."[20]

During the preproduction phase of *Menace II Society*, Albert and Allen Hughes cast Shakur as Sharif, the observant Muslim continually trying to get his crime-obsessed friends to walk a straighter path. Having angled for the meatier role of the dead-eyed killer O-Dog, which went to teen-age TV actor Larenz Tate, Shakur didn't make it past an acrimonious table read, during which he stormed off the set, never to return. Though Allen Hughes would later claim that Shakur's star presence would have "overwhelmed" the film's sense of realism,[21] it was also true that the inspiration for O-Dog seemed to be Shakur himself. Early in the film, O-Dog is introduced via voice-over as "America's nightmare: young, Black, and didn't give a fuck"—those last four words a variation on a key Bishop line from *Juice* and a line from a *2Pacalypse Now* track. Even more than John Singleton for *Boyz n the Hood*, the Hughes brothers drew from the deep bench of California reality rappers to cast their film. The platinum-selling Oakland pimp-rapper Too $hort played the minor role of Lew-Loc, a year after the Hugheses shot the black-and-white video for his *Shorty the Pimp* single "I Want to Be Free (That's the Truth)." Echoing their treatment for "Brenda's Got a Baby," the Hugheses crafted "I Want to Be Free" as a faux documentary, segueing from a brief street interview with $hort into slow-motion, black-and-white recreations of police harassing Black motorists around Oakland.

The Hughes brothers cast MC Eiht as the gregarious elder A-Wax, an apt choice, because few rappers had as firm a grasp on the aesthetics of reality rap as Eiht's Compton's Most Wanted. The group's 1992 video for "Hood Took Me Under" was not directed by the Hughes brothers, but it had all the hallmarks of their realist touch: it opened with a disclaimer that "the video you are about to view contains frank discussions by street gang members about gang life," intercut performance clips with crime reenactments, and, most strikingly, featured a focus group of actual gang members recounting the stark realities of street life. "Yeah, you know when you go to get your points back," one gang member tells the camera, "when you go to even the score up, you can't worry about who out there with him, his momma, his daddy, his kids. It's on, it's just on right there on the spot." From that quote, which could effectively summarize the dramatic final scene of *Menace II Society*, the video cuts to a mocked-up wanted poster of Eiht, while an on-screen text graphic proclaims, "Gang warfare is the number one cause of death for black youth age 13–25." Compton's Most Wanted were not nearly as famous as their reality rap peers, but the video for "Hood Took Me Under" was a perfect fusion of documentary, dramatization, and rap stardom.

Menace II Society draws a direct historical line from Watts in 1965 to the gang-dominated reality of 1993. The film opens with a brief montage of TV clips from the uprising, then jumps to the late 1970s, when, in voice-over, the lead character of Caine laments, "When the riots stopped, the drugs started." After young Caine watches his father (Samuel L. Jackson) shoot and kill a man who insulted him during a card game, the action jumps to the present day, with the Hughes brothers appropriately introducing modern Watts through a helicopter-mounted camera: the gaze of the police. The film is told through the experiences of Caine, a character played by a relative unknown, South Central native Tyrin Turner. Though he had a minor part in the 1992 LA cop film *Deep*

Cover, Turner's most relevant pre-*Menace* experience was his role as Charlie Green, the reluctant teenage Crip in the July 15, 1990, episode of *America's Most Wanted* that featured the Sedrick Scott case. His *Menace* character, Caine, is a far more complex figure than Charlie, but in both roles, Turner plays a young Black man lured toward violent street crime by a charismatic figure. *Menace* itself is excessively stylized, with Caine's voice-over narration pairing with the Hugheses' hyperdramatic lighting and constantly roving camera to create a sensationalistic aesthetic halfway between an *America's Most Wanted* reenactment and a rap video. Where *Wanted* exploited Reaganist law-and-order anxieties that malevolent forces were threatening the sanctity of the suburbs and required constant vigilance, *Menace* casts Watts as a drug-and-crime-glutted dystopia, where Black enemies from the block over could attack at any time.

Unlike *Boyz n the Hood*, there is no redemptive character like Tre or Furious Styles in *Menace*. "*Boyz N the Hood* got made cuz it was 100 percent street with a sympathetic character," Albert Hughes told the *Source*. "You can't tell no Black story without one."[22] Embracing a more gangsta take on John Singleton's "hip-hop director" claim, the Hughes brothers started a beef with their Black filmmaking peers in the press, claiming that Spike Lee needed to go to "ending school" and that Matty Rich's 1991 indie *Straight Out of Brooklyn* was "the worst piece of shit [Allen had] ever seen."[23] According to the brothers, Singleton started sniping at them in the press after learning they weren't from the hood but had grown up in mostly white Pomona, and his dislike only ramped up after their falling out with Singleton's friend Shakur. While the Hughes brothers rightfully despised being compared only to other Black directors, the fact that it was even possible to do so was an unimaginable reality even five years earlier. And Singleton's example gave Albert and Allen a benchmark to exceed, anyway: in early interviews, the pair claimed that *Menace* was going to make *Boyz* look like *Mary Poppins*.

Like reality rappers and *America's Most Wanted* reenactment producers, the Hugheses obsessed over the verisimilitude of their violence. Their influences were white filmmakers—Martin Scorsese's *Goodfellas* and Quentin Tarantino's *Reservoir Dogs*—who were granted the latitude to show extremely realistic torture and killing without worrying about creating empathy with an audience. "One thing we knew about violence . . . is that it's never like in the movies," Allen said. Instead of the dramatic heroism of action films, he explained, real-life violence is "short and sporadic and when it's done there's usually someone on the ground pissing himself."[24] This fixation comes full flower in *Menace*'s final scene, as visually hideous as it is narratively cruel. Caine has decided to move with his girlfriend, Ronnie (Jada Pinkett), to Atlanta, and Sharif and O-Dog are helping them pack their moving van. Then, out of nowhere, Caine's adversary drives by and sprays the front yard with semiautomatic gunfire, murdering Sharif and Caine, who dove to protect Ronnie's toddler, who was innocently pedaling down the sidewalk on his Big Wheel. The brief shot of an overturned, broken child's toy tumbling into the frame was a sensationalistic cousin of the empty playground swing rocking back and forth in *America's Most Wanted*'s opening credit sequence. The Hughes brothers aren't finished, though: they end the film by slowly zooming in on Caine's face during the agonizing final seconds of his life, as he graphically contorts in pain while spitting up a foamy combination of blood and saliva: an R-rated version of Charlie Green's Wichita warehouse torture from three years earlier, but without offering viewers the option of helping to find the killer.

Seconds later, Caine's voice-over—revealed to have been posthumous for the entire film—sums it up matter-of-factly: "It was funny like that in the hood sometimes. I mean, you never knew what was gonna happen, or when. . . . My grandpa asked me one time if I care whether I live or die. Yeah, I do. Now, it's too late." There is no full-screen message tying the film to the political present, as in *New Jack City* or *Boyz n the Hood*, and *Menace*'s ending is a direct rebuke to the conclusion of *Boyz*, which ends with Tre and Brandi escaping to Atlanta to attend two prestigious HBCUs. The Hughes brothers made no pretense toward positivity: "If you hate blacks, this movie will make you hate them more," Allen said at the 1992 Cannes Film Festival.[25] Their over-the-top approach and political ambivalence earned them fans across the ideological spectrum, including a tempered rave from George Will, who agreed with the Hugheses' description of *Menace* as an *anti*-violent movie: "I wish for *Menace* a huge audience of young inner-city males who need to see violence drained of all traits or consequences that could make it charismatic," he wrote.[26] The *New York* magazine critic David Denby, who four years earlier had predicted that the conclusion of *Do the Right Thing* would trigger Black riots, raved about the far more violent *Menace*, calling it "the most striking directorial debut in the history of black cinema."[27] Noting the "almost documentary manner" of the Hughes brothers' directorial touch, Henry Louis Gates Jr. asserted that "you don't know whether you're watching a nightmare or the nightly news."[28]

Or a convenience-store surveillance video. In *Menace*'s vicious opening sequence, Caine and O-Dog are profiled by the Korean American owners of a local convenience store. Their frustration at being followed around the store comes to a head when the proprietor mutters, "I feel sorry for your mother," as O-Dog turns to leave. Infuriated, O-Dog shoots him in the head at point-blank range, a morbid spin on Ice Cube's sinister "Black Korea" threats and a grotesque bit of cinematic payback for Latasha Harlins's murder. The sequence concludes with O-Dog clearing out the cash register after retrieving the most important bit of loot: the incriminating surveillance tape. For the rest of the film, that VHS tape functions as two types of evidence: legal proof of O-Dog's double murder and visual confirmation of his street authenticity. Committing a random act of murder is one thing, but rewatching it on television, over and over again, makes O-Dog feel like a hood celebrity. Though his friends warn him to pipe down, he screens the tape for groups of friends, jokes that he's going to start selling copies for $59.95, and brags to A-Wax that "I'm larger than that nigga Steven Seagal. I'm gonna be a big-ass movie star off that shit." Though the police hound O-Dog and Caine throughout the film, Caine is confident that "without the tape, they ha[ve] nothing." The same could be said for the tape's role in creating O-Dog's own credibility to *Menace* viewers. Gates argues that O-Dog's rewatching of the "film within the film...ultimately implicates us, the audience," who, after all, are asking the Hughes brothers to provide the same kind of violent authentication for O-Dog's character.[29] The gory killing and its videotaped proof were the latest hyperreal chapter in the ongoing multimedia saga based around the undeniable entertainment value of mediated Black criminality.

While reporting a profile of Snoop Doggy Dogg for the *Source*, dream hampton was being driven with the rapper through the Baldwin Hills neighborhood of Los Angeles, otherwise known as the Blood-controlled "Jungle" that John Singleton had been forced to abandon for Ice Cube's safety during the *Boyz n the Hood* shoot:

> At a stop sign a young brotha waiting for a bus recognized Snoop, a Long Beach Crip, and tied his red bandanna over his face. He pulled out a *.22* and pointed it at Snoop Doggy Dogg, one of the most anticipated rap artists in hip-hop history. Dre's car swerved slightly. Snoop told the Cross Colours rep who was driving his car to "just keep on driving." He sang it in his laid back, distinctive LA twang, *nuthin' but a G thang, baby*. He pulled out his two .380s, uncocked both of them and stared at the Blood. The Blood kept his shit up until Snoop's car and his .380s were around the bend.

The next day, Snoop regaled his Death Row associates with the story. "He ain't want none," he told them with a laugh. Indeed, a key part of Snoop's image from the moment he surfaced as a star was his negotiation of the very blurry line between performative and actual violence, especially when actual gang members were constantly throwing up sets while he was on set. "The other day we were in Compton shooting this short film with Dre," he told hampton. "I wasn't even thinking. I show up to this mothafucka... with a blue comb in my hair, blue khakis, blue sneakers, blue mothafuckin' shoe laces!" They were in Blood territory. "They're strapped. They got bats and they're like whazzup, Blood? Y'all gotta leave." The Bloods left without incident, but the larger lesson of the story was Snoop's self-consciousness about telling it. "I don't know if you should write that I'm a Crip, cuz then lil' niggas'll think it's cool," he told hampton.[30]

Unlike Shakur, Snoop came to gang life organically. Born in 1971, he grew up in Long Beach with an absent biological father and a strict mother, and though his childhood was happy, he recalls everything coming to a halt in 1987. "I was too old to be a youngblood anymore, and too young to be able to take charge of my game," he remembered. "It was as if a switch got turned off... or maybe on."[31] Soon, the lanky, soft-voiced young man who sang in his church choir and starred on the Long Beach Polytechnic High School basketball team fell in with the Rollin 20s

Crips, before moving on to the more violent Insane Crips. By 1988, Snoop was making his living on the streets and, in the wake of Ice-T and N.W.A, trying to record a rap demo. He did so with some friends: the producer Warren Griffin, a.k.a. Warren G, who happened to be Dr. Dre's half brother; and the rapper and singer Nathaniel Hale, a.k.a. Nate Dogg. The trio called themselves 213, after their area code, and sent their tape to Dre, who passed. Snoop was still making his living selling drugs on corners, and one fateful afternoon he was caught with a handful of vials and charged with intent to distribute. He pleaded down to simple possession and served a bid in Wayside Jail. Snoop took advantage of his imprisonment to refine his rapping, with lyrics that blended personal experience and others' passed-down lore. "At Wayside I listened to all the stories people told, wrote them down on my note pad and turned them into raps," he told Touré in 1993. "The older inmates would take me aside and say, 'Youngster, you don't need to be inside this place. God gave you some talent, and you ought to use it.' "[32]

Upon his release, Snoop redoubled his efforts to enter the record business. After hearing a tape of a freestyle Snoop had performed at a party, Dre invited him to sit in on the *Niggaz4Life* sessions. The next year, Snoop wrote the lyrics and contributed a verse and the singsong chorus to Dre's one-off soundtrack contribution "Deep Cover," released while Dre's lawyers were fighting Ruthless Records in court. The same summer that "Cop Killer" turned Ice-T into a law-and-order pariah, Snoop's smooth, menacing voice was crooning the California penal code for murder: "It's 1-8-7 on an undercover cop." Snoop was a new kind of rap star: never before had the performative menace of Black criminality been delivered so soulfully, with a drawl that was part Slick Rick, part Stylistics, part Mississippi twang derived from his southern-born parents. Snoop became Dre's protégé, ghostwriter, and, in the "Nuthin' but a 'G' Thang" and "Fuck wit Dre Day" videos, his costar. He estimates that he penned 70 percent of Dre's lyrics for *The Chronic*, and the album track "Lil' Ghetto Boy," based on a Donny Hathaway sample, stands as *The Chronic*'s most potent moment of soulful introspection. Snoop's character is an exaggeration of his real-life rap sheet ("Murder was the case that they gave me"), but his descriptions of the daily horrors of life behind bars were drawn from direct experience.

The incredible success of *The Chronic* created an unprecedented level of anticipation and hype for Snoop's solo debut. He had undeniable street credibility, a surfeit of personal magnetism, and a novel approach to flow and timbre, but critics, journalists, and fans were most interested in his realness. "If you want a rapper that dramatizes the harshness of ghetto life, this is it," wrote Powell in his *Vibe* profile.[33] In a *Spin* feature titled "Sir Real," Charles Aaron located Snoop's personal authenticity in the call-and-response chorus of his first solo single, "Who Am I (What's My Name)?": "This bold attempt to spark a remark from the audience, to get the issue of identity out in the street, shoots to the heart of hip-hop's power. It's a music that begs the question every single day: 'Who am I?' . . . And Snoop's still asking, waiting for an answer, waiting for his audience to acknowledge him. Waiting, ultimately, for them to help him feel real."[34] The music video for "Who Am I?" planted Snoop atop the Long Beach music store V.I.P. Records—in whose small recording studio Snoop had cut his first demo a few years earlier—with a large, adoring crowd looking up at him from below, visually confirming his status. Though the vibe of the music video was undeniably upbeat—Snoop and his friends being chased through the city by dogcatchers—the shoot was plagued by an overzealous police presence, with hovering helicopters monitoring the gang members wandering through nearby King Park. When gunfire erupted, the shoot turned into chaos. "It was like my success was counted on the Crip side of the ledger, and until some Blood made it like I had, there was going to be a score that needed settling," Snoop explained. "My past was following me into my future, breathing down my neck."[35] Though the Blood-affiliated Suge Knight overlooked Snoop's Crip connections in favor of his obvious commercial value, anywhere else he went, the rapper's status as a celebrity Crip exposed him not only to the prying eyes of the press and the police but to rivals who saw him as the ultimate target.

For his safety, Snoop had moved from Long Beach to an apartment in Los Angeles's middle-class Palms neighborhood, where he stayed with his bodyguard, McKinley Lee. His location was an open secret in Los Angeles, which Snoop did not mind: occasional visits from locals kept him apprised about the street reality that existed outside his relative isolation. This suddenly changed on the afternoon of August 25, when a car full of Bloods pulled up outside the apartment. Lee shoved Snoop aside to confront the three men, but Snoop could make out one in the back seat as a local gang member who had shown up waving a gun at an earlier video shoot. Lee sent the car on its way, but returning from errands later that day, they encountered the same crew at the park across the street from Snoop's apartment. According to Snoop, he and Lee were again confronted by the man he recognized from the back seat, whose name was Philip Woldemariam and who was reaching for his gun. Lee shot and killed him, and Snoop drove away. While Suge Knight and David Kenner secreted Snoop away to the Beverly Garland Hotel to lie low and determine the best way to negotiate the rapper's surrender, Snoop's face was on the cover of *Vibe*. Snoop's next public appearance would be not in a courtroom but, two weeks after Lee killed Woldemariam, on the stage of the Universal Amphitheatre at the 1993 MTV Video Music Awards, where, along with Dr. Dre and Parliament-Funkadelic icon George Clinton, he presented the trophy for Best R&B Video to En Vogue. The shooting was not yet public knowledge, and the second Snoop was done, he jumped into an idling car at the back of the venue and left, barely avoiding the Los Angeles police who had shown up to arrest him. Hours later, he surrendered to police, was charged with murder, and posted $1 million bail. He was indicted on November 19, and four days later, *Doggystyle* debuted at no. 1, selling eight hundred thousand copies in its first week. "Snoop is part of the most dramatic confluence of violent art and violent reality the modern pop world has ever witnessed: gangsta rap," wrote one critic.[36] In his four-star *Rolling Stone* review of *Doggystyle*, Touré included a quote from Snoop comparing his plight to the assassinations of John F. Kennedy and Martin Luther King Jr.: "It would sound hella good, according to the streets, to kill me."[37]

Snoop's paranoia and unprecedented pop notoriety notwithstanding, the rapper's fame exploded in 1994 thanks to the convivial side of his image, which was on full display in the video for *Doggystyle*'s second single, "Gin and Juice." The next episode of the laid-back Black suburban vibe of "'G' Thang" and "Who Am I?," the "Gin and Juice" music video was shot on location in Compton, depicting Snoop as "Homeboy Alone" after his parents leave for the weekend. Just as iconic as the video's portrayal of a suburban living room as dance club—like *House Party* with more indo, Tanqueray, and (safe) sex—are the day-in-the-hood images of Snoop lazily riding down the street on the handlebars of a friend's bicycle and a woman braiding his hair on a front porch. The police appear only during a brief sequence where Snoop de-escalates a fight between two women, and another comical sequence staged at a drive-in theater (the double feature is the "Who Am I?" video and *Menace II Society*) shows two Cheech-and-Chong-style stoners stumbling out of a Volkswagen Beetle, followed by a plume of weed smoke. After MTV's censors significantly edited the clip, it was an absolute smash. Suburban white kids who would never see an Uzi could certainly identify with getting buzzed with their friends when their folks were out, helping "Gin and Juice" join "Who Am I?" as a *Billboard* Top 10 pop crossover. Dre and Cube had sold millions of records to white listeners, Eazy had laid the groundwork for gangsta entrepreneurialism, and Shakur was a movie star, but in 1994, Snoop's street credibility, sui generis delivery, and wry sense of teenage humor had made him reality rap's first pop star.

In late 1993, Shakur was attempting to strike Snoop's balance between convivial and intimidating, following *Poetic Justice* with a menacing role in the Harlem street basketball film *Above the Rim*. Penned by *New Jack City*'s Barry Michael Cooper and directed by *The Fresh Prince of Bel-Air* cocreator Jeff Pollack, the film showcased Shakur as Birdie, a neighborhood criminal trying to convince a local hoops star to work for him. As always, Shakur based his character on traits he picked up from someone in his immediate orbit, and this time, it was the shady, high-rolling music promoter Jacques "Haitian Jack" Agnant, with whom he had recently become friendly. During the shoot, Shakur was regularly hitting New York clubs with Haitian Jack and his crew, and on one of those nights, he became amorous with a woman on the dance floor, and the two exchanged personal information. A few days later, the woman, Ayanna Jackson, found herself in Shakur's suite at the Parker Meridien Hotel, where he, Haitian Jack, and some other friends were partying. The night ended with Jackson running from the suite crying and ordering the hotel's security to call the police. Jackson said she had been forced to perform oral sex on Shakur and one of his friends, while others watched and groped her. Shakur, Haitian Jack, and another associate were arrested. As he was led out of the hotel's lobby in handcuffs, in full view of the

New York press, Shakur shifted into unrepentant tabloid-star mode: "I'm young, I'm black... I'm making money and they can't stop me. They can't find a way to make me dirty.... I'm clean."[38]

Jackson's credible allegations came when Shakur was on the cusp of a crossover to the mainstream of Black popular entertainment. His portrayal of Lucky in *Poetic Justice* had earned him a nomination for an NAACP Image Award, putting him in the company of Denzel Washington, who had played Malcolm X in Spike Lee's heavily hyped 1993 biopic. But one civil rights veteran with deep political connections was deeply displeased that Shakur might represent the Black cultural elite at the January 1994 awards ceremony. To reinvent her three-decade-long political career, C. Delores Tucker reemerged in 1993 as the lead moral entrepreneur shaming hip-hop stars into cleaning up their act. Tucker spoke loudest among the numerous representatives of the Black bourgeoisie who believed that the respectability politics of the 1960s civil rights battles still applied to the hip-hop generation. After Snoop and Shakur's rise in 1993, Black radio stations in several major cities announced they would no longer play street rap; the NAACP, the National Urban League, and Jesse Jackson's Operation PUSH started holding patronizing "youth forums" across the country; and the Reverend Calvin Butts of Harlem's Abyssinian Baptist Church hired a steamroller and called the press to watch him annihilate dozens of rap albums outside his church. Then Tucker took over. At her first press conference in late 1993, she displayed a photo-enlarged *Doggystyle* album cover and cited the lyrics from the Geto Boys' "Mind of a Lunatic," both of which she classified as pornographic. She was arrested and fined for protesting in front of Washington, DC, record stores that sold the music, and though the NAACP never replied to her protest, the award that Shakur was nominated for was won by Denzel Washington.

Tucker's campaign found common cause across the political spectrum, with Democratic moderates such as Senator Joe Lieberman and Al Gore joining GOP standard-bearer Bob Dole and cultural conservative William Bennett in support of her cause. In early 1994, Tucker's publicity campaign found its way to Capitol Hill, where Congresswoman Cardiss Collins and Senator Carol Moseley Braun convened hearings to discuss rap's impact on American youth. Tucker's own testimony boiled down to the familiar conflation of incitement and obscenity, and she cited two recent examples of such dubious cultural causation:

> In one case, a 16-year-old from New Mexico, along with two of his friends, stabbed to death the boy's 80-year-old grandparents in a dispute over beer. A lieutenant investigating the case said that the teenagers worked themselves up by listening to a tape of Snoop Doggy Dogg entitled "Serial Killer." The second incident just occurred last week when an 11-year-old Dayton, Ohio boy accidentally killed his 3-year-old sister and injured another 5-year-old sister while brandishing a gun and imitating the actions of Snoop Doggy Dogg.[39]

Tucker's rhetorical playbook extended to the 2 Live Crew case, but not by citing the rappers' ultimate victory over industry censorship. Instead, she cited the notorious legal decision that permitted the spectacle to start in the first place: "As U.S. District Judge Jose Gonzalez explained in his opinion in the 2 Live Crew case, obscenity is not a protected form of speech under the U.S. Constitution," Tucker declared.[40]

In the end, however, the renewed controversy spurred by the hearings only deepened the gap between those who framed rap as an epidemiological crisis and those who saw it as a product of deeper social and economic maladies that can't just be swept under the rug. Brown University professor Michael Eric Dyson argued the latter position in his testimony, asserting that the "cultural distancing by Black bourgeois culture" happened "because we were ashamed about the vulgarity and the explicit lyrics... because they pointed to things we were embarrassed to deal with."[41] Aligning with Dyson's perspective was that of California congresswoman Maxine Waters, who read her defense of reality rap as documentary into the Senate record:

> Let us not lose sight of what the real problem is. It is not the words being used. It is the reality they are rapping about. For decades, many of us have talked about the lives and the hopes of our people, the pain and the hopelessness, the deprivation and destruction. Rap music is communicating that reality in a way we never have. Someone

has described it as the CNN of the black community, causing people from every sector, including black leadership, to sit up and take notice.[42]

In an interview after the hearing, Waters stressed that this moment was not a simple rehash of 1990's First Amendment battles. "It scares the hell out of people when young black males get aggressive. It isn't just free speech that we're talking about defending here, it's a social movement. And that's what people can't stand to confront."[43] Waters also read the lyrics of Snoop's hit single "Murder Was the Case" into the record, defining them as evidence that he and his peers "paint the world as they see it with their words and their music, and they feel the pain," Waters said. "They long for hope. They despair of change. They long for meaning."[44]

At a hearing two weeks earlier, Maine senator William Cohen cited an editorial from the previous day's *Washington Post* about the rapper Bo$$, whose 1993 Def Jam debut *Born Gangstaz* had made her the nation's most popular female exponent of the deeply masculinist genre. The editorial was responding to a *Wall Street Journal* profile published earlier that month in which the reporter, Brett Pulley, had ostensibly pulled back the curtain on the gun-toting, cop-hating Los Angeles rapper's middle-class past, revealing that she was raised as Lichelle Laws in Detroit by two loving parents, went to private school, and studied dance and piano. Around 1989, Pulley noted, Laws became obsessed with rappers like Ice-T and N.W.A, enough to move to Los Angeles, adopt the gangsta persona, and land a lucrative record deal. To Cohen, Laws was not a tried-and-true success story of grabbing a piece of the cultural industries for herself but a cautionary tale of an impressionable young Black woman taken advantage of by a ruthless record industry marketing violence for profit. In her testimony, Tucker echoed Cohen, claiming that Laws had "been turned into a gangster" by an industry that insisted on "placing profit ahead of social obligation" and had forced a sweet young woman to debase herself through pornography. But in his testimony, president of Rush Associated Labels David Harleston compared Bo$$ to white artists like David Bowie and Madonna who were granted a distinction between their on- and offstage personas. "In hip hop, people have a little more of a tough time doing that," he said. "I am not quite sure why."[45]

The success of Bo$$ and *Born Gangstaz* was plain evidence of just how deeply reality or gangsta rap had rooted itself in the pop-cultural firmament. By moving from middle-class Detroit to the streets of Los Angeles, investing in baggy pants, prison-style work shirts, and skull-caps, even affiliating with Bloods and selling crack out of hotel rooms, Laws was participating in the latest version of the pop pilgrimage. In the 1960s, aspiring folkies flooded New York's Greenwich Village folk scene, in the 1970s, wannabe punks looked toward the Bowery District, and in the 1980s, heavy metal aspirants flooded LA's seedy Sunset Strip bars. The same year that *Born Gangstaz* came out, a flood of grunge pilgrims were buying flannel and saturating Seattle, seeking record deals from grunge-obsessed A&R employees. Just like all of these previous spectacular subcultures, reality rap was a fashion system, comprising recorded music, industry vultures, trendy clothes, hard drugs, and various other vices. Lichelle Laws was not even trying to disguise any of this either: six months before Pulley's putative exposé, Laws gave an interview to the *Los Angeles Times* where she admitted that she had moved to LA because it was a good business decision. Moreover, the opening skit on *Born Gangstaz* is an answering machine message from Laws's mother, chiding her for not acting like "a young lady who was brought up in Catholic school for 12 years." To a rebellious twenty-something, that was exactly the point.

At a much higher level of cultural prominence, that was Suge Knight's point too. To capitalize on Snoop's disrepute, Death Row released *Murder Was the Case*, a seventy-three-minute "soundtrack album." It opened with the *Doggystyle* single, featured the first post-N.W.A collaboration between Dr. Dre and Ice Cube, and was padded out with more than an hour of filler material from the Death Row stable, more than enough to debut at no. 1 on the *Billboard* album chart, a position it held for two weeks. Knight also commissioned an eighteen-minute short film for "Murder Was the Case," directed by Dr. Dre, who made a reality rap "Thriller"—part gothic horror, part action-packed B movie—which simultaneously elaborated on Snoop's most ambitious lyrics and promoted Death Row's largesse. Early in the film, Snoop is shot by a rival

(Charlie Murphy) in a parking lot, a trope familiar to viewers of *Boyz n the Hood* and *Menace II Society*. At death's door, his character prays for a resurrection and is answered by a metaphysical figure—part devil, part Christ—from whom he accepts a luxurious lifestyle in exchange for abandoning his street life. When Snoop falls off the wagon, however, the figure returns and restages the shooting with Snoop as the culprit, which sends him to hell on earth: the men's prison in Chino, California. The theological lesson was blurry: Had Snoop been punished by a vengeful God, or had he been tricked by a devious devil? Either way, "Murder" was, more compellingly, a moral fable about Snoop's conflicted relationship with his own fame. His authentic connection to gang life and the drug trade had played a significant role in building his image, which had made him a target for the same gangstas he had left behind.

Months earlier, Snoop had agreed to perform "Murder" at MTV's September 1994 Video Music Awards—almost a year to the day after presenting an award while the LAPD were on his trail. MTV executives knew they were taking a risk by showcasing a man facing murder charges on the network's biggest night, but as executive Judy McGrath told a *New Yorker* reporter, if they wanted to maintain their position at the cutting edge of music culture, they had to give Snoop the stage. "Musically, Snoop is happening now, and we have a responsibility to our viewers to show that," she explained. "It is sort of scary that this is the direction the music is taking us, but we're not really in control of that. Plus, it's a lot more meaningful to show this stuff—it's real." The story then cuts to McGrath meeting Snoop and his entourage backstage, after which she comments to an assistant, "You didn't tell me how cute he is."[46]

MTV had given Snoop a platform, and Snoop had given MTV credibility, and for the performance, they combined forces to pull out all the stagecraft stops. Snoop's performance opens with a reverend presiding over his funeral—mourners wailing as they walk by his open casket—while a full gospel choir backs him up. As the "Murder" music kicks in, the choir segues into polyrhythmic throes, and the star, clad head to toe in blue, is pushed onstage in a wheelchair. Once he hits center stage, he stands up dramatically, as if suddenly healed. Where the recorded version of "Murder" mapped Snoop's fame insecurity onto a combination of Black Christianity, *Faust*, and Delta blues mythology, he was now, live on MTV, bringing the full weight of the African American musical and spiritual tradition to bear on his pending trial as an accessory to murder. It would be another year before Snoop's trial would start in a Los Angeles courtroom, but his incredible VMA performance spoke directly to the equally important court of popular opinion. As "Murder" ratchets up to its fervent conclusion, the music suddenly drops out, and Snoop's voice is left alone: "I'm innocent . . . I'm innocent."

CHAPTER 7

2 OF AMERIKAZ MOST WANTED

▼

On December 1, 1994, Tupac Shakur made one of the most dramatic public appearances of his career. Against his doctor's wishes, he had checked himself out of Bellevue Hospital a day after being shot multiple times at point-blank range, and he was pushed into a courtroom in a wheelchair, his head wrapped in bandages, to hear a judge read the jury's decision in the Ayanna Jackson sex abuse case, a year after his arrest. Shakur had been recording guest verses and new tracks throughout his trial, to help defray his mounting legal costs and the growing public impression that his criminal exploits had overwhelmed, if not *become*, his creative output. Early in the morning of November 30, Shakur showed up to Quad Studios in Times Square, having been promised $7,000 for a verse on a song by Little Shawn, part of the newly minted Brooklyn rap star Notorious B.I.G.'s crew. He would not get to record his verse. In Quad Studios' lobby, Shakur was confronted by several men who brandished pistols and demanded money. Before he could pull the loaded and cocked gun in his waistband, Shakur was shot five times. The assailants robbed him and ran away. The next day, while sitting silently in the wheelchair, Shakur was acquitted of the three sodomy counts and the weapons charges but convicted of two counts of sexual abuse. His bail was set at $3 million, and he was immediately incarcerated to await sentencing. Two months later, Shakur was sentenced to serve one and a half to four and a half years at the maximum-security Clinton Correctional

Facility in Upstate New York. To many observers, Shakur's punishment far outweighed his crime, the result of Assistant District Attorney Melissa Mourges's conflation of his public persona as a cocky, political rapper with the facts of the case. During the trial, Mourges referred to Shakur as a "thug" (obviously not aligning with Shakur's definition of the term) and cited his lyrics about shooting police officers and rival gang members as evidence of his guilt and his danger to society.

A few days after Shakur was wheeled out of the courtroom, Touré reviewed his appearance in the December 14 issue of the *Village Voice* as the rapper and actor's greatest-yet performance, the culmination of a series of run-ins with the law that had been designed to distract from, or at least bolster, his on-record work. "Despite being, along with Snoop, one of the two most famous rappers in the world, he is merely an average vocalist and lyricist," Touré argued. On the other hand, Shakur's off-record "performance art" was "dangerously compelling and ecstatically brilliant," enough to keep "his lackluster professional work artistically interesting and commercially viable." Touré not only viewed Shakur's bandaged, wheelchair-bound appearance in the Manhattan court as a transparent attempt to generate juror and journalist sympathy but went so far as to suggest that the shooting might have simply been part of the rapper's act. "It doesn't matter who shot Tupac or why," he added, "and the lack of clarity and attendant controversy only add to his myth and heighten the dramatic impact of the most enigmatic and climactic part of the show." Even the prospect of imprisonment would not bring Shakur's performance to a conclusion, Touré wrote, but would simply necessitate a change of setting: "When you're perpetually on stage, you never get off. The stage simply comes with you."[1]

Touré's critical opinions notwithstanding, he was onto something in his critique: Shakur had revolutionary blood but had been swallowed by celebrity and had grown to value notoriety over anything else. Unlike any other pop-music star before him, Shakur insisted on bringing his offstage life squarely to center stage, blending his public image as a platinum-selling rapper and respected actor with his ostensibly private image as a playboy and thug-life folk hero. Though he counted actresses Jasmine Guy and Jada Pinkett among his dearest personal friends, he was more known for cavorting with controversy-courting celebrities like Mickey Rourke and Madonna (whom he briefly dated). He never stopped trying to live up to the impossible heights of his mother's Black Panther lineage, but by the early 1990s, the idea of radical Black liberation had been fully engulfed by late-capitalist consumerism—radical chic as a million-dollar brand identity—and redefined as the freedom for a Black man to become famous by not giving a fuck. Shakur could have easily segued out of music and into a comfortable career onscreen, like Ice-T's mid-1990s transition to sci-fi action films with *Surviving the Game, Tank Girl,* and *Johnny Mnemonic.* But rap as a medium gave Shakur a much looser set of performative parameters to break down the walls between his commercial output and offstage life—and gave the authorities an opportunity to come after him. "I never had a record until I made a record," he was known to say.

Though he presented himself as a strident revolutionary, Shakur never articulated a coherent political ideology. As Touré wrote, "Tupac's character is far from Huey Newton the revolutionary leader and political organizer, and a lot closer to Huey Newton the chauvinist pig and self-destructive rebel. He is Huey with the misogyny, the sex appeal, and the guns without the 10-point plan."[2] Increasingly, Shakur's music shifted far away from the Public Enemy–inspired calls to action of "Holler if Ya Hear Me" and toward more self-pitying and score-settling content. Kevin Powell opened Shakur's first magazine profile in *Vibe* with a judge reading the rapper his charges, which drained Shakur of his machismo and made him look like "a lost little boy." But Shakur coaxed Powell into detailing his personal anguish, a combination of childhood trauma and mass-media notoriety that Shakur claimed "separates me from other rappers."[3] In the wake of his sexual assault charges, Shakur appeared on *Arsenio* to brazenly and callously paint himself as the true victim, using his personal agony as his defense. "It bothers me so much to go through my life . . . coming out of a family and a household with just women, to get to this point, to have a woman say I took something from her." Hall then brought up Shakur's first sexual encounter with Ayanna Jackson, giving Shakur the opportunity to obliquely slut-shame her. The interview ended with Shakur comparing the sexual assault case to the next day's scheduled sentencing for his assault of the Hughes brothers. "All the cases where I'm so-called guilty, they're tomorrow. All the cases I can fight . . . they'll deal with me in the newspapers."

At the same moment that Shakur was painting himself as the victim of a lying Black woman, his landmark rap single celebrating the innate resilience of Black women was one of the year's biggest hits. "Keep Ya Head Up" had reached no. 12 on the *Billboard* Hot 100 a few months earlier, propelled by the first lyrics by a major hip-hop artist to express heartfelt respect for women's struggles, not just a begrudging acceptance of their equality. "I wonder why we take from our women / Why we rape our women—do we hate our women?" he asked. Yet there was no doubt that Shakur took a purely transactional view of feminism, like when he positioned "Keep Ya Head Up" as a moral quid pro quo in a 1994 interview with BET's Ed Gordon: "I did that from my heart, so if they do try to put a rape charge on me my sisters can say, 'He ain't 'bout that.' Now if my sisters can't say that, you won't hear another motherfucking 'Keep Ya Head Up' out my mouth."[4] Less than three years earlier, Shakur's first single had been inspired by the New York tabloid story of a teenage mother killing her baby. Now, he himself was embroiled in tabloid infamy, assailing the press outside of the Manhattan courtroom for devoting their coverage to him instead of to "people throwin' babies outta windows, and puttin' them in incinerators." While the jury deliberated his fate in late November 1994, Shakur held court to a scrum of courthouse reporters: "Y'all cover murders…every day, and y'all treat me like I'm New York's most notorious criminal."[5]

It was no coincidence that Shakur's rise to A-list notoriety coincided with the decline in popularity of the group that had inspired him to rap, Public Enemy. More than any rapper before him, Shakur believed his hype, and the spectacle he personified so absorbed the national attention that PE's fifth album, *Muse Sick-n-Hour Mess Age*, released in August of 1994, nearly three years after their previous LP, got lost in the noise. The group was "knee-deep in the age of gangsta," the *Spin* review noted, a fact that Chuck and company ruefully acknowledged on the single "So Whatcha Gone Do Now?"[6] On that song's refrain, Chuck laments that "everybody talkin' that gangsta shit," calling them "slaves to the rhythm of the master" for selling out to white-owned record companies who profited from negative and violent images of African American life. The music video was one of PE's most high-concept works yet: a detailed reimagining of the Kennedy assassination fast-forwarded to the current moment, with a Black president leading a motorcade winding through Dallas. As gangstas clad in bold colors obliviously throw gang signs at one another, a white supremacist with a sniper rifle takes position in a nearby building, inspired by a talk-radio host with a Nazi badge on his sleeve. Chuck and his black-clad mercenaries spring into action, subduing the shooter, kidnapping the radio host, and saving the life of the president. PE's potent message had not changed a bit since the group's breakthrough: while too many Black Americans were wasting time fighting one another, PE were the only political program that could successfully subdue white-supremacist threats to Black authority. The rap world itself had changed far too much, however. *Muse Sick* was the group's first album not to sell platinum since their 1987 debut, and it would be the last Public Enemy album for five years. Public Enemy had been eclipsed by a new hip-hop era, just as they'd witnessed the same thing happen to Run-DMC after *Raising Hell*.

In the meantime, a new empire had emerged in New York City. The Notorious B.I.G. was one of the country's most popular and critically acclaimed rappers, on the strength of his LP *Ready to Die*, which *Rolling Stone's* Cheo Hodari Coker proclaimed "the strongest solo rap debut since Ice Cube's *AmeriKKKa's Most Wanted*."[7] He was the brightest star signed to Bad Boy Records, founded by Sean "Puffy" Combs, whose rapid ascent up the rap industry ladder began as an A&R for Uptown Records, where he managed the nascent careers of the R&B stars Mary J. Blige and Jodeci. Combs had personal aspirations for stardom: he scored a feature profile (in the same debut issue of *Vibe* in which Kevin Powell profiled Snoop) that described the aspiring mogul as "quite possibly...the only A&R executive with as many groupies as his artists."[8] B.I.G. was a peerless lyricist and hip-hop purist from Bedford-Stuyvesant who, along with the dizzyingly productive Staten Island collective the Wu-Tang Clan and the gifted Queens-born rapper Nas, had shifted the national hip-hop focus back to New York after several years of West Coast supremacy—thanks in large part to positive notices in the *Source* and *Vibe*. Yet while in many ways B.I.G. was a far more compelling and nuanced rapper than the LA reality rappers, he also understood who had recently paved his way: he and Combs sampled the *Doggystyle* track "Tha Shiznit" and *The Chronic's* "Lil' Ghetto Boy" within the first few minutes of *Ready to Die*. More than anyone, though, B.I.G. liked Shakur—and the feeling was mutual. The two struck up a friendship in 1993 and wowed a Madison Square Garden crowd with back-to-back freestyles at a rap showcase that year. At that time, Shakur was a huge star and B.I.G. was a relative unknown, and as Ben Westhoff has chronicled, "Biggie and other young rappers assembled in record studios or hotel rooms to hear Tupac lecture about how to make it in the game."[9] Before *Ready to Die*, with Bad Boy still a fledgling startup, B.I.G. even asked Shakur to manage him, an offer that Shakur declined.

In the September 1996 *Vibe* (the immediately infamous East-versus-West issue with Combs and B.I.G. on the cover), Chuck D sat with Ice-T for an interview about the idea of "juice"—power—within the record business and society at large. They did not hold back. "It's simulated," T said. "We think we got juice in the music industry but in reality we have none. Michael Jordan don't own the team, and Oprah don't own the network. We simulate it." Chuck agreed: "People try to measure power and juice by a verse, or a fucking hit record. . . . That shit is what you call bread and circuses." When T was asked about hip-hop's East/West beef, he was similarly perceptive about the larger issues: "Why can't *Vibe* talk positively about *The Source*? Because it's competition. Right now, rap is business, millions of dollars are exchanging hands."[10]

Six months earlier, Shakur, who had just signed a Faustian deal with Death Row that felt like Snoop's "Murder Was the Case" pact come to life, had told the *Source* that the most important thing to him was "making sure every single human being in the United States and the world knows who Tupac is, who Death Row is, and where Los Angeles, California is."[11] A similar drive for national recognition had once compelled N.W.A, Ice Cube, and Ice-T to launch West Coast reality rap: in the "Straight Outta Compton" video, the anonymous police literally consult maps showing them, and the viewing audience, the location of Compton. But as Chuck D and Ice-T remorsefully acknowledged, the battlefield had dramatically expanded in just a few years. Death Row was worth more than $100 million, and Suge Knight had the Bad Boy upstarts in his sights. The reality rap world that had launched itself as a sensationalistic, quasi-journalistic response to institutionalized racism and police brutality would find itself ensnared in a gargantuan tabloid rap war between the coasts—started by Knight, fueled by Shakur, and nourished by the *Source*, *Vibe*, and a drama-hungry mainstream press. If 1993 and 1994 were the years that reality rap reached its tabloid peak with the true-crime superstardom of Snoop Doggy Dogg and Tupac Shakur, 1995 and 1996 saw the empire develop a stand-alone reality system, and crumble under its own weight.

By some estimates, hip-hop accounted for a full 10 percent of the entire recording industry by 1994, and the growth and influence of its two native-born publications reflected its takeover. The *Source*, which spoke to its readers in hip-hop argot and dispensed with journalistic pieties for street-level signifying, had become a full-fledged kingmaker. A short, glowing March 1992 review of a four-song Notorious B.I.G. mixtape first brought the rapper to Combs's attention, and the magazine's review of Nas's 1994 debut, *Illmatic*, given five out of five "mics," lent the album "instant classic" status. But the *Source* had to keep up with the more polished and professional *Vibe*, which was published by magazine-industry veterans. The *Source* was grittier and less grammatical, but it was also *just* about rap: the heads' bible. In *Vibe*'s universe, rap was one of the brightest stars in a vast constellation of Black popular culture and lifestyle coverage, sharing space with ads for the Gap and Versace. While the *Source* made room for three thousand words on Too $hort, Spice 1, and MC Eiht, *Vibe* gave covers to En Vogue, Boyz II Men, and Rosie Perez. By 1997, *Vibe* had started outselling *Rolling Stone* on newsstands, and its owners bought *Spin* outright for $43 million that year.[12]

In early 1995, one of the most fervent readers of the hip-hop press was imprisoned on Rikers Island, awaiting his transfer upstate to the maximum-security Clinton Correctional Facility. Shakur read the February 1995 issue of *Vibe*, which contained a three-page spread detailing Shakur's career high points and legal troubles, complete with a computer-generated graphic recreating the Quad Studios shooting. As part of the package, Kevin Powell described Shakur as a one-man condensation of the questions that dogged rap music in his wake: Does life imitate art or vice versa? Does music condone violence or reflect it? The answers, Powell concluded, "don't lie as much in Shakur's music as in his life," which "was a symbol of black resistance, even if it's not always clear what it is he's resisting."[13] After reading Touré's *Village Voice* takedown of his life/art performance, Shakur knew who his most sympathetic audience was and granted Powell an exclusive jailhouse interview, which ran in the April 1995 *Vibe*. In it, Shakur presented himself not as a canny performance artist but as a misunderstood rebel who had been chastened by jail and was changing for good. He told Powell that the "thug life" portion of his career was over and promised that upon his release from prison, he was starting an organization for Black street youth called Us First with Mike Tyson and Sanyika Shakur (a.k.a. Monster Kody, the formidable former Crip OG who had released a well-received memoir in 1993). But the part of the conversation that earned the most notice was Shakur's detailed account of, and personal perspective on, the events at Quad Studios. While Shakur stopped short of accusing Puffy, B.I.G., Uptown Records founder Andre Harrell, and others of setting up his ambush a bit more than a month earlier, he did note that they were acting mysteriously calm when he entered the eighth-floor studio, bleeding from his head and leg. He told Powell, "Nobody approached me. I noticed that nobody would look at me."[14]

The *Vibe* interview coincided with Interscope's release of Shakur's third album, *Me Against the World*. When it debuted at no. 1, granting Shakur the debased distinction of being the first imprisoned artist to top the charts, some critics saw a validation of his performative authenticity. "As other rappers strive to prove their 'realness,' 2Pac has become a certified outlaw, with bullet wounds and a . . . prison sentence to prove it," wrote Jon Pareles in the *New York Times*.[15] But while *Me Against the World* opened with a skit of fictional newscasters reporting on Shakur's real legal troubles, the album dialed in on the self-reflection and anguish that had comprised the most solemn moments of *Strictly 4 My N.I.G.G.A.Z.* . . At *Vibe*, Danyel Smith called it "a mass of sad songs rapped over plodding beats" that suffered in comparison to the more indignant and extreme *N.I.G.G.A.Z.*[16] Cheo Hodari Coker heard the opposite, praising *Me Against the World* in *Rolling Stone* as Shakur's best album for the way it "lets the listener look at the roots of his anger" and examines "some of the results of the gangsta lifestyle."[17] One thing was certain: *World* presented Shakur as a chastened convict seeking redemption. Its first single "Dear Mama," which hit the *Billboard* Top 10, was illustrated by a video that resembled a TV docudrama about Tupac's relationship with his mother. Opening with the real Afeni recalling her pregnancy while on trial with the Black Panthers, the clip was structured as a trip through an old photo album, with actors dramatizing various moments from the mother's and son's lives together. "Dear Mama" was affecting melodrama and Shakur's first full attempt at autobiographical self-mythologization, his life story retold as a loving son trying to live up to his imperfect mother's ideal image of him. But his attempt at redirecting his public image did not go unchallenged. In its June issue, *Vibe* ran a full-page rebuttal to Powell's Shakur feature from an anonymous Ayanna Jackson, the woman he had been convicted of sexually assaulting. "Tupac knows exactly what he did to me," she wrote. "I admit I didn't make the wisest decisions, but I did not deserve to be gang-raped."[18]

Though the Bad Boy collective initially declined comment on Shakur's jailhouse *Vibe* interview, in the magazine's August issue they accused him of conducting a grand performance of which he might not even be fully conscious. Combs acknowledged that "he definitely brought the theatrics" and warned, "If you gonna be a motherfuckin' thug, you gots to live and die a thug.... There ain't no jumpin' in and out of thugism." Fellow performer Notorious B.I.G. was sympathetic. "With the shit he was talking in *Vibe*, he was just confused more than anything. You get shot and then you go to jail for something you ain't even do—that could twist a nigga's mind up." But then B.I.G. addressed the elephant in the room, the rap-world controversy over his latest single, "Who Shot Ya?" While the single had not yet been released at the time of Shakur's interview, B.I.G.—like everyone reading *Vibe* and the *Source*, and especially everyone listening to New York rap radio—knew that it was being widely interpreted as a coy admission of Bad Boy's role in the Quad City shooting. "That shit is crazy. That song was finished way before Tupac got shot," B.I.G. proclaimed.[19] That was easy to believe—songs about gunning down rivals were not exactly rare in the 1994 rap world—but if it was not about Shakur, the timing of its release was the worst possible promotional move. Regardless, there was an irony to the fact that the "Who Shot Ya?" lyrics were feeding rap's increasingly vigorous gossip mill and Shakur's own sense of persecution. Believing that the song equated to an admission of guilt required exactly the kind of literalist lyric interpretation that had been pioneered by rap's self-appointed enemies.

Shakur's ongoing saga paralleled an even more absorbing tabloid story, which began when the National Football League Hall of Fame running back and longtime commercial spokesman O. J. Simpson was charged with the brutal murder of his ex-wife, Nicole Brown, and her friend,

Ron Goldman, outside her Brentwood condominium. Ten years earlier, O. J. Simpson's story might well have never escaped the supermarket tabloids. But in 1994, it was the perfect storm of celebrity, gory murder, and, once the case got to court in 1995, a tale of the racist Los Angeles Police Department framing a Black man. Simpson was far from a civil rights icon—he had consistently resisted calls to join with his Black activist peers during his playing days—but with the Rodney King video and the LA riots still a recent memory, his expensive legal team quickly turned his murder trial into a referendum on racist policing. Defense attorneys F. Lee Bailey and Johnnie Cochran focused their efforts on discrediting Mark Fuhrman, the white officer who had discovered the bloody black glove on Simpson's estate. One of the trial's key moments came when Simpson's team introduced recorded interviews Fuhrman had given an author for background research on a story, during which the officer repeatedly said the word "nigger" and asserted that when dealing with certain suspects "you don't need probable cause. You're God." In court, Fuhrman claimed he was voicing a composite character comprised of multiple racist colleagues in his past, and even though Black LAPD chief Willie Williams defended Fuhrman in the press, the recorded evidence spoke for itself in the court of public opinion, and Fuhrman became the latest avatar caught on tape proving the department's deep-rooted racism.

Cochran's closing statement, watched by tens of millions of Americans, doubled down on the danger of racist cops: "A racist is somebody who has power over you, who can do something to you. . . . A police officer in the street, a patrol officer, is the single most powerful figure in the criminal justice system. He can take your life." Essentially an extended version of Ice Cube rapping in "Fuck tha Police" that cops "have the authority to kill a minority," Cochran's statement was the clearest evidence yet that the concerns of reality rappers had been molded into a rhetorical weapon, strong enough to generate a not-guilty verdict despite mountains of evidence to the contrary. Simpson was an imperfect icon, but for many Black Americans the verdict meant that a Black man had finally done what white people had been doing for years: used his race to *avoid* prison. The verdict split the country: Oprah Winfrey devoted a broadcast to the live announcement of the verdict, and when the words "not guilty" were uttered, cameras cut to a group of Black women leaping into the air, screaming and waving their hands in celebration. The next shot showed several white women shaking their heads in disbelief.

From summer 1994 to October 1995, the lurid, compelling twists and turns of the Simpson trial revealed America as a tabloid nation, obsessed with the kinds of violent, titillating, celebrity-fixated spectacles that had grown out of the intertwined worlds of reality rap and reality television. Events that would have previously been relegated to supermarket rags or *A Current Affair* were unavoidable on the nightly news and CNN: the murderous suburban affair of Amy Fisher and Joey Buttafuoco, Lorena Bobbitt castrating her abusive husband, the Menendez brothers murdering their parents, Tonya Harding's figure-skating rival Nancy Kerrigan being kneecapped before the Winter Olympics. In August 1994, the era was duly satirized in Oliver Stone's *Natural Born Killers*, in which "white trash" outlaws Mickey and Mallory Knox (Woody Harrelson and Juliette Lewis) become tabloid superstars during a three-week murder spree. They are tailed during their rampage by the blustery Australian host of *American Maniacs*, Wayne Gale (Robert Downey Jr.), a character inspired by Steve Dunleavy, the real-life star reporter of *A Current Affair*. The film's narrative peak comes during Gale's exclusive live interview with an incarcerated Mickey, which airs in the prime post–Super Bowl slot. When Mickey unapologetically defends murder as part of the natural order of all living beings, he triggers a prison riot that allows him and Mallory to escape with Gale as their hostage. "You want reality, you got it," Mickey tells Gale as they leave the prison, with cameras rolling. Though Gale comes to fully identify with the killers—to Stone, the scandal-obsessed media were *Natural Born Killers'* real villains—they deny his offer to stage a national tour on *Oprah* and *Donahue* and instead murder the host while his camera records it. Stone edits that bloody scene into a channel-flipping montage that clicks between footage of the Menendez brothers, Rodney King, Tonya Harding, the burning Branch Davidian compound, Lorena Bobbitt, and O. J. Simpson.

Stone's hyperstylized camerawork and rapid-fire editing on *Killers* simulated a deep immersion within the dizzying electronic nightmare world of trash television. His constant switching between angles, lenses, film stocks, tints, even genres (Mickey and Mallory's courtship is portrayed as a trashy sitcom) was unparalleled in mainstream cinema, but it did have a precedent in the violent, postmodern TV collage of reality rap albums like *AmeriKKKa's Most Wanted* and *The Chronic*. It was just as fitting that the film's soundtrack would include Dre's "The Day the Niggaz Took Over" as it was that Dre and Cube would collaborate on a single, released a few months later, titled "Natural Born Killaz." In one verse that attempts to reassert rap's dominion over mass-mediated violent entertainment, Cube links Reginald Denny's beating to the nation's most cultishly admired serial killer: "So fuck Charlie Manson / I snatch him out his truck, hit him with a brick, and I'm dancin'." The real shocks came through the exorbitantly budgeted video, in which the rappers portray serial killers—they briefly dramatize the O. J. Simpson and Menendez brothers murders—holed up in an abandoned warehouse, while dozens of police swarm outside (Shakur even makes a preprison cameo as a sniper lying in wait). "Shock value—that's what it's about," Dre told the *Los Angeles Times*. "The most exciting thing going down in the news right now is O.J.'s case. So we decided to play on that and the Menendez trial too—and just have a little fun with it all." Cube concurred: "The point of the song is to poke fun at serial killers, like Oliver Stone's movie did. It's supposed to be humorous."[20] The characters might have shifted, but the song remained the same.

In March 1995, Cube showcased the other side of his public persona with *Friday*, a feature-length expansion of the day-in-the-hood narrative format that he had pioneered four years earlier. F. Gary Gray, who had helmed Cube's "It Was a Good Day" and "True to the Game" videos, shot *Friday* on the block the director grew up on: 126th and Normandie, just west of Compton and four miles south of the Florence and Normandie intersection. The film's plot was simple: after being caught on surveillance video for the minor transgression of stealing boxes at work, newly unemployed Craig (Cube) is drawn in by his weed-puffing best friend, Smokey (Chris Tucker), to a series of schemes to acquire the $200 that Smokey owes the flamboyant local weed dealer Big Worm (Faizon Love), while avoiding being robbed by the neighborhood bully Deebo ("Tiny" Lister). There are no police in *Friday*, and the film allows Cube to address the issues plaguing his community—joblessness, gun violence, drugs, broken families—through a Cheech-and-Chong-style plot and a form of conflict resolution decided on the neighborhood's own terms, not the cops'. Though Craig keeps a 9 mm in his dresser drawer, his father (John Witherspoon) convinces him to settle the film's climactic dispute with his fists. Where "Natural Born Killaz" was the most graphic extension of the "gangsta" persona he had created seven years earlier, *Friday* expressed Cube's deep affection for South Los Angeles's Black suburbs, populated by regular families trying to get by and filled with the hilarious, harmless nonsense of young people with nothing better to do.

While Cube and Dre had established themselves as solo stars in the mainstream of American entertainment, N.W.A's original entrepreneur was living a far more chaotic life. In Black Los Angeles Eazy-E was a living legend who was generous with his money and time for his vast set of friends and associates. But he had also fathered nine children by numerous women and was regularly taking paternity tests and being hit up for late child support payments. His politics remained just as idiosyncratic as they had been when he and Jerry Heller appeared at a 1991 GOP fundraiser, underscored by his attendance at the 1993 federal trial of Theodore Briseno, one of the officers who was acquitted of criminal charges in the beating of Rodney King. Eazy shared a lawyer with Briseno, and he seemed as eager to remix the meaning of the Rodney King video as the Simi Valley jurors, telling reporters outside the courthouse that "out of the four, he was the only one I saw who was trying to stop the beating." The Geto Boys' Willie D was appalled, calling Eazy a "sellout" and claiming that "he ain't about nothin' but money."[21] But Ruthless Records was a minor player in the reality rap game compared to Death Row, which was raking in profits (part of which went to Ruthless) and scoring the sensationalistic headlines that Eazy wanted for himself. He released an October 1993 EP titled *It's On (Dr. Dre) 187um Killa*, with Dre's name crossed out: Blood code for someone marked for death. The EP was successful, but Eazy was foundering in the public eye. A December 1993 *Vibe* profile by Kevin Powell opened with the rhetorical question, "Is there a more reviled name in hip hop than Eazy-E?"[22] Despite it all, Eazy remained steadfast in his commitment to personal authenticity and regional diplomacy, no matter where it led him. In late 1994, he released "Tha Muthaphukkin Real," a slow-burning collaboration with MC Ren, on which he asserted his legacy: "And it's a fact, to be exact, my tombstone should read / 'He put Compton on that map.'"

Eazy was a wild card, but not even his closest friends predicted the sudden announcement made by his attorney in March 1995, five weeks before *Friday*'s premiere, that he had contracted HIV, which had developed into full-blown AIDS. A statement putatively written by the rapper framed the disease as the unforeseen product of a life lived *too* real. "Yeah, I was a brother on the streets of Compton doing a lot of things most people look down on, but it did pay off," read the statement, which doubled as a career retrospective. "Then we started rapping about real stuff that shook up the LAPD and the FBI. But we got our message across big time, and everyone in America started paying attention to the boys in the 'hood." AIDS, in Eazy's view, was punishment for his lifestyle of "fancy cars, gorgeous women, and good living" and cosmic retribution for having seven children with six different women. "Maybe success was too good to me," he speculated, before concluding with a mission statement for his followers: "It's your real time and your real life."[23] Eazy died ten days later, and while the rap community mourned and paid tribute to Eazy's unparalleled influence, it conducted a reality check of its own. "It's time for the hip-hop world to pull themselves out of their petty, microcosmic world of beef, beer, and boom and take a careful look at the rest of the world surrounding them," read an editorial in the June issue of the *Source*.[24]

Eazy-E's career and image were, in a way, testament to one young Black man's ability not only to evade death, by cop or street rival, but to aestheticize and capitalize that very evasion. If he died young, it was supposed to be because he was shot to death, not succumbed to AIDS. But though it significantly deviated from Eazy's stardom, his death adhered to the data. In 1993, the Centers for Disease Control had named AIDS as the leading killer of African American men aged twenty-five to forty-four. Though AIDS was largely ignored by the Reagan and Bush administrations—for whom the health of Black men, intravenous drug users, and homosexuals was not a policy priority—activists and independent journalists spent the 1980s forcing it into the national conversation. Early on, they were assisted by two tabloid culture icons: Phil Donahue, who devoted an episode to AIDS in 1982, and Geraldo Rivera, who gave AIDS its first national prime-time broadcast mention in a 1983 story on the ABC newsmagazine *20/20*. A year before Eazy's death, the third season of MTV's *The Real World*, set in San Francisco, starred the gay HIV-positive activist Pedro Zamora, who was applauded for raising international awareness about the disease and died that November, months after shooting wrapped. But though it was situated in the same tabloid mindset and pop culture circles, reality rap was not part of the solution. Only five years after rap's elder statesman Chuck D dismissed AIDS as a government conspiracy on *Fear of a Black Planet*, and despite the Black Los Angeles basketball icon Magic Johnson revealing his own HIV diagnosis a year later, reality rap was woefully underprepared to deal with a world in which an invisible virus was one of Black America's biggest threats. Heroin addicts were weak pawns in the dope man's game, and impugning a rival's heterosexuality was perhaps a rapper's most commonly used insult. In a *Doggystyle* skit, Daz Dillinger lambasted "busta-ass, HIV pussy-ass motherfuckers" and was interrupted by Dre, who told Daz, "Easy come, easy . . ." before he was cut off, the implication clear to anyone who was following his beef with Eazy.

Though reality rappers occasionally advocated for safe sex in their own language (Ice Cube advised listeners to "put a sock on the pickle" in "Look Who's Burnin'"), it was women who forced an adult discussion of responsible sex and AIDS into hip-hop's mainstream. It began with Salt-N-Pepa's 1990 single "Let's Talk About Sex"—a title that could have been drawn from a daytime talk show—and continued with the trio's remake of the song as "Let's Talk About AIDS" for Peter Jennings's 1992 ABC News town hall telecast about the disease. The group even included a public service announcement dramatization created by Boston high schoolers, titled "I Have AIDS," as the final track on their multiplatinum 1993 album *Very Necessary*. The trio's hip-hop/R&B counterparts TLC were outspoken advocates of safe sex as well. The group's gregarious lead rapper, Lisa "Left Eye" Lopes, wore a condom as an eye patch, and their smash 1995 single "Waterfalls" was themed to overcoming AIDS ignorance. A smarter and more mature strain of journalistic critique came from dream hampton in *Spin*, who duly highlighted Eazy's "aggressively heterosexual public statement" and quoted GLAAD associate director Donald Suggs: "It's sad that he felt (Black) people wouldn't be compassionate toward him unless he insisted on his heterosexuality. . . . To imply that this disease was spread by the uncontrollable sexual appetite of hip hop's female fans spreads ignorance."[25] In *Vibe*, Joan Morgan pushed back against the idea that Eazy's death was merely a tragic part of the rap game. Blaming his diagnosis and death on his "unrepentantly promiscuous" status as a young Black gangsta rapper was simply another racist stereotype that stopped people from understanding the reality of the AIDS epidemic, Morgan wrote. It was no more illuminating than arguing that AIDS was the province of "faggots" or "junkies," and it was especially galling given that hip-hop artists promoted safe sex more than did musicians working in any other popular genre.[26] Despite the forceful words of hip-hop's most prominent women, the response from the rest of the rap community was mournful but muted. In the same way that executives and politicians were careful to split rhetorical hairs by defending "free speech" without addressing the content of rap music threatened with censorship, most of the rap community warned the public about AIDS while carefully evading its stigmatized reality.

That August, Eazy received a hero's send-off at the second annual Source Awards. He was paid tribute with a lifetime achievement award and a performance from Bone Thugs-n-Harmony, the Cleveland-based group whom Eazy had signed to Ruthless and who had dedicated their second album, which hit no. 1 the week after the ceremony, to their mentor. The *Source* had started the award ceremony the year before as a form of self-coronation; it not only conferred prestige on the most noteworthy performers and producers but cast the magazine itself as hip-hop's foremost authority. While the telecast displayed the industry's geographic and stylistic diversity—Atlanta's Outkast won Best New Rap Group, and Miami dance-rappers 69 Boyz performed their hit "Tootsee Roll"— the evening belonged to Death Row and Bad Boy. The ceremony was held at New York's Madison Square Garden, but it opened with a medley of Death Row's latest hits, concluding with Snoop delivering a particularly fervent rendition of "Murder Was the Case." The night's most intriguing drama, however, was not in who won but in the victors' acceptance speeches, which doubled as tabloid-style rhetorical warfare. Accepting the trophy for Motion Picture Soundtrack of the Year for *Above the Rim*, Suge Knight gave a Death Row recruitment speech that both acknowledged Shakur ("I'd like to tell Tupac, keep his guards up, we ridin' with him") and fired a thinly veiled shot at Bad Boy and Combs. Knight said, "Any artist out there that want to be an artist and stay a star, and don't have to worry about the executive producer trying to be all in the videos, all on the record, dancing: come to Death Row!"

Combs was well aware of Shakur's increasing Bad Boy paranoia but did not know that Knight was playing along. (It was later revealed that Knight had flown to the ceremony after visiting Shakur upstate in prison.) Later in the evening, Combs was much more magnanimous in his remarks before he presented the Solo Artist of the Year award: "I'm the executive producer that a comment was made about a little bit earlier. . . . Contrary to what other people may feel, I'm very proud of Dr. Dre, of Death Row, and Suge Knight for their accomplishments. . . . All this East and West, it needs to stop." Combs presented the award to Snoop Doggy Dogg, and the two embraced—quite the tonal shift from Snoop's own heated comments from the stage toward the New York audience a bit earlier: "The East Coast ain't got no love for Dr. Dre and Snoop Dogg and Death Row? Y'all don't love us? . . . Well, let it be known, then!" That evening's animosities were performative, but that was not the case a month later, when a fight broke out at a party for Atlanta producer Jermaine Dupri that was attended by both Knight and Combs. In the melee that followed, one of Knight's friends was shot and killed by one of Combs's bodyguards. Combs claimed ignorance, but Knight took to the *Source* to directly blame his rival for the shooting.

If there was a single figure to match Shakur's relentless megalomania while serving as the worst possible authority figure for the emotionally vulnerable superstar, it was Knight. After the Atlanta shooting, the Death Row leader had all the ammunition he needed to wage a lucrative media war with the East Coast—and in October 1995, he landed his most important soldier. After months of negotiations between Death Row lawyer David Kenner and the Manhattan District Attorney's Office, and after Shakur signed a legally dubious "memo" binding him to Death Row for three albums, the rapper was released on appeal, his $1.4 million bail funded by Interscope. When the *LA Times* caught up with him six days later, Shakur was back to his old self. He had already recorded fourteen songs and described his prison bid in media terms: "It was tough sitting in jail listening to Jay Leno and Rush Limbaugh and everybody making jokes about me getting shot. And watching the media report all kinds of lies about me."[27] But his comeback single was neither the reality rap of his first two albums nor the resentful self-loathing of *Me Against the World* but the epic "California Love," a cocky, rollicking ode to West Coast supremacy supported by a *Mad Max*–inspired video that cost Interscope more than half a million dollars to produce. The single hit no. 1 in July 1996, four months after Shakur's equally gargantuan 130-minute double album *All Eyez on Me* debuted at the top of the album chart. While he did not exactly bask in the glare of publicity on *Eyez*, the album signaled an overbearing edge absent from *Me Against the World*. Suffused with imagery of law-enforcement surveillance and paparazzo photography, *Eyez* existed within a fog of paranoid publicity unlike anything that pop had ever seen. "I got the police watching me, the feds," Tupac told MTV about his choice of album title. "I got the females that want to charge me with false charges and sue me and all that. I got the females that like me. I got the jealous homeboys and I got the homies that roll with me. Everybody's looking to see what I'ma do now so, *All Eyez on Me*."

As early as the November 1992 issue of the *Source* (the cover of which showed Dre holding a gun to his head and which coincided with Dre's twinned peaks of tabloid infamy and hip-hop production), Dre insisted that *The Chronic* was going to be his lone solo album before he shifted to producing and perhaps a career in real estate. True to his word, at least for the time being, Shakur's comeback was Dre's last project for the label. Wanting no part of Knight's ever-heightening transcontinental drama, Dre left in March 1996 to start his own label with Interscope, called Aftermath. His first solo single for his new venture, "Been There, Done That," signaled his belief that he had nothing left to prove and underscored his long-expressed desire to sink his rap profits into a quieter, more secluded existence: the exact opposite of Knight's and Shakur's dreams. Dre wouldn't release another single for three years.

While Shakur was imprisoned, C. Delores Tucker's antirap campaign had gained significant momentum, earning the activist a brief, vulgar acknowledgment on Tupac's *All Eyez on Me* single "How Do U Want It." In June 1995, Tucker had teamed up with the cultural conservative William Bennett for the *New York Times* opinion piece "Lyrics from the Gutter," which insisted that Time-Warner should immediately stop its "sponsorship and promotion of lyrics that celebrate rape, torture and murder."[28] Shortly thereafter, Interscope postponed *Dogg Food*, the heavily hyped debut from Tha Dogg Pound, the duo of Death Row rising stars Kurupt and Daz, set for July. Furious, Suge Knight took to the pages of the *Source* for his rebuttal, paying for a two-page ad titled "Freedom Fighters," which listed the names of Martin Luther King Jr., Nelson Mandela, Malcolm X, and C. Delores Tucker but, in Knight's finest act of provocative yellow journalism, crossed out Tucker's with a red line: like Eazy with Dre, it was Blood code that she was marked for death. But though Tucker claimed victory that September, when Time-Warner sold its Interscope stake back to owners Ted Field and Jimmy Iovine, she was no closer to stanching the flood of reality rap: *Dogg Food* was released in October and debuted at no. 1. Though the album's first single, "New York, New York," did not take specific lyrical aim at the city or any of its rappers, rap fans recognized the music as the same track B.I.G. had earlier rapped over in a St. Ides ad, and B.I.G. himself called in to a local radio station to voice his complaints when he heard that Snoop, Daz, and Kurupt were filming the song's video in Red Hook, Brooklyn. Inspired by the rapper or not, an anonymous person fired shots at the "New York" video crew's on-set trailer and sped off. Tha Dogg Pound replied to the provocation in postproduction, inserting crudely green-screened footage of the group rampaging through the city and kicking over its skyscrapers.

Time-Warner might have left the reality rap recording industry, but *Vibe*, one of the crown jewels of the company's publishing empire, was deeply invested in the tawdry, violent soap opera spawned by its most powerful figures. "There was nobody that our readership cared about and reacted to the way that they responded to [Shakur]," said *Vibe* editor Alan Light. "Every cover we did with him was bigger each time."[29] The larger-than-life Suge Knight was a close second to Shakur's popularity, and the cover of *Vibe*'s February 1996 issue featured an image shot by Death Row's in-house photographer that portrayed those two with Snoop and Dre in a dark, dramatic framing, like a B-level *Godfather* remake. "This is an especially hectic time for Knight and Death Row, whose 'keepin' it real' mentality has the industry all shook up," wrote Kevin Powell in the accompanying story, which recapped the past year's drama, homing in on Knight's definition of "real." To Knight, being real meant maintaining loyalty to those he came up with and deploying "ghetto politics" to conduct business. He hired his Compton cronies no matter their criminal background or industry intelligence and operated his multimillion-dollar company with the pitiless tactics of a street shakedown. Knight's tactics had clearly rubbed off on Shakur, whose postprison image was one not of reform or regret but of score settling—both to save face and to generate lucrative publicity. Powell caught up with Shakur on the set of "California Love" and asked him about the supposed East/West feud. "It's gonna get deep," Shakur replied. Powell ended the article with a dramatic prediction: "The tragedy here is that two of the most successful young black entrepreneurs ever could possibly end up hurt or dead over God only knows what."[30]

For the same story, Powell also reported from the Los Angeles County criminal court building where jury selection was taking place for Snoop's long-delayed murder trial; the building had recently been occupied, Powell noted, by O. J. Simpson, "Hollywood madam" Heidi Fleiss, and Michael Jackson (the latter accused of child sexual abuse). The courtroom would again be visited by Johnnie Cochran, whom one of Snoop's codefendants had retained as counsel. Prospective jurors were asked for their opinions on Simpson and Rodney King, though Snoop's attorney David Kenner was more worried that they would confuse the nonviolent man with his occasionally bloodthirsty on-record persona. "Snoop Doggy Dogg is not on trial here; Calvin Broadus is," Kenner told Powell. "When you reach to a performer's interviews or their songs and try to extrapolate from that perceptions that you want to draw about the real person, to me it would be no different than saying Arnold Schwarzenegger is a cold-blooded murderer because of his last movie."[31] Not quite the spectacle of its tabloid predecessors, Snoop's trial ran from November to February and was covered extensively by MTV, which aired a show called "Murder Is the Case: The Trial of Snoop Doggy Dogg" and filed regular reports on the network's recently launched website. With a reality rapper on the stand and with Rodney King, the LA rebellion, and O. J. Simpson still a recent memory, Snoop's defense initially tried to "play the L.A.P.D. card," as the LA Times put it, by attacking officers' mishandling of crucial evidence.[32] The attorneys painted Philip Woldemariam as a gun-toting gangster threatened by Snoop's accidental incursion into his territory and McKinley Lee as a family man who was merely doing his job as a bodyguard. The prosecution's case was hampered by witness accounts that had grown hazy in the three years since the shooting and by the fact that the average gang-affiliated Black man was not going to tell the entire truth to the police, leading to contradictory witness-stand narratives. In late February, the jury acquitted Snoop of murder and accessory after the fact and deadlocked on the charge of manslaughter, leading the judge to declare a mistrial on the latter charge. Snoop had been exonerated, and it appeared that his performative notoriety did not harm his case at all but might have actually helped him. It was reported in the case's aftermath that one of the jurors had performed a self-written rap song in the judge's chambers that poked fun at the prosecution and had performed it again at a Death Row celebration party at a Westwood bar soon after the acquittal—an event also attended by at least half the jurors.[33]

That May, Shakur and Snoop were back in court—in the video for their first collaborative single, "2 of Amerikaz Most Wanted," recorded immediately after Shakur's release from prison, while Snoop was still awaiting his legal fate. Snoop's first verse opens with a line from the proto-reality rap song "The Message" ("I keep my hand on my gun / 'Cause they got me on the run"), not as a warning about the harmful effects of ghetto life but to describe his high-profile legal predicament: "Now I'm back in the courtroom, waitin' on the outcome." Shown flipping through stacks of hundreds and sitting around a lavishly decorated dining table, both rappers are celebratory and cocky, "two multi-millionaires catchin' cases" while enjoying the high life. But amid the celebratory scenarios, Shakur still had scores to settle. The video opens with a short, fantasized dramatization of what Shakur clearly wished could have happened the night after the Quad Studios shooting. Echoing a scene from the 1983 *Scarface* remake, a heavily bandaged Shakur walks into a well-appointed office and confronts Combs and Biggie, named "Buff" and "Piggy," after they finish discussing what they assume was a successful hit. When Shakur appears to reach for a gun, a terrified Piggy stammers out a confession and pins the blame on Buff. But Shakur is merely pulling out a cigarette lighter, and he shakes his head in disappointment at the revelation he has just triggered. "We was homeboys once, Pig. Once we homeboys, we always homeboys. Even if you is a fat phony." High-concept reality rap without any political undertones, the opening to "2 of Amerikaz Most Wanted" existed wholly on the other side of the celebrity looking glass. It was Hollywood reality as publicity, a celebrity sampling *Scarface* to save face.

That fall, it appeared that the TV version of *America's Most Wanted* had reached the end of its run. Though John Walsh's program had helped to capture 431 fugitives during its eight years on Fox, the network was more concerned with the program's declining ratings. Unlike *Cops'* more generalizable scenarios, the extreme timeliness of *Wanted*'s reenactments did not lend themselves to the lucrative postbroadcast world of syndication, and Fox's new programming head saw reality shows as a trend that had run their course. Fox scheduled the final *Wanted* episode for September 21, which Walsh planned to devote to the story that first brought him to public attention: his own son Adam's still-unsolved kidnapping and murder. Yet once Fox publicized its intentions, *Wanted* fans around the country started vociferously expressing their objections. A North Carolina woman whose murdered brother had been profiled on the show protested outside Fox's TV lot for a week, and thousands of other passionate viewers sent supportive letters to Walsh. Numerous public officials joined fans in disparaging Fox's decision: the FBI issued a sympathetic statement, the governor of Nevada rallied thirty-seven of his fellow state leaders in support, and numerous victims' advocacy groups and local law enforcement officers spoke up as well. It worked: in early October, Fox announced a "major" prime-time overhaul that involved canceling some low-performing shows, moving others, and rebranding *America's Most Wanted* as the more vigilante-centric *America's Most Wanted: America Fights Back*. The show's low ratings couldn't compete with the deep affective connection it had engendered among viewers and the law enforcement community, who banded together to resurrect it.

The world of daytime talk had reached a similar turning point. Having played in the tabloid TV mud pit for nearly a decade, the format's progenitor, Phil Donahue, had lost the energy to keep up with his low-brow competition and hung up his microphone in May, after twenty-nine years on the air. While Oprah had pivoted her show into a form of New Age consumerist feminism a couple of years earlier, the daytime talk format that she and Donahue popularized had generated its own talent ecosystem of fame seekers from society's fringes and a new crop of hosts eager to gain a foothold in the carnivalesque public sphere. The previous year and a half had seen the debut of new daytime talk shows from Ricki Lake, Charles Perez, Montel Williams, Tempestt Bledsoe, Gabrielle Carteris, Rolonda Watts, and Carnie Wilson. While Geraldo Rivera was promising to devote more time on his program to investigations of global import (he took a trip to war-torn Bosnia that year), his trash-TV legacy was duly upheld by upstarts Richard Bey and Jerry Springer, who booked guests willing to debase themselves by actually fighting one another on television. The new regime of confrontational tabloid talk came to a head in March 1995, when, three days after Scott Amedure surprised Jonathan Schmitz with a profession of love on *The Jenny Jones Show*, Schmitz shot and killed Amedure at his home. The performative emotional outbursts, shocking revelations, and sordid crimes of passion that had become tabloid television's profitable stock-in-trade had crossed over into a real-life murder.

In a shocking move that could have been drawn directly from a sordid talk show stage, Shakur opened "Hit 'Em Up," the B side to his smash single "How Do U Want It," with a surprise revelation aimed at the Notorious B.I.G.: "I fucked your bitch, you fat motherfucker!" B.I.G. had married the Bad Boy–signed R&B singer Faith Evans in August 1994, but the rising rapper had almost immediately been unfaithful, travails that were captured and tracked in a hip-hop media ecosystem hungry for lurid tabloid headlines. Convincing himself in prison that B.I.G. and Combs had been responsible for his shooting at Quad Studios, Shakur decided that the best revenge against his rival would be to sleep with his wife. In the March 1996 issue of the *Source*, Shakur added fuel to the fire, claiming his rival was falsely presenting himself as a player on club tracks like "Big Poppa," which was Shakur's lane. "Stole my lyrics, I stole his bitch," Shakur explained. "If he talk all that shit about being a player and I got at his wife two days after I got outta jail, imagine that gangsta shit he's talking, how plastic that shit is."[34] After his release, Shakur publicly affiliated himself with Evans in the press and convinced her—without telling her the album was on Death Row, she claims—to add vocals to the *All Eyez on Me* track "Wonda Why They Call U Bitch," on which he chastises an anonymous woman for sleeping her way to fame and fortune. Suddenly, Evans found herself squarely in the center of a tabloid-rap love triangle and the subject of coverage that gave her little agency apart from a trophy traded between two powerful men. "Is the new, slimmer Faith losing weight from all that running back and forth between the Notorious B.I.G. and Tupac?" asked *Vibe* in a March 1996 "20 Questions" feature.[35] A short piece in the May issue was more supportive: "Like Anita Hill and Robin Givens, Faith is portrayed in terms that are repeatedly used to devalue black womanhood."[36] The seedy scenario even made its way into the *New York Times Magazine* as part of a feature profile on Suge Knight. While he and Shakur were getting dressed for a night out, Knight told the reporter that Evans had bought Shakur the shirt he was wearing and then asked Shakur what he did in return. "'I did enough,' he [said], rather salaciously."[37]

"Hit 'Em Up" went further than accusations of cuckolding. With the chorus couplet "Who shot me? But you punks didn't finish / Now you 'bout to feel the wrath of a menace," Shakur was publicly daring Bad Boy to reply in kind. Puffy and B.I.G. would not respond in their music or in person, but the July issue of *Vibe* solidified the beef with the instantly notorious cover line "East vs. West." In the story, B.I.G. came across less angry than disconsolate: "Honestly, I didn't have no problem with the nigga," he said. Puffy felt the same toward Knight's Source Awards remarks: "I couldn't believe what he said. I thought we was boys." Regardless, the 3,600-word story recounted every detail of the feud to date and even delved into rumors, like one about a mocked-up advertisement Death Row had commissioned that showed Suge with Puffy's wife, Misa, holding the couple's two-year-old son, with the caption "The East Coast can't even take care of their own." Though B.I.G. was not interested in recording a response track to what was a fairly one-sided fight, he got a dig in at Shakur's obsession with him. "My niggas is, like, 'Fuck dat nigga, that nigga's so much on your dick, it don't even make no sense to say anything.'" For his part, Puffy—whose father, Melvin, had been an associate of the Harlem drug lord Frank Lucas and had been murdered when Combs was two years old—drew a clear distinction between violent entertainment and reality. "What it's been right now is a lot of moviemaking and a lot of entertainment drama. Bad boys move in silence. If somebody wants to get your ass, you're gonna wake up in heaven. There ain't no record gonna be made about it."[38] It was increasingly clear that Shakur did not share this assessment.

On September 3, Shakur and Snoop attended the MTV Video Music Awards on Bad Boy's turf at Radio City Music Hall. "2 of Amerikaz Most Wanted" was not nominated (Coolio's hit "Gangsta's Paradise" beat "California Love" to take home the Best Rap Video trophy), but the duo walked out to the strains of their hit single to announce the winner for Best Hard Rock Video. A postbroadcast interviewer asked whether they had been hesitant to come to the East Coast, given the status of their Bad Boy animosities. Shakur quickly responded, "We are businessmen, we are not animals. It's not like we're gonna see them, and rush them, and jump on them." He was also quick to note that the "wanted" part of "2 of Amerikaz Most Wanted" was less about being wanted by the law than desired by a consumer public. "We got beef with the people we got beef with. But we could go anywhere in the country, because we are America's most wanted," Shakur said.[39] At its core, he stressed, the rivalry was about market share, and if capitalism knew no geographic boundaries, why should they?

Four nights later, Shakur and Knight flew to Las Vegas. At the MGM Grand, they watched Mike Tyson walk to the ring to the strains of Shakur's song "Let's Get It On (Ready 2 Rumble)," which the rapper had recorded for the boxer a day earlier, and then knock out Bruce Seldon one minute and forty-nine seconds into the first round to win the WBA Heavyweight Championship. Shakur, Knight, and their entourage headed out, with plans to attend a show at Knight's Club 662 featuring Run-DMC, whom Knight was trying to recruit to the newly announced Death Row East. In the lobby of the Grand, one of Knight's Blood comrades told him he had just seen a Southside Crip named Orlando Anderson, who not only had snatched his Death Row chain in a recent altercation but was also rumored to have been present at the 1995 Atlanta shooting. Shakur took off running after Anderson, and he, Knight, and the rest of their crew stomped him before being chased off by hotel security. After changing clothes at Knight's nearby home, Knight and Shakur drove toward the club in Knight's BMW, while listening to an early version of Shakur's forthcoming album, *The Don Killuminati: The 7 Day Theory*, tailed by an entourage of about ten other cars. At a stoplight, a white Cadillac pulled up next to the car containing Knight and Shakur, and someone inside opened fire. Shakur tried diving into the back seat but was hit by four .40 caliber Glock rounds. Knight started speeding toward a nearby hospital while his Death Row enforcers tried in vain to retaliate against the shooter, who drove off. When Knight ran over a curb and blew out his car's tires, he found himself splayed out on the street by the Las Vegas Police Department, who aimed their guns at the crew, while asking about their gang affiliations and the meanings of their tattoos.

Shakur was rushed to University Medical Center, where he lay in critical condition while police and the Fruit of Islam security team stood guard and television news cameras, paparazzi, and concerned fans swarmed outside. Though the rap community assumed that Shakur would pull through, like he had after the Quad Studios shooting, he died six days later. He was twenty-five years old. The investigation into Shakur's murder was slowed by mutual mistrust between the police, Death Row, and the gang-affiliated witnesses to the crime. "In my opinion, it was black-gang related and probably a Bloods-Crips thing," Sgt. Chuck Cassell of the Las Vegas Police Department's gang unit told Kevin Powell for Powell's *Rolling Stone* cover story. "Look at [Shakur's] tattoos and album covers. . . . It looks like a case of live by the sword, die by the sword."[40] Another officer told Powell that there had been three related Crip shootings the week after Shakur's murder, a connection that a Compton officer laughed off. The lack of solid leads generated a wealth of conspiracy theories. Powell dismissed the idea that Puffy and B.I.G. had been involved and noted that others were wondering if the killer might have been aiming for Knight himself, or if Knight had somehow himself arranged the murder out of his fear that Shakur would soon leave Death Row.

When Knight rushed *Don Killuminati* to stores two months after Shakur's death, the fact that the album was released under a new performative identity, complete with a liner-note blurb that read, "Exit—2Pac / Enter—Makaveli," generated rumors that Shakur had faked his death. Given Shakur's uninterrupted fixation on the album with vanquishing his industry rivals, it certainly *felt* like he was still around. *Killuminati* opens with a replica newscast framing the album itself as an unsolved murder: "Although no one knows the exact cause of the new album," a reporter asserts, "resources tell me a number of less fortunate rappers have joined together in conspiracy to assassinate the character of not only Mr. Shakur but of Death Row Records as well." It was surreal and sad but also morbidly appropriate that Shakur's posthumously released album was themed to the murder of his reputation. The "alleged ringleader" was Nas, in cahoots with New York rappers "Mobb Sleep" (a.k.a. Mobb Deep), "Notorious P.I.G.," Jay-Z, and Big L. On the album's concluding track, "Against All Odds," Shakur took direct lyrical aim at Jacques "Haitian Jack" Agnant and Combs for their roles in the

Quad Studios shooting and directly asked Nas why a few lyrics of "The Message," from his second album, *It Was Written*, seemed to directly correspond to those events. To Nas, his detail-rich song was broadly metaphoric, aimed at the rising crop of New York street rappers threatening his supremacy. In Shakur's worldview, these two things were inextricable: misquoting *Scarface* in your lyrics was equivalent to putting out a hit on a real rival.

With Knight's assistance, Shakur had pushed his career as close as possible to the invisible line separating mediated crime from its real-world equivalent. "Now it's real," a hip-hop journalist told *Vibe* in the hours after Shakur died. "The shit people have been talking in the past five years, all the dissing and posturing, has led to this. Hip hop has crossed a line, and it's gonna be hard to cross back."[41] The only way to discover that line, and expose it, was to kill or be killed, and Shakur had finally achieved true realness in death. "Like Kurt Cobain before him, Shakur had become a living symbol of his generation's angst and rage, and for that he is now looked upon as a martyr," Powell wrote.[42] Where Cobain's suicide coalesced in a single tragedy of the disaffection and pain of millions of white fans, Shakur's death solidified his status as "the most important solo artist in the history of rap," Powell wrote, "not because he was the most talented (he wasn't) but because he, more than any other rapper, personified and articulated what it was to be a young black man in America." In his death, Shakur had become a one-man representation of the everyday terror internalized by the nation's young Black men, that they could die at any moment—whether from the police, an enemy, or a stray bullet—and that there was a good chance their killer would never be found. Shakur was, Powell specified, "a product of a post–civil rights, post–Black Panther, post–Ronald Reagan American environment ... [who] kept it real for a lot of folks who didn't believe that anyone like him (or like themselves) could do anything with his life." Shakur was also a million-selling pop superstar, and his iconography certainly registered differently to the millions of white consumers who absorbed his every word, action, and visual. "There may never have been a pop star who signified so differently for so many different people," wrote R. J. Smith in the *Spin* obituary. "The more his fame grew, the more the split widened." Countless Americans knew Shakur, Smith wrote, only as the vulgar criminal antagonist who "changed the direction of hip-hop—hijacked it, some would say—and ceremonialized its status as the art politicians love to hate."[43]

To Powell, Shakur's lifetime of fame and controversy was cut short by a sudden death that rendered him "an enigma," like Cobain, Marvin Gaye, James Dean, Jimi Hendrix, Jim Morrison, and Malcolm X. Like those icons who died too soon before him, there would be interminable questions about what Shakur could have done with the rest of his career. In the bootlegged iconography that would circulate long after his death, Shakur's visage would be constantly linked to these other cultural martyrs. Yet the video rushed to MTV and BET while the world was freshly mourning his death established a different canon of Shakur's afterlife peers. Like Snoop's character in "Murder Was the Case" and B.I.G. on *Life after Death*, Shakur predicted his own demise in the music video for the *All Eyez on Me* single "I Ain't Mad at Cha," complete with a dramatized murder, unsuccessful resuscitation attempts, and ascent to a dry-ice–filled heaven, where he was greeted by impersonators portraying Hendrix, Redd Foxx, Miles Davis, and Sammy Davis Jr. "It may steal its idea from a better Bone Thugs-N-Harmony video," Smith wrote, comparing it to "Tha Crossroads," but he insisted that Shakur's final video is "sentimental kitsch" that "steals its soul from Vegas."[44] Indeed, in the aftermath of Shakur's death, he was on his way to becoming rap's version of rock's ultimate tabloid tragedy, Elvis Presley, who spent the latter half of his life surrounded by the glitzy squalor of Sin City. Like the King, Shakur's posthumous existence was nearly as busy as his short time on earth. Amid countless articles and books speculating about the true cause of Shakur's death and the estate-sanctioned albums that would come to outnumber those that were released while he was alive, there were tabloid stories that claimed to have spotted Shakur at a fast-food restaurant or speculated that he was holed up in Cuba with Assata.

Shakur's death in Vegas mirrored his public image in a more metaphysical sense as well. Now known as the "Entertainment Capital of the World," Las Vegas—more specifically, the Las Vegas Strip—is in many ways the quintessential American environment, built in the middle of nowhere by capitalist pioneers taking advantage of Nevada's libertarian approach to vice. In and around the flashy casinos, the Las Vegas Strip, near where Shakur was gunned down, is laden with hyperrealistic replicas of everything from the Egyptian pyramids to the Eiffel Tower, the

Venice canals to the New York City skyline. Vegas is the absolute fake, the single American geographical location whose architectural landscape is built out of knockoffs and whose entertainment culture is pure, uncut capitalist spectacle for spectacle's sake. According to the influential 1972 study *Learning from Las Vegas*, the Strip's status as pure kitsch, a facsimile of cosmopolitanism and wealth, makes it the frontier of postmodern American populism; it is thus a sprawling cousin to tabloid television, which translated a highbrow journalism into a vehicle for lowbrow stories and perspectives. Las Vegas was where Suge Knight attended college and started his career as a nightclub bouncer and where, after the success of Death Row, he returned to purchase the Las Vegas home that he'd watched Robert DeNiro's character Sam Rothstein occupy in the 1995 film *Casino*. Unlike N.W.A, who were straight outta Compton, Shakur had no home to call his own: he was born in Harlem, raised in Baltimore, and shuttled off to Marin City before reinventing himself as a rapper/ spectacle in Los Angeles, itself a land of Hollywood hyperreality, a blank slate on which average Americans have rewritten their life stories for generations.

Just as there was no more appropriate place for rapper/spectacle Tupac Shakur to meet his tragic fate than Las Vegas, there was no more appropriate outlet to take the investigative lead than the freshly resurrected *America's Most Wanted*, which devoted the first episode of its new iteration to the investigation into Shakur's murder. "As a performer, Tupac Shakur often lived out the fears of his life in the fiction of his videos," Walsh noted to open the November 9 segment, before cutting to clips from the music videos for "2 of Amerikaz Most Wanted" and "I Ain't Mad at Cha." The ironic similarity of the first clip's title to Walsh's own program was not noted, while the second video's reenactments looked for all intents and purposes like they could have been staged and shot by *America's Most Wanted*'s own production staff. The segment's reporting coup was never-before-seen casino surveillance video showing the moments after Shakur and Knight's brawl with Orlando Anderson and the Las Vegas detectives' first televised interviews since the murder. "That East Coast / West Coast stuff was a lot of hype," one officer opines, pinning Shakur's death on Orlando Anderson and casting it, ten years after the gangs had first infiltrated hip-hop at Run-DMC's Long Beach concert, as a Vegas extension of the Bloods and the Crips' Los Angeles rivalry. Back in the high-tech confines of what Walsh called "the crime center"—surrounded by massive, glowing video walls, banks of phone operators, and a massive *America's Most Wanted* logo—Walsh posed a rhetorical question to the story's lead reporter: "Wouldn't you hope that someone would have the guts to call this hotline because they can remain anonymous and solve this case?" It was as much an attempt to break the case open as it was to reroute the significant attention surrounding Shakur's murder investigation to Walsh's hypermediated posse.

The Shakur murder investigation, and Suge Knight's possible involvement, became the nation's latest tabloid fixation. The *Wanted* report noted that Knight, who was jailed for a probation violation in the Anderson assault, was being mum on any details of the case. A few months later, Knight told the ABC newsmagazine *Primetime Live* from prison that even if he knew who had shot Shakur, he would not say. "I don't get paid to solve homicides," he said. That same story revealed that one of Knight's earliest forays into the rap recording business was shaking down Vanilla Ice—literally dangling him over a balcony—for his "Ice Ice Baby" royalties. But Knight had larger problems to deal with: federal agents were probing Death Row's connections to organized crime, a charge that Knight characterized as racially motivated in an interview where he compared himself to Martin Luther King Jr. and Malcolm X. "A black brother from Compton creates a company that helps people in the ghetto, so what does the government do? They try to bring him down."[45] Knight retained Rodney King's lawyer Milton Grimes, who contended that Interscope higher-ups were equally worthy of investigation. "Their money came from Interscope... so if there are going to be indictments, let them take on the industry—not just this one black business."[46] In March, Knight was sentenced to nine years in prison for his probation violation, but investigations into Knight and Death Row would soon expand to the LAPD itself. Though it was not a secret that Knight used off-duty officers as Death Row security, it was not until the department was rocked by the Rampart scandal, which erupted in late 1997 and continued for several years, that the public learned the degree to which at least two officers in the LAPD's CRASH unit (the antigang force started by Daryl Gates) were involved in everything from a massive bank robbery to theft and resale of confiscated cocaine and also had direct financial connections to Knight and Death Row. While

Knight took the fall, Interscope heads Ted Field and Jimmy Iovine were untouched.

Amid the November 1996 tumult, Snoop Doggy Dogg released his second album, T*ha Doggfather*, three years after his first, bearing a title that signaled his embrace of the emergent East Coast mafioso image. It sold well (after Shakur's two albums, it had the highest first-week numbers of any album that year), but it was swallowed by the drama surrounding Shakur and Death Row. The following February, Snoop guest starred as himself on a first-season episode of *The Steve Harvey Show*, a sitcom on the WB, Warner Bros.' newly launched broadcast network designed to replicate Fox's success in attracting young Black audiences. Harvey played Steve Hightower, an out-of-work musician teaching high school music appreciation in Chicago, and Snoop shows up early in the episode, to the delight of Hightower's students and the studio audience, to request that Hightower let Snoop sample his song "When the Funk Hits the Fan." Soon after Snoop's request, Puffy shows up later to ask the same question, leading Hightower's friend Cedric Robinson (Cedric the Entertainer) to warn him, "Don't you know about the East Coast / West Coast rivalry?" Harvey responds, "No...I must've missed that, along with Michael Jackson having a baby and that whole O. J. thing." Late in the episode, with both rap icons in the same room, Hightower delivers a brief lecture on their responsibility as role models. Snoop and Puffy were way ahead of him though. "All that East Coast / West Coast stuff is a bunch of media hype," Combs tells him. "We make music for everybody," Snoop concurs, as the studio audience erupts into applause. Hightower convinces the two to deliver the same message in front of his class—and, for Snoop and Combs's sake, a national television audience of young Black viewers.

Three weeks later, the Notorious B.I.G. was murdered in a vehicle while leaving a *Vibe*-sponsored party the night after the Soul Train Awards in Los Angeles. Two weeks after that, his second album, the two-hour-long double LP *Life after Death*, was released. With a garish, pop-influenced production style that flaunted the expensiveness of its samples, *Life after Death* both commemorated the life of its creator and foretold a new era for rap. Predicted by Death Row and Bad Boy's corporate war, hip-hop's ambition and style was moving from the street to the suite. The video for the album's second single, "Mo Money Mo

Problems," directed by up-and-coming auteur Hype Williams, looked like few rap videos before it. Combs and Bad Boy signee Ma$e wore shiny, colorful suits and floated in a zero-gravity space capsule, while B.I.G. delivered his posthumous verse from a futuristic video monitor. Bad Boy had taken over not just rap but the entire record industry. The label's output owned the *Billboard* Hot 100 for nearly half of 1997, with "Mo Money Mo Problems," the B.I.G. tribute "I'll Be Missing You," Biggie's "Hypnotize," and the Combs single "Can't Nobody Hold Me Down" trading off the top spot from mid-March to mid-September, interrupted for three weeks by Hanson's teen-pop earworm "MMMBop."

On his first solo single "Can't Nobody Hold Me Down," Combs flipped the patient zero of reality rap, "The Message," from a tabloid narrative of an economically decimated Black New York into a number one single themed to hyperreal, Black capitalistic excess. As Combs and Ma$e sped through the desert in a Rolls-Royce, it was impossible not to see that 1997 heralded a new era. Shakur and Eazy were dead, Knight was sentenced to nine years in prison, Dre was focusing on Aftermath production and A&R, Snoop shared a bill with Korn and Tool as part of the alt-rock festival Lollapalooza, Ice Cube appeared in the action thrillers *Dangerous Ground* and *Anaconda*, Ice-T starred in a short-lived Dick Wolf crime drama called *Players*, and Public Enemy kept plugging away at a much lower level of visibility. Reality rappers had helped usher hip-hop to the center of popular culture and political debate, but its newest crop of organic executives—Combs, Jay-Z, the New Orleans upstart Master P—were less interested in tabloid stardom than in conquering the pop charts and making inroads into other consumer markets. Black-owned labels were flourishing, and hip-hop had redefined the pop charts on its own terms. For the next several years, hip-hop would be dominated by the kind of flash and glamour that reality rap had temporarily vanquished a decade earlier, while the most outspoken political voices were relegated to the warrens of a rapidly expanding underground, and Atlanta, New Orleans, Memphis, and Virginia Beach emerged as the newest industry hot spots. Just below the surface, the remains of the reality rap empire smoldered, waiting for a resurrection.

CONCLUSION

DEEPER THAN RAP

▼

In April 2012, more than fifteen years after his death, Tupac Shakur once again performed "2 of Amerikaz Most Wanted" with his erstwhile collaborator, who by then was going by the name Snoop Dogg. The setting was the thirteenth annual Coachella Festival, the multiday music and arts event that drew fans from around the world to the rolling green hills of Indio, California, two hours east of Los Angeles. Shakur's presence came courtesy of an expensive, realistic holographic projection that replicated his vocal timbre and body movements with eerie accuracy. When the reconstituted Shakur appeared onstage and yelled, "What the fuck is up, Coachella?!" the effect was uncanny and, for many, quite moving. Lindsay Zoladz compared the effect to the Notorious B.I.G.'s posthumous appearance in Puff Daddy and Ma$e's 1997 "Mo Money Mo Problems" video and the glowing ghost of Eazy-E in Bone Thugs-n-Harmony's "Tha Crossroads" clip. (Zoladz also noted that Eazy-E had been revitalized by the same technology, with motion-capture performances staged by his children and supervised by his widow, Tomica.)[1] "Holography could prosper only in America, a country obsessed with realism," wrote Umberto Eco in an essay about wax museums. "If a reconstruction is to be credible, it must be absolutely iconic, a perfect likeness, a 'real' copy of the reality being represented."[2] The man who had devoted the final five years of his life to a performative project of scandalous Black American realism had been resurrected by holography, a technological phenomenon that made him even more quintessentially American than his Las Vegas death.

Well before his 2012 performance, Shakur had ascended to a rarefied level of American cultural memory: the eternal presentness of the prematurely dead. As Greil Marcus wrote about Elvis's second life, Shakur "made history" while he was alive, and "when he died, maybe people found themselves caught up in the adventure of remaking his history, which is to say their own."[3] By 2012, Tupac's posthumously released albums outnumbered those issued during his short life. His image and "thug life" mantra had reached iconographic status in officially sanctioned and bootleg form, and because his murder was still unsolved, numerous documentaries and homemade YouTube videos had proffered their own theories about what really happened in Las Vegas. In 2003, Shakur's story was made into an Oscar-nominated documentary and book, aptly titled *Resurrection*, with both productions supervised by his mother. Five years after Coachella, Shakur was granted pop music's two most hallowed forms of cultural enshrinement: he was inducted into the Rock and Roll Hall of Fame, with a moving induction speech delivered by Snoop, and had his story retold through the biopic *All Eyez on Me* (also supervised by Afeni), which was, appropriately enough, acclaimed less for its screenplay or direction than for Demetrius Shipp Jr.'s uncannily accurate embodiment of Shakur.

Hip-hop is known for paying loving tribute to its fallen soldiers, and Kendrick Lamar's 2015 revivification of Shakur at the end of his album *To Pimp a Butterfly* provided a sonic equivalent of the Coachella hologram. After reading a brief spoken-word piece titled "Mortal Man," Lamar channels the spirit of Shakur, in a way. Lamar had found an unpublished audio interview with Shakur from November 1994, two weeks before the rapper's life and career were irrevocably altered by the Quad Studios shooting. With Afeni's blessing, Lamar spliced in his own questions to Shakur's responses, characterizing himself in one pseudo prompt as "one of your offsprings of the legacy you left behind." The conversation, so to speak, touches upon some of Shakur's favored topics: how the American system "take[s] the heart and soul out of a [Black] man," how one needed to balance self-enrichment with the good of the community, and how the next Black revolution would be infinitely more deadly than the 1992 LA uprising. Like the hologram, Lamar's conversation with Shakur was more impressive for its technological novelty than its actual content. "The excitement you feel while listening to it comes from the *idea* of the two talking, not from what's actually said," wrote Jay Caspian Kang.[4] After the pair's brief exchange, Lamar reads a poem written by a friend but finds Shakur unresponsive when he finishes, as if the medium has lost contact with the spirit. The album concludes with Lamar urgently reaching out: "Pac? Pac?! Pac?!!"

Though their music and public personas were quite different, it wasn't out of character for Lamar to position himself as Shakur's heir apparent. The magnetic, Compton-raised rapper's critically adored 2012 breakthrough LP, *Good Kid, M.A.A.D. City*, established him as what Kang called hip-hop's latest messiah figure. More than any Black artist since Shakur and the Notorious B.I.G., Kang wrote, post–*Good Kid* Lamar was faced with the impossible burden of representation: "He must create something that feels as though it has grown organically out of his city, but that is at the same time universal. His work must feel political, but not overtly political. He should be an example and a savior to the young Black people who listen to his music. It's an impossible role to inhabit—at least while the hip-hop messiah is alive."[5] As with Shakur, the messiah crown—previously granted to Rakim, the Notorious B.I.G., Nas, Shakur, and one of Lamar's most prominent inspirations, Eminem—weighed heavily on its recipients. Correspondingly, a prominent theme of Lamar's *Good Kid* follow-up, *To Pimp a Butterfly*, was the emotional toll of his status during a time of incredible tumult in Black communities across the country. Combined, the two albums launched Lamar's career and resurrected Compton as one of hip-hop's most hallowed real-world stages after a decade and a half of relative invisibility.

Born in Compton during the summer that Ice-T released *Rhyme Pays* and Eazy-E dropped "Boyz-n-the-Hood," Lamar came of age not during the heyday of Los Angeles reality rap but after the legend had been established. His streets were controlled by Bloods and Crips and poisoned by crack, but to the rest of the country, they could have been a film studio's back lot. Subtitled "A Short Film by Kendrick Lamar," *Good Kid* sounded nothing like N.W.A's sensationalistic tabloid rap, but more like the hood neorealism of the Watts-raised director Charles

Burnett, whose films shunned violence, comedy, stars, and happy endings for a quasi-documentary, psychologically complex presentation of Black lives. In his predecessors' tradition, Lamar incorporates skits into the album, but they are not comedic and sound nothing like news reports. Instead, they trace the contours of the mind of a young man trying to balance responsibility and social conformity. Seamlessly sequenced into the flow of the music, which is more brooding and darker than the bright G-funk of *The Chronic* or *Doggystyle*, the skits include an answering machine message from his hectoring parents and a detailed portrayal of his friends plotting a crime. Distrustful of gang life's nihilistic machismo, surrounded by various forms of extreme addiction, and fixated on achieving an affective equilibrium, *Good Kid* codifies a millennial gangsterism, expressing "the vulnerabilities of young Black men at risk and as risk in the postindustrial ghettos of urban America."[6]

Though Lamar chose mostly to work with unknown collaborators on *Good Kid*, a few reality rap OGs appear on the album: MC Eiht shows up on the album's title track—which shifts midway to a beat that recreates Ice Cube's "Bird in the Hand"—and Dr. Dre appears on the album-closing track, "Compton." Dre had spent most of the 2000s holed up in the studio, taking business meetings, helping launch the careers of superstars Eminem and 50 Cent, and founding the Beats by Dr. Dre headphone line with Interscope and Aftermath partner Jimmy Iovine. In January 2014, Dre and Iovine launched the music streaming service Beats Music, which was bought by Apple a few months later, along with Beats Electronics, for $3.2 billion, making Dre, he claimed in a viral video, rap's first billionaire. Dre's Aftermath label released *Good Kid*, and as Jayson Greene noted, Dre was the album's "most visible benefactor and most unsettled presence," having "availed himself of the fresh-career oxygen Kendrick's rise has pumped into his atmosphere, lumbering out of his corporate airlock to stand with Lamar on magazine covers."[7] Indeed, "Compton" was *Good Kid*'s sole inauthentic moment, a bright, wide-screen victory lap at the end of an album that otherwise communicated precious little that warranted celebration.

Dre was not there to play a role in Lamar's passion play but to portray Dr. Dre, the entertainment mogul and industry icon. The same year that Lamar released *To Pimp a Butterfly*, Dre and Cube used their industry might to will the long-gestating N.W.A biopic into existence. Released in August 2015, *Straight Outta Compton* wove the narrative threads and urban legends surrounding the "World's Most Dangerous Group" into a carefully curated Hollywood narrative. Directed by *Friday*'s F. Gary Gray and executive-produced by Dre, Cube, and Eazy's widow, Tomica, *Straight Outta Compton* portrayed a series of momentous events in the life of the group, each of which was freighted with the burden of historical importance. The film's opening scene, set in the mid-1980s, sees Eazy confront some uncooperative, heavily armed customers in a Compton rock house. What is shaping up to be a deadly interpersonal battle is quickly interrupted by state-sanctioned violence when one of Daryl Gates's batter rams barrels through the home, allowing Eazy to make his dramatic escape—and for N.W.A to eventually exist. The film also retrofits the group's lyrics and other iconic terminology into its dialogue: Eazy is called "ruthless" at one point, and Cube, played by the real Cube's son O'Shea Jackson Jr., mutters "Fuck tha Police" lyrics while being slammed on the hood of a car. One of the film's most noticeable nods to period-specific jargon comes during its first pivotal moment, when Eazy bails Dre out of jail, and the budding producer tries to convince the budding entrepreneur of a business opportunity. "That shit, the reality raps? That's what I'm talkin' about, man. That's *it*," Dre tells Eazy.

Much more than reintroducing N.W.A to a new generation, *Straight Outta Compton* was critically and financially successful: it was named one of the National Board of Review's top ten films of 2015, and its screenplay was nominated for an Academy Award. With worldwide receipts of more than $200 million, *Straight Outta Compton* surpassed *Walk the Line* as Hollywood's highest-grossing music biopic and bettered Keenen Ivory Wayans's 2000 horror parody *Scary Movie* as the highest-grossing film helmed by a Black director. The film's theatrical release was accompanied by the kind of promotional tie-ins that showed just how deeply the iconography of N.W.A had been incorporated into popular culture and the synergistic reality of the twenty-first-century entertainment industries. To coincide with the film's release, Dre put out his first album in sixteen years, simply titled *Compton*, with a long list of cameos that cast Black Los Angeles as a wellspring of diverse musicianship—Kendrick Lamar, the Oxnard-raised multi-instrumentalist Anderson Paak, and the Compton-born rapper the Game—and reintroduced several reality rap charter members, including Ice Cube, Snoop Dogg, and Above the Law's Cold 187um. *Compton* reached no. 2 on the *Billboard* album chart, but anyone seeking to stream it had to create a paid account with Dre's corporate home of Apple Music, which was seeking to boost its subscription numbers by affiliation. Streaming services were not the only online platforms involved in the film's rollout: Beats by Dre partnered with Universal to release a promotional app called Straight Outta Somewhere, which allowed fans to reconfigure the film's title logo into a reflection of their own hometown and post it on Twitter, Facebook, or Instagram. "It wasn't about Compton as a place anymore, it became about being proud of where you're from," a Beats employee said.[8] On social media platforms, even the most geographically and culturally specific identities become pliable forms of self-expression, and *Straight Outta Compton* was no exception. Six million people downloaded and personalized the graphic in the app's first week alone, turning a tabloid-saturated statement of civic pride and vulgar protest into the dominant communication form of the 2010s: a viral meme.

The press surrounding the film wasn't all celebratory, however. The *Straight Outta Compton* promotional blitz also had to account for a significant element of the N.W.A story: Dre's 1991 assault of Dee Barnes. At the time, the group had blithely incorporated the beating into their star image of pitiless Black antiheroes, but the mid-2010s were a very different landscape for conversations about violence against women. The *Los Angeles Times* reported that while the original *Straight Outta Compton* screenplay contained a scene depicting the Barnes assault in which Dre "fling[s] her around like a rag-doll, while she screams, cries, begs for him to stop," Gray said it was cut from the film "because they wanted to focus tightly on the group."[9] Four days after the film's premiere, Barnes herself wrote a stirring article for *Gawker* that reflected on the film and offered her depiction of the event that was left on the cutting-room floor. "I didn't want to see a depiction of me getting beat up, just like I didn't want to see a depiction of Dre beating up [the Ruthless-signed R&B singer] Michel'le, his one-time girlfriend. . . . But what should have been addressed is that it occurred. . . . Like many of the women that knew and worked with N.W.A., I found myself a casualty of *Straight Outta Compton*'s revisionist history."[10] A couple of days later, Dre issued a formal apology, followed by an official statement from Apple, the world's largest technology company, which counted Dre among its most prominent spokespeople.

In 2016, Kendrick Lamar inducted N.W.A into the Rock and Roll Hall of Fame. "It was dubbed gangsta rap, but what it was for me was an intimate look at what was actually happening in our community," Lamar said. "Chuck D once said that hip-hop was the Black CNN, and N.W.A represent that to the fullest: bringing inner-city life to the forefront and making the world pay attention to our realities." The next year, Snoop inducted Tupac Shakur as the sixth rap act to earn the honor, joining Grandmaster Flash and the Furious Five (inducted in 2007), Run-DMC (2009), the Beastie Boys (2012), and Public Enemy (2013). The Notorious B.I.G. was inducted in 2020. Like the transformation of "rock star" into a generic descriptor of skill in any field, the acceptance of hip-hop into the Hall of Fame coincided with "gangsta" being turned into a synonym for "badass," used as an ironic nod toward one's whiteness, or simply used to express enthusiasm. In the online DIY marketplace Etsy, one can purchase a baby onesie reading "gangsta napper," yoga gear proclaiming oneself a "spiritual gangsta," and coffee mugs emblazoned with the motivational phrase, "Drink some coffee, put on gangsta rap, and handle it." Gangsta rap had not only ascended what the cultural theorist Stuart Hall called the escalator of cultural prestige (biopics, Hall of Fame coronations) and been transformed into raw material for digital reappropriation but had fully crossed the linguistic threshold into a casual component of everyday vernacular.

Whether "gangsta" was fated for such a transition or it was triggered by the career choices of the rappers themselves is an unanswerable question, but it is fair to excuse millennial and younger fans of Ice Cube, Ice-T, and Snoop Dogg for their ignorance of the fact that these men were once among the nation's most provocative and scandalous public figures. Though he still released the occasional album and toured, by the late 2010s Ice Cube had long transitioned from gangsta notoriety to mainstream Hollywood bankability with *Friday* (which spawned two sequels) and the 2002 film *Barbershop* (which also generated two follow-ups). In the early 2010s, a meme circulated online comparing two photos of Cube: In the "then" image, Cube brandished an AK-47 with a terrifying glare in his eyes. In the "now" shot, he struck the same position with a fishing rod and a goofy smile, in a still from the 2005 family caper *Are We*

There Yet? While the current generation knows Cube as much for playing Captain Dickson in the reboot of *21 Jump Street* as for writing "Fuck tha Police," Ice-T, who once threatened the profits of a global corporation with a song about killing police, has proven even more willing to play against type, portraying NYPD officer Fin Tutuola on the NBC police drama *Law and Order: Special Victims Unit* since 2000. Of all the reality rappers to have parlayed their 1990s ignominy into twenty-first-century pop-cultural omnipresence, Snoop Dogg's trajectory has been the most unpredictable and enjoyable. He has cohosted multiple seasons of a cooking show with Martha Stewart, as well as hosted a TBS reboot of the 1970s game show *The Joker's Wild*. Unlike Cube or T, however, Snoop maintains an active recording schedule, releasing thirteen full-length albums since the turn of the millennium, in genres ranging from reggae (2013's *Reincarnated*, as Snoop Lion) to funk (2015's *7 Days of Funk*, with Dam-Funk) and gospel (2018's *Bible of Love*).

While reality rap was transformed into light entertainment fare and nostalgia, multiple new forms of reality programming took over television. In May 2015, the *Washington Post* published an online story commemorating the fifteenth anniversary of the pioneering reality game show *Survivor* that chronicled the breadth of twenty-first-century reality television programming. "The extreme success of *Survivor* officially ushered in the era of reality television, and nothing has ever really been the same," the story opened. "It opened the floodgates. Everyone, particularly broadcast networks, wanted a piece of the success and massive fortune they sensed was around the corner." By 2015, the story's headline noted, there were more than three hundred reality shows on offer, on broadcast and cable networks alike, which the authors split into ten formats: competing for prizes, talent competitions, dating and love, family, autobiographical, ridiculous people, life improvement, businesses and careers, hidden camera and trickery, and shows about wives.[11] Though the piece briefly noted *The Real World* in its introduction, it made no mention of reality television's formative tabloid era in the late '80s and early '90s. *Survivor*'s cultural ubiquity and influence were powerful enough to erase the memory of the crop of programs that invented the format.

A close look at the *Washington Post* story's accompanying time lines, however, revealed that the first wave of reality rappers had adapted well to the new televisual landscape. The "family" category included Joseph Simmons's MTV show *Run's House*; Snoop Dogg's *Father Hood*, which aired on the E! network; and Luther Campbell's *Luke's Parental Advisory*, which aired for a single season on VH1; while neglecting to include *Ice Loves Coco*, which ran on E! for three seasons. In the "dating and love" category was *Flavor of Love*, VH1's take on NBC's sensation *The Bachelor*, spawned by Flavor Flav's relationship with the actress Brigitte Nielsen, which itself began on another reality show, VH1's *Real World*–inspired *The Surreal Life*. *Flavor of Love*'s March 2006 season finale drew nearly six million viewers, the highest-rated show in VH1's history. The *Post* article's "talent" category contained *Making the Band*, which was overseen starting in its second season by the executive then known as P. Diddy, whose playfully domineering tone earned its own satire on Dave Chappelle's eponymous sketch comedy show. The story left out VH1's soapy *Love and Hip Hop*, which traced the dramatic lives of people in and around the industry's New York base. An immediate hit, *Love* spun off subsequent versions set in Atlanta, Hollywood, and Miami, and a season-six star turn helped launch the career of future chart-topping rapper Cardi B.

Two decades into the twenty-first century, it's hard to find two sectors of popular culture that reflect the democratic possibilities, consumerist ideologies, and emotional flare-ups of American life more than reality TV and reality rap. Is there any more fitting predecessor for reality television's mantra "I'm not here to make friends!" than the performative pugnacity of hip-hop beefs?[12] In the first decade of the 2000s, hip-hop culture and reality television climbed to the forefront of technological changes and popular trends. While reality producers were pioneering TV-internet convergence, user-generated content, and corporate synergy, rap became "the most accurate arbiter of the zeitgeist, of the consciousness of the people and the age," as Greg Tate put it in 2016: "Insofar as this moment is defined by sex, shopping, terror, and virtual life and death, hip-hop remains our most prophetic cultural pulse taker, raker, and shaker. Bush, bin Laden, 50 Cent, Paris Hilton, Fox News, ringer tones, and the iPod shuffle—these are actually what constitute our real world, people—a world of loops, break beats, random bombings, bootleg videos, faked realness, and manipulated fears; it's all of a piece, it all runs together nicely."[13]

The dizzying, endlessly recombined modern world of culture, technology, and politics was born from the tabloid culture that exploded in 1986 and collapsed under its own weight in 1996. That era's fusion of technologies and industries, information and entertainment, acting and being, hard news and light distractions has so thoroughly permeated the mass communications ecosystem that it evades recognition. What reality rap and reality TV created then is the taken-for-granted way that we learn about distant others, distract ourselves, and participate in political discourse today. Out of this landscape emerged Donald Trump, a pure product of 1980s and '90s tabloid culture and its 2000s reinvention as a vehicle for celebrity rehabilitation, who used social media to avoid the prying political press and give his millions of followers the populist sense that he was talking directly to them. While Ronald Reagan used racial dog whistles and TV spectacle to make himself the first hyperreal president, Trump directly appealed to the racist fears of a population unwilling to accept the nation's first Black president to make himself the nation's first reality president.

More than twenty years after Ice Cube asked, "Who got the camera?" the answer is, "Everyone, everywhere, at all times." The talk shows and camcorders that revealed hidden truths about the darker corners of 1980s and '90s American life are the smartphone cameras and social media platforms of today, only orders of magnitude more accessible and pervasive. While the widespread use of these technologies and platforms transformed the conduct of social life and helped eviscerate the economic infrastructures supporting print media, they were also revealing the horrifying extent of police brutality and murder that made Rodney King's 1991 beating look comparatively tame. While Barack Obama served his second term in office, a new generation of political activists wrangled these platforms to organize for infrastructural change in a nonhierarchical, intersectional way and were attacked in the streets by local police departments that had been militarized beyond even Daryl Gates's wildest dreams, by officers who increasingly imagine themselves "as soldiers in a battle with the public rather than guardians of public safety."[14] In 2020, the most politically contentious year since 1968, the thirty-two-year-old song "Fuck tha Police" felt more terrifyingly relevant than ever.

$$\ast \qquad \ast \qquad \ast$$

The first bridge between 1990s tabloid culture and twenty-first-century rap was built by a white kid from postindustrial Detroit who reignited the culture wars at the turn of the millennium. Trained as a battle rapper in a Black milieu, Eminem could outrap his peers, but that alone was not enough to make him a star. Encouraged by Dre and Jimmy Iovine, who signed him to Aftermath on the strength of a 1997 mixtape, Eminem conquered popular culture by translating his "white trash" image for a hip-hop world that valued underclass voices who spoke vulgar truth to thin-skinned power. Drawn as much from the trailer-park public sphere of *The Jerry Springer Show* and the lurid murder dramatizations of *A Current Affair* as from N.W.A and the Geto Boys, Eminem's image was fittingly introduced to the world through the boob tube. In his 1999 debut video, "My Name Is," a junk-food-eating, cigarette-smoking married couple watch his alter ego, Slim Shady, in a living room decked out in the kitschy redneck squalor of *Natural Born Killers*. Over a midtempo Dre track that flipped an obscure funk break into what sounded like the theme from a cartoon or a family sitcom, Eminem takes gleefully vulgar aim at various female pop-culture icons (Pamela Anderson, the Spice Girls), cavalierly mentions his mother's drug addiction, and even stages a *Cops*-style dramatization where he stumbles drunkenly out of a car on the side of the road. Underscored by his impression of shock-rock provocateur Marilyn Manson in the clip, Eminem had instantly established himself as an expert media "troll" before that word had entered the popular lexicon, punctuated by the final line of the song's first verse: "I don't give a fuck, God sent me to piss the world off."

Released in May 2000 as the presidential campaign was entering its final stages, Eminem's second album, *The Marshall Mathers LP*, seemed tailor-made to play as large a role in the election as Ice-T and Sister Souljah had in 1992. The album opened with "Kill You," a horrifying fantasy about Eminem raping and murdering his mother. In true self-reflexive fashion, Eminem steps back and comments on his own outrageousness:

> "Oh, now he's raping his own mother
> Abusing a whore, snorting coke
> And we gave him the *Rolling Stone* cover?"
> You're goddamn right, bitch, and now it's too late
> I'm triple platinum and tragedies happened in two states

Not only would *Mathers* improve on its predecessor's sales numbers, but by selling 1.76 million copies in its first week, it annihilated the previous record holder for fastest-selling rap album: *Doggystyle*. It would eventually sell more copies than any rap album before or since. Because Eminem's unequaled popularity was a product of his whiteness, his videos were pulling mainstream pop down into the gutter with them, especially MTV's teen-aimed viewer-voting phenomenon *Total Request Live*. Enter Lynne Cheney, wife of vice presidential candidate Dick, who handed the Senate Commerce Committee the lyrics to "Kill You" during her September 2000 testimony in front of them. Her terse review: "It is despicable. It is horrible. This is dreadful. This is shameful. This is awful." She was joined in her crusade against Seagram—which had bought Universal Entertainment, which owned Interscope Records, which distributed Aftermath—by Democratic senator Joe Lieberman, Al Gore's running mate and Tipper Gore's media-panic heir apparent.

But Eminem's own take on the vagaries of rap's deep connections with its audience would prove far more influential than Cheney's election-year gambit. *The Marshall Mathers LP*'s most enduring song is "Stan," a rap epistolary with a plangent pop hook on which Eminem plays two roles: himself and the role of his most intense, troubled admirer. "See, everything you say is real / And I respect you 'cause you tell it," the titular superfan writes to the rapper, who is too busy to reply. As the song progresses, the fan grows more desperate, eventually killing himself by driving off a bridge. Superficially empathetic toward its tragic protagonist, at its core "Stan" asserts that music—or, more specifically, a charismatic musician—has the power to drive its listeners to acts of (self-) violence. But it offers a twist on the incitement argument pioneered by Tipper Gore more than a decade earlier: no specific lyric drove Stan to kill himself, but he was instead done in by his inability to forge an authentic connection with the *real* Marshall Mathers. That was Eminem's counterargument to Lynne Cheney: the power of his stardom was far more potent a cultural toxin than his vulgar music. Eminem was fond of portraying his legion of admirers as an army of clones with a uniform of dyed blond hair, white T-shirts, and permanent scowls. With "Stan," he played into the entrenched societal belief that fandom, with its focus on uncovering the star's *true* self, was a form of pathological derangement, inextricable from fanaticism.[15] In the ensuing years, as rap arguments moved out of the *Source* and *Vibe* and onto blogs, message boards, and social media platforms, "Stan" appropriately evolved into a derisive slang term for any overly obsessive fan of a particular rap star. In a 2020 retrospective, Charles Aaron aptly summarized the *Mathers* gestalt: "Eminem was a one-man internet before the internet really became the internet."[16]

In the 2002 video for "Without Me," Eminem played his mother on an episode of "The Sandy Messy Lezbial Show" titled "When Sons Go Bad" and inserted himself into parodies of *The Real World* and *Survivor* with veterans of those pioneering reality shows. That same year, Eminem heard a different vision of reality rap on a mixtape recorded by a hotly tipped Queens rapper and ex–drug dealer named 50 Cent. Wowed, Eminem immediately arranged for 50 to fly to Los Angeles and meet with him and Dre. A year later, Aftermath released the Dre-produced *Get Rich or Die Tryin'*, which made 50 Cent, for a brief time, the biggest rapper in the world. Far from the hellish tabloid rap of Eminem, 50 was Tupac Shakur as comic-book superhero: all of the credibility and charisma, a WWE wrestler's body protected by a bulletproof vest, but with the code of the street superseding revolutionary politics. Born Curtis Jackson in Jamaica, Queens, 50 was orphaned at eight, sold crack by twelve, and was making $5,000 a day by the time he was eighteen. Thanks to early mentorship from Jam Master Jay, 50 was set to release his debut, *Power of the Dollar*, on Columbia, but when the label kept him hovering in release-date limbo, he engineered a new form of grassroots publicity. He cut the track "How to Rob," in which he fantasized about sticking up several of hip-hop's most popular and powerful figures. When Columbia declined to promote it, 50 and his team took it straight to influential rap DJs like Hot 97's Funkmaster Flex, and it immediately established 50 as a fearless, talented upstart. "Viral wasn't a word then," said executive Cory Rooney, "but that's what 50 was trying to achieve."[17]

It worked. But when *Power of the Dollar* was finally granted a release date, violent reality intruded: 50 was shot nine times outside his grandmother's home in Queens, with one bullet piercing his left cheek. Wanting nothing of the controversy, Columbia dropped him, leaving 50 to redouble his DIY path to fame, this time through New York's underground mixtape market. Mixtapes had been an unofficial part of New York's hip-hop culture for more than a decade, but 50 changed the game with 2002's *50 Cent Is the Future*. "Instead of just spitting a 16, he started to re-do people's hooks and make his own songs to the point where as DJs we wanted to play his versions in the club," recalled mixtape icon DJ Drama.[18] The tape sold Eminem and Dre on 50 Cent's marketability and helped introduce hip-hop to a medium that offered rappers a new format for low-risk demo tapes—and, with the rise of MP3 files, a medium with instant global distribution—which permitted them to report more directly from the streets to their listeners, without the major labels' bureaucratic red tape.

Fifty's first single, "In Da Club," was a crossover smash, its video positioning him as Shady/Aftermath's impossibly toned Frankenstein's monster. A revivified gangsta rap had its first authentic icon of the twenty-first century, and 50 knew exactly who he wanted to be: "In the hood in LA they sayin', '50, you hot' / They like me, I want 'em to love me like they love Pac," he rapped. Eminem agreed: "That's the thing with 50. That same aura...that's been missing since we lost Pac and Biggie. The authenticity, the realness behind it."[19] A 2003 *Spin* profile went a step further: "At a time in America's history when planes crash into towers that collapse in plain view of the nation, and when reality TV shows like *Survivor* and *Joe Millionaire* take the place of real living, listeners of popular music expect their gangsta rappers to deliver a certain truth. Pop in a 50 Cent CD and you, too, can be gangsta for 70 minutes."[20] Though 50's image was a product of digital technology and personal biography, his stardom was increasingly cast in the language of competitive reality programming and corporate brand synergy. Following Puff Daddy's entrepreneurial lead, 50 diversified his celebrity portfolio, investing in the Queens-based startup Vitamin Water and becoming the company's spokesperson, a choice that turned a huge profit when the brand was purchased by Coca-Cola for $4 billion in 2007. In 2008, with deep pockets and an entrepreneurial mindset, he took the logical next step and launched his own competitive reality show, *50 Cent: The Money and the Power*, which aired for a season on MTV.

With his third album, *Curtis*, set for release in September 2007, 50 decided to stage a competitive media spectacle with the one rapper who threatened his sales supremacy: Kanye West, whose third album, *Graduation*, was scheduled to drop on the same day. Though 50 reneged on his pledge to retire if West outsold him, it didn't much matter. While 50's success was rooted in his successful update of the gangsta archetype, West was the most sui generis mainstream rapper since Eminem. His 2004 debut, *The College Dropout*, introduced him to the world as a cerebral, middle-class, preppy son of an English professor single mother who had *a lot* to say. Where 50 Cent translated his prefame shooting into evidence of his invincibility, West recorded his first single, "Through the Wire," with his mouth partially wired shut after a car crash, and apologized on the song's chorus for his lack of lyrical clarity. His impulsiveness was his greatest gift, and when he ad-libbed "George Bush doesn't care about Black people" during a 2005 Hurricane Katrina benefit, he was cast as an outspoken political icon and spokesperson for a generation of unheard Black voices. That was short-lived, however: he apologized to President George W. Bush a few days later on the *Today* show. With *Graduation*, the 2007 conclusion to his career-opening trilogy that included *Dropout* and 2005's *Late Registration*, West had made himself into a gregarious, widely beloved superstar. But after his mother's sudden death on a plastic surgeon's table in late 2007, West's public persona dramatically shifted inward. He released an Auto-Tuned R&B album, *808s and Heartbreak*, and then largely disappeared from the public eye, save his notorious interruption of Taylor Swift's acceptance speech at the 2009 MTV Video Music Awards.

When West reappeared in summer 2010, it was not in a music video or an exclusive interview, but on Twitter, the social media platform that exploded in popularity by shrinking blog posts down to 140 character aphorisms and ordinary updates. The first star to maximize the platform's potential, West translated his motormouth tendencies into exclusive peeks at his opulent lifestyle, turning Twitter into his personal reality show. Though few could relate to West's luxurious jet-setting, he had tapped into one of the platform's most powerful affordances: a potent sense of constant, ersatz intimacy dubbed "ambient awareness" by social scientists. West's Twitter account was proof of concept that fans were eager not just for information about new singles or albums but for access to celebrities' mundane, everyday activities too. This notion wasn't new, but dated back to the 1960s rise of "direct cinema," the American take on European cinema verité that revolutionized the dry documentary form by turning it into a behind-the-scenes peek at public figures like John F. Kennedy, Jane Fonda, and Bob Dylan in their off-camera "real" lives.

Half a century later, with *The Real World* entering its third decade on MTV and *Big Brother* creating a TV sensation by simply installing surveillance cameras to monitor people chosen to live together in a house they cannot leave, a new crop of reality aspirants ventured that by strategically opening their lives to video cameras, they could become celebrities by dint of sheer exposure. As Mark Andrejevic has explained, the promise of democratic participation on reality television is contingent on allowing oneself to be constantly surveilled. Writing before the rise of social media, he predicts the platforms perfectly in his gloss on reality TV: "It is perhaps not a coincidence that the emergence of relatively inexpensive highly sophisticated technologies for comprehensive consumer monitoring coincides with a trend in popular culture toward the portrayal of surveillance as a means of self-expression and a shortcut to fame and fortune."[21] Andrejevic locates the point of overlap shared by reality TV fame aspirants and prospective social media "influencers": the intimate details of one's everyday life are packaged by platforms and sold to their advertisers. The basis of reality/tabloid television from the late 1980s onward comprises the economic model of Facebook, Instagram, and Twitter.

The key figure who linked social media's and reality TV's consumer surveillance models was Kim Kardashian (the daughter of O. J. Simpson attorney Robert Kardashian), whose series *Keeping Up with the Kardashians* debuted in 2007, months after her 2002 sex tape was leaked online. Though *Kardashians* was panned as the latest iteration of public figures who were "famous for being famous" (the *New York Times* said the show was "purely about some desperate women climbing to the margins of fame"), the show was a ratings hit.[22] Over multiple seasons, numerous spin-offs, and countless brand tie-ins, *Kardashians* capitalized on the same tweak of reality culture that West had brought to Twitter and that Kim Kardashian took to Instagram: people loved behind-the-scenes peeks at celebrities doing and saying mundane, "real" things. In April 2012, the tabloids announced that West and Kardashian were dating, and though he initially blanched at a supporting role in a reality show he did not control, West slowly ramped up his participation over the next few years.

As West's reality-fueled second career was taking off, his mentor Jay-Z was settling into a comfortable status as hip-hop's diplomat to the rest of the world, a position that had changed quite a bit since Run-DMC first assumed the position in 1985. Jay-Z had come a long way since his 1996 debut, *Reasonable Doubt*, which positioned him as a smooth, un-flappable Black Mafia don who told his stories with an uncommonly dense thicket of allusions and acrobatic shifts of meter that reportedly wowed his Brooklyn contemporary Notorious B.I.G., who appeared on a track. Off-record, Jay was a budding entrepreneur in the Eazy-E, Suge Knight, and Puff Daddy mold, and one who was cocky enough to call the self-released *Reasonable Doubt* a one-off album, strictly intended to pub-licize the launch of his brand empire. Though a string of pop hits made him a superstar, and he started multiple product lines bearing his brand, Jay's street credibility was upheld on record (by dissing Nas on 2001's *The Blueprint*) and off, when he pled guilty to stabbing a record producer at a bar. By 2003, Jay's influence was unparalleled enough that even a brief response to 50 Cent's playful jab at him on "How to Rob" at that year's Hot 97 Summer Jam concert was enough to establish 50's career. That same year, Jay announced his retirement with *The Black Album*, which contained a Rick Rubin–produced remake of Ice-T's 1993 album track "99 Problems," and threw himself a going-away party at Madison Square Garden that was filmed and released in theaters. Jay-Z's story was a classic American bootstraps bildungsroman, taking him from the Marcy Projects to Madison Square, to paraphrase *The Black Album*'s "Encore." In a guest verse on a remix of Kanye West's "Diamonds from Sierra Leone," recorded a few years later, Jay summarized hip-hop's self-branding mandate in eight words: "I'm not a businessman / I'm a business, man!"

Jay's corporate savvy didn't detract from his skill as a rap critic: the most scathing part of the Nas-dissing "The Takeover," after all, is his scathing, point-by-point takedown of Nas's ostensibly spotty dis-cography. Jay finally realized his literary aspirations with *Decoded*, his 2010 memoir / literature seminar / hip-hop mini history, which offers lyric-by-lyric interpretations of a handful of his most memorable songs, complete with footnotes. With *Decoded*, Jay was positioning himself not just as a legendary rapper or a successful one-man brand but as a man of letters, the music's cultural translator, all in one. "Jay-Z is a great

American artist—and he'd be the first to tell you so," opened the *LA Times* review.[23] The timing was apt: the same year, two English professors released *The Anthology of Rap* for Yale University Press, raising rap lyrics to the level of classic American poetry. To be sure, Jay (and Nas and B.I.G.) pioneered a lyricism that rewarded close reading. Jay's early career benefactor DJ Clark Kent summarized his approach by comparison: "When you hear NWA, you hear gun killin', drug sellin', but you hear it in such a very plain English. . . . [Jay-Z is] saying it in a way that you have to practically be a drug dealer to understand it."[24]

Sprinkled among the song-by-song breakdowns, Jay writes his autobiography, establishing his origin story as the unaddressed midpoint of the swagger of "Sucker M.C.'s" and the social conscience of "The Message." "What was missing was what was happening in between those two images," he wrote. "How young cats were stepping through the broken glass and into the Caddy. The missing piece was the story of the hustler." He nods to Ice-T's formative influence and acknowledges the godfather of reality rap's epochal quote: "Chuck D famously called hip-hop the CNN of the ghetto, and he was right, but hip-hop would be boring as the news if all MCs did was report. Rap is also entertainment—and art."[25] It was also controversy, as he noted in the section addressing N.W.A's FBI letter and the 2 Live Crew's obscenity trial. "But the attempts at censorship only made the targets bigger stars," he warned. "In the end, you can't censor the truth, especially when it comes packaged in hot music."[26] *Decoded*'s main appeal, however, was Jay's lyrical self-analysis. Like an English BFA student, he explains that the line "I got 99 problems but a bitch ain't one," borrowed from Ice-T's 1993 original, "works on all these levels, in its literal meaning, its ironic meaning, and in its sonic power." Like his own publicist, Jay writes that "99 Problems" is "a not-quite-true-story" about "the anxiety of hustling" but is not, despite the hook, a diss at women.[27] A *New York Times* bestseller that helped elevate its author to the rarefied level of cultural commentator, *Decoded*'s larger accomplishment was entrenching the notion that rappers themselves are the only ones who can decipher the truth behind their lyrics.

By the time *Decoded* was published, Jay's assertion that rappers were the sole decoders of lyrical meaning was already under fire by a radically decentralized rap internet. A prominent example of autodidactic interpretation surfaced in late January 2012, when a rap blogger wrote a post titled "I Found Ice Cube's 'Good Day.'" Using freely available internet research resources, the blogger took the lyrics to Cube's hit 1993 single literally and claimed to have located the *actual* day Cube was rapping about. After laying out his evidence, he concludes:

> The ONLY day where:
> *Yo MTV Raps* was on air
> It was a clear and smogless day
> Beepers were commercially sold
> Lakers beat the SuperSonics
> and Ice Cube had no events to attend was . . .
> JANUARY 20 1992
> National Good Day Day[28]

The post had the perfect blend of amateur research and nostalgic cultural relevance to go viral. Cube was asked to verify the claim in several interviews, and he set the record straight during the February press cycle for his upcoming film *21 Jump Street*: "It's a fictional song. It's basically my interpretation of what a great day would be. . . . So, you know, it's a little of this and a little of that. I don't think you can pinpoint the day."[29] Though Cube deflated the post's factual claims, "National Good Day Day" stuck around: in 2014, a few people created an online campaign to raise $25,000 for a South Central charity pegged to the "holiday," and Ice Cube appeared at a photo op pseudo-event sponsored by Goodyear (whose promotional blimp is prominently mentioned in the "It Was a Good Day" lyrics) to sign an oversized check. Though all involved knew that January 20 was not the actual "day" of Cube's song, they had used social media to invest that date with a significance that belonged as much to them as to Cube.

Much more than a viral gimmick or promotional ploy, the "Good Day" post was evidence of a growing understanding among rap fans that by harnessing the collective energy and boundless resources of the internet, they could create a Rosetta Stone to decode the truth of any rap lyric. The desire to create such a library had been present since the early days of the text-centric public internet, epitomized by the Original Hip-Hop Lyrics Archive (OHHLA.com), a bare-bones site to which any listener with an email account could contribute. As the new millennium dawned, as MP3 files deflated the exchange value of the music commodity and

Google established itself as the web's default search engine, lyrics became a valuable commodity in their own right, and dozens of fly-by-night lyric sites sprouted up, selling cheap ads against fans' search queries. By the 2010s, however, the internet was taken over by platforms, and lyric transcription started to emulate Facebook, Instagram, and Twitter, becoming a game that rewarded its players with ephemeral social capital. Thus was born Rap Genius in 2009. The site's founders populated their platform with thousands of rap lyrics (many of which were copy-pasted from OHHLA), turning each bar of each verse into a puzzle to be decoded for "Rap IQ" points, and a landing page with its own URL, the better to game Google's search algorithm. Rap Genius's scale and ambition derived from the economic model known as "platform capitalism," which doesn't derive profits from extracting natural resources to manufacture goods but instead collects and processes the data created by users who perform various forms of pleasurable social labor within a private virtual space. Rap Genius exploded in popularity, earning tens of millions of dollars of Silicon Valley investment and dramatically expanding its lyrical corpus and user base. Its expansion led to the company simultaneously dropping the "Rap" prefix and coaxing rappers to annotate their own lyrics with "Verified" accounts.

More than the latest killer app, Genius marked a profound shift in the basic understanding of rap's putative truths. While 1980s and '90s reality rappers borrowed from journalism to bolster their truth claims, and Jay-Z revived the centrality of authorial intent in *Decoded*, Genius investor Ben Horowitz compared the site to the Talmud, a tool for translating a dense text (the Torah) into something accessible and knowable, which echoed Google cofounder Sergey Brin's claim that "the perfect search engine would be like the mind of God."[30] To the Genius generation, rap lyrics are sets of enigmas waiting to be unlocked by reading and researching, not poetic expressions of more ambiguous truths. Ice Cube packed a world of emotion, experience, and hope into his lyrics for "It Was a Good Day," but the capsule description on the song's current Genius page boils the song down to a list of ingredients: "Ice Cube describes his ideal day: a pork-free breakfast, *Yo MTV Raps!*, gambling, and a sexual rendezvous." Genius also doesn't account for rappers who use words not for semantic purposes but because they sound good or fit neatly within a cadence. After observing the rap internet's response to a meaningless neologism, "fanute," used by French Montana on the Rick Ross single "Stay Schemin'," Willy Staley rebuked Genius's insistence on turning every lyric into a question with an answer. "Fanute" was likely contrived by Montana to merge the sounds of two adjacent words into a bar, yet Staley noted with some resignation that legions of online rap fans nonetheless took it upon themselves to create a dictionary entry for it. One of the pleasures of pop music, Staley argued, was the misheard lyric, which Genius destroyed by turning musical engagement into boring homework. "The Internet is a powerful research tool," he concluded, "and apparently we've decided to use it to enable crowdsourced pedantry of the most obnoxious sort."[31]

In the years preceding the rise of Rap Genius, a generation who had grown up watching reality rap videos on MTV and BET and reading rap coverage in the *Source* and *Vibe* came online. They started blogs, posted on lengthy message board threads, and took paid positions at online music publications, quickly shifting the critical conversation about what "quality" rap was.[32] In 2004, the indie-rock-focused online music publication *Pitchfork*, which had come to national prominence with career-boosting raves for bookish, white indie-rock acts like Sufjan Stevens, Arcade Fire, and the Decemberists, started devoting significant coverage to rap, but not the kind of heady, political "backpack rap" that its readership preferred. Instead, the new wave of *Pitchfork* rap critics preferred the image-driven, crime-themed, lyrically inventive rap that was popular among the new online cognoscenti. Informally known as "coke rap" and christened "don rap" by one scholar to account for the larger-than-life mafioso kingpin archetypes that populated the music,[33] it had swelled in popularity as reality rap declined, spurred by albums such as Jay-Z's *Reasonable Doubt*, Notorious B.I.G.'s *Life after Death*, and Raekwon's *Only Built 4 Cuban Linx*. When *Pitchfork*'s 2004 year-end "best of" list mixed in coke-rap albums from Virginia Beach's Clipse, Atlanta's Young Jeezy, and Harlem's Cam'ron with its typical indie-rock fare, the site's die-hard fans exploded. One commenter on another indie-rock blog took *Pitchfork* to task for its broadened ambit, writing, "I think [*Pitchfork*] could have made separate lists—One for indie and one for rap. That way the genres are separated, like they should be. Indie kids could read one list and not bitch about rap, and rap fans could do vice versa. Problem solved." In his daily blog for the *Village Voice*'s website, part-time *Pitchfork* rap critic Tom Breihan curtly retorted, "Yes. Segregation solves all problems."[34]

The biggest beneficiary of coke rap's critical approval was Rick Ross. Born William Roberts and raised in the Carol City neighborhood of Miami Gardens, Florida, Ross borrowed his moniker from "Freeway" Rick Ross, the legendary cocaine trafficker whose 1980s Los Angeles empire (which used the Bloods and the Crips for distribution) was worth hundreds of millions before he was sentenced to life in prison in 1996. Following appeals, Ross was released in 2009, three years after his hip-hop namesake debuted at *Billboard*'s top spot with his first LP, *Port of Miami*.[35] Although his albums sold well (his 2008 follow-up also entered the charts at no. 1), Rick Ross was not an immediate critical favorite, a situation that was compounded when the website The Smoking Gun revealed that the rapper not only was not a cocaine tycoon but had actually worked as a prison corrections officer in the mid-1990s. The revelation, which was denied at first by Ross, until the site produced photographic documentation, was, according to Jon Caramanica, "the most spectacular and public implosion of a rapper's self-styled tough-guy image... since *The Dallas Morning News* picked apart the looser sections of Vanilla Ice's biography." With a new album of his own to promote, 50 Cent started a beef with Ross that assailed his inauthenticity, but it didn't stick in the marketplace: Ross's 2009 album, *Deeper Than Rap*, still debuted at no. 1. "Impenetrability of image, that old signal of hip-hop authenticity, somehow no longer seems to count," observed Caramanica. "And what a relief that is. Like all great pop music, rap is theater, and Rick Ross... is one of its most ambitious characters."[36] Caramanica, a Harvard graduate who came to the *New York Times* in 2010 after a stint editing *Vibe*, was perhaps the preeminent representative of rap's critical new school, who scornfully dismissed previous generations' metrics of authenticity—largely decided by rock critics who dabbled in rap—while embracing well-constructed artifice. Revelations about Ross's past notwithstanding, *Deeper Than Rap* was his first critical hit, with critics crediting his improved rapping and the sheer sonic extravagance of his production. "Treated with the same suspension of belief accorded a summer blockbuster, *Deeper Than Rap* succeeds in its baroque but basic goals," wrote Jeff Weiss.[37] Upon the release of Ross's 2012 mixtape album *Rich Forever* (the tape with Montana's "fanute" line on it), Sasha Frere-Jones wrote that "Ross may represent the final abandonment of hip-hop's mandate to 'keep it real.' "[38]

Though Rick Ross had never presented himself as a deep thinker on representation and authenticity, the title *Deeper Than Rap* signaled otherwise. "In an age of routine tabloid invasions and the microrevelation as celebrity news, it's become commonplace to expect access to all aspects of the lives of the famous," wrote Jon Caramanica, who then coaxed an oblique disclosure out of Ross. "Right now as we speak, I got two of my best friends that's on the run from two separate cocaine conspiracy indictments," Ross explained. "This is a reality that I can't glorify. The relationship I have with these people is deeper than rap."[39] Ross's explanation echoes Ice-T's 1987 acknowledgment that there was a limit to reality rap, that certain details of his past life would never make it onto an album because he didn't want to snitch or expose himself to criminal liability. Ross's interview was conducted a quarter-century later, when the legal stakes around rap lyrics were far steeper, with prosecutors and judges increasingly agreeing that there was *nothing* deeper than rap. "Rather than treating rap music as an art form whose primary purpose is to entertain," two legal scholars observed in 2014, "prosecutors have become adept at convincing judges and juries alike that the lyrics are either autobiographical confessions of illegal behavior or evidence of a defendant's knowledge, motive, or identity with respect to the alleged crime."[40] For decades, the most famous Black popular musicians have borne the burden of double representation: with so few Black artists at the highest echelons of visibility, those who make it there find it incumbent to represent *the world* through their creativity and to represent *their community* through their mass-media presence. But the worrying escalation of the legal belief that rap lyrics constitute legal evidence effects those at the *lowest* levels of visibility. For up-and-coming street rappers with little social or economic power, the burden of representation is purely legalistic: what they say on record becomes a direct report of what they did in real life. Rappers trying to use the medium as an escape from the lure of criminality are increasingly being held legally responsible for the creative ways they're reimagining their world.

According to dozens of prosecutors who use them in court, the debate around the reality of rap lyrics is settled: they're an authentic piece of evidence tying a person to an action or a mindset. They're a confession note. More than any other genre of music or form of cultural expression, according to the American Civil Liberties Union, rap lyrics "have been the focus of the vast majority of cases analyzing the use of fictional expressions as evidence of character or motive and intent in criminal proceedings."[41] Unlike Tupac Shakur or Snoop Doggy Dogg, the rappers who have their words used against them in court do not have access to expensive legal teams and are subject to having their lyrics read to judges and juries as words on paper, the medium of written confession, and not heard as part of a musical composition created to entertain and to shock. In 2006, some rap lyrics written by Ronell Wilson were convincingly argued to be confessional in nature, and he was convicted of murdering two police officers. Aspiring rapper Vonte Skinner's lyrics were read to a jury to establish his motive and intent in a 2008 murder case, and he was convicted. His case was later overturned by the New Jersey Supreme Court, the judge offering the commonsense comment, "One would not presume that Bob Marley, who wrote the well-known song 'I Shot the Sheriff,' actually shot a sheriff."[42] But the cases kept coming. In 2013, prosecutors played some drug-themed rap videos made by Clyde Smith, who was charged with intent to distribute despite the fact that the drugs found in his car were all legally prescribed to him. He was convicted, and his attorney blamed the videos for swaying the jury. That same year, rap label owner Anthony Johnson claimed that he had shot his business partner in self-defense, but the jury rejected his claim after being provided lyrics he wrote while in jail awaiting trial and sentenced him to forty years.

In 2013, Jamal Knox, a.k.a. Mayhem Mal, was convicted of two counts of making terroristic threats and two counts of witness intimidation for posting the original track "Fuck the Police" on YouTube and Facebook. The track contained lyrics that fantasized about committing acts of violence against two police officers who had previously arrested Knox, which the court determined posed a "true threat" to the officers and thus did not warrant First Amendment protection. In 2019, several famous rappers (including Chance the Rapper, Killer Mike, and Meek Mill) contributed to an amicus brief filed with the US Supreme Court on Knox's behalf that contained "a primer on hip-hop." In an attempt to convince the court that rap lyrics were not factual statements or un-filtered autobiography, but a creative outlet for tension release, they re-visited the peak period of reality rap. They described N.W.A's original "Fuck tha Police" as "a fictional trial where rappers play the roles of judge and prosecutors, while the defendant is the police department," stating that "no one would objectively take it as threatening"; they reminded the court that Ice Cube mentioned killing LAPD officers Laurence Powell and Stacey Koon on the million-selling *Predator* without those officers filing suit; and they quoted the section of Ice-T's 2011 autobiography that discussed the "Cop Killer" furor: "If you believe that I'm a cop killer, you believe David Bowie is an astronaut."[43] A victory in the case would have held out the possibility that threatening-sounding rap lyrics could be classified as a form of protected political speech, the goal that Ice-T, Ice Cube, and Tupac Shakur had fought for in the tabloid decade's court of public opinion. It was not to be. Thirty years after N.W.A's infamous summer tour saw the group hounded by police for the mere threat of uttering a three-word title, the Supreme Court declined to take Jamal Knox's case, leaving him to sit in prison for the crime of releasing a song called "Fuck the Police."

Michael Brown did not have any anticop rap posted on his SoundCloud page. Though his technologies were raw, the eighteen-year-old Ferguson, Missouri, native who recorded as Big'Mike was confident in his voice. "BODY Baq," uploaded on July 31, 2014, was a swaggering, double-timed tour through his mind and hometown; and on "Forgiveness," uploaded a week later, he bared his emotions (his stepmother had recently been diagnosed with a chronic heart condition) over a sample of the Chi-Lites' "Have You Seen Her" in a way that recalled Tupac Shakur at his most poignant. Brown was living in Ferguson's Canfield Green apartment complex with his grandmother, where he had set up an ad hoc studio in a small room, and on August 11, he was going to start attending Vatterott School, with the hopes of turning his degree into a blue-collar job. He had recently gotten into an argument with his father over his desire to make a career as a rapper. "One day, the world is gonna know my name," he told his father. "I'll probably have to go away for a while, but I'm coming back to save my city."[44] On August 9, a Saturday, Brown met up with his friend Dorian Johnson, and the two walked to the Ferguson Market to pick up some Swisher cigarillos. An argument ensued between Brown and the cashier, and the surveillance camera recorded Brown shoving the clerk and walking out of the store with the Swishers. Seven minutes later, Ferguson police officer Darren Wilson pulled up beside Brown and Johnson as they were walking down the middle of Canfield Drive. Wilson, who is white, confronted the two young men, and an altercation ensued between Brown and him. Wilson fired two shots at Brown, who was unarmed—one missed him, and the other grazed him—causing him to take off running down Canfield, his Nike slippers coming off as he fled. When Brown stopped and briefly turned toward Wilson, the officer fired several shots, killing him.

None of this was captured on video, but the incident was broadly witnessed, and photos of the aftermath quickly proliferated on Twitter. "I JUST SAW SOMEONE DIE OMFG," Twitter user @TheePharaoh posted two minutes later. He then uploaded a photo, taken with his phone, of two Ferguson policemen standing over Brown's lifeless body, with the caption "Fuckfuckfuck." Residents started flooding the area, and graphic photos of Brown's dead body spread through social media. It was twenty minutes before police covered Brown's body with a sheet, ninety before forensic detectives appeared on the scene, and more than four hours before his corpse was removed from the street. News cameras showed police standing guard around Brown's body, refusing to allow his family to see him. In a few hours, members of a local racial justice organization were making signs and querying the cops. Soon, they started marching and setting up memorials near the site of the shooting. One police officer allowed his dog to urinate on one of the memorials, and some others crushed them while driving away from the scene. As the number of protesters increased, news organizations spilled in from around the country, and Black reporters from other beats asked their editors to send them to Ferguson.

The next day, they all witnessed local and regional authorities dramatically escalate a tense but peaceful situation with an overwhelming show of military force: SWAT teams shot tear gas and rubber bullets at the growing crowd, helicopters cleared the airspace above the city, and armored personnel carriers rolled down the street. Individual officers obscured their badge numbers and wore armbands reading "I AM DARREN WILSON." A CNN camera caught one officer yelling, "Bring it, all you fucking animals!" at a group of protesters.[45] Journalists were arrested, some protesters lit a gas station on fire, and photographers occasionally captured dramatic footage that looked like an action movie, including a photo of a young Black man, Edward Crawford, throwing a tear gas cannister back at police while holding a bag of chips in his other hand. Unconfirmed word had spread that Brown had raised his hands to Wilson before the officer opened fire, and protesters adopted "Hands Up! Don't Shoot!" as a chant when confronting police. In a day, Ferguson became the most dramatic mass-mediated spectacle of Black Americans' exasperation and anger at police racism since Los Angeles in 1992. It would grow in the weeks to come as well: according to the St. Louis reverend-activist Osagyefo Sekou, Ferguson became "the longest rebellion in the history of the United States against police brutality."[46]

As the #Ferguson hashtag spread through Twitter on August 10, 2014, so did #BLM. Black Lives Matter had been established a year earlier after the acquittal of George Zimmerman, the neighborhood-watch coordinator for a Sanford, Florida, gated community. In 2012, Zimmerman shot and killed an unarmed seventeen-year-old, Trayvon Martin, whom Zimmerman had profiled as dangerous for being Black and wearing a hoodie in a predominantly non-Black neighborhood. The killing garnered national attention, spurring debate about Florida's vigilante-endorsing "Stand Your Ground" law and prompting many Black celebrities and public officials, including the entire Miami Heat basketball team and Illinois congressman Bobby Rush, to publicly don a hoodie or post a photo on social media of themselves in a hoodie so as to demonstrate the dangerous ignorance of such profiling while rearticulating the symbol's meaning. After so much media buildup, Zimmerman's acquittal was an especially harsh blow. Oakland activist Alicia Garza learned of the verdict through Facebook and wrote an impassioned post that ended, "Black people. I love you. I love us. Our lives matter." In Los Angeles, Garza's friend, community activist and prison reform advocate Patrisse Cullors, moved the conversation to Twitter, adding the hashtag #BlackLivesMatter. The two reached out to Phoenix-based activist and community organizer Opal Tometi, who bought the domain name. When Ferguson erupted in protest, the trio organized a Black Lives Matter Freedom Ride to Ferguson, a tribute to the civil rights–era pilgrimages to register southern Black voters. The Black Lives Matter movement differed from the 1960s civil rights movement in many ways: it was not interested in Black respectability politics or in directly lobbying to pass new laws but was a liberation movement that resisted following top-down commands, affirming singular messiah figures, kowtowing to white anxieties, or waiting for the mass media's blessing. It was also profoundly intersectional. As Reverend Sekou explained, "I take my orders from 23-year-old queer women."[47] Black Lives Matter was more diverse, and dispersed, than any of its civil rights predecessors, and it moved the issue of racist policing squarely into the center of American political debate.

In late November 2014, when a grand jury announced it would not indict officer Darren Wilson for shooting and killing Michael Brown, protesters returned to the streets, and President Barack Obama took to the airwaves to urge calm. "There will inevitably be some negative reaction, and it will make for good TV," Obama said. But while Obama spoke, TV and Twitter were combining to undermine his message. Television producers had turned Obama's address into a split screen, with the president calling for peace on one side, while the other showed police firing tear gas at protesters. The tragic irony of the contrast made it a perfect screen cap to circulate through Twitter, as a form of live metacommentary that underscored the insufficiency of Obama's rhetoric at this moment. During Obama's presidency, social media platforms had taken over for reality television as the primary media space for ordinary Americans to stake a claim to mass-media discourse. Facebook, Instagram, and Twitter offered numerous affordances: they helped reporters find sources, provided a space for marketers to astroturf social participation, and served as the primary organizational and messaging platforms for activist groups. They also constituted a standing archive of Black death at the hands of police officers.

A few weeks before Michael Brown's shooting death, a video went viral of a forty-three-year-old Black Staten Island resident, Eric Garner, being choked to death by a New York Police Department officer, Daniel Pantaleo, who had confronted Garner for selling untaxed cigarettes. As Pantaleo wrenches Garner's last words from his lungs (Garner repeats "I can't breathe!" eleven times), the voice of Ramsey Orta, a member of the national police-monitoring organization Copwatch, can be heard.

"Once again, police beatin' up on people," Orta says, while filming the killing on his phone, before an officer tells him to move back. Orta doesn't yet know Garner will die, and the fact that he wasn't screaming the words but simply describing the scene reflects a sense of mundane frustration. *This shit again.* The videos proliferated, from numerous sources: squad-car dashcam footage of Chicago police shooting and killing Laquan McDonald while he lay on the ground; a surveillance camera capturing officers shooting and killing twelve-year-old Tamir Rice; a bystander recording a South Carolina police officer shooting Walter Scott multiple times in the back; Diamond Reynolds livestreaming her boyfriend Philando Castile's final moments on earth on Facebook Live, seconds after he was shot seven times at point-blank range by a St. Anthony, Minnesota, police officer. None of the officers involved in these shooting deaths were found guilty of criminal acts.

By mid-decade, Twitter and Facebook had usurped print, television, and radio to become the primary news source for tens of millions of Americans, and social media's deployment by activists and average folks alike had forced the nation to confront Black death at the hands of the state, which placed them in a dreadful lineage of mass-media witnessing. In August 1955, the fourteen-year-old Black Chicago native Emmett Till was kidnapped, beaten, shot in the head, and dumped into Mississippi's Tallahatchie River, all for the alleged crime of not showing proper deference to a local white woman. Days later, Till's mother, Mamie, insisted on an open-casket funeral and contacted several members of the press to photograph it, knowing that the act of bearing visual witness to her son's mutilated body would be the most powerful way to commemorate his tragic death. "I knew that I could talk for the rest of my life about what happened to my baby . . . [but] people would still not get the full impact," she wrote in her memoir. "If people opened the pages of *Jet* magazine or the *Chicago Defender*, if other people could see it with their own eyes, then together we would find a way to express what we had seen."[48] A month after Till's murderers were acquitted, Rosa Parks cried when she read the *Jet* story and listened to T. R. M. Howard deliver a powerful speech about Till at Martin Luther King Jr.'s church in Montgomery, Alabama. Four days later, with Till's memory still on her mind, Parks defied the city's segregation laws and refused to give up her seat on a city bus to a white man.[49]

The organizers of the southern civil rights movement that grew in the wake of Parks's action sought to capitalize on the then-new medium of television news to stage dramatic interactions with racist police. The Southern Christian Leadership Conference (SCLC) and the Student Nonviolent Coordinating Committee (SNCC) planned their face-offs with segregationist law enforcement with full knowledge that white America would best understand Black terror if it was viscerally demonstrated as it happened. King saw television news as a powerful medium for vicarious participation and was intent on using it to transport a regional movement into the virtual world. "As the broadcasting profession will confirm, no shows are so successful as those which allow for audience participation," he wrote. "In order to be somebody, people must feel themselves part of something."[50] King also believed that the bright lights of national media spectacle would shame the racist police into changing their ways: "The brutality with which officials would have quelled the black individual became impotent when it could not be pursued with stealth and remain unobserved. It was caught—as a fugitive from a penitentiary is often caught—in gigantic circling spotlights. It was imprisoned in a luminous glare revealing the naked truth to the whole world."[51] On a Sunday evening in March 1965, all three broadcast networks broke into their prime-time Sunday programming with shocking footage of SNCC voting-rights marchers being violently beaten and gassed by Alabama police officers. The terrifying event, later dubbed "Bloody Sunday," was captured for the nation by a new innovation: handheld 16 mm cameras that provided footage from a number of angles, with a shocking proximity to a conflict that looked like civil war. Representative John Lewis directly credited television news coverage with the passage of the 1965 Voting Rights Act.

The civil rights movement came of age with broadcast journalism, and the two relied on one another for credibility. Decades later, Black Lives Matter was inextricable from social media, while the news media establishment faced a reckoning about the future of the profession. As Catherine Knight Steele has explained, the additive and redundant nature of social media discourse combined with an expressive tradition rooted in orality to make Twitter and Facebook logical and ideal spaces for numerous forms of Black communication, including political protest.[52] Print circulation had been plummeting for a decade, and after

Facebook and Google seized the majority of online advertising revenue, news organizations laid off thousands of reporters. The situation was dire, but the journalists left standing realized that, at a time when videos of Black death at the hands of the state were proliferating, they needed to simultaneously embrace digital technologies and ditch the twentieth century's objectivity mantra, which was increasingly seen as a useless "view from nowhere." As two scholars noted in a 2019 book, social media and the internet were much less the *cause* of journalism's crisis as they were its most effective diagnostic, surfacing new truths and vociferous publics eager to have their voices heard. As #BLM and numerous other social-media-fueled accountability movements proved, the distortions of "both sides" balance and the overwhelming whiteness of newsrooms were unacceptable servants of a racist status quo. If journalism was going to maintain relevance as the democratic voice of a rapidly diversifying population who imagined themselves as citizen-reporters, the profession would have to adapt accordingly.[53] Behind the scenes, communications firms and public relations experts were training reporters to pry themselves away from their overreliance on police press releases and connecting them to on-the-ground sources who could explain the causes and effects of Black deaths with much more nuance.[54] One such journalist was Wesley Lowery, a Black *Washington Post* reporter whose perspective was transformed after Ferguson, leading him to devise the "Fatal Force" project, an online database that tracked the nation's mortal police shootings, information that had not otherwise been provided anywhere, to expose the sheer extent of the nation's problem. The project won the 2016 Pulitzer Prize for National Reporting.

Less than a year after Ferguson, President Obama, deep in his second term, gave a speech commemorating the fiftieth anniversary of the "Bloody Sunday" march. "We honored those who walked so we could run. We must run so our children soar," Obama said. He later acknowledged that the line was a slimmed-down appropriation of a Jay-Z verse on a remix of Young Jeezy's "My President," which was released to coincide with Obama's historic 2008 election.[55] The Selma speech, and its Jay-Z sample, bridged the two broad views of Obama's presidency: a long-delayed victory for the 1960s civil rights movement and the ultimate ascendance of hip-hop culture to the highest echelon of political life.

Attempts by the right to paint Obama as a far-leftist, linking him to the 1960s radical Bill Ayers and even the revivified Black Panthers, shriveled against his overwhelming charisma and message of hope. After Obama's election, Al Sharpton, who had his own hour-long show on the newly left-leaning MSNBC, predicted a new era of moderation for hip-hop: "Here's the greatest political victory in the history of black America, and the thug rappers can't come near it. They will have to change or become irrelevant."[56] Sharpton was clearly unaware that Young Jeezy's own 2005 breakthrough album was subtitled *Thug Motivation 101*, but the mainstreaming of "thug" was far from hip-hop's only shift. By the time of Obama's speech, rap had no single center of discursive or geographic power, and the heyday of Public Enemy, N.W.A, Ice Cube, and Tupac Shakur was further from 2015 than James Brown, Curtis Mayfield, and Marvin Gaye were from the dawn of reality rap. Kendrick Lamar might have been the most critically acclaimed rapper of the moment, but the most *popular* rapper was Drake, a former child actor from Toronto whose brooding, internally directed music fit perfectly with a listening culture shaped by streaming platforms like Spotify, Apple Music, and Tidal (in which Jay-Z owned a financial stake), where mood-setting capabilities overrode music's capacity for political agitation.

A bit more than three months after Obama's speech, Lamar performed his *To Pimp a Butterfly* single "Alright" at the 2015 BET Awards, standing atop a vandalized police car with the American flag waving in the background. As a protest anthem, "Alright" was no "Fuck tha Police," but a midtempo, jazz-derived track on which Lamar stresses resilience in the face of insurmountable obstructions and Pharrell Williams croons a chorus that hews closer to Bob Marley than Ice Cube. Still, the night after the BET performance, a Fox News panel homed in on the song's prechorus: "Nigga, and we hate po-po / Wanna kill us dead in the street fo sho'." Geraldo Rivera, who had joined the right-wing news network in 2001, reactivated the "Cop Killer" strategy of rerouting the problems *exposed* by rappers onto rap itself, claiming that "hip-hop has done more damage to young African-Americans than racism in recent years."[57] Lamar replied, "Hip-hop is not the problem. Our reality is the problem of the situation."[58]

A month later, a fourteen-year-old Black teenager was arrested during a Black Lives Matter conference at Cleveland State University. When the teenager was released to his family instead of taken to jail, protesters started singing the "Alright" chorus, and video of the event went viral. A few days later, the Black cultural critic Aisha Harris wondered if "Alright" had become the new Black national anthem. "It's been a long and difficult year since Ferguson, and the world sometimes seems like a terrible place, and I need Lamar's reminder that we've been down before," Harris wrote, filing "Alright" alongside "Mississippi Goddam," "Say It Loud—I'm Black and I'm Proud," and "Fight the Power" as a classic work of Black pop protest.[59] It was fitting that a song about resilience in the face of structural oppression would become the defining protest anthem of the Obama presidency, which missed multiple opportunities to forcefully counteract the hypermilitarized and often plainly racist culture of American policing. By 2015, the idea of resilience had come to signify the *opposite* of resistance. Instead of fighting back, Americans were encouraged to bounce back from crisis after crisis and to sublimate their anger in consumerism instead of destroying its brick-and-mortar avatars in the interest of deep structural change.[60] Those who don't bounce back, like those who angrily took to the streets to protest Baltimore police's murder of twenty-five-year-old Freddie Gray a month after Obama's Selma speech, were described by the president himself as "criminals and thugs."

"Alright" had plenty of fans, including Obama himself, but on the ground in Ferguson and at the subsequent protests it inspired, not to mention on Twitter, "Fuck the Police" rang out far more often. It wasn't N.W.A's original that was galvanizing the protests, however, but a track of the same name released by the Baton Rouge rapper Boosie Badazz (formerly Lil Boosie) and his collaborator Webbie on a 2009 MP3 mixtape. Boosie's track sounded nothing like the lush, jazzy bohemia of "Alright" or the tabloid reenactments of its N.W.A namesake, and a lot like a southern rap mixtape of its era: blunt drum-machine handclaps mixed with ultradeep sub-bass, a high-pitched melodic line played on a synthesizer, and occasional shouts of the DJ's name accompanied by an air-horn blast. The meager production made it easier to focus on the lyrics, a straightforward and uncompromising litany of personal wrongs:

> They killed Venelle when I was 12, turned me against 'em
> Sent me to my first funeral now I'm a victim

My daddy called 'em pigs, I'll neva forget
He went to jail on Highland road, for tryna piss
Kicked my auntie Trina door, lookin' for my cousin
Looked at me 'cross tha street and said, "Boy, you ugly"

Boosie's chorus is much easier to chant at a rally than N.W.A's version, while retaining MC Ren's combative spirit: "Without dat badge you a bitch and a half," Boosie raps.

Though he was far from a household name in 2014, Boosie had become a living symbol of twenty-first-century rap reality for countless fans. After five years behind bars, he was paroled from the Louisiana State Penitentiary a few months before Ferguson, a sentence that had generated a widespread "Free Boosie" campaign on social media. His case, and his cause, were derived from the wrongheaded legal conflation of rap celebrity and criminality. He was initially arrested in 2009 on a gun and marijuana charge, and because it was his third conviction, he got four years; but in 2010, he was charged with having paid a hitman to murder a rival a few years earlier and was suddenly facing life. During his 2012 murder trial, a judge ruled that while Boosie's song "187" could not be played in its entirety, nor could the lyrics be read aloud to the jury, the prosecution could use the slang terms "187," "murk," and "cake" as evidence of his guilt. It did not matter much: after the killer recanted his confession, the jury deliberated for an hour before delivering a not-guilty verdict. After serving out his drug sentence, Boosie hit the streets in March 2014 as what Jeff Weiss called "a folk hero hovering somewhere between 2Pac and Lead Belly," the blues icon "discovered" at the very same prison by the folklorists John Lomax and Alan Lomax in 1933. Boosie's music would never reach Kendrick Lamar's level of mainstream respectability, but his image as an outlaw survivor relating unvarnished truths in a simple, forceful fashion resonated deeply with those taking to the streets to protest infrastructural injustice. As he told Weiss, "If you can understand reality, you can understand my music."[61]

As the 2012 US presidential election season was heating up, Donald Trump was considering a run for the highest political office, an idea he had toyed with for nearly as long as he had been in the public eye. At the time, Trump was most recognizable from *The Apprentice*, the popular business-themed reality series developed by *Survivor* producer Mark Burnett. Trump had used his TV character—an all-powerful American business tycoon who dispatched the unworthy from his gaudy boardroom with the catchphrase "You're fired"—to reinvent his public image, which had taken a hit with the late-1990s rise of the internet-age tech mogul. In the early 2000s, Trump's image as a real estate baron had been reduced to that of "a museum piece with no more grip on the popular imagination than a railroad tycoon."[62] But as a public figure who had long pitched himself as the walking embodiment of late-capitalist hyperreality, Trump had reinvented himself before, and reality television was the perfect format for his latest shift. "Most of us knew he was a fake. He had just gone through I don't know how many bankruptcies," one of Burnett's longtime editors explained. "But we made him out to be the most important person in the world. It was like making the court jester the king."[63] Each episode ended in a hyperstylized, flamboyantly decorated "boardroom," which, James Poniewozik writes, "embodies the highest value of reality TV and a key to Trump's persona: being 'real,' which is different from being honest."[64] Being "real" meant being one's most *entertaining* and *combative* self, which, as *The Real World* had proven in 1992, was what played best on TV. As *Apprentice* ratings dropped, NBC launched *The Celebrity Apprentice* in 2008, in which a string of B-list public figures competed with one another to do what Trump himself had mastered: turn their dwindling celebrity into a new revenue stream.

No single figure predicted hyperreal twenty-first-century reality culture more than Trump, who used television and the tabloid press to establish himself as a walking, talking hyperrealistic brand in the 1980s and 1990s. With a small fortune inherited from his landlord father, Trump became the embodiment of Reagan-era entrepreneurial individualism, a one-man *Lifestyles of the Rich and Famous* who bought skyscrapers and casinos just to slap his last name on them. The tabloids and entertainment press lavished attention on Trump's ostentatious lifestyle and very public relationships, shaping his image as "The Donald," a wealthy, egocentric, hypermasculine embodiment of the American Dream—even viewed as a sex symbol by *People* magazine—who was hated by more-wealthy establishment figures for his success. In a 1990 interview with *Playboy*, he freely admitted that his yacht, Trump Tower, and his casinos were all "props for the show" that was his public persona.

"The show is *Trump*," he added, "and it is sold-out performances every-where."[65] As one scholar explains, Trump's ease at pulling back the curtain on his own self-creation "was well-calibrated for a tabloid discourse that itself routinely shifts among realist and fictive modes of representation."[66] When an economic recession hit, Trump was forced to dramatically scale back his economic activities, while keeping up appearances to the public, both for his sake and his creditors'. If Trump in the 1980s was a businessman who used celebrity for promotion, by the 1990s he had become a celebrity "whose calling card was the ability to play the figure of a businessman."[67] Trump's image was every bit the postmodern *projection* of wealth, a simulacrum of affluence as inspired by schmaltzy Las Vegas glitz as were Tupac Shakur and Suge Knight. From the 1990s onward, Trump's last name alone was used as a shorthand for showy affluence by a number of rappers, including Ice Cube, Scarface, Raekwon, Nas, Jay-Z, 50 Cent, and Kanye West.

Though Trump's racism was never a major part of his image through the 2000s, it had also never been concealed: his first appearance in the *New York Times* came in 1973, defending his landlord father, Fred, in a story about accusations that the elder Trump had violated the Fair Housing Act by refusing to rent to Black tenants. In 1989, Trump chimed in on the case of the "Central Park Five," the Black youths accused of raping and assaulting a white woman, by taking out full-page ads in four New York newspapers calling for the return of the death penalty (the men were later exonerated). But in the early years of Obama's presidency, Trump took to Fox News to fully pull back the curtain on his disdain for Black people. Launched in 1996, Fox News was Rupert Murdoch's attempt to use his vast American media influence to boost conservative political fortunes against what he saw as an overtly liberal journalistic landscape. To oversee the upstart cable news network, Murdoch brought in Roger Ailes, the pugnacious former media consultant to Richard Nixon, Ronald Reagan, George H. W. Bush, and New York City mayor Rudy Giuliani. As the new century dawned, Fox News merged right-wing politics with tabloid sensationalism and the 1990s' moral entrepreneurship, welcoming Geraldo Rivera, conservative columnist Juan Williams, *Inside Edition* host Bill O'Reilly, Oliver North, and numerous former GOP politicians and consultants. By the turn of the century, Fox News had reinvented the conservative political movement as a powerful *cultural* force, by combining political populism with tabloid journalism and positioning partisanship not only as an ideological force but as an identity *style* counter to the so-called liberal elites.[68] The tabloid 1990s had spawned a cultural juggernaut: the propaganda wing of the Republican Party was the most-watched cable network in the country.

During Obama's first term, Fox News personalities Glenn Beck and Sean Hannity spread numerous conspiracy theories about the nation's first Black president, mirroring the barely concealed racism of the insurgent right-wing Tea Party movement. Trump became a frequent guest on Fox News' daytime talk show *Fox and Friends* in 2010, where he began publicizing a conspiracy theory that questioned Obama's country of birth. On his Twitter account and at press conferences (they quickly became indistinguishable), Trump demanded to see Obama's birth certificate. Though the barely concealed racism of the request outraged millions, the GOP power center that refused to even negotiate with Obama on his policy ideas kept its distance, aware of numerous polls revealing that Trump's racism resonated with a not-insignificant number of Republican voters. In 2015, Trump launched his presidential campaign by appending to his racist demonization of Obama other forms of ethnic and nationalist bigotry aimed at Muslim Americans and Spanish-speaking immigrants. Though decades of research had debunked "Black-on-Black crime" as a fallacy (most homicide victims are killed by people they know or who live near them), and few in the Black community used the phrase anymore, Trump and Fox News doubled down on it, particularly toward Obama's adopted hometown of Chicago.

Trump's 2016 election shocked politicians and the media commentariat. Soul-searching Democrats and gobsmacked pundits blamed pro-Trump "fake news" stories that spread through Facebook and Twitter in the waning months of the campaign, seeded by foreign intermediaries sowing discord in the populace. While such stories did circulate, claims of fake news shifting the election were wishful thinking—issued, and believed the most, by liberals who assumed that the centrist institutions comprising the American public sphere had been assailed from the outside instead of existing largely as a nostalgic figment of a simpler information era. As researchers pointed out, Trump's victory reflected a much longer shift in American civic life toward a situation in which "sizeable portions of the citizen public are demonstrating not only a tolerance for candidates who bend the norms of political and civil discourse but a will to celebrate such transgressive performative acts."[69] Trump won not because centrist, objective journalism had been infiltrated by foreign forces using social media. Instead, his victory was the most prominent product of the tabloidification of popular culture and politics that had launched his career thirty-plus years earlier. Trump had teased a presidential run in a 1988 appearance on *Oprah*, and the radio shock jock Howard Stern had predicted in 1999 that "President Trump will be a reality."[70] From the New York gossip rags to the *National Enquirer* through *The Apprentice*, tabloid culture and reality media not only made Donald Trump into a celebrity but primed a significant number of Americans to believe that he was a commanding authority figure with the gravitas to become a political leader—most of which was invisible to pollsters and media pundits. Trump knew less about policy than any of his predecessors, but like Reagan, he knew how to pretend like he did through photo ops and television appearances. Far more than Reagan's reliance on C-SPAN to keep tabs on Congress, Trump watched Fox News so much that his Republican colleagues appeared on *Fox and Friends* to get his attention.

Trump's bigotry and xenophobia isolated him from most of the entertainment establishment, but in the weeks after his electoral college victory of November 2016, he found one willing supporter: Kanye West. Though the two are different in obvious ways, the least of which being that West made his own way in the world and has contributed meaningfully to it, their similarities are telling. Both are headline-hungry, egocentric reality TV veterans married to glamorous models. West's 2010 critical high-water mark, *My Beautiful Dark Twisted Fantasy*, was described in one rave review as "a hedonistic exploration into a rich and famous American id," a phrase that could be extracted and reappropriated to describe Trump's own self-made iconography.[71] Two months after Trump's 2015 announcement of his presidential candidacy, West ended a digressive thirteen-minute lifetime-achievement acceptance speech at the MTV Video Music Awards by announcing that he was going to run for president in 2020 (his abridged candidacy was supported by Geraldo Rivera, who also endorsed Trump). Both Trump and West are prone to flights of incoherent rambling, often via lengthy

Twitter diatribes waged against their perceived enemies, and spur-of-the-moment decision-making, whether something as mild as finishing and releasing an album or as vital as international diplomacy. Trump and West are informational chaos agents, unable or unwilling to distinguish between provable facts and fringe ideas that position them as freethinking iconoclasts. In October 2018, West took to the offices of the celebrity gossip empire *TMZ* to argue that slavery was a "choice," six months after tweeting that his support for Trump was less a matter of ideology than alignment with another maverick that everyone assumed he should hate: "You don't have to agree with trump but the mob can't make me not love him. . . . I don't agree with everything anyone does. That's what makes us individuals. And we have the right to independent thought." West's embrace for his own purposes of what a Trump spokeswoman dubbed the administration's favored "alternative facts" arose not only from the entitlement granted the wealthy, famous, and isolated but from the much vaster confluence of a social media–fueled informational miasma with a resentment-fueled populism.

More broadly, Trump's election came as the result of a curious American amnesia. In numerous ways, the 2010s looked a lot like the 1990s, from the endless run of rebooted TV shows and films (a product of risk-averse cultural industries that have ramped up the 1990s consolidation craze) to the nostalgic embrace of reality rap's icons and the resurgence of South Los Angeles as a rap hotbed, launching Kendrick Lamar, Vince Staples, YG, Nipsey Hussle, and Lamar's labelmates Schoolboy Q and Ab-Soul, leading Tom Breihan to remark in 2016 that the world's best rap music is rooted "in the ancestral G-funk of the '90s."[72] But the most crucial legacy of the American period between the fall of the Berlin Wall and the national trauma of the 9/11 attacks was the significant amount of social and political business that America left unfinished. That period comprised what Tony Judt called "the years the locusts ate: a decade and a half of wasted opportunity and incompetence," derived from the belief that the victory of liberal democracy and capitalism in 1989 had left America with nothing to do but expand its economy and turn its bellicose tendencies inward.[73] The September 11, 2001, terrorist attacks led president George W. Bush to shift the national priorities from wars on crime and drugs to terrorism, fostering the rapid rise of anti-Muslim hatred and, after the bipartisan passage of the Patriot Act, a vast surveillance state that predicted the forthcoming privacy invasions sponsored by Google and social media platforms.

President Bush's most notorious solution to the terrorism problem, however, was market driven. Two weeks after the attacks, President Bush recommended that Americans return to normalcy by supporting the struggling airline industry and flying to Disney World. The twentieth century's victorious ideology, as Gary Cross has argued, was not democracy but consumerism, which has "no interest in linking the present to the past and future," except for nostalgia and fantasy. Cross saw in the end of communism the rise of an "enemy crisis" that generated the culture wars and facilitated an unending political stalemate.[74] Indeed, the stark, GOP-driven political polarization that skyrocketed during Obama's tenure and defined the vicious 2016 election cycle could be traced to Newt Gingrich's demonization of Democrats as socialist traitors, which led to the GOP's epochal 1994 takeover of Congress and the Fox News–supported Clinton impeachment that ended the century in tawdry tabloid spectacle. But while the nation was distracted by political infighting, a booming economy, and a flourishing commercial internet, homegrown white antigovernment sentiment exploded from Ruby Ridge to Waco, spawning a terrorist bombing in Oklahoma City, while President Clinton, forced by the GOP to govern like a Republican, focused his legislative energy on the specter of Black crime. Clinton's 1994 federal crime bill included the "three strikes" law and promised billions in funding to build new prisons and hire one hundred thousand new police officers nationwide, all of which disproportionately affected Black communities and solidified a punitive, law-and-order approach to crime as a bipartisan reality. Hillary Clinton being repeatedly forced to answer for a 1996 reference to Black "superpredators" during the election twenty years later was further proof that the 2010s were a dark echo of the 1990s, America's holiday from history.

George Floyd grew up in Houston's Third Ward and made a name for himself in that city's hip-hop community in the 1990s. He cut numerous recordings with the Screwed Up Click, a collective led by the influential DJ Screw, who pioneered a slowed-down production style that mimicked the narcotic effects of the codeine-laced cocktail popular in the region. As

Big Floyd, George appeared on six DJ Screw tapes before the producer's 2000 death and earned admirers among Houston's hip-hop luminaries, including Trae tha Truth, UGK, and Scarface. A devout Christian and a prominent member of his church, Floyd spoke some words of inspiration to his city on a 1998 tape, over an instrumental of the Notorious B.I.G.'s "One More Chance." "Everybody gotta stick together, mane, know what I'm sayin'? All this motherfuckin' hatin' man, people coming up dead man. Let a nigga shine. That's for real." Floyd moved to Minneapolis in 2014 to start a new life and found work as a bouncer at a local nightclub that also employed Minneapolis police officer Derek Chauvin as security detail. Just after 8:00 p.m. on May 25, 2020, Floyd was approached by officers after passing a suspicious-looking twenty-dollar bill to a convenience store clerk. Floyd was handcuffed but struggled with the officers, leading Chauvin to force him to the ground and press his knee into the back of Floyd's neck. Seventeen-year-old Darnella Frazier quickly pulled out her phone and started recording while several other onlookers protested and Floyd repeatedly pleaded that he could not breathe. Chauvin kept his leg pressed into Floyd's neck for nearly nine minutes, killing him. The initial charging document elided Chauvin's responsibility, and the first autopsy ascribed Floyd's death to preexisting health conditions. But, as had been the case since Rodney King, Darnella Frazier's video was all the evidence most people needed to see.

President Trump was deeply enamored of wielding state violence against ostensibly disobedient American citizens. During a 2017 address to law enforcement, he removed all subtext from the "law and order" rhetoric that dated back to Nixon. "The laws are so horrendously stacked against us, because for years and years, they've been made to protect the criminal . . . not the officers. You do something wrong, you're in more jeopardy than they are," he said. The phrase that circulated afterward was characteristically blunt and unfeeling: "Please don't be too nice." But in the wake of the Floyd video, a vociferous nationwide counterargument to law-and-order culture quickly emerged. In a matter of days, the George Floyd protests dwarfed even Ferguson, with millions of people taking to the streets in all fifty states, from major metropolitan areas to Simi Valley and even small towns with Klan histories, to protest infrastructural racism and demand police reform. Though slogans varied, the

Floyd protests were an outgrowth of Black Lives Matter, which had nestled into the American vernacular in the post-Ferguson years. Powered in part by a broad antipathy toward President Trump—who tweeted the phrase "LAW AND ORDER" from the White House—and executed safely in the midst of a global pandemic, the Floyd protests were bigger than any racial justice movement since the 1960s.

Still, the police reacted with stubborn intransigence and frequent violence, confronting peaceful protesters with rubber bullets and tear gas, beating them with billy clubs, kicking and shoving them. Much of this brutality was captured on smartphone cameras, which spread the word through Facebook, Instagram, and Twitter, providing a necessary contrast to national journalistic coverage focused on violence and property destruction. The protests swallowed the national discourse, leading the massive multinational conglomerates who had taken over American consumer culture and its public sphere to scramble to issue public affirmations of solidarity. The mostly white, Democratic US House leadership staged an awkward Afrocentric photo op of their own, wearing kente-cloth stoles while announcing their Justice in Policing Act of 2020. Meanwhile, the protesters were quickly achieving their goals: within days, Minnesota's attorney general upgraded Officer Chauvin's charges to second-degree murder and second-degree manslaughter, and numerous US cities—Minneapolis, New York City, Seattle, Sacramento, and Washington, DC, among others—announced reform initiatives to shift funds from bloated police department budgets to social services and education.

A lesser but still significant impact of the Floyd protests resonated throughout the television industry. Many longtime TV critics noted that the medium, and they themselves, had long been complicit in misrepresenting the internal culture and external effects of American policing. "TV has long had a police's-eye perspective that helps shape the way viewers see the world, prioritizing the victories and struggles of police over communities being policed," wrote one critic in the midst of the protests.[75] Actors who had played police in the past promoted their donations to social justice causes on Twitter, and when the NBA restarted its season in Orlando, Florida, four months after suspending it due to the COVID-19 pandemic, the league put the words "Black Lives Matter" on every court for its telecasts, meeting a demand from its mostly Black players. Along with "Black Lives Matter" and "ACAB" (All Cops Are Bastards), one of the Floyd protests' most common refrains was "Fuck 12," the number derived from the TV police procedural *Adam-12*, executive-produced by *Dragnet*'s Jack Webb. Even *Cops*, which was set to start its thirty-third season on the Paramount network in mid-June, could not survive the moment. Though the show's ratings were paltry (after twenty-five years on Fox, it had moved to Spike TV, which morphed into Paramount), the symbolism was significant. For three decades of new episodes and syndicated repeats, *Cops* had served as ambient propaganda for American policing, now simply reduced to "copaganda." The Floyd protests and the establishment of Black Lives Matter as a potent force in American discourse cast in sharp relief the truism that popular culture is a space for social struggle: Who gets to speak, about what, and for whom? But while the summer of 2020 went "a long way toward undoing the conditioning of decades of televised stories of heroic cops," in the words of another critic, television had not been revolutionized.[76] Four out of the top five prime-time network programs of 2020—*Chicago P.D.*, *Blue Bloods*, *FBI*, and *NCIS*—were narrated from the perspective of heroic law enforcement officials.

In December 1991, the near midpoint between the release of the Rodney King video and the LAPD officers' acquittal, "Fuck tha Police" had become a menacing, anticop folk anthem on the streets of Los Angeles. "At 51st and Avalon, the words are scrawled on the wall of a market," an *LA Times* story noted. "Officers driving through the Nickerson Gardens housing project in South Central hear elementary school kids sing its taunting tag line in reedy voices."[77] Extracted from its formative context but always nodding back to it, "Fuck the police" had, by 2020, become part of the American protest vernacular, every bit as potent as "No justice, no peace," but much more intense and single-minded in its rhetorical aim. In the midst of the Floyd protests, the Compton-born rapper and Tree Top Pirus member YG released the one-off single "FTP." The acronym was obvious to everyone: it was spray-painted on countless walls across the country, and President Trump was even photographed strolling past one such instance on his way to a photo op in the midst of the protests. The last line of YG's first verse, "Without that badge, you's a bitch and a half," was a nod to Boosie's 2009 adaptation, itself audible at many of the protests. A few days after "FTP" dropped, YG worked with the Los Angeles chapter of Black Lives Matter to stage a massive protest march in Hollywood that drew an estimated one hundred thousand participants. He filmed the event for the "FTP" music video, which opens with Martin Luther King Jr.'s quote "A riot is the language of the unheard" and mixes YG's performance footage at the protest rally with a montage of police violence, all of which had been shot in the previous few days.

Since civil rights protesters marched while singing "We Shall Overcome" in full view of the handheld film cameras of network news photographers; since the Impressions urged Black Americans to "Keep on Pushin'" and Sam Cooke promised "A Change Is Gonna Come"; since the Black Panthers staged their hyperreal interventions into mainstream news discourse; and since the title of Marvin Gaye's *What's Going On* combined a journalistic statement of reality with an existential query, Black music and an ever-shifting landscape of visual media have been intertwined components of modern American protest. In 2020, Black protest music exploded with a force unseen since the late 1960s, from the countless tracks rush-released by street rappers to the more abstract meditations proffered by a new crop of Black nationalist jazz musicians. On the streets and through the air, the George Floyd protesters broadcast their demands and footage of their forceful standoffs with the cops, from the same smartphones that streamed their music and captured Floyd's murder, and through the same social media platforms that surveilled and tracked them to more specifically pinpoint ads to their user profiles. "The most urgent filmmaking anybody's doing in this country right now is by black people with camera phones," wrote Wesley Morris at the height of the protests.[78] A few years before the Floyd protests, when videos of Black death by white police started flooding social media, the Americans of the Black Lives Matter generation picked up the Panthers' legacy of policing the police, fighting a grassroots media war against those sworn to serve and protect, armed with the expensive gadgets in their pockets. Like the reality rappers of the 1980s and '90s, they have little interest in respectability politics or the solemn admiration of white America, and they deeply believe in the combined power of the moving image and protest music to force social change in the hyperreal war zone of popular culture. Many of them are printing out pamphlets to carry in their pockets that outline their legal rights, offer tips for interacting with officers, and contain advice for capturing the best footage. One of the most popular of these guides is titled "Film the Police."

NOTES

▼

Preface

1. bell hooks, *Outlaw Culture: Resisting Representations* (London: Rout-ledge, 1994), 150.

Introduction: The Strength of Street Knowledge

1. Bill Carter, "Police Dramas on TV Were Always Popular; Now They're Real," *New York Times*, October 17, 1990, C13.
2. John Leland, "Armageddon in Effect," *Spin*, September 1988, 48.
3. Frank Owen, "Hangin' Tough," *Spin*, April 1990, 34.
4. Ice-T and Douglas Century, *Ice: A Memoir of Gangster Life and Redemption—from South Central to Hollywood* (New York: Ballantine, 2011), 53.
5. Dennis Hunt, "The Rap Reality: Truth and Money," *Los Angeles Times*, April 2, 1989.
6. Jacob Hoye and Karolyn Ali, *Tupac: Resurrection 1971–1996* (New York: Atria, 2011), 27.
7. Chuck D, *Lyrics of a Rap Revolutionary: Volume One*, ed. Yusuf Jah (Beverly Hills, CA: Off Da Books), 120.
8. Tom Matthews and Daniel Glick, "Fine Art or Foul?," *Newsweek*, July 2, 1990, 46.
9. Francis Fukuyama, "The End of History?," *National Interest* 16 (Summer 1989): 3.

10. James Rowley, "300 FBI Agents Turn Efforts from Spies to Street Gangs," *Austin American-Statesman*, January 10, 1992, A4.

11. David Kamp, "The Tabloid Decade," *Vanity Fair*, February 1999.

12. Kevin Glynn, *Tabloid Culture: Trash Taste, Popular Power, and the Transformation of American Television* (Chapel Hill, NC: Duke University Press, 2002), 2.

13. Carl Bernstein, "The Idiot Culture: Reflections on Post-Watergate Journalism," *New Republic*, June 8, 1992.

14. Chuck D and Yusuf Jah, *Fight the Power: Rap, Race, and Reality* (New York: Delta, 1997), 10.

15. Jonathan Katz, "Rock, Rap and Movies Bring You the News," *Rolling Stone*, March 5, 1992.

16. Joshua Meyrowitz, *No Sense of Place: The Impact of Electronic Media on Social Behavior* (Oxford, UK: Oxford University Press, 1986), 90.

17. Meyrowitz, 90.

18. Meyrowitz, 311.

19. Todd Gitlin, *Inside Prime Time* (New York: Pantheon Books, 1983), 10.

20. Gitlin, 250.

21. Henry Louis Gates Jr., *The Signifying Monkey: A Theory of African-American Literary Criticism* (Oxford, UK: Oxford University Press, 1988), xxiv.

22. Henry Louis Gates Jr., "2 Live Crew, Decoded," *New York Times*, June 19, 1990.

23. Christine Acham, *Revolution Televised: Prime Time and the Struggle for Black Power* (Minneapolis: University of Minnesota Press, 2004), 1.

24. Marcus Baram, *Gil Scott-Heron: Pieces of a Man* (New York: St. Martin's Press, 2014), 73.

25. Jeff Chang, *Can't Stop Won't Stop: A History of the Hip-Hop Generation* (New York: Picador, 2005), 93–94.

26. David Hepworth, *Uncommon People: The Rise and Fall of the Rock Stars* (New York: Henry Holt, 2017), 209.

27. John Leland, "Do the Right Thing," *Spin*, September 1989, 70.

28. Lou Cannon, *President Reagan: The Performance of a Lifetime* (New York: Simon and Schuster, 2000), 38.

29. Dudley Clendinen, "Reagan and Television: How His Image Leaves Him Vulnerable in Debates," *New York Times*, October 20, 1984, 9.

30. Cannon, *President Reagan*, 58.

31. Howard Kurtz, *Hot Air: All Talk, All the Time* (New York: Times Books, 1996), 163.

32. Steven R. Weisman, "Reagan's Misstatements Getting Less Attention," *New York Times*, February 15, 1983, A20.

33. Andrew Hartman, *A War for the Soul of America: A History of the Culture Wars* (Chicago: University of Chicago Press, 2015), 121.

34. Herman Gray, *Watching Race: Television and the Struggle for Blackness* (Minneapolis: University of Minnesota Press, 1995), 17.

35. Robert M. Entman, "Modern Racism and the Images of Blacks in Local Television News," *Critical Studies in Mass Communication* 7, no. 4 (1990): 332.

36. Mary Beth Oliver and G. Blake Armstrong, "Predictors of Viewing and Enjoyment of Reality-Based and Fictional Crime Shows," *Journalism and Mass Communication Quarterly* 72, no. 3 (1995): 560, 565.

Chapter 1: Peace Is a Dream, Reality Is a Knife

1. Ed Kiersh, "Beating the Rap," *Rolling Stone*, December 4 1986, 60.

2. Patrick Goldstein, "Can Rap Survive Gang War?," *Los Angeles Times*, August 24, 1986.

3. Pete Bishop, "Rocky Rock Scene," *Pittsburgh Press*, July 15, 1986, B5.

4. Goldstein, "Can Rap Survive."

5. Richard Harrington, "Run-D.M.C. and the Rap Flap," *Washington Post*, August 29, 1986.

6. Kurt Loder, "A Message for the Times," *Rolling Stone*, September 16, 1982, 52.

7. Damien Love, "Rap Moves On: The Making of The Message by Grandmaster Flash and the Furious Five (An Oral History)," August 2013, https://damienlove.com/writing/rap-moves-on-the-making-of-the-message-by-grandmaster-flash-and-the-furious-five-an-oral-history/.

8. Dennis Anderson, "Teen Warlords Rule the Night—Fear Grips South Los Angeles," *Orlando Sentinel*, April 7, 1985, G11.

9. Kiersh, "Beating the Rap," 62.

10. Kiersh, 60.

11. Kiersh, 104.

12. Todd Boyd, *Am I Black Enough for You? Popular Culture from the Hood and Beyond* (Bloomington: Indiana University Press, 1997), 17–18.

13. Stanley Cohen, *Folk Devils and Moral Panics: The Creation of the Mods and Rockers* (London: Routledge, 2002).

14. Howard S. Becker, *Outsiders: Studies in the Sociology of Deviance* (New York: Free Press, 1963), 147–164.

15. Geoff Edgers, *Walk This Way: Run-DMC, Aerosmith, and the Song That Changed Music Forever* (New York: Penguin, 2019), 10–11.

16. Jerry Cohen, "Black Youth Gangs: Is Threat Overstated?," *Los Angeles Times*, March 19, 1972.

17. Cohen, "Black Youth Gangs."

18. Daryl F. Gates, with Diane K. Shah, *Chief: My Life in the LAPD* (New York: Bantam, 1992), 291.

19. Mike Davis, *City of Quartz: Excavating the Future in Los Angeles* (London: Verso, 1990), 293.

20. Ward Churchill and Jim Vander Wall, *The COINTELPRO Papers: Documents from the FBI's Secret Wars against Dissent in the United States* (Cambridge, MA: South End Press, 2002), 130.

21. Davis, *City of Quartz*, 299.

22. Sanyika Shakur, *Monster: The Autobiography of an L.A. Gang Member* (New York: Grove Press, 1993), 56.

23. Steven R. Cureton, "Something Wicked This Way Comes: A Historical Account of Black Gangsterism Offers Wisdom and Warning for African American Leadership," *Journal of Black Studies* 40, no. 2 (2009): 352.

24. Shakur, *Monster*, 57.

25. Max Felker-Kantor, *Policing Los Angeles: Race, Resistance, and the Rise of the LAPD* (Chapel Hill: University of North Carolina Press, 2017), 6.

26. Brian Cross, *It's Not About a Salary: Rap, Race and Resistance in Los Angeles* (London: Verso, 1993), 180.

27. *Breakin' 'N' Enterin'*, directed by Topper Carew (1985).

28. Scott Menho, "Going Schooling," *Spin*, October 1986, 16.

29. Ice-T and Douglas Century, *Ice: A Memoir of Gangster Life and Redemption—from South Central to Hollywood* (New York: Ballantine, 2011), 93.

30. Ronin Ro, *Have Gun, Will Travel: The Spectacular Rise and Violent Fall of Death Row Records* (New York: Doubleday, 1998), 4.

31. "Panel Urged to Curb Police Use of Battering Ram," *Los Angeles Times*, February 12, 1985.

32. Andrew Nosnitsky, "That Motherfucker Sound Like a Trash Truck: Toddy Tee's OG 'Batterram Tape,'" *Light Sleeper*, February 5, 2020, https://lightsleeper.substack.com/p/that-motherfucker-sound-like-a-trash.

33. Kinohi Nishikawa, *Street Players: Black Pulp Fiction and the Making of a Literary Underground* (Chicago: University of Chicago Press, 2018), 50.

34. Ice-T and Century, *Ice*, 41.

35. Jeff "Chairman" Mao, "Ice-T," *Red Bull Music Academy*, 2017, https://www.redbullmusicacademy.com/lectures/ice-t.

36. Seymour Stein, *Siren Song: My Life in Music* (New York: Doubleday, 2018), 254.

37. Dick Hebdige, *Cut 'n' Mix: Culture, Identity, and Caribbean Music* (London: Routledge, 1987), 73.

38. Dennis Hunt, "Rhyme Pays for Ice-T," *Los Angeles Times*, August 2, 1987.

39. Robert Christgau, "Ice-T," n.d., https://www.robertchristgau.com/get_artist.php?name=Ice-T.

40. "Gigography" (June 16, 1987, Seattle, WA), Beastiemania, n.d., http://www.beastiemania.com/gigog/show.php?g=19870616.

41. John M. Glionna, "A Murder That Woke Up L.A.," *Los Angeles Times*, January 30, 1998.

42. Peter J. Boyer, "Bad Cops," *New Yorker*, May 21, 2001.

43. Bob Pool, "Police Call Gang Sweep a Success; 1,453 Are Arrested," *Los Angeles Times*, April 12, 1988.

44. Bill Kelley, "'Colors,' Controversy, and Hopper," *Fort Lauderdale News / Sun-Sentinel*, April 17, 1988, F1.

45. Two years later, Mejía dropped the last name and reached the *Billboard* Top 10 with the Spanglish pop-rap single "Rico Suave."

46. Hal Hinson, "Colors," *Washington Post*, April 15, 1988; Sheila Benson, "Complexity and Context Washed Out of 'Colors,'" *Los Angeles Times*, April 15, 1988.

47. Deborah Caulfield, "'Colors' Director Hopper Defends His Movie on L.A. Gangs," *Los Angeles Times*, March 25, 1988, J18.

48. "'Colors' Yanked from Stockton Movie House Following Shooting," *United Press International*, April 26, 1988.

49. Iceberg Slim, *Pimp: The Story of My Life* (New York: Cash Money Content, 2011), xiii.

50. Cary Darling, "Former Hustler Ice-T Raps Out a Strong Message," *Detroit Free Press*, January 2, 1989, 6B.

51. Mark Christensen, "True Glitz," *Rolling Stone*, May 8, 1986, 36.

52. "West 57th Opens to Mixed Reviews," *Broadcasting*, August 19, 1985, 68.

53. Steve Weinstein, "'48 Hours,' CBS Focus on L.A. Gangs," *Los Angeles Times*, June 30, 1988.

54. Léon Bing, *Swans and Pistols: Modeling, Motherhood, and Making It in the Me Generation* (New York: Bloomsbury, 2009), 104.

55. Léon Bing, "Confessions from the Crossfire," *LA Weekly*, May 12, 1988, 23.

56. Robert Hilburn, "Run-D.M.C. Struggles to Hold Rap Title," *Los Angeles Times*, June 29, 1988.
57. Cary Darling, "Tougher Than Leather," *Rolling Stone*, July 14, 1988, 142; Nelson George, "Stars Begin to Fade for Some Artists," *Billboard*, October 1, 1988, 27.
58. Richard Harrington, "Tougher Than Leather," *Washington Post*, September 17, 1988.

Chapter 2: Don't Quote Me, Boy, 'Cause I Ain't Said Shit

1. Robert Hilburn, "N.W.A Show at Anaheim a Reality Rap," *Los Angeles Times*, March 25, 1989.
2. Bud Wilkinson, "'COPS': Taking It to the Streets," *Arizona Republic*, March 10, 1989.
3. Tom Jicha, "'Cops' Captures Big Ratings in Major Cities," *South Florida Sun-Sentinel*, March 14, 1989.
4. Harry F. Waters, "TV's Crime Wave Gets Real," *Newsweek*, May 15, 1989, 72.
5. John J. O'Connor, "'Cops' Camera Shows the Real Thing," *New York Times*, January 6, 1989, L50.
6. Dave Marsh and Phyllis Pollack, "Wanted for Attitude: The Right-Wing Attack on Rock," *Village Voice*, October 10, 1989.
7. Christopher Weingarten, *It Takes a Nation of Millions to Hold Us Back* (New York: Bloomsbury, 2010), 25.
8. Steve Daley, "'Capone's Vaults' a Mint to Producers Only," *Chicago Tribune*, April 24, 1986.
9. Howard Rosenberg, "Rivera's Drug Report Is a Bust," *Los Angeles Times*, December 4, 1986.
10. David Toop, *Rap Attack 3: African Rap to Global Hip-Hop*, expanded 3rd ed. (London: Serpent's Tail, 2000), 180.
11. Toop, 181.
12. Davey D and Keith Moorer, "N.W.A.—Art or Irresponsibility?," *BAM*, April 21, 1989.
13. Davey D and Moorer, "Irresponsibility."
14. Toop, *Rap Attack 3*, 181.
15. John Leland, "Noise Annoys," *Village Voice*, April 21, 1987.
16. Jeff Chang, *Can't Stop Won't Stop: A History of the Hip-Hop Generation* (New York: Picador, 2005), 251.
17. John Leland, "Singles: Column by John Leland," *Spin*, February 1988.

18. Greg Tate, "The Devil Made 'Em Do It: Public Enemy," in *Flyboy in the Buttermilk: Essays on Contemporary America*, ed. Greg Tate (New York: Fireside, 1992), 125.
19. Owen Murphy, "Bring the Noise: Chuck D Discusses Making *It Takes a Nation of Millions to Hold Us Back*," KEXP, June 21, 2018, https://www .kexp.org/read/2018/6/21/bring-noise-chuck-d-discusses-making-it -takes-nation-millions-hold-us-back/.
20. Chuck D, *Lyrics of a Rap Revolutionary: Volume One*, ed. Yusuf Jah (Beverly Hills, CA: Off Da Books, 2006), 91.
21. Earlier that year, they released a cheaply made clip for "Don't Believe the Hype" that did not gain much airplay.
22. Tricia Rose, *Black Noise: Rap Music and Black Culture in Contemporary America* (Middletown, CT: Wesleyan University Press, 1994), 119.
23. Rose, 119.
24. Chang, *Can't Stop Won't Stop*, 239.
25. Daniel Boorstin, *The Image: A Guide to Pseudo-Events in America* (New York: Vintage Books, 1992), 39.
26. Sol Stern, "The Call of the Black Panthers," *New York Times Magazine*, August 6, 1967.
27. Radley Balko, *Rise of the Warrior Cop: The Militarization of America's Police Forces* (New York: PublicAffairs, 2014), 79.
28. Weingarten, *Nation of Millions*, 12–13.
29. Chuck D, *Lyrics*, 78.
30. Chang, *Can't Stop Won't Stop*, 251.
31. John Leland, "Armageddon in Effect," *Spin*, September 1988, 76.
32. Jack Breslin, *America's Most Wanted: How Television Catches Crooks* (New York: Harper, 1990), 93.
33. David Friedman, "Wanted: Lowlifes and High Ratings," *Rolling Stone*, January 12, 1989, 34.
34. Jane Feuer, *Seeing Through the Eighties: Television and Reaganism* (Durham, NC: Duke University Press, 1995), 20.
35. Breslin, *America's Most Wanted*, 168.
36. Michael Mariott, "One Is Killed and 12 Are Injured as L.I. Rap Concert Turns Violent," *New York Times*, September 12, 1988, A1.
37. Chang, *Can't Stop Won't Stop*, 274.
38. Nelson George, *Stop the Violence: Overcoming Self-Destruction* (New York: Pantheon, 1990), 13.
39. George, 51.

40. David Wilson, *Inventing Black-on-Black Violence: Discourse, Space, and Representation* (Syracuse, NY: Syracuse University Press, 2005).

41. John H. Johnson, "Publisher's Statement," *Ebony*, August 1979, 32.

42. George, *Stop the Violence*, 23.

43. Joshua Clover, *1989: Bob Dylan Didn't Have This to Sing About* (Berkeley: University of California Press, 2009), 14.

44. Jeff Weiss, "A History of the Hip Hop Skit," *Red Bull Music Academy*, July 7, 2015, https://daily.redbullmusicacademy.com/2015/07/hip-hop -skits-history.

45. Jonathan Gold, "N.W.A: A Hard Act to Follow," *LA Weekly*, May 5, 1989.

46. Joseph P. Kahn, "The Right to Be Secure," *Boston Globe*, April 7, 1991, 30.

47. Guy Padula, *Colorblind Racial Profiling: A History, 1974 to the Present* (London: Routledge, 2018), 120.

48. Padula, 121.

49. Karen Herman, "Interview with John Langley," Television Academy Foundation, The Interviews, May 22, 2009, http://www.emmytvlegends .org/interviews/people/john-langley.

50. Warren Richey, "Navarro's Crack Lab Upheld by Federal Judges," *South Florida Sun-Sentinel*, February 19, 1995.

51. Avido D. Khahaifa, "Crackdowns Change Drug Scene," *Fort Lauderdale News*, September 6, 1987, 4B.

52. Renee Krause and Steven Wissink, "Sheriff Invites Media to Witness Drug Raids," *Fort Lauderdale News*, July 9, 1988.

53. Rick Pierce, "Tent Houses Prisoners," *South Florida Sun-Sentinel*, July 13, 1988.

54. Mike Pulfer, "From Pulpit, a Song of Values, Restraint," *Cincinnati Enquirer*, June 10, 1989.

55. Mary McDonald, "Rapping Out Messages of Hate," *Cincinnati Enquirer*, June 14, 1989.

56. Frederick Bermudez, "N.W.A. Says It's Getting a Bum Rap," *Cincinnati Enquirer*, June 13, 1989.

57. Bob Weston, "Judge Fines 3 Rappers for Obscenity," *Cincinnati Enquirer*, September 13, 1989.

58. Dave Marsh and Phyllis Pollack, "The F.B.I. Hates This Band," *Village Voice*, October 10, 1989.

59. R. J. Smith, "The Enemy Within," *Village Voice*, June 20, 1989.

60. Marc Dollinger, *Black Power, Jewish Politics: Reinventing the Alliance in the 1960s* (Waltham, MA: Brandeis University Press, 2018), 7.

61. Clayborne Carson, ed., *The Autobiography of Martin Luther King, Jr.* (New York City: IPM, 1998), 461.

62. Tynnetta Muhammad, "Brief History on Origin of the Nation of Islam," Nation of Islam, March 28, 1996, https://www.noi.org/noi-history/.

63. Juan Williams, "Farrakhan's 'Death Threat' Is Disputed," *Washington Post*, May 4, 1984.

64. "Muslim Accuses Press of Twisting His Comments," *New York Times*, April 12, 1984, B12.

65. Tate, "Public Enemy," 125.

66. Smith, "Enemy Within."

67. R. J. Smith, "Public Enemy: Bring the Goys," *Village Voice*, June 27, 1989.

68. John Leland, "Do the Right Thing," *Spin*, September 1989, 72.

69. Leland, 68.

70. Spike Lee, with Lisa Jones, *Do the Right Thing* (New York: Simon and Schuster, 1989), 19–21.

71. David Denby, "He's Gotta Have It," *New York*, June 26, 1989, 53; Joe Klein, "Spiked?," *New York*, June 26, 1989, 14.

72. Logan Hill, "How I Made It: Spike Lee on 'Do the Right Thing,'" *New York*, April 3, 2008, http://nymag.com/anniversary/40th/culture/45772/.

73. Douglas Kreutz, "Television Show's Dragnet Reels in Prime-Time Collars," *Arizona Daily Star*, September 12, 1989, A2.

74. David Freed, "TV Making the Long Arm of the Law Longer," *Los Angeles Times*, September 18, 1989.

75. James Endrst, "The Envelope? No, Thanks," *Hartford Courant*, September 16, 1989, D2.

76. Michael Isikoff, "Drug Buy Set Up for Bush Speech," *Washington Post*, September 22, 1989, A1.

77. Maureen Dowd, "White House Set Up Drug Buy in the Park for Bush TV Speech," *New York Times*, September 23, 1989, A1.

Chapter 3: Get Me the Hell Away from This TV

1. Paolo Carpignano, Robin Andersen, Stanley Aronowitz, and William Difazio, "Chatter in the Age of Electronic Reproduction: Talk Television and the 'Public Mind,'" *Social Text*, nos. 25–26 (1990): 51.

2. "Roy Innis Pushes Al Sharpton," *Washington Post*, August 11, 1988.

3. Tom Shales, "Talk Is Cheap," *Washington Post*, November 18, 1988.

4. Harry F. Waters, "Trash TV," *Newsweek*, November 14, 1988, 72.

5. Elayne Rapping, "Daytime Inquiries," *Progressive*, October 1991, 37.

6. Jane Shattuc, *The Talking Cure: TV Talk Shows and Women* (New York: Routledge, 1997), 18, 19.

7. Jerry Adler, "The Rap Attitude," *Newsweek*, March 19, 1990, 56.

8. Patrick Goldstein, "Rappers Don't Have Time for Newsweek's Attitude," *Los Angeles Times*, March 25, 1990.

9. Robert Christgau, "Jesus, Jews, and the Jackass Theory," *Village Voice*, January 16, 1990, 83.

10. Frank Owen, "Public Service," *Spin*, March 1990, 58.

11. Alan Light, "Brothers from a Black Planet," *Rolling Stone*, May 17, 1990, 141.

12. Robert Hilburn, "Rap—The Power and the Controversy," *Los Angeles Times*, February 4, 1990.

13. Greg Kot, "A+ for Chuck D," *Chicago Tribune*, July 8, 1990.

14. Tom Moon, " 'Fear of a Black Planet'—Concept Rap from Public Enemy," *Philadelphia Inquirer*, April 10, 1990, 7-D.

15. Robert Christgau, "Jews, Jesus, and the Jackass Theory," *Village Voice*, January 16, 1990.

16. J. Powers, "Public Enemy: the Politics of Compromise," *Word Up!*, April 1990, 23.

17. Greg Sandow, "Public Enemy: Fear of a Black Planet," *Entertainment Weekly*, April 27, 1990, 62.

18. Bernard R. Ortiz de Montellano, "Melanin, Afrocentricity, and Pseudo-science," *Yearbook of Physical Anthropology* 36 (1993): 35, 36.

19. Frances Cress Welsing, *The Isis (Yssis) Papers: The Keys to the Colors* (Chicago: Third World Press, 1991), 4–5.

20. Molefi Kete Asante, *The Afrocentric Idea*, rev. and expanded ed. (Philadelphia: Temple University Press, 1998), 1.

21. Welsing, *Isis Papers*, 84–85.

22. Welsing, 300.

23. Chuck D, *Lyrics of a Rap Revolutionary: Volume One*, ed. Yusuf Jah (Beverly Hills, CA: Off Da Books, 2006), 122.

24. Marc Gunther, " 'Rescue 911' May Do More Harm Than Good," *Detroit Free Press*, August 23, 1989, 6B.

25. Fred Schruers, " 'Fear' Strikes Out—An Assessment of the Importance of Public Enemy's 'Fear of a Black Planet,' " *Entertainment Weekly*, Spring 2000, 55.

26. Aaron Applegate, "The Painful Legacy of 1989's Greekfest Endures," *Virginian-Pilot*, September 8, 2009, https://www.pilotonline.com/news/article_0292b5dd-7bb3-5553-8bee-48d23635ca53.html.

27. B. Drummond Ayres Jr., "Virginia Beach Is Quiet after Violence," *New York Times*, September 5, 1989, A12.
28. Mike Sager, "Cube: The World According to Amerikkka's Most Wanted Rapper," *Rolling Stone*, October 4, 1990, 83.
29. Brian Coleman, *Check the Technique: Volume 2* (Berkeley, CA: Gingko, 2014), 241.
30. David Toop, *Rap Attack 3: African Rap to Global Hip-Hop*, expanded 3rd ed. (London: Serpent's Tail, 2000), 183.
31. Jack Breslin, *America's Most Wanted: How Television Catches Crooks* (New York: Harper, 1990), 292.
32. Robert Hilburn, "Notorious Ice Cube: Still the 'Most Wanted,'" *Los Angeles Times*, May 27, 1990.
33. Greg Tate, "Ice Cube," in *Flyboy 2: The Greg Tate Reader* (Durham, NC: Duke University Press, 2016), 98.
34. Greg Kot, "Rap Is All the Rage," *Chicago Tribune*, June 14, 1990.
35. Neil Postman and Steve Powers, *How to Watch TV News* (New York: Penguin, 1992), 92.
36. Luther Campbell, *The Book of Luke: My Fight for Truth, Justice, and Liberty City* (New York: Amistad, 2015), 111.
37. Chuck Philips, "The 'Batman' Who Took On Rap," *Los Angeles Times*, June 18, 1990.
38. Barbara Walsh, "2 Live Crew Getting Bad Rap, Musician Says," *South Florida Sun-Sentinel*, March 17, 1990, 4B.
39. Warren Richey, "2 Live Crew Rap Group Defends Its Lyrics as Humorous, Artistic," *South Florida Sun-Sentinel*, May 15, 1990.
40. Brian O'Gallagher and David P. Gaertner, "2 Live Crew and Judge Gonzalez Too: 2 Live Crew and the Miller Obscenity Test," *Journal of Legislation* 18, no. 1 (1992): 107–108.
41. Mike Billington, Barbara Walsh, and Warren Richey, "2 Live Crew Lyrics Obscene," *South Florida Sun-Sentinel*, June 7, 1990.
42. Avido D. Khahaifa et al., "Some Retailers Refuse to Halt Sale of Album," *South Florida Sun-Sentinel*, June 8, 1990, 13A.
43. George Will, "America's Slide into the Sewer," *Newsweek*, July 29, 1990.
44. Campbell, *Book of Luke*, 162.
45. Henry Louis Gates Jr., "2 Live Crew, Decoded," *New York Times*, June 19, 1990.
46. Ice Cube, "Black Culture Still Getting a Bum Rap," *Los Angeles Times*, June 25, 1990.
47. Campbell, *Book of Luke*, 117.

48. Tom Davidson and Barbara Walsh, "Jurors Convict Record's Seller," *South Florida Sun-Sentinel*, October 4, 1990, 1A.

49. Barbara Walsh, "Lyric Laughter," *South Florida Sun-Sentinel*, October 18, 1990, 9B.

50. Barbara Walsh, "Defense, State Rest Crew Case," *South Florida Sun-Sentinel*, October 20, 1990, 7B.

51. Barbara Walsh and Bob Knotts, "Crew Beats the Rap," *South Florida Sun-Sentinel*, October 21, 1990, 1A.

52. Jon Pareles, "Distributor Withdraws Rap Album over Lyrics," *New York Times*, August 28, 1990.

53. Patrick Goldstein, "Geffen vs. Geto Boys: Double Standard?," *Los Angeles Times*, August 26, 1990, 76.

54. Steve Hochman, "Maybe They Should Issue Stickers for Everyone's Ears," *Los Angeles Times*, July 22, 1990.

55. Jon Pareles, "Gangster Rap: Life and Music in the Combat Zone," *New York Times*, October 7, 1990.

56. Tricia Rose, *Black Noise: Rap Music and Black Culture in Contemporary America* (Middletown, CT: Wesleyan University Press, 1994), 150.

57. Michele Wallace, "When Black Feminism Faces the Music, and the Music Is Rap," *New York Times*, July 29, 1990, H20.

58. Kimberlé Crenshaw, "Beyond Racism and Misogyny: Black Feminism and 2 Live Crew," *Boston Review*, December 1991, 6.

59. Crenshaw, 31; emphasis added.

60. Tate, "Ice Cube," 98–99.

61. Jill Young Miller, "A Slap in the Face," *South Florida Sun-Sentinel*, February 27, 1991.

62. Rose, *Black Noise*, 164.

63. Rose, 152.

64. Jonathan Gold, "Dr. Dre's Expanding Sphere of Influence," *Los Angeles Times*, July 7, 1990, F4.

65. Jeff Chang, "Word Power: A Brief, Highly Opinionated History of Hip-Hop Journalism," in *Pop Music and the Press*, ed. Steve Jones (Philadelphia: Temple University Press, 2002), 66.

66. J. the Sultan, "Rakim on the Cut," *Source*, Summer 1990, 18.

67. Bill Stephney, "Funda-Mental Hip-Hop," *Source*, January 1991, 36.

68. Robert Hilburn, "Why Is Everyone Still Fussing about Ice?," *Los Angeles Times*, March 17, 1991.

69. James Bernard, "Why the World Is After Vanilla Ice," *New York Times*, February 3, 1991.

70. Kembrew McLeod, "Authenticity within Hip-Hop and Other Cultures Threatened with Assimilation," *Journal of Communication* 49, no. 4 (December 1999): 139.

71. David Mills, "The Gangsta Rapper: Violent Hero or Negative Role Model?," *Source*, December 1990, 40.

72. Mills, 36.

73. Mills, 40.

Chapter 4: I'm Gonna Treat You Like King!

1. Daryl F. Gates, with Diane K. Shah, *Chief: My Life in the LAPD* (New York: Bantam, 1992), 4.

2. John Fiske, *Media Matters: Race and Gender in US Politics* (Minneapolis: University of Minnesota Press, 1996), 2.

3. Fiske, 2.

4. John Caldwell, *Televisuality: Style, Crisis, and Authority in American Television* (New Brunswick, NJ: Rutgers University Press, 1995), 305.

5. Fiske, *Media Matters*, 127.

6. After serving a prison term, Barry was reelected in 1994.

7. Chuck Philips, "Rodney King Gets Rap Offer," *Los Angeles Times*, March 20, 1991.

8. Richard Harrington, "Guns N' Roses' Thorny Contract," *Washington Post*, May 29, 1991.

9. "Rap Group's Video Will Include Snippets of Rodney King Tape," *Washington Post*, June 1, 1991.

10. William Raspberry, "The Chief and the Choke Hold," *Washington Post*, May 17, 1982.

11. Sylvia Wynter, "No Humans Involved: An Open Letter to My Colleagues," *Forum N.H.I.: Knowledge for the 21st Century* 1, no. 1 (Fall 1994): 42.

12. Josh Meyer, "Rise in Violence Worries Trendy Westwood Village," *Los Angeles Times*, March 11, 1991.

13. Alan Light, "Rapper Ice-T Busts a Movie," *Rolling Stone*, May 16, 1991, 85.

14. Nelson George, "Box Office Riot," in *Buppies, B-Boys, Baps, and Bohos: Notes on Post-Soul Black Culture* (New York: Harper Perennial, 1993), 153.

15. Jake Paine, "New Jack City Is Turning 25; New Revelations from Its Writer Will Blow Your Mind," *Ambrosia for Heads*, March 2, 2016, https://ambrosiaforheads.com/2016/03/new-jack-city-is-turning-25-new-revelations-from-its-writer-will-blow-your-mind/.

16. Paine, "New Jack City."
17. Barry Michael Cooper, "Kids Killing Kids: New Jack City Eats Its Young," *Village Voice*, December 1, 1987, 23.
18. Craigh Barboza, *John Singleton: Interviews* (Jackson: University Press of Mississippi, 2009), xv.
19. Thomas Golianopoulos, "How John Singleton Made 'Boyz n the Hood,'" *The Ringer*, May 1, 2019, https://www.theringer.com/movies/2019/5/1/18525191/john-singleton-boyz-n-the-hood-oral-history-ice-cube.
20. Sam Kashner, "Hollywood in the Hood," *Vanity Fair*, September 2016.
21. Ras Baraka, "Mo' Dialogue: Ice Cube," *Source*, September 1990, 32.
22. Baraka, "Mo' Dialogue."
23. Alan Light, "Not Just One of the Boyz," *Rolling Stone*, September 5, 1991, 74.
24. Golianopoulos, "John Singleton."
25. Karen Grigsby Bates, "They've Gotta Have Us," *New York Times*, July 14, 1991.
26. David Hinckley, "Making Men of 'Boyz,'" *New York Daily News*, July 11, 1991.
27. Patrick Goldstein, "His New Hood Is Hollywood," *Los Angeles Times*, July 7, 1991.
28. Baraka, "Mo' Dialogue."
29. Robert Reinhold, "Near Gang Turf, Theater Features Peace," *New York Times*, July 15, 1991.
30. Louis Sahagun, "More Than 'Plain Folks,'" *Los Angeles Times*, April 6, 1991.
31. dream hampton, "Hip-Hop Cinema . . . South Central Style," *Source*, September 1991, 33.
32. Simone Browne, *Dark Matters: On the Surveillance of Blackness* (Durham, NC: Duke University Press, 2015), 10.
33. David Fricke, "The Year in Records," *Rolling Stone*, December 12–26, 1991, 165; Jon Pareles, "Should Ice Cube's Voice Be Chilled?," *New York Times*, December 8, 1991.
34. "Editorial," *Billboard*, November 23, 1991, 8.
35. Pareles, "Ice Cube's Voice."
36. Jon Leland, "Cube on Thin Ice," *Newsweek*, December 2, 1991, 69.
37. Greg Kot, "Ice Cube's Rage," *Chicago Tribune*, December 15, 1991.
38. Dennis Hunt, "Outrageous as He Wants to Be," *Los Angeles Times*, November 3, 1991.
39. Anthony DeCurtis and Alan Light, "Opinion," *Rolling Stone*, September 19, 1991, 32.

40. Jon Shecter, "Real Niggaz Don't Die," *Source*, September 1991, 24.
41. Chuck Philips, "N.W.A's Dr. Dre Target of Suit by Host of Rap Show," *Los Angeles Times*, July 23, 1991.
42. Mark Blackwell, "NIGGAZ4DINNER," *Spin*, September 1991, 57.
43. Alan Light, "N.W.A. Beats Up the Charts," *Rolling Stone*, August 8, 1991, 66.
44. Kirk Honeycutt, " 'Terminator's' Generator," *Los Angeles Times*, July 2, 1991, F1.
45. Honeycutt, " 'Terminator's' Generator."
46. Eric Ducker, "A History of Famous White Guys in Public Enemy T-Shirts, or Stories of How a Revolutionary Rap Group Infiltrated the Mainstream," *Pitchfork*, January 28, 2015, https://pitchfork.com/thepitch /649-a-history-of-famous-white-guys-in-public-enemy-t-shirts-or -stories-of-how-a-revolutionary-rap-group-infiltrated-the-mainstream/.
47. James Bernard, "Editorial: Terminator," *Source*, October 1991, 4.
48. Dennis Hunt, "Chuck D. Stands Up for Cube's 'Certificate,' " *Los Angeles Times*, November 24, 1991.
49. Simon Reynolds, "Chuck D. Interview," *Melody Maker*, October 12, 1991.

Chapter 5: Who Got the Camera?

1. Robert Hilburn, "The Rap Is: Justice," *Los Angeles Times*, May 31, 1992, 4.
2. *LA 92*, directed by Daniel Lindsay and T. J. Martin (National Geographic Documentary Films, 2017).
3. Norman Klein, *The History of Forgetting: Los Angeles and the Erasure of Memory* (London: Verso, 1997), 224.
4. Mike Davis and Jon Weiner, *Set the Night on Fire: L.A. in the Sixties* (London: Verso, 2020), 215.
5. Davis and Weiner, 209–210.
6. Davis and Weiner, 210.
7. Davis and Weiner, 204.
8. Doug Smith, "Stunned by the Watts riots, the L.A. Times Struggled to Make Sense of the Violence," *Los Angeles Times*, August 12, 2015, https:// graphics.latimes.com/watts-annotations/.
9. Christine Acham, *Revolution Televised: Prime Time and the Struggle for Black Power* (Minneapolis: University of Minnesota Press, 2004), 35.
10. Andrew Hartman, *A War for the Soul of America: A History of the Culture Wars* (Chicago: University of Chicago Press, 2015), 46.
11. Elizabeth A. Wheeler, "More Than the Western Sky: Watts on Television, August 1965," *Journal of Film and Video* 54, nos. 2–3 (1992): 12.

12. Lou Cannon, *Official Negligence: How Rodney King and the Riots Changed Los Angeles and the LAPD* (New York: Random House, 1997), 263.

13. Cannon, 271.

14. Cannon, 300.

15. Erna Smith, "Transmitting Race: The Los Angeles Riot in Television News" (Joan Shorenstein Center on the Press, Politics and Public Policy, Discussion Paper Series, no. R-11, May 1994), 9.

16. Marc Cooper and Greg Goldin, "Some People Don't Count," in *Inside the L.A. Riots: What Really Happened—and Why It Will Happen Again* (Institute for Alternative Journalism, 1992), 42.

17. Chris Wilder, "L.A. Story," *Source*, August 1992, 6.

18. James Bernard, "The L.A. Rebellion: Message behind the Madness," *Source*, August 1992, 41.

19. David Shaw, "Onetime Allies: Press and LAPD," *Los Angeles Times*, May 24, 1992, A1.

20. David Shaw, "Times Coverage of LAPD, Minority Areas," *Los Angeles Times*, May 26, 1992, A20.

21. Qtd. in Robert Ferguson, "Reading the Riots Act: Oprah Winfrey in Los Angeles," *Changing English* 2, no. 2 (1995): 61–62.

22. Alan Light, "Rappers Sounded Warning," *Rolling Stone*, July 9–23, 1992, 17.

23. Robert Hilburn and Chuck Philips, "For 'Gangsta' Style Rappers, Urban Explosion Is No Surprise," *Los Angeles Times*, May 2, 1992, A7.

24. Light, "Rappers Sounded Warning," 17.

25. Hilburn, "Justice," 4.

26. John Leland, "The Word on the Street Is Heard in the Beat," *Newsweek*, May 11, 1992, 52.

27. Michael Sragow, "King James and Prince Charlie," *New Yorker*, December 28, 1992, 202.

28. Dan Charnas, *The Big Payback: The History of the Business of Hip-Hop* (New York: New American Library, 2010), 375–376.

29. Chuck Philips, "The Uncivil War," *Los Angeles Times*, July 19, 1992.

30. Gerald M. Levin, "Why We Won't Withdraw 'Cop Killer,'" *Wall Street Journal*, June 24, 1992.

31. David Mills, "Sister Souljah's Call to Arms," *Washington Post*, May 13, 1992.

32. Thomas B. Edsall, "Clinton Stuns Rainbow Coalition," *Washington Post*, June 14, 1992.

33. Sheila Rule, "Rapper, Chided by Clinton, Calls Him a Hypocrite," *New York Times*, June 17, 1992.
34. John Leland, "Rap and Race," *Newsweek*, June 29, 1992.
35. Alan Light, "The Rolling Stone Interview: Ice-T," *Rolling Stone*, August 20, 1992.
36. Richard N. Clurman, "Pushing All the Hot Buttons," *New York Times*, November 29, 1992.
37. Chuck Philips, "Ice-T Pulls 'Cop Killer' Off the Market," *Los Angeles Times*, July 29, 1992.
38. Reginald Dennis, "The Cops Gag Ice-T: Is Rap Dead?," *Source*, October 1992, 6.
39. Gregory Lewis, "Paris' Blues," *Image: The Magazine of the San Francisco Examiner*, February 21, 1993, 9.
40. Ben Westhoff, "'West Coast Walter Cronkite': Meet the Man Who Captured NWA on Camera," *Guardian*, August 10, 2015, https://www.theguardian.com/music/2015/aug/10/west-coast-walter-cronkite-nwa-straight-outta-compton.
41. Robin D. G. Kelley, "Kickin' Reality, Kickin' Ballistics: Gangsta Rap and Postindustrial Los Angeles," in *Droppin' Science: Critical Essays on Rap Music and Hip Hop Culture*, ed. William Eric Perkins (Philadelphia, PA: Temple University Press, 1996), 137.
42. Bernard, "L.A. Rebellion," 45.
43. Bernard, 46.
44. Bernard, 48.
45. Jonathan Gold, "Day of the Dre," *Rolling Stone*, September 30, 1993, 41.
46. Jeff Chang, *Can't Stop Won't Stop: A History of the Hip-Hop Generation* (New York: Picador, 2005), 420.

Chapter 6: Stop Being Polite and Start Getting Real

1. Kevin Powell, *The Education of Kevin Powell: A Boy's Journey into Manhood* (New York: Atria Books, 2015).
2. Daniel Cerone, "MTV's Sort-Of Real 'World,'" *Los Angeles Times*, May 28, 1992, F12.
3. Powell, *Education of Kevin Powell*.
4. Powell, *Education of Kevin Powell*.
5. Jeff Chang, *Can't Stop Won't Stop: A History of the Hip-Hop Generation* (New York: Picador, 2005), 423.
6. Kevin Powell, "Hot Dogg," *Vibe*, September 1993, 52.

7. Powell, 52.
8. Kevin Powell, "This Thug's Life," *Vibe*, February 1994.
9. Chris Willman, "Rap Attack, Take Two," *Los Angeles Times*, March 14, 1993.
10. John Leland, "Criminal Records: Gangsta Rap and the Culture of Violence," *Newsweek*, November 29, 1993.
11. Chuck Philips, "Music to Kill Cops By? Rap Song Blamed in Texas Trooper's Death," *Los Angeles Times*, September 20, 1992.
12. Philips, "Texas Trooper's Death."
13. John Broder, "Quayle Calls for Pulling Rap Album Tied to Murder Case," *Los Angeles Times*, September 23, 1992.
14. Ben Westhoff, *Original Gangstas: The Untold Story of Dr. Dre, Eazy-E, Ice Cube, Tupac Shakur, and the Birth of West Coast Rap* (New York: Hachette, 2016), 296.
15. Connie Bruck, "The Takedown of Tupac," *New Yorker*, July 7, 1997, 51.
16. Chuck Philips, "2Pac's Gospel Truth," *Rolling Stone*, October 28, 1993, 22.
17. Kim Green, "War Stories," *Source*, August 1993.
18. Westhoff, *Original Gangstas*, 295.
19. Pamela Ward, "Jury to Start 'Rap Murder' Sentencing Deliberations," *Austin American-Statesman*, July 9, 1993, B5.
20. Pamela Ward, "Howard Gets Death Sentence," *Austin American-Statesman*, July 15, 1993, B5.
21. Rob Markman, "Tupac Would Have 'Outshined' *Menace II Society*, Director Admits," *MTV News*, May 30, 2013, http://www.mtv.com/news/1708225/menace-ii-society-tupac-shakur/.
22. Judi McCreary, "Hughes' Bad," *Source*, October 1992, 24.
23. Henry Louis Gates Jr., "Niggaz with Latitude," *New Yorker*, March 21, 1994, 143.
24. Sarah Goldstein, "The Verge Q+A: The Hughes Brothers on Violence," *GQ*, January 14, 2010, https://www.gq.com/story/the-verge-qa-the-huges-brothers-on-violence.
25. Roger Ebert, "Armed with a Video Camera and Spunk, the Hughes Bros. Take On the Film 'Society,'" *Daily News*, May 21, 1993.
26. George Will, "Menace II Society: Violence Therapy," *Washington Post*, June 17, 1993.
27. David Denby, "Mean Streets," *New York*, May 31, 1993, 54.
28. Gates, "Latitude."
29. Gates, "Latitude."
30. dream hampton, "G Down," *Source*, September 1993.

31. Snoop Dogg, with Davin Seay, *Tha Doggfather: The Times, Trials, and Hardcore Truths of Snoop Dogg* (New York: William Morrow, 1999), 71.

32. Touré, "Snoop Dogg's Gentle Hip-Hop Growl," *New York Times*, November 21, 1993.

33. Powell, "Hot Dogg."

34. Charles Aaron, "Sir Real," *Spin*, October 1993, 56.

35. Snoop Dogg, *Doggfather*, 183.

36. Chuck Philips, "Rap Charts, Rap Sheet," *San Francisco Examiner*, December 12, 1993, 39.

37. Touré, "Snoop and Cube," *Rolling Stone*, January 27, 1994, 52.

38. Powell, "This Thug's Life."

39. *Shaping Our Responses to Violent and Demeaning Imagery in Popular Music: Hearing before the Subcommittee on Juvenile Justice of the Committee on the Judiciary*, S. Hrg. 103-1005, 103rd Cong. (February 23, 1994).

40. *Shaping Our Responses*, S. Hrg. 103-1005.

41. *Shaping Our Responses*, S. Hrg. 103-1005.

42. *Shaping Our Responses*, S. Hrg. 103-1005.

43. Chuck Philips, "Rap Finds a Supporter in Rep. Maxine Waters," *Los Angeles Times*, February 15, 1994, F8.

44. *Shaping Our Responses*, S. Hrg. 103-1005.

45. *Music Lyrics and Commerce: Hearings before the Subcommittee on Commerce, Consumer Protection, and Competitiveness of the Committee on Energy and Commerce*, H. Hrg. 103-112, 103rd Cong. (February 11 and May 5, 1994).

46. John Seabrook, "Rocking in Shangri-La," *New Yorker*, October 10, 1994, 64.

Chapter 7: 2 of Amerikaz Most Wanted

1. Touré, "The Professional," *Village Voice*, December 13, 1994, 75.

2. Touré, "The Professional."

3. Kevin Powell, "This Thug's Life," *Vibe*, February 1994.

4. "2Pac - BET Interview with Ed Gordon (1994)," YouTube video, uploaded by Hip-Hop Universe, October 5, 2016, https://www.youtube.com/watch?v=HWNwvBrUUGQ&feature=youtu.be.

5. "Full Interview: Tupac Outside Courthouse, N.Y. - November 29, 1994," YouTube video, uploaded by 2PAClegacy_net, December 17, 2016, https://www.youtube.com/watch?v=o9j8fs6SSfc&feature=youtu.be.

6. Brian Keizer, "Muse Sick N Hour Mess Age," *Spin*, August 1994, 86.

7. Cheo Hodari Coker, "Ready to Die," *Rolling Stone*, November 3, 1994, 96.

8. Scott Poulson-Bryant, "Puff Daddy," *Vibe*, September 1993, 90.

9. Ben Westhoff, *Original Gangstas: The Untold Story of Dr. Dre, Eazy-E, Ice Cube, Tupac Shakur, and the Birth of West Coast Rap* (New York: Hachette, 2016), 300.

10. Danyel Smith, "Ice-T and Chuck D. Rap about Life in the Hip Hop Trenches," *Vibe*, September 1996, 159.

11. Adario Strange, "Death Wish," *Source*, March 1996, 111.

12. Jeff Chang, "Word Power: A Brief, Highly Opinionated History of Hip-Hop Journalism," in *Pop Music and the Press*, ed. Steve Jones (Philadelphia: Temple University Press, 2002), 68–69.

13. Kevin Powell, "2Pacalypse Now," *Vibe*, February 1995, 21.

14. Kevin Powell, "Ready to Live," *Vibe*, April 1995.

15. Jon Pareles, "Confessions of a Rapper Who Done Wrong," *New York Times*, April 9, 1995.

16. Danyel Smith, "Me Against the World," *Vibe*, April 1995.

17. Cheo Hodari Coker, "2Pac: Me Against the World," *Rolling Stone*, May 4, 1995, 69.

18. Anonymous, "Mail," *Vibe*, June 1995, 21.

19. The Blackspot, "Stakes Is High," *Vibe*, September 1996.

20. Chuck Philips, "Is America Ready for 'Natural Born Killaz'?," *Los Angeles Times*, October 20, 1994.

21. Chuck Philips, "Rapper Takes Officer's Side," *Los Angeles Times*, April 6, 1993.

22. Kevin Powell, "Little Big Man," *Vibe*, December 1993–January 1994, 76.

23. Lisa Respers, "Rap Star Eazy-E Says He Has AIDS," *Los Angeles Times*, March 17, 1995.

24. Marc Landas, "A Cure for AIDS?," *Source*, June 1995, 60.

25. dream hampton, "Eazy-E: 1963–1995," *Spin*, June 1995, 42.

26. Joan Morgan, "Start," *Vibe*, June–July 1995, 29.

27. Chuck Philips, "I Am Not a Gangster," *Los Angeles Times*, October 25, 1995, F1.

28. C. DeLores Tucker and William Bennett, "Lyrics from the Gutter," *New York Times*, June 2, 1995, A29.

29. Justin Tinsley, "All Eyez on Vibe Magazine's 1996 Death Row Cover," The Undefeated, April 20, 2017, https://theundefeated.com/features/all-eyez-on-vibe-magazines-1996-death-row-cover/.

30. Kevin Powell, "Live from Death Row," *Vibe*, February 1996.

31. Powell, "Death Row."

32. Tina Daunt and Chuck Philips, "Playing the L.A.P.D. Card," *Los Angeles Times*, October 26, 1995.

33. Tina Daunt, "Another Victory for Rapper," *Los Angeles Times*, February 22, 1996, B3.

34. Strange, "Death Wish," 86.

35. "20 Questions," *Vibe*, March 1996, 131.

36. Karen R. Good, "Faith; Fully," *Vibe*, May 1996.

37. Lynn Hirschberg, "Does a Sugar Bear Bite?," *New York Times Magazine*, January 14, 1996, 50.

38. Blackspot, "Stakes Is High."

39. "2Pac and Snoop Dogg Interview at the MTV Video Music Awards 1996," YouTube video, uploaded by 2pacshakur, November 23, 2013, https://www.youtube.com/watch?v=6WP6iQSVTBo&feature=youtu.be.

40. Kevin Powell, "Bury Me Like a 'G,'" *Rolling Stone*, October 31, 1996, 40.

41. Rob Marriott, "Ready to Die," *Vibe*, November 1996.

42. Powell, "Like a 'G,'" 40.

43. R. J. Smith, "All Eyez on Him," *Spin*, December 1996, 57.

44. Smith, 57.

45. Chuck Philips and Alan Abrahamson, "U.S. Looks for Rap Label Ties to Organized Crime," *Los Angeles Times*, December 29, 1996, A38.

46. Connie Bruck, "The Takedown of Tupac," *New Yorker*, July 7, 1997, 64.

Conclusion: Deeper Than Rap

1. Lindsay Zoladz, "Ghost Riding," *Pitchfork*, November 21, 2013, https://pitchfork.com/features/ordinary-machines/9265-ghost-riding/.

2. Umberto Eco, *Travels in Hyperreality: Essays* (New York: Harcourt Brace Jovanovich, 1986), 4.

3. Greil Marcus, *Dead Elvis* (New York: Doubleday, 1999).

4. Jay Caspian Kang, "Notes on the Hip-Hop Messiah," *New York Times Magazine*, March 24, 2015.

5. Kang.

6. Sarah Lappas, "Vocal Vulnerabilities: The New Masculinities of Millennial Hip Hop," in *The Oxford Handbook of Hip Hop Music*, ed. Justin D. Burton and Jason Lee Oakes (New York: Oxford University Press, 2018), 1.

7. Jayson Greene, "Kendrick Lamar—good kid, m.A.A.d. city," *Pitchfork*, October 23, 2012, https://pitchfork.com/reviews/albums/17253-good-kid-maad-city/.

8. Rebecca Ford, "How 'Straight Outta Compton' Viral Marketing Became a Sensation," *Hollywood Reporter*, August 14, 2015, https://www.holly woodreporter.com/news/how-straight-outta-compton-viral-815390.

9. Gerrick D. Kennedy, "Dr. Dre's Assault on Dee Barnes Was Once Included in 'Straight Outta Compton,'" *Los Angeles Times*, August 19, 2015.

10. Dee Barnes, "Here's What's Missing from Straight Outta Compton: Me and the Other Women Dr. Dre Beat Up," *Gawker*, August 18, 2015, https://gawker.com/heres-whats-missing-from-straight-outta-compton -me-and-1724735910.

11. Emily Yahr, Caitlin Moore, and Emily Chow, "How We Went from 'Survivor' to More Than 300 Reality Shows: A Complete Guide," *Washington Post*, May 29 2015, https://www.washingtonpost.com/graphics/enter tainment/reality-tv-shows/.

12. Rich Juzwiak, "I'm Not Here to Make Friends!," *fourfour*, July 2008, https://fourfour.typepad.com/fourfour/2008/07/im-not-here-to.html.

13. Greg Tate, "Ice Cube," in *Flyboy 2: The Greg Tate Reader* (Durham, NC: Duke University Press, 2016), 5.

14. Alex S. Vitale, *The End of Policing* (London: Verso, 2017), 3.

15. Joli Jenson, "Fandom as Pathology: The Consequences of Characterization," in *The Adoring Audience: Fan Culture and Popular Media*, ed. Lisa A. Lewis (London: Routledge, 1992), 9–29.

16. Charles Aaron, "Before and After: 'The Marshall Mathers LP,'" *New York Times*, May 18, 2020, https://www.nytimes.com/interactive/2020 /05/18/arts/music/eminem-marshall-mathers-lp.html.

17. Thomas Golianopoulous, "Robbing Celebs and Shooting the Mayor: The Story behind the Two Most Controversial Rap Songs of 1999," *The Ringer*, August 1, 2019, https://www.theringer.com/music/2019 /8/1/20749275/50-cent-how-to-rob-screwball-who-shot-rudy-1999 -music-controversy.

18. Dan Rys, "The Evolution of the Mixtape: An Oral History with DJ Drama," *Billboard*, January 26, 2017, https://www.billboard.com/articles /columns/hip-hop/7669073/history-dj-drama-mixtape-evolution.

19. Touré, "The Life of a Hunted Man," *Rolling Stone*, April 3, 2003, 48.

20. Sasha Jenkins, "Urban Legend," *Vibe*, May 2003, 100.

21. Mark Andrejevic, *Reality TV: The Work of Being Watched* (Lanham, MD: Rowman and Littlefield, 2004), 8.

22. Ginia Bellafante, "The All-Too-Easy Route to Stardom," *New York Times*, October 13, 2007.

23. Evelyn McDonnell, "Book Review: 'Decoded' by Jay-Z,'" *Los Angeles Times*, December 3, 2010.

24. Zack O'Malley Greenburg, *Empire State of Mind: How Jay Z Went from Street Corner to Corner Office* (New York: Portfolio/Penguin, 2011), 34.

25. Jay-Z, *Decoded* (New York: Spiegel and Grau, 2010), 18.

26. Jay-Z, 155.

27. Jay-Z, 57.

28. Donovan Strain, "I FOUND ICE CUBES 'GOOD DAY.'" *Murk Avenue*, January 27, 2012, https://murkavenue.tumblr.com/post/16553509655/i-found-ice-cubes-good-day.

29. Kyle Anderson, "Ice Cube Finally Resolves 'It Was a Good Day' Theories: 'It's a Fictional Song,'" *Entertainment Weekly*, March 5, 2012, https://ew.com/article/2012/03/05/ice-cube-it-was-a-good-day-theory/.

30. Josh Constine, "Ben Horowitz and the Founders Explain Why A16Z Put $15M into Rap Genius: "Knowledge about Knowledge,'" *TechCrunch*, October 3, 2012, https://techcrunch.com/2012/10/03/rap-genius-andreessen-horowitz/.

31. Willy Staley, "Lady Mondegreen and the Miracle of Misheard Song Lyrics," *New York Times Magazine*, July 13, 2012.

32. The new wave of online rap critics were themselves white (overwhelmingly so), as is the author of this book.

33. Adam Krims, *Rap Music and the Poetics of Identity* (London: Cambridge University Press, 2000), 83.

34. Tom Breihan, "Pitchfork's Year-End List vs. Haters," *Village Voice*, December 28, 2005, https://www.villagevoice.com/2005/12/28/pitchforks-year-end-list-vs-haters/.

35. In 2010, the former drug dealer filed a trademark-infringement suit against the rapper, which was dismissed by a judge.

36. Jon Caramanica, "Beyond Authenticity: A Rapper Restages," *New York Times*, April 22, 2009.

37. Jeff Weiss, "Album Review: Rick Ross' 'Deeper Than Rap,'" *Pop and Hiss: The LA Times Music Blog*, April 24, 2009, https://latimesblogs.latimes.com/music_blog/2009/04/album-review-rick-ross.html#more.

38. Sasha Frere-Jones, "The Sound of Success," *New Yorker*, February 13, 2012.

39. Caramanica, "Beyond Authenticity," 2009.

40. Charis E. Kubrin and Erik Nielson, "Rap on Trial," *Race and Justice* 3, no. 4 (2014): 186.

41. American Civil Liberties Union of New Jersey, *Brief of Amicus Curiae: State of New Jersey versus Vonte L. Skinner*, July 29, 2013.

42. Rebecca Everett, "No New Trial for Shooter Who Already Had Three," *NJ*, December 1, 2017, https://www.nj.com/burlington/2017/12/no_new_trial_for_shooter_who_already_had_three.html.

43. Travis M. Andrews, "Killer Mike, Chance the Rapper and others file Supreme Court brief to educate justices about rap music," *Washington Post*, March 6, 2019, https://www.washingtonpost.com/arts-entertainment/2019/03/06/killer-mike-chance-rapper-others-file-supreme-court-brief-educate-justices-about-rap-music/.

44. Jeff Chang, *We Gon' Be Alright: Notes on Race and Resegregation* (New York: Picador, 2016), 134.

45. Amanda Terkel, "Police Officer Caught on Video Calling Michael Brown Protesters 'F***ing Animals,'" *Huffington Post*, August 12, 2014, https://www.huffpost.com/entry/michael-brown-protests_n_5672163.

46. Sarah Van Gelder, "Rev. Sekou on Today's Civil Rights Leaders: 'I Take My Orders from 23-Year-Old Queer Women,'" *Yes!*, July 22, 2015, https://www.yesmagazine.org/social-justice/2015/07/22/black-lives-matter-s-favorite-minister-reverend-sekou-young-queer/.

47. Van Gelder, "I Take My Orders."

48. Mamie Till-Mobley and Christopher Benson, *Death of Innocence: The Story of the Hate Crime That Changed America* (New York: One World, 2004), 139.

49. Timothy B. Tyson, *The Blood of Emmett Till* (New York: Simon and Schuster, 2017), 210–211.

50. Martin Luther King Jr., *Why We Can't Wait* (New York: Signet Classics, 2000), 25.

51. King, 25.

52. Catherine Knight Steele, "Black Bloggers and Their Varied Publics: The Everyday Politics of Black Discourse Online," *Television and New Media* 19, no. 2 (2018).

53. Candis Callison and Mary Lynn Young, *Reckoning: Journalism's Limits and Possibilities* (London: Oxford University Press, 2019).

54. Lewis Raven Wallace, *The View from Somewhere: Undoing the Myth of Journalistic Objectivity* (Chicago: University of Chicago Press, 2019), 24–29.

55. Travis Andrews, "Obama Describes His Bond with Jay-Z," *Washington Post Morning Mix*, June 16, 2017, https://www.washingtonpost.com/news/morning-mix/wp/2017/06/16/obama-describes-his-bond-to-jay-z/.

56. Greg Kot, "Will Obama's Victory Force Hip-Hop to Change Its Tune?," *Chicago Tribune*, November 9, 2008.

57. Peter Helman, "You'll Never Guess What Fox News Thinks of Kendrick Lamar," *Stereogum*, June 30, 2015, https://www.stereogum.com/1812647/youll-never-guess-what-fox-news-thinks-of-kendrick-lamar/video/.

58. Colin Stutz, "Kendrick Lamar Responds to Geraldo Rivera: 'Hip-Hop Is Not the Problem, Our Reality Is,'" *Billboard*, July 2, 2015, https://www.billboard.com/articles/columns/the-juice/6620035/kendrick-lamar-responds-geraldo-rivera-alright-bet-awards.

59. Aisha Harris, "Has Kendrick Lamar Recorded the New Black National Anthem?," *Slate*, August 3, 2015, https://slate.com/culture/2015/08/black-lives-matter-protesters-chant-kendrick-lamars-alright-what-makes-it-the-perfect-protest-song-video.html.

60. John Patrick Leary, *Keywords: The New Language of Capitalism* (Chicago: Haymarket, 2018), 150.

61. Jeff Weiss, "The Definitive Lil Boosie Story," *XXL*, June/July 2014.

62. James Poniewozik, *Audience of One: Donald Trump, Television, and the Fracturing of America* (New York: Liveright, 2019), 76.

63. Patrick Radden Keefe, "How Mark Burnett Resurrected Donald Trump as an Icon of American Success," *New Yorker*, January 7, 2019.

64. Poniewozik, *Audience of One*, 135.

65. Glenn Plaskin, "The Playboy Interview with Donald Trump," *Playboy*, March 1990.

66. Geoffrey Baym, "'Think of Him as the President': Tabloid Trump and the Political Imaginary, 1980–1999," *Journal of Communication* 69, no. 4 (2019): 406.

67. Poniewozik, *Audience of One*, 64.

68. Reece Peck, *Fox Populism: Branding Conservatism as Working Class* (Cambridge, UK: Cambridge University Press, 2019), 10.

69. J. L. Mast, "Action in Culture: Act I of the Presidential Primary Campaign in the US, April to December, 2015," *American Journal of Cultural Sociology* 4, no. 3 (2016): 281.

70. Baym, "Tabloid Trump," 408.

71. Ryan Dombal, "Kanye West: My Beautiful Dark Twisted Fantasy," *Pitchfork*, November 22, 2010, https://pitchfork.com/reviews/albums/14880-my-beautiful-dark-twisted-fantasy/.

72. Tom Breihan, "The World's Best Rap Music Comes from California," *Stereogum*, October 19, 2016, https://www.stereogum.com/1905847

/the-worlds-best-rap-music-comes-from-california/franchises/
columns/status-aint-hood/.

73. Tony Judt, *Reappraisals: Reflections on the Forgotten Twentieth Century*
(New York: Penguin, 2008), 1–2.

74. Gary Cross, *An All-Consuming Century: Why Commercialism Won in
Modern America* (New York: Columbia University Press, 2000), 3, 8.

75. Kathryn VanArendonk, "Cops Are Always the Main Characters," *Vulture*,
June 1, 2020, https://www.vulture.com/2020/06/tv-cops-are-always
-the-main-characters.html.

76. Alan Sepinwall, "A History of Violence: Why I Loved Cop Shows,
and Why They Must Change," *Rolling Stone*, August 9, 2020,
https://www.rollingstone.com/tv/tv-features/cops-on-tv-holly
wood-policing-sepinwall-1039131/.

77. Stephen Braun, "Tensions Mount on L.A. Streets," *Los Angeles Times*,
December 15, 1991, A1.

78. Wesley Morris, "The Videos That Rocked America . . . and the Song That
Knows Our Rage," *New York Times*, June 4, 2020, C1.

INDEX

▼

Moore, Rudy Ray, 15, 36, 120. *See also* Dolemite
moral panics, 22, 30–32, 48–49, 54, 86, 163
Morgan, Joan, 233–234
"Mortal Man" (Kendrick Lamar), 252
Mourges, Melissa, 220
"Move Somethin'" (2 Live Crew), 117
Moynihan, Daniel Patrick, 166–167
Moynihan Report, 52
MTV News, ix, 89, 191, 238
MTV Video Music Awards, 1, 191, 210, 216, 242, 265, 288
Muhammad, Elijah, 89–90
Muhammad, Khalid Abdul, 151–152
Muhammad Speaks (Nation of Islam), 90
Muhammad, Wallace Fard, 89–90
"Murder Rap" (Above the Law), 129
Murder, Teenage Style (CBS), 27
Murder Was the Case (Death Row artists), 215
"Murder Was the Case" (Snoop Dogg), 214–215, 224, 234, 246
Murphy, Charlie, 194, 216
Murphy, Eddie, viii, 118
Murray, Jonathan, 190
Muse Sick-n-Hour Mess Age (Public Enemy), 222–223
"My Adidas" (Run-DMC), 23
My Beautiful Dark Twisted Fantasy (Kanye West), 288
"My Name Is" (Eminem), 261
"My Philosophy" (KRS-One), 78
"My President" (Young Jeezy), 281
Mystery of Al Capone's Vaults, The (NBC), 61
"My Summer Vacation" (Ice Cube), 151
mythologizing, 6, 39–40, 59, 91, 220, 227

NAACP, 89, 212
Narcs (Coram), 84
Nas, 223, 225, 244–245, 253, 267–268, 286
Nassau Coliseum, 75–76
Nate Dogg (Nathaniel Hale), 208
National Black Police Association, 175

National Good Day Day, 269
nationalism in rap, viii, 4, 54, 67, 176–183
National Rifle Association, 176–178
National Urban League, 76–77, 212
Nation of Islam, viii, 167, 179, 184; and anti-Semitism, 89–92; and Chuck D, 11, 106; on *Donahue*, 111; and Five Percent theology, 59, 108; and Ice Cube, 145, 150–154; and sexism, 126–127, 147
Native Tongues collective, 108
"Natural Born Killaz" (Dr. Dre and Ice Cube), 230–231
Natural Born Killers (Stone), 229–230, 261
Navarro, Nick, 8, 56, 83–86, 95, 103, 116–122, 135, 198
Negro World (Garvey), 90
Nelson, Jack, 11
New Black Panthers, 69
New Edition, 133
New Jack City (Van Peebles), 142–143, 147–148, 205, 211
"New Jack Hustler (Nino's Theme)," 144, 177
"New News," 12
New Right, 20–22, 77, 102–103
Newton, Huey, 60, 69–71, 91, 167, 200, 221
"New York, New York" (Tha Dogg Pound), 237
"NHI" ("no humans involved"), 141
Niggaz4Life (N.W.A), 154–155, 183, 208
Nightline (ABC), 4, 12, 50, 120, 159
"Night of the Living Baseheads" (Public Enemy), 68, 109
"Nighttrain" (Public Enemy), 158
Nixon, Richard, 20, 286, 291
Norwood, Jennifer, 88
"No Sell Out" (Geto Boys), 123
Notorious B.I.G., 219, 223–227, 237, 239, 241–246, 249–251, 253, 264, 267, 291; *Life after Death*, 246, 249, 271; *Ready to Die*, 223–224
"No Vaseline" (N.W.A), 153